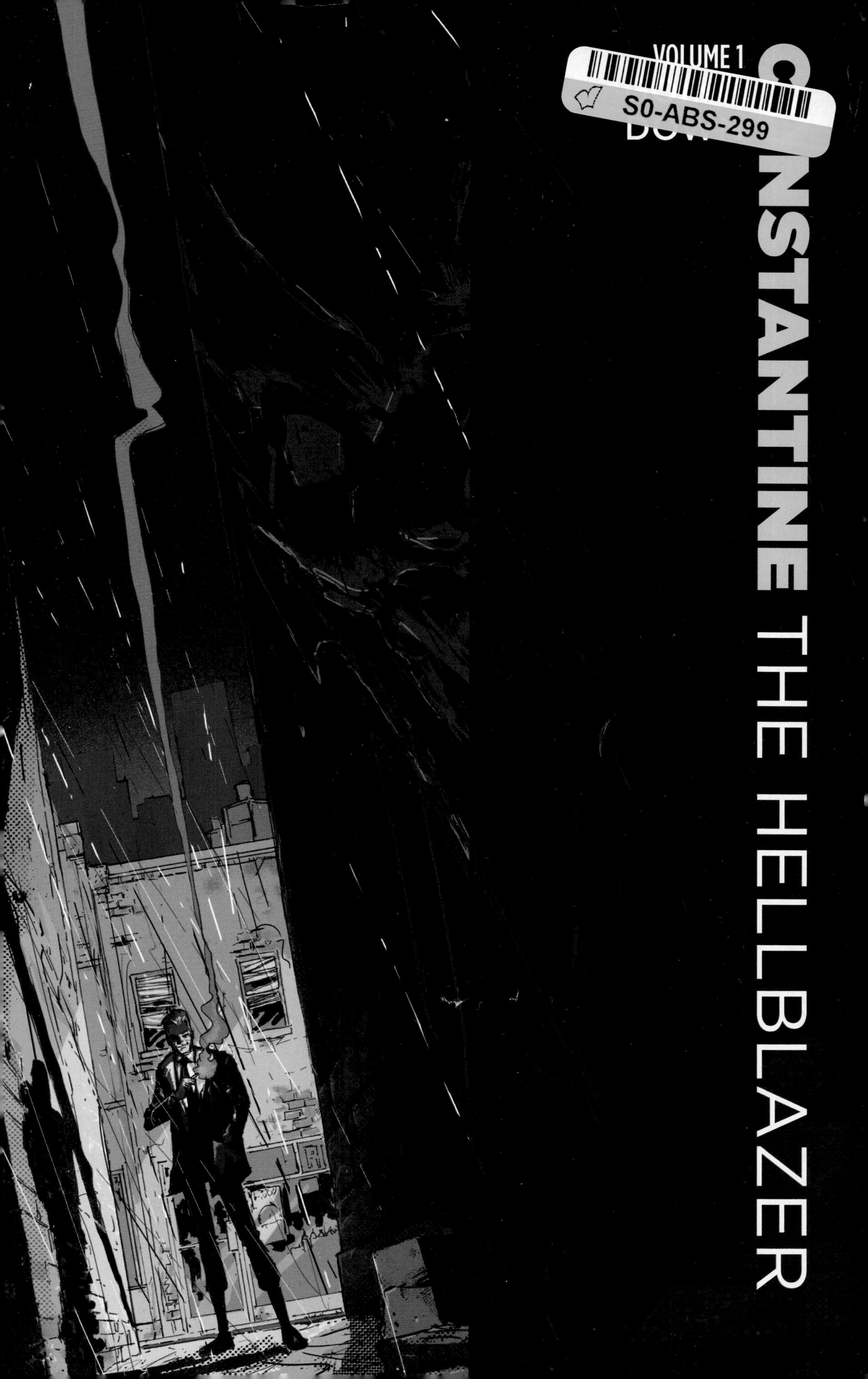
VOLUME 1
CONSTANTINE THE HELLBLAZER

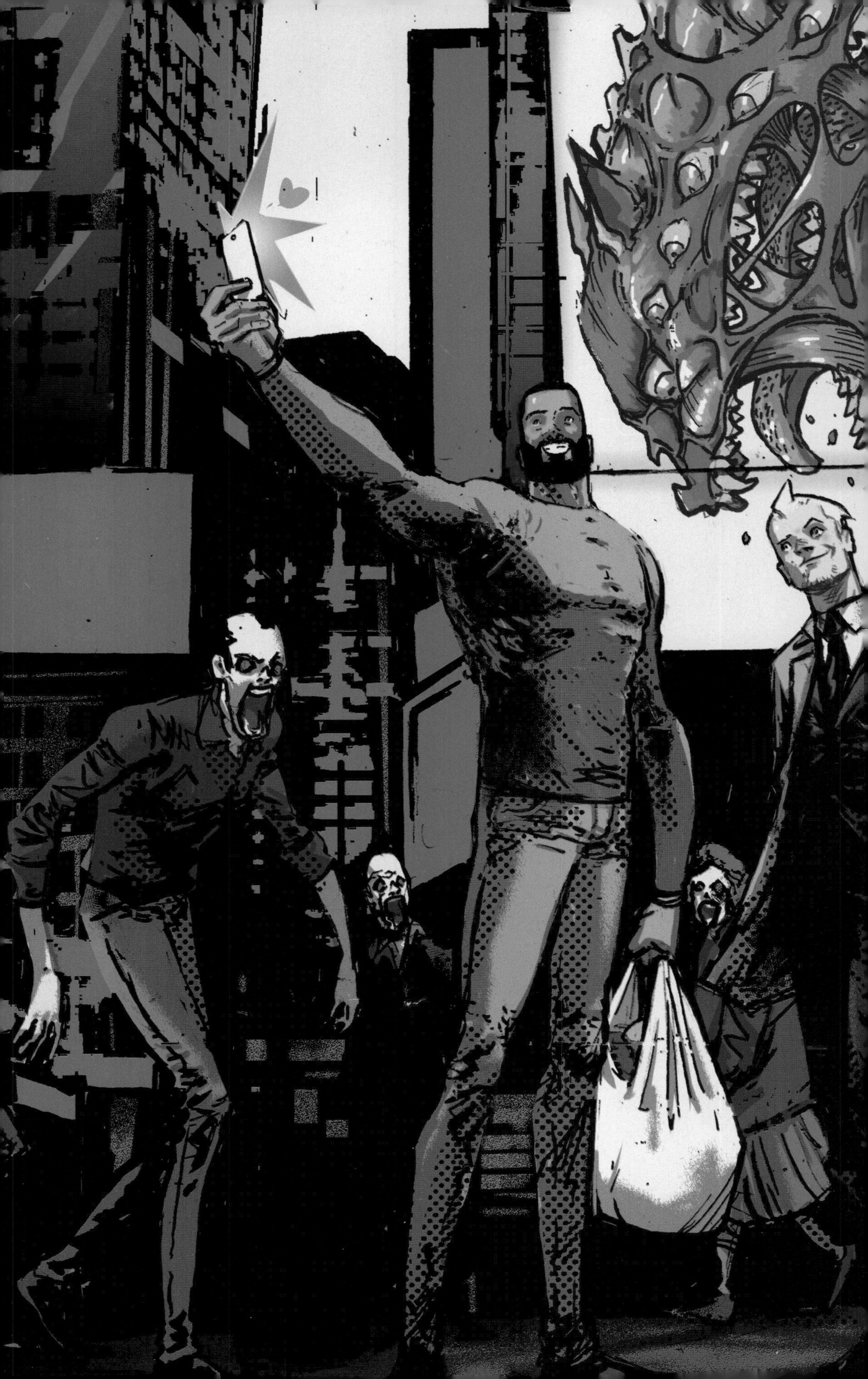

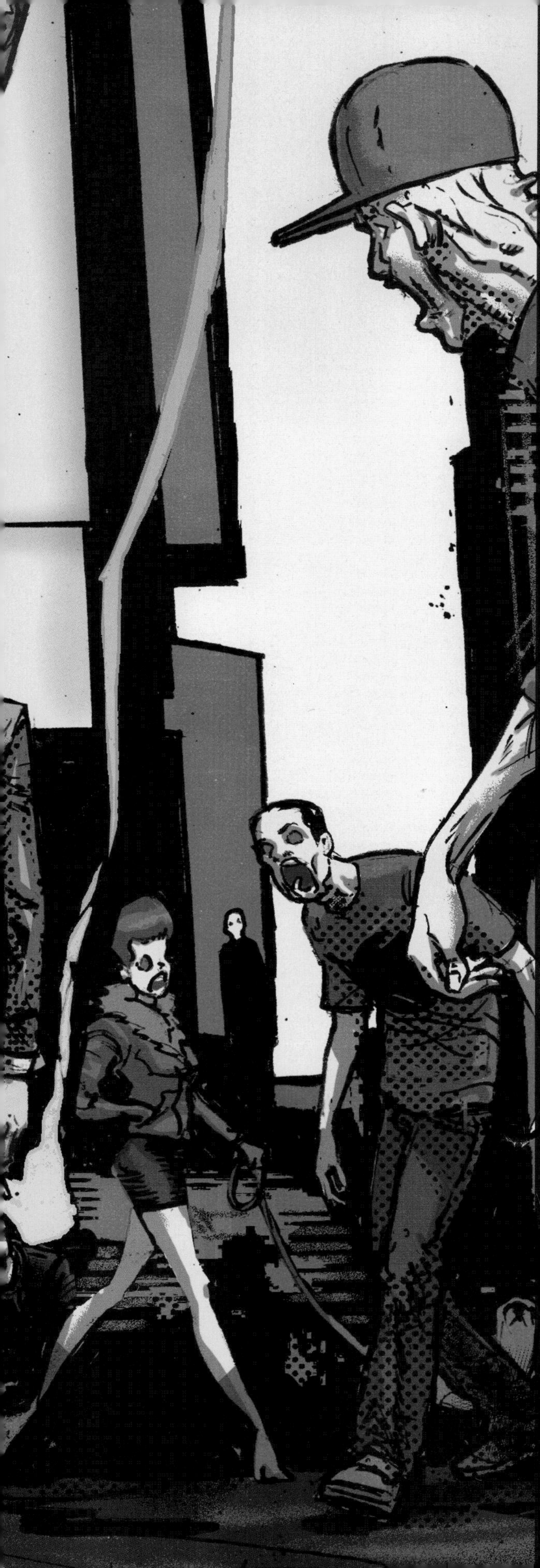

CONSTANTINE THE HELLBLAZER

VOLUME 1
GOING DOWN

WRITTEN BY
MING DOYLE
JAMES TYNION IV

ART BY
RILEY ROSSMO
MING DOYLE
VANESA DEL REY
CHRIS VISIONS
SCOTT KOWALCHUK

COLOR BY
IVAN PLASCENCIA
LEE LOUGHRIDGE

LETTERS BY
TOM NAPOLITANO
SAL CIPRIANO

COVERS BY
RILEY ROSSMO

ANDY KHOURI Editor – Original Series
AMEDEO TURTURRO Assistant Editor – Original Series
JEB WOODARD Group Editor – Collected Editions
ROBIN WILDMAN Editor – Collected Edition
STEVE COOK Design Director – Books
DAMIAN RYLAND Publication Design

BOB HARRAS Senior VP – Editor-in-Chief, DC Comics

DIANE NELSON President
DAN DIDIO and JIM LEE Co-Publishers
GEOFF JOHNS Chief Creative Officer
AMIT DESAI Senior VP – Marketing & Global Franchise Management
NAIRI GARDINER Senior VP – Finance
SAM ADES VP – Digital Marketing
BOBBIE CHASE VP – Talent Development
MARK CHIARELLO Senior VP – Art, Design & Collected Editions
JOHN CUNNINGHAM VP – Content Strategy
ANNE DEPIES VP – Strategy Planning & Reporting
DON FALLETTI VP – Manufacturing Operations
LAWRENCE GANEM VP – Editorial Administration & Talent Relations
ALISON GILL Senior VP – Manufacturing & Operations
HANK KANALZ Senior VP – Editorial Strategy & Administration
JAY KOGAN VP – Legal Affairs
DEREK MADDALENA Senior VP – Sales & Business Development
JACK MAHAN VP – Business Affairs
DAN MIRON VP – Sales Planning & Trade Development
NICK NAPOLITANO VP – Manufacturing Administration
CAROL ROEDER VP – Marketing
EDDIE SCANNELL VP – Mass Account & Digital Sales
COURTNEY SIMMONS Senior VP – Publicity & Communications
JIM (SKI) SOKOLOWSKI VP – Comic Book Specialty & Newsstand Sales
SANDY YI Senior VP – Global Franchise Management

CONSTANTINE: THE HELLBLAZER VOLUME 1: GOING DOWN

Originally published in single magazine form and online as CONSTANTINE: THE HELLBLAZER 1-6, DC SNEAK
PEEK: CONSTANTINE 1 © 2015 DC Comics. All Rights Reserved. All characters, their distinctive
likenesses and related elements featured in this publication are trademarks of DC Comics.
The stories, characters and incidents featured in this publication are entirely fictional.
DC Comics does not read or accept unsolicited ideas, stories or artwork.

DC Comics, 2900 West Alameda Avenue, Burbank, CA 91505
Printed by RR Donnelley, Salem, VA, USA. 1/8/16. First Printing.
ISBN: 978-1-4012-5972-3

Library of Congress Cataloging-in-Publication Data is available.

PEFC Certified

Printed on paper from
sustainably managed
forests and controlled
sources

PEFC/29-31-75   www.pefc.org

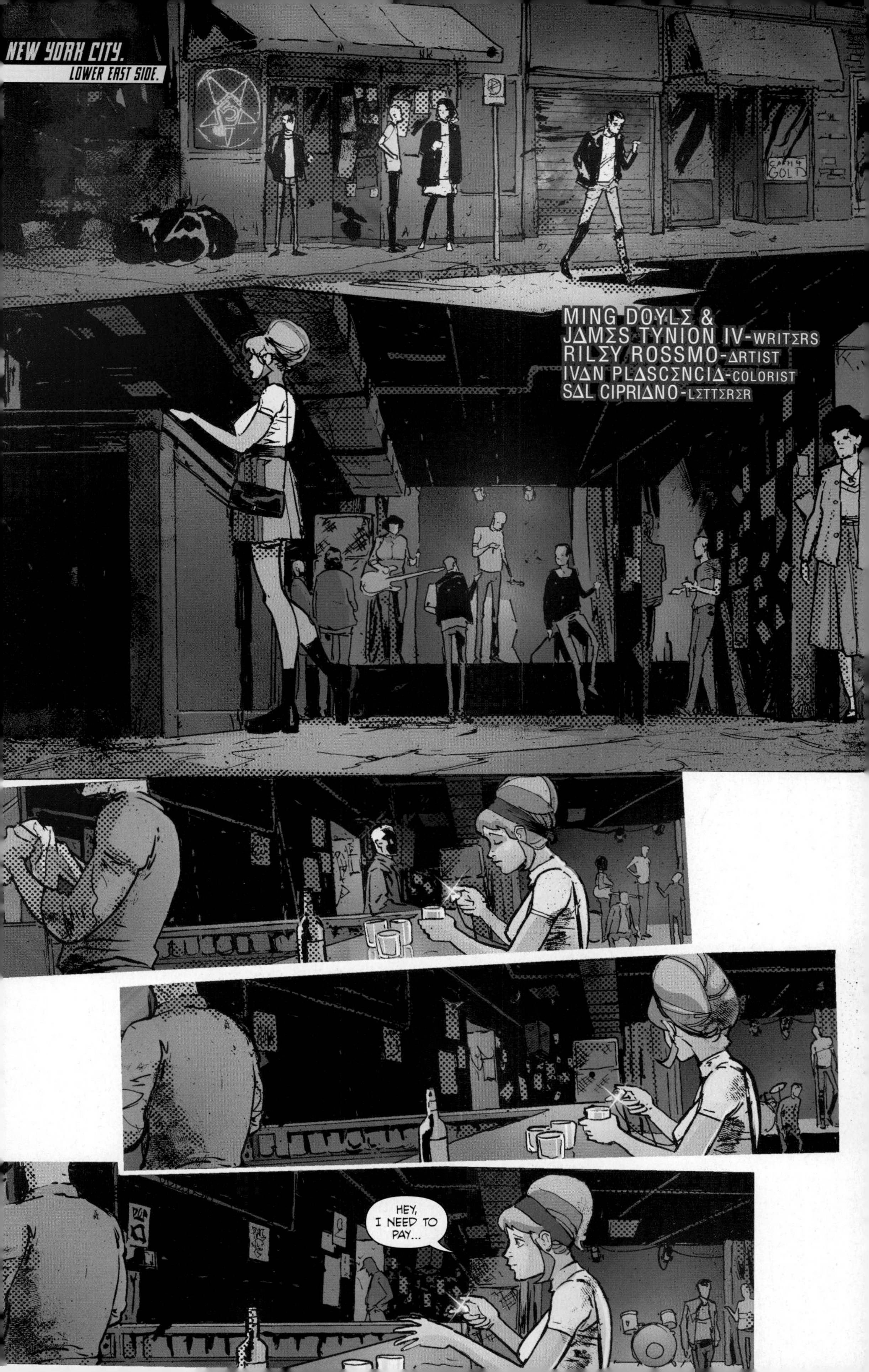
NEW YORK CITY.
LOWER EAST SIDE.
CASH 4 GOLD
MING DOYLE &
JAMES TYNION IV-WRITERS
RILEY ROSSMO-ARTIST
IVAN PLASCENCIA-COLORIST
SAL CIPRIANO-LETTERER
HEY, I NEED TO PAY...

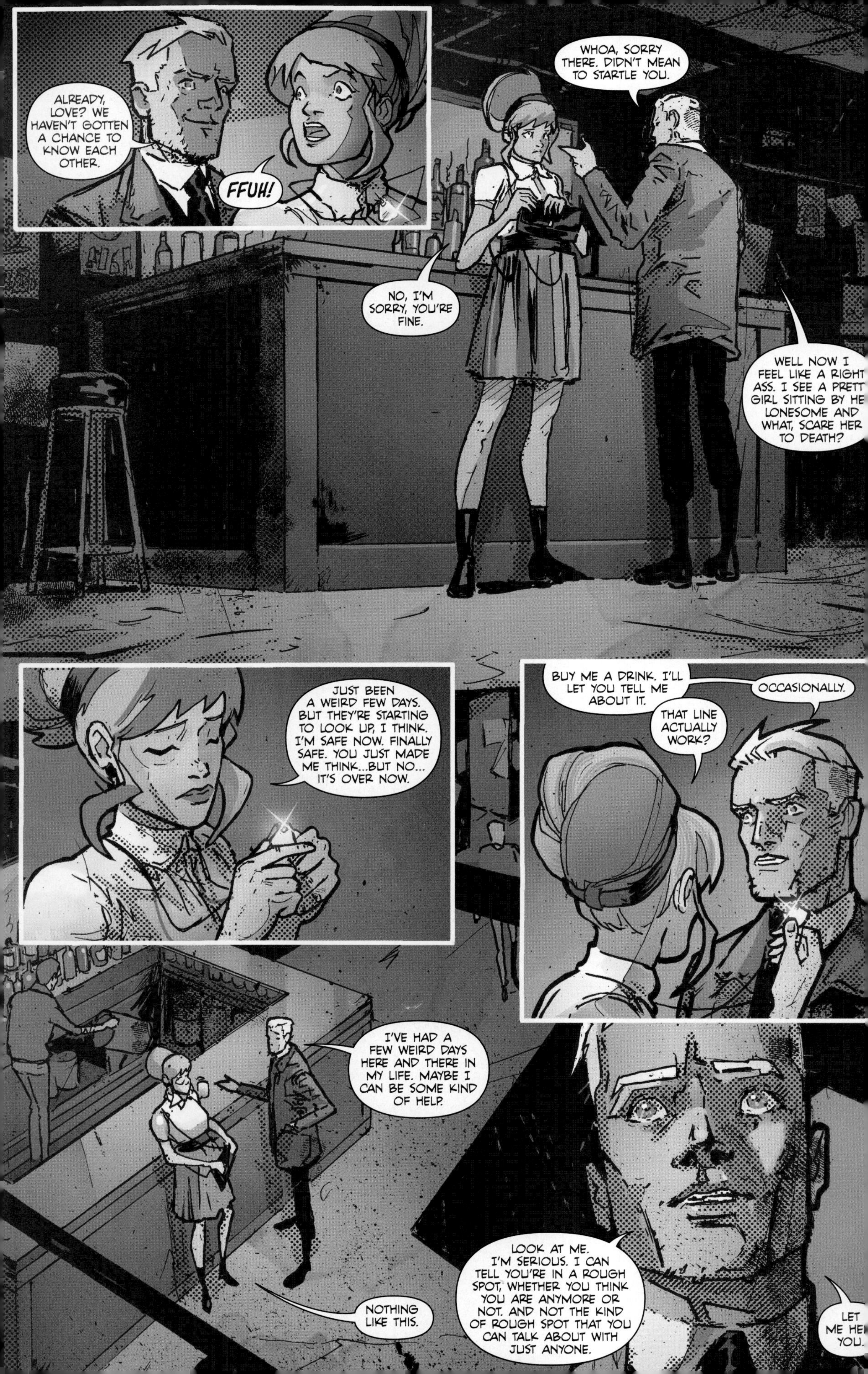
ALREADY, LOVE? WE HAVEN'T GOTTEN A CHANCE TO KNOW EACH OTHER.
FFUH!
WHOA, SORRY THERE. DIDN'T MEAN TO STARTLE YOU.
NO, I'M SORRY, YOU'RE FINE.
WELL NOW I FEEL LIKE A RIGHT ASS. I SEE A PRETT GIRL SITTING BY HE LONESOME AND WHAT, SCARE HER TO DEATH?
JUST BEEN A WEIRD FEW DAYS. BUT THEY'RE STARTING TO LOOK UP, I THINK. I'M SAFE NOW. FINALLY SAFE. YOU JUST MADE ME THINK...BUT NO... IT'S OVER NOW.
BUY ME A DRINK. I'LL LET YOU TELL ME ABOUT IT.
THAT LINE ACTUALLY WORK?
OCCASIONALLY.
I'VE HAD A FEW WEIRD DAYS HERE AND THERE IN MY LIFE. MAYBE I CAN BE SOME KIND OF HELP.
NOTHING LIKE THIS.
LOOK AT ME. I'M SERIOUS. I CAN TELL YOU'RE IN A ROUGH SPOT, WHETHER YOU THINK YOU ARE ANYMORE OR NOT. AND NOT THE KIND OF ROUGH SPOT THAT YOU CAN TALK ABOUT WITH JUST ANYONE.
LET ME HE YOU.

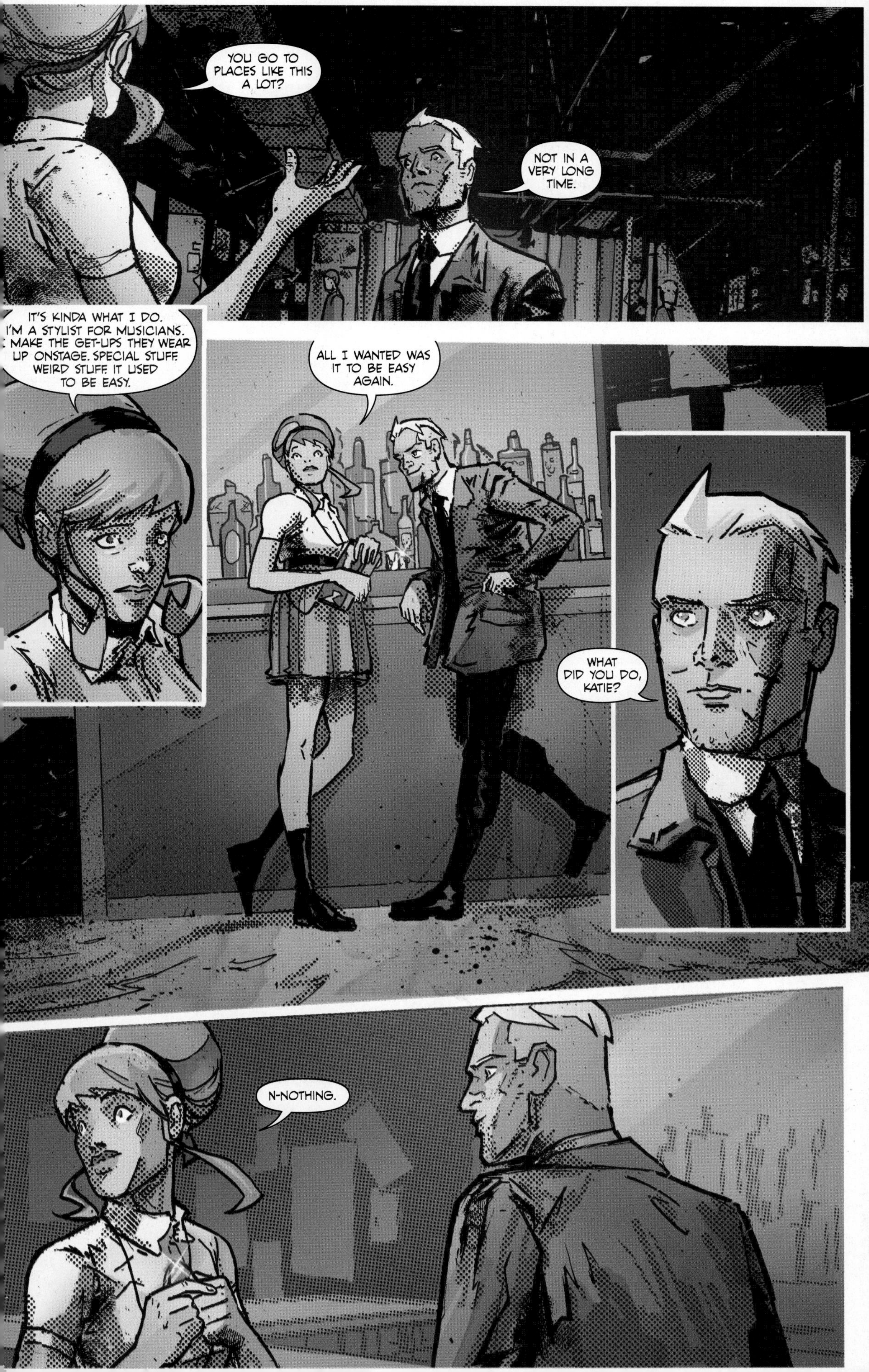
YOU GO TO PLACES LIKE THIS A LOT?
NOT IN A VERY LONG TIME.
IT'S KINDA WHAT I DO. I'M A STYLIST FOR MUSICIANS. I MAKE THE GET-UPS THEY WEAR UP ONSTAGE. SPECIAL STUFF. WEIRD STUFF. IT USED TO BE EASY.
ALL I WANTED WAS IT TO BE EASY AGAIN.
WHAT DID YOU DO, KATIE?
N-NOTHING.

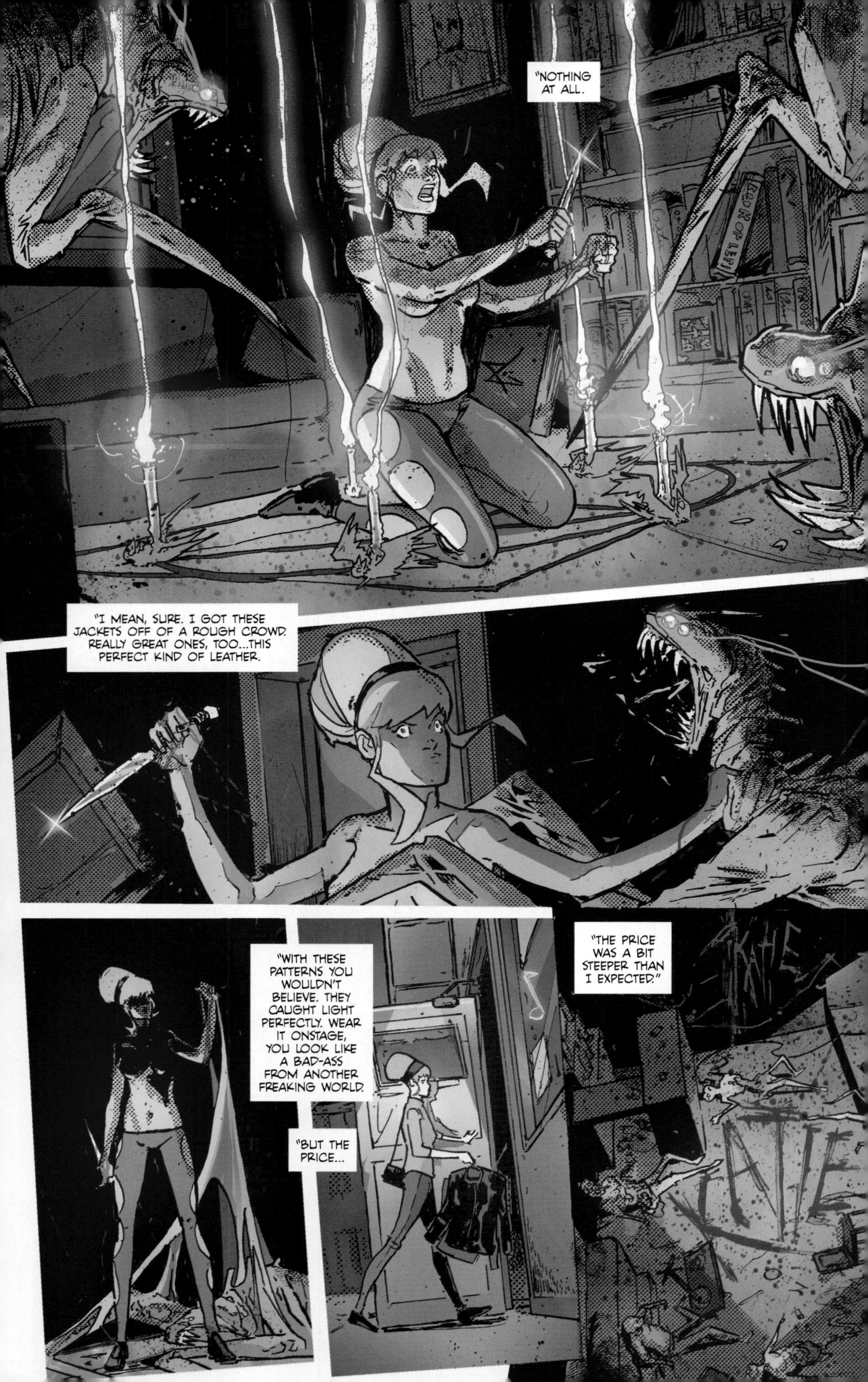
"NOTHING AT ALL.
"I MEAN, SURE. I GOT THESE JACKETS OFF OF A ROUGH CROWD. REALLY GREAT ONES, TOO...THIS PERFECT KIND OF LEATHER.
"WITH THESE PATTERNS YOU WOULDN'T BELIEVE. THEY CAUGHT LIGHT PERFECTLY. WEAR IT ONSTAGE, YOU LOOK LIKE A BAD-ASS FROM ANOTHER FREAKING WORLD.
"BUT THE PRICE...
"THE PRICE WAS A BIT STEEPER THAN I EXPECTED."

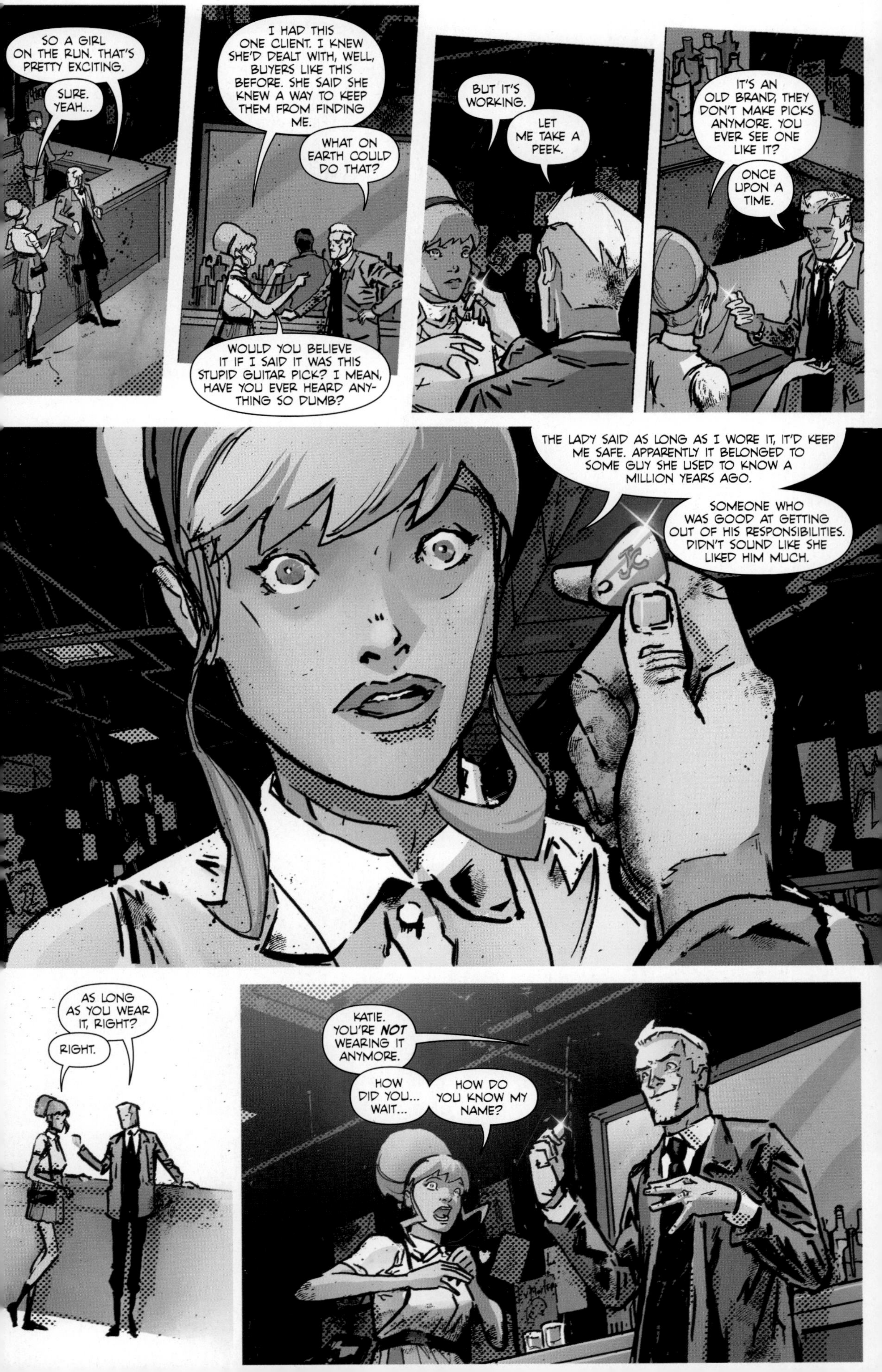

SO A GIRL ON THE RUN. THAT'S PRETTY EXCITING.
SURE. YEAH...
I HAD THIS ONE CLIENT. I KNEW SHE'D DEALT WITH, WELL, BUYERS LIKE THIS BEFORE. SHE SAID SHE KNEW A WAY TO KEEP THEM FROM FINDING ME.
WHAT ON EARTH COULD DO THAT?
WOULD YOU BELIEVE IT IF I SAID IT WAS THIS STUPID GUITAR PICK? I MEAN, HAVE YOU EVER HEARD ANY-THING SO DUMB?
BUT IT'S WORKING.
LET ME TAKE A PEEK.
IT'S AN OLD BRAND, THEY DON'T MAKE PICKS ANYMORE. YOU EVER SEE ONE LIKE IT?
ONCE UPON A TIME.
THE LADY SAID AS LONG AS I WORE IT, IT'D KEEP ME SAFE. APPARENTLY IT BELONGED TO SOME GUY SHE USED TO KNOW A MILLION YEARS AGO.
SOMEONE WHO WAS GOOD AT GETTING OUT OF HIS RESPONSIBILITIES. DIDN'T SOUND LIKE SHE LIKED HIM MUCH.
AS LONG AS YOU WEAR IT, RIGHT?
RIGHT.
KATIE. YOU'RE **NOT** WEARING IT ANYMORE.
HOW DID YOU... WAIT...
HOW DO YOU KNOW MY NAME?

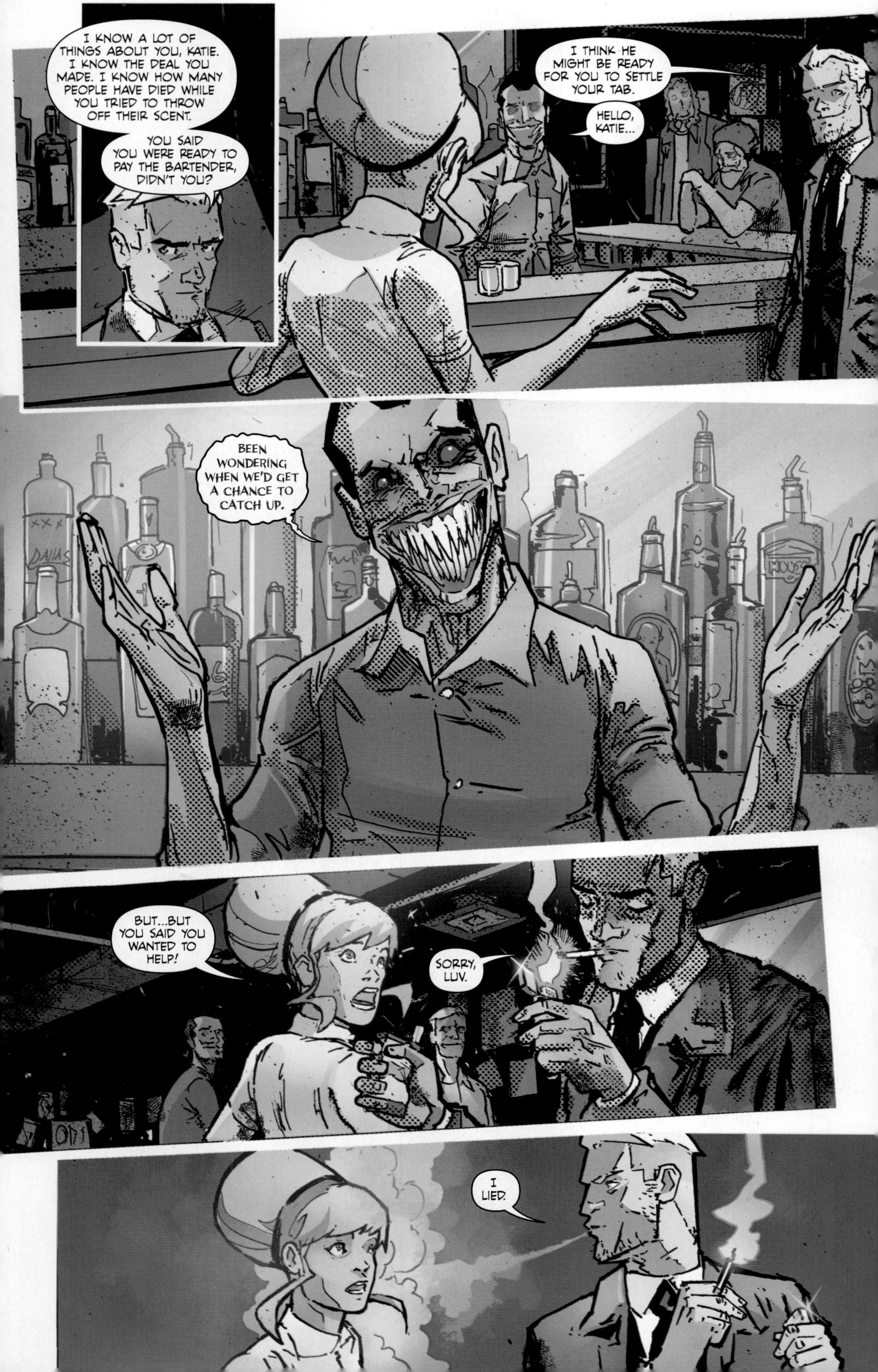
I KNOW A LOT OF THINGS ABOUT YOU, KATIE. I KNOW THE DEAL YOU MADE. I KNOW HOW MANY PEOPLE HAVE DIED WHILE YOU TRIED TO THROW OFF THEIR SCENT.
YOU SAID YOU WERE READY TO PAY THE BARTENDER, DIDN'T YOU?
I THINK HE MIGHT BE READY FOR YOU TO SETTLE YOUR TAB.
HELLO, KATIE...
BEEN WONDERING WHEN WE'D GET A CHANCE TO CATCH UP.
BUT...BUT YOU SAID YOU WANTED TO HELP!
SORRY, LUV.
I LIED.

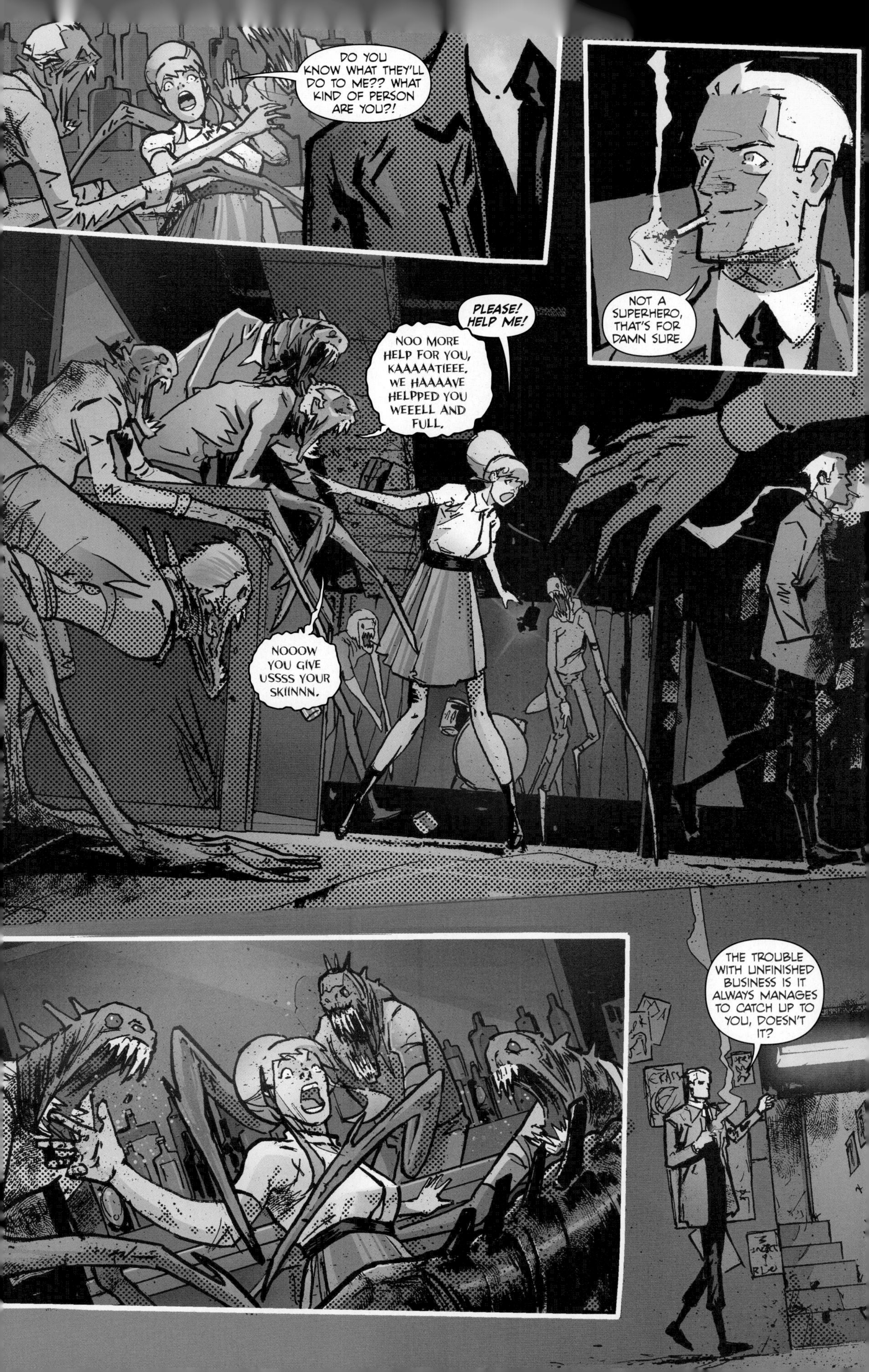

DO YOU KNOW WHAT THEY'LL DO TO ME?? WHAT KIND OF PERSON ARE YOU?!
NOT A SUPERHERO, THAT'S FOR DAMN SURE.
PLEASE! HELP ME!
NOO MORE HELP FOR YOU, KAAAAATIEEE. WE HAAAAVE HELPPED YOU WEEELL AND FULL.
NOOOW YOU GIVE USSSS YOUR SKIINNN.
THE TROUBLE WITH UNFINISHED BUSINESS IS IT ALWAYS MANAGES TO CATCH UP TO YOU, DOESN'T IT?

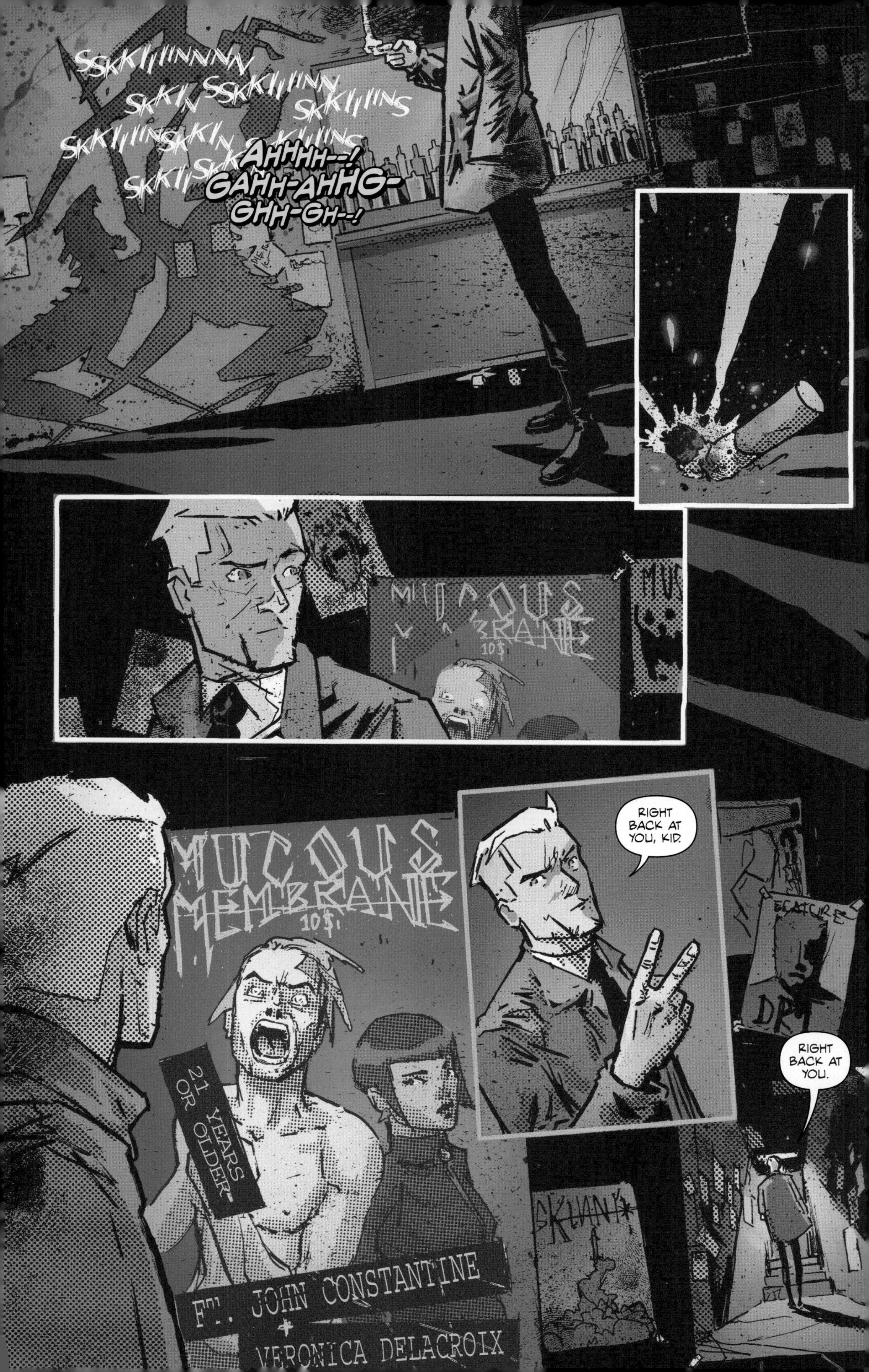
SSKKIIIINNNN
SKKIN SSKKIIIINN SKKIIIINS
SKKIIINSKKIN SKKIIINS
SKKIISKK
AHHHH--! GAHH-AHHG-GHH-GH--!
MUCOUS MEMBRANE
10$
MUC
MUCOUS MEMBRANE
10$
21 YEARS OR OLDER
FT. JOHN CONSTANTINE
+
VERONICA DELACROIX
RIGHT BACK AT YOU, KID.
FEATURE
DR
SKUNK
RIGHT BACK AT YOU.

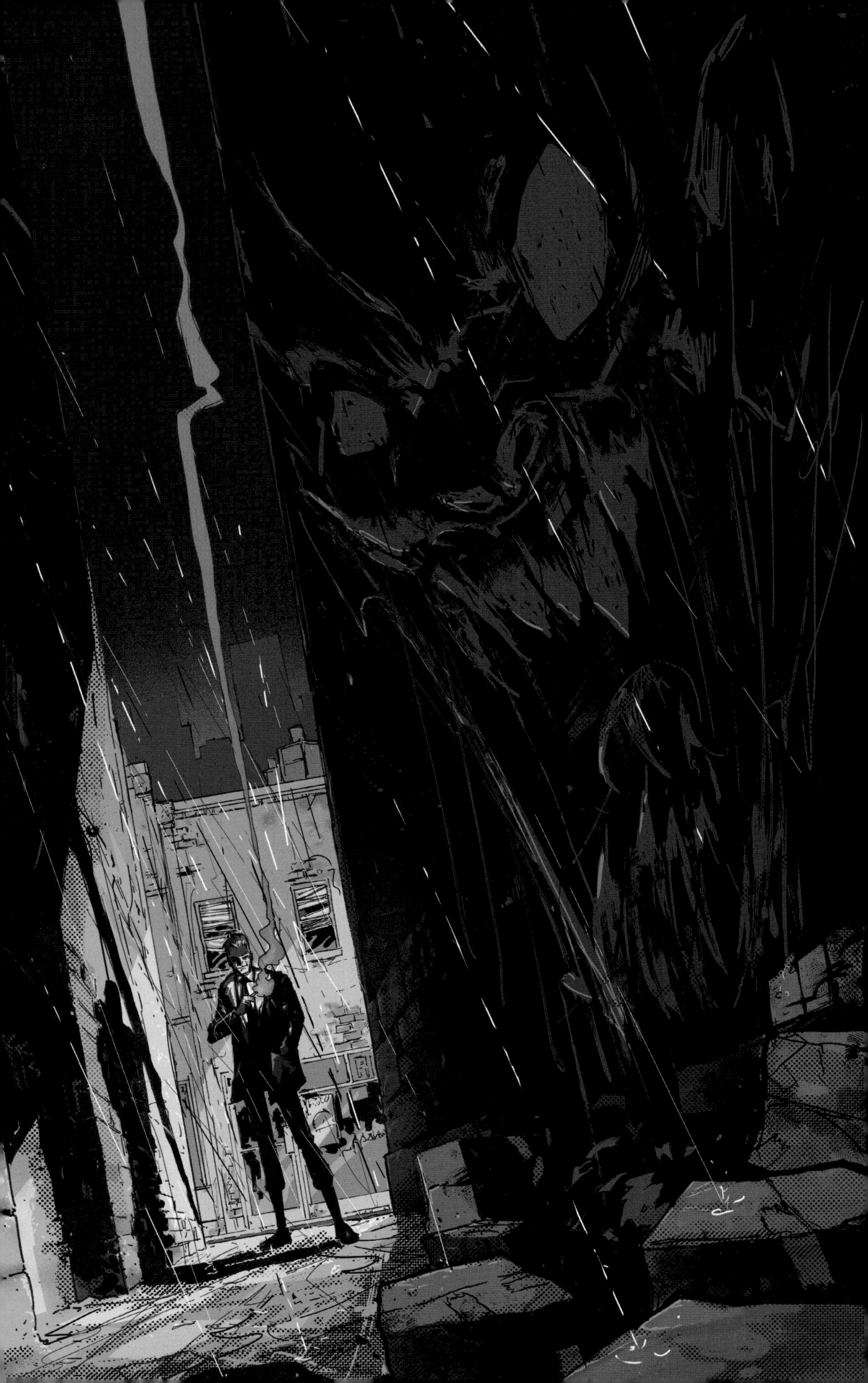

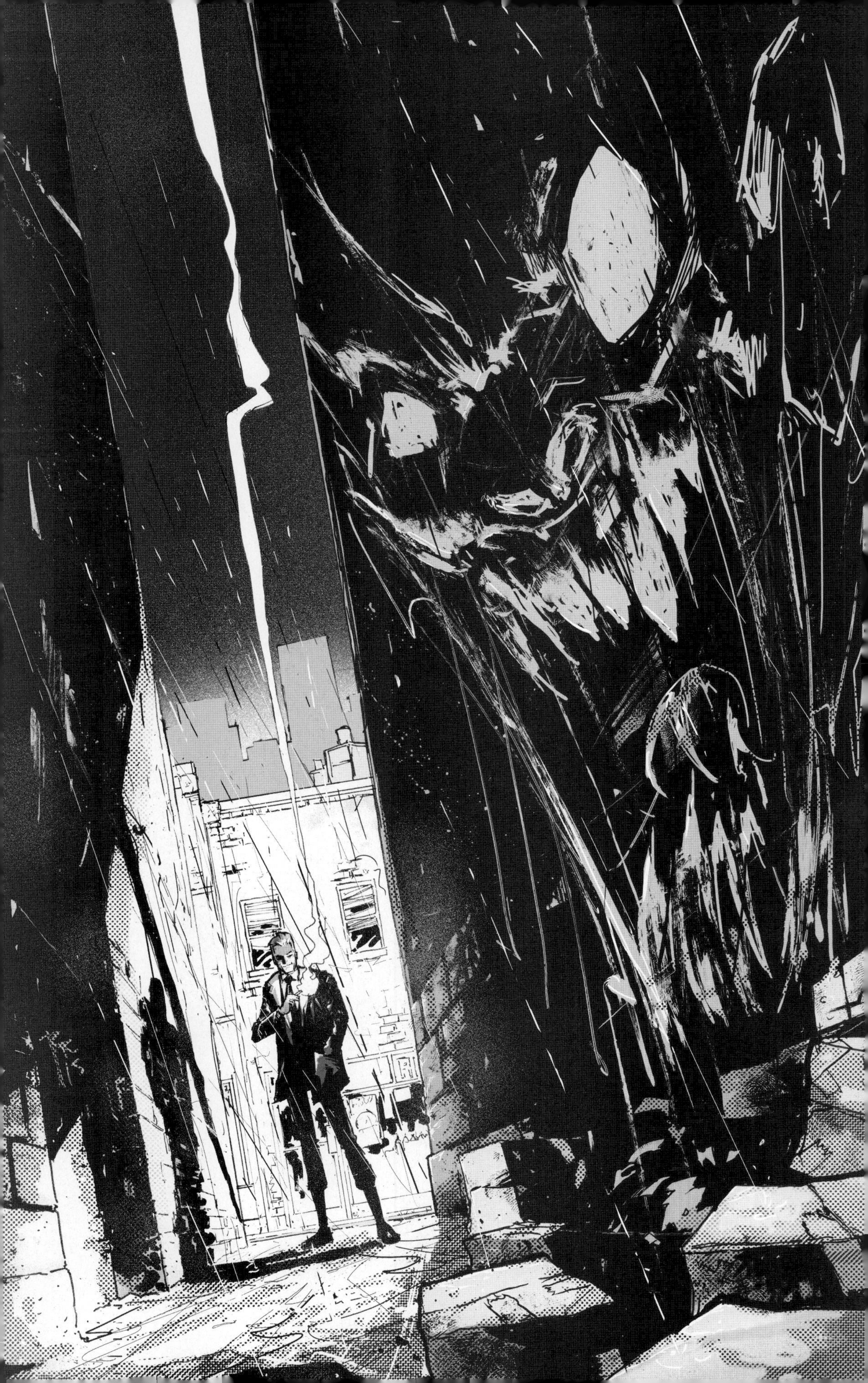

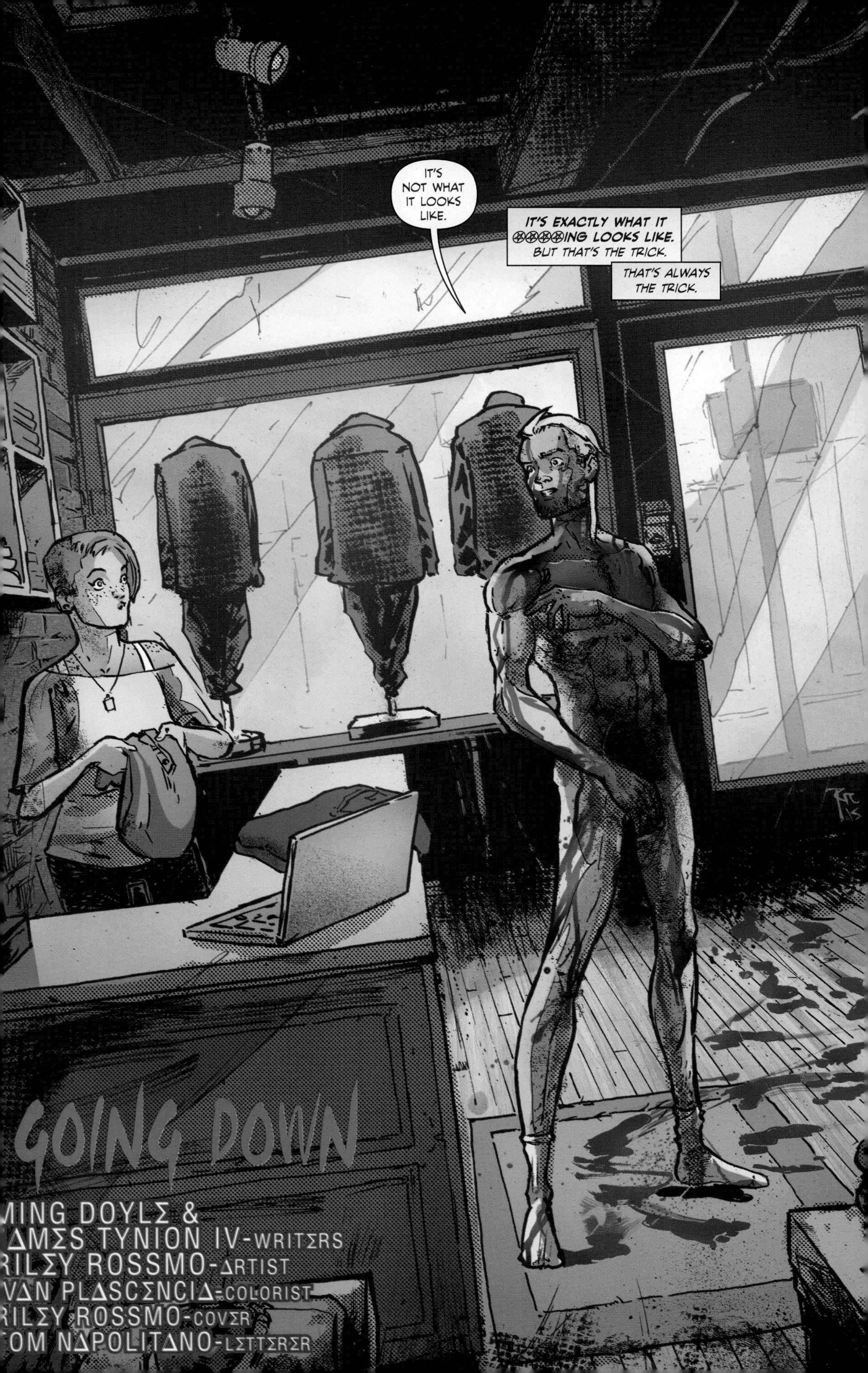

IT'S NOT WHAT IT LOOKS LIKE.
IT'S EXACTLY WHAT IT ⊗⊗⊗⊗ING LOOKS LIKE. BUT THAT'S THE TRICK.
THAT'S ALWAYS THE TRICK.
GOING DOWN
MING DOYLE &
AMES TYNION IV-WRITERS
RILEY ROSSMO-ARTIST
VAN PLASCENCIA-COLORIST
RILEY ROSSMO-COVER
TOM NAPOLITANO-LETTERER

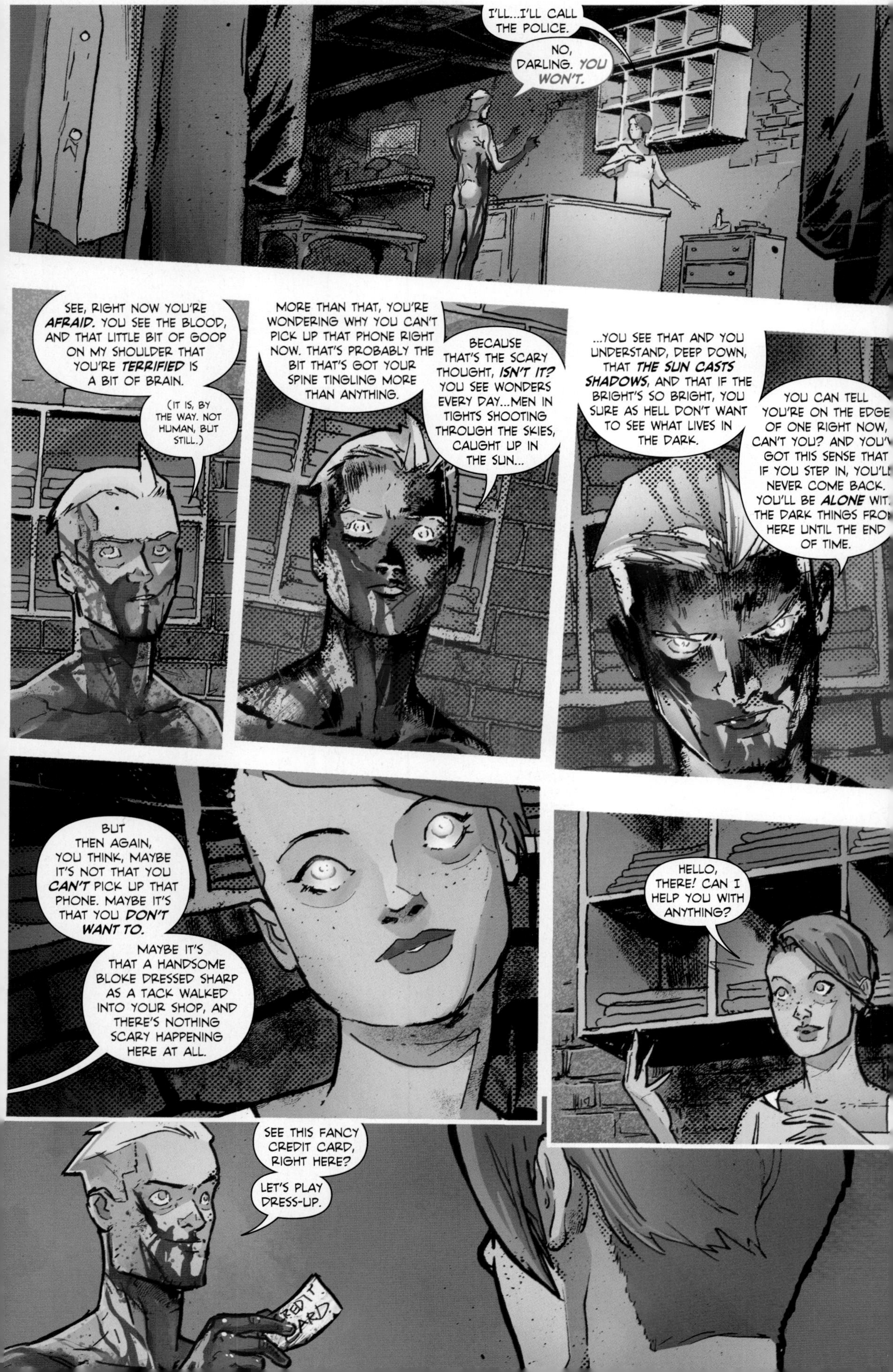
I'LL...I'LL CALL THE POLICE.
NO, DARLING. YOU WON'T.
SEE, RIGHT NOW YOU'RE AFRAID. YOU SEE THE BLOOD, AND THAT LITTLE BIT OF GOOP ON MY SHOULDER THAT YOU'RE TERRIFIED IS A BIT OF BRAIN.
(IT IS, BY THE WAY. NOT HUMAN, BUT STILL.)
MORE THAN THAT, YOU'RE WONDERING WHY YOU CAN'T PICK UP THAT PHONE RIGHT NOW. THAT'S PROBABLY THE BIT THAT'S GOT YOUR SPINE TINGLING MORE THAN ANYTHING.
BECAUSE THAT'S THE SCARY THOUGHT, ISN'T IT? YOU SEE WONDERS EVERY DAY...MEN IN TIGHTS SHOOTING THROUGH THE SKIES, CAUGHT UP IN THE SUN...
...YOU SEE THAT AND YOU UNDERSTAND, DEEP DOWN, THAT THE SUN CASTS SHADOWS, AND THAT IF THE BRIGHT'S SO BRIGHT, YOU SURE AS HELL DON'T WANT TO SEE WHAT LIVES IN THE DARK.
YOU CAN TELL YOU'RE ON THE EDGE OF ONE RIGHT NOW, CAN'T YOU? AND YOU'VE GOT THIS SENSE THAT IF YOU STEP IN, YOU'LL NEVER COME BACK. YOU'LL BE ALONE WITH THE DARK THINGS FROM HERE UNTIL THE END OF TIME.
BUT THEN AGAIN, YOU THINK, MAYBE IT'S NOT THAT YOU CAN'T PICK UP THAT PHONE. MAYBE IT'S THAT YOU DON'T WANT TO.
MAYBE IT'S THAT A HANDSOME BLOKE DRESSED SHARP AS A TACK WALKED INTO YOUR SHOP, AND THERE'S NOTHING SCARY HAPPENING HERE AT ALL.
HELLO, THERE! CAN I HELP YOU WITH ANYTHING?
SEE THIS FANCY CREDIT CARD, RIGHT HERE?
LET'S PLAY DRESS-UP.
CREDIT CARD

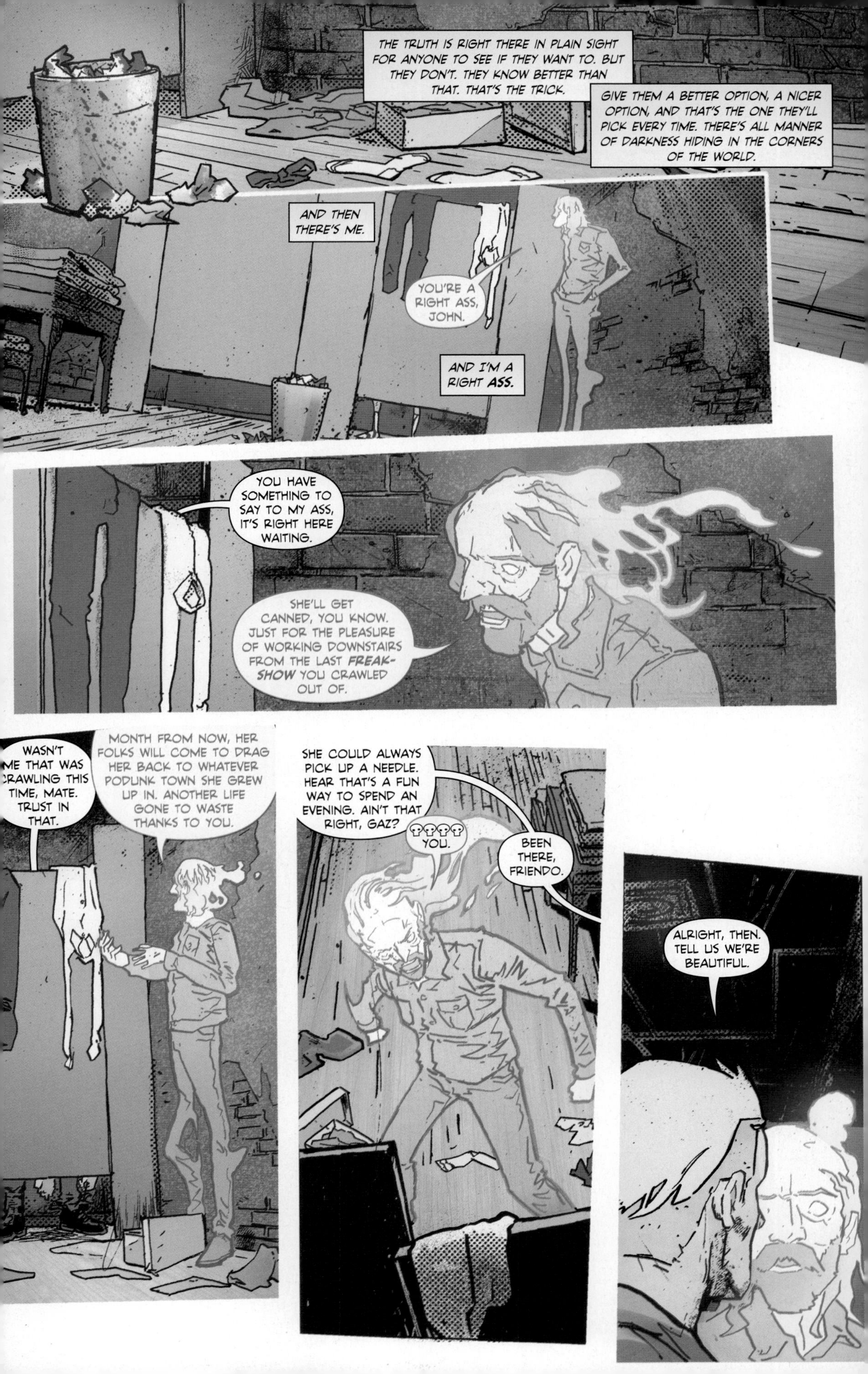

THE TRUTH IS RIGHT THERE IN PLAIN SIGHT FOR ANYONE TO SEE IF THEY WANT TO. BUT THEY DON'T. THEY KNOW BETTER THAN THAT. THAT'S THE TRICK.
GIVE THEM A BETTER OPTION, A NICER OPTION, AND THAT'S THE ONE THEY'LL PICK EVERY TIME. THERE'S ALL MANNER OF DARKNESS HIDING IN THE CORNERS OF THE WORLD.
AND THEN THERE'S ME.
YOU'RE A RIGHT ASS, JOHN.
AND I'M A RIGHT ASS.
YOU HAVE SOMETHING TO SAY TO MY ASS, IT'S RIGHT HERE WAITING.
SHE'LL GET CANNED, YOU KNOW. JUST FOR THE PLEASURE OF WORKING DOWNSTAIRS FROM THE LAST FREAK-SHOW YOU CRAWLED OUT OF.
WASN'T ME THAT WAS CRAWLING THIS TIME, MATE. TRUST IN THAT.
MONTH FROM NOW, HER FOLKS WILL COME TO DRAG HER BACK TO WHATEVER PODUNK TOWN SHE GREW UP IN. ANOTHER LIFE GONE TO WASTE THANKS TO YOU.
SHE COULD ALWAYS PICK UP A NEEDLE. HEAR THAT'S A FUN WAY TO SPEND AN EVENING. AIN'T THAT RIGHT, GAZ?
YOU.
BEEN THERE, FRIENDO.
ALRIGHT, THEN. TELL US WE'RE BEAUTIFUL.

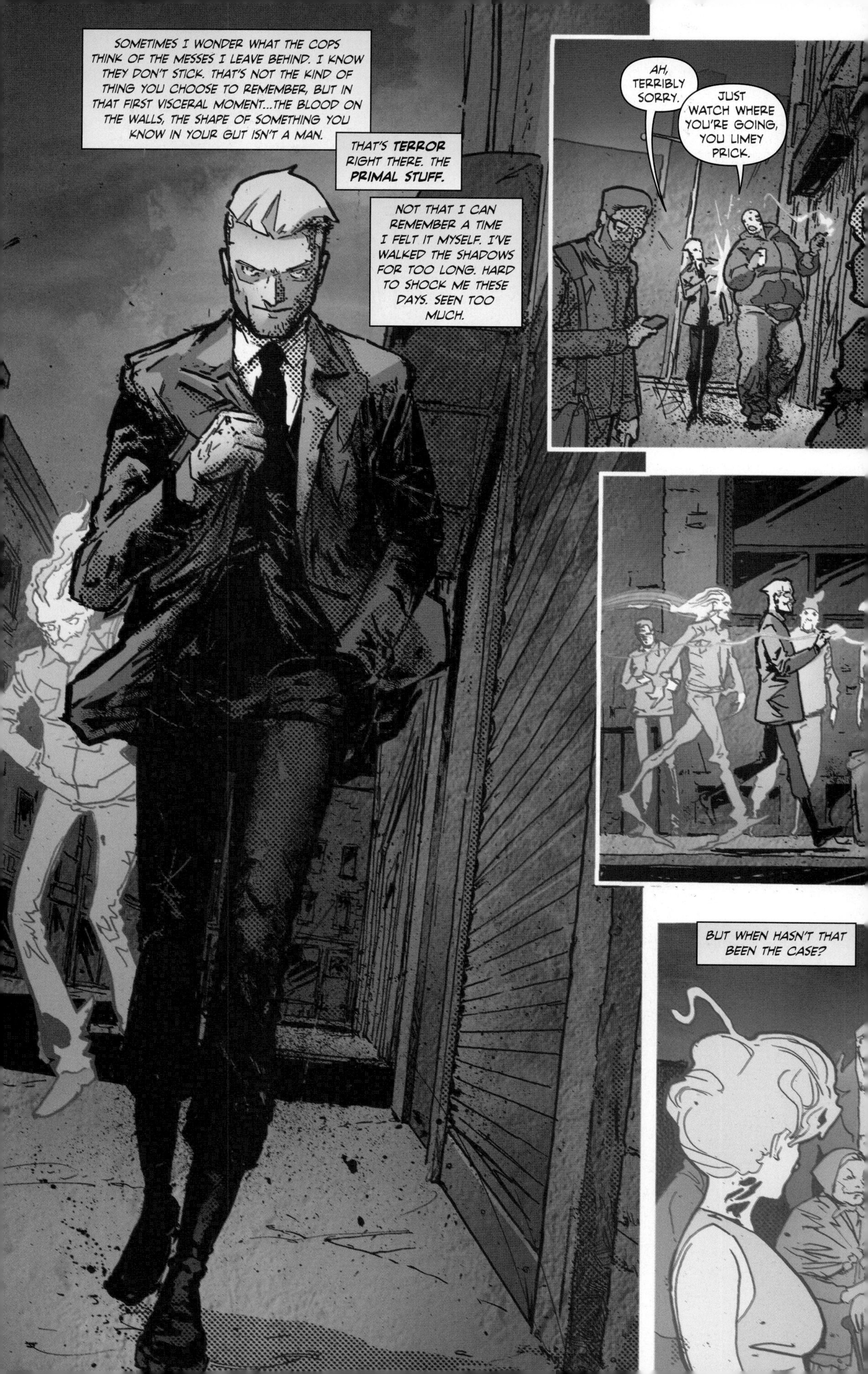
SOMETIMES I WONDER WHAT THE COPS THINK OF THE MESSES I LEAVE BEHIND. I KNOW THEY DON'T STICK. THAT'S NOT THE KIND OF THING YOU CHOOSE TO REMEMBER, BUT IN THAT FIRST VISCERAL MOMENT...THE BLOOD ON THE WALLS, THE SHAPE OF SOMETHING YOU KNOW IN YOUR GUT ISN'T A MAN.
THAT'S TERROR RIGHT THERE. THE PRIMAL STUFF.
NOT THAT I CAN REMEMBER A TIME I FELT IT MYSELF. I'VE WALKED THE SHADOWS FOR TOO LONG. HARD TO SHOCK ME THESE DAYS. SEEN TOO MUCH.
AH, TERRIBLY SORRY.
JUST WATCH WHERE YOU'RE GOING, YOU LIMEY PRICK.
BUT WHEN HASN'T THAT BEEN THE CASE?

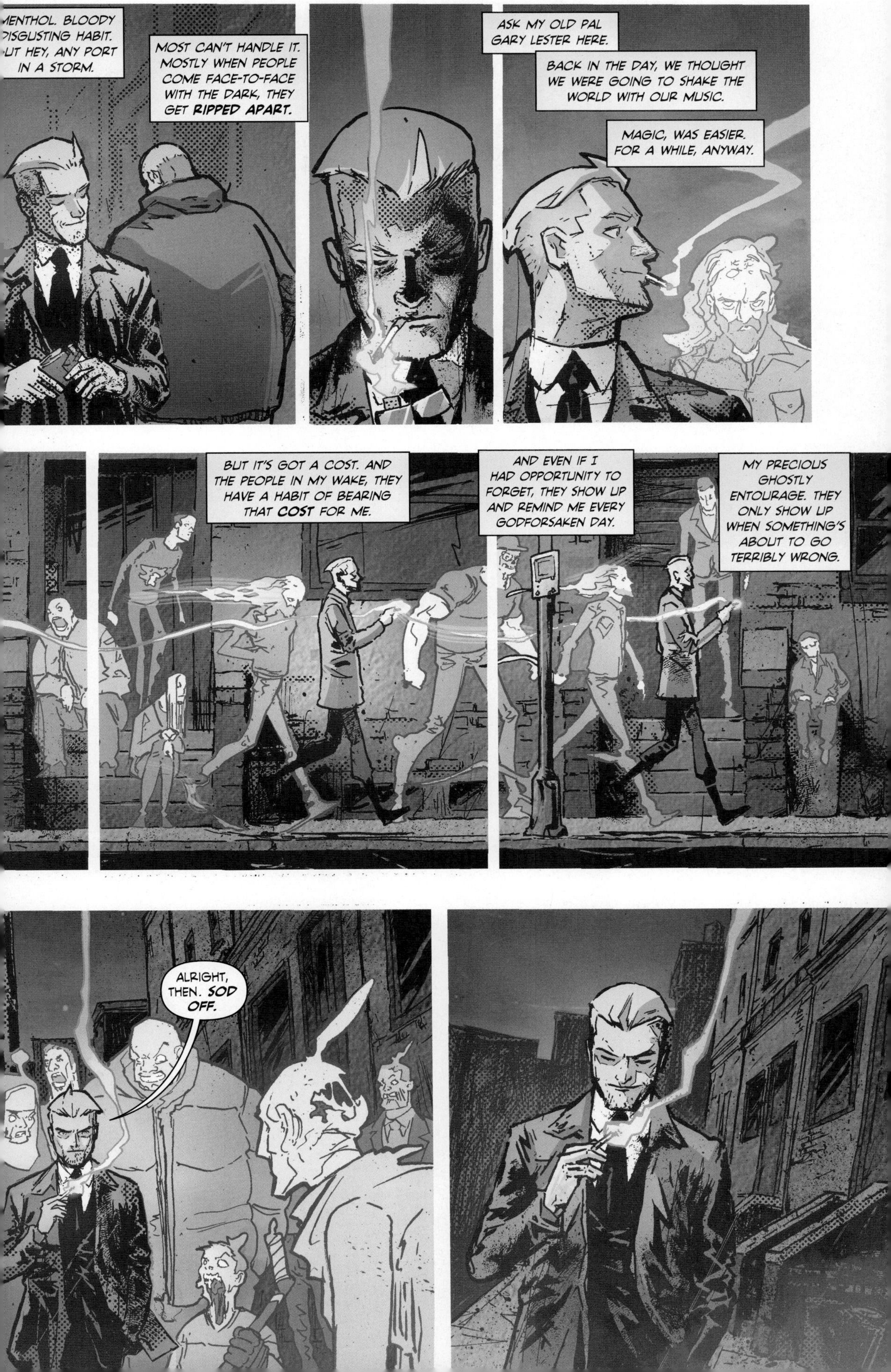

MENTHOL. BLOODY DISGUSTING HABIT. BUT HEY, ANY PORT IN A STORM.
MOST CAN'T HANDLE IT. MOSTLY WHEN PEOPLE COME FACE-TO-FACE WITH THE DARK, THEY GET RIPPED APART.
ASK MY OLD PAL GARY LESTER HERE.
BACK IN THE DAY, WE THOUGHT WE WERE GOING TO SHAKE THE WORLD WITH OUR MUSIC.
MAGIC, WAS EASIER. FOR A WHILE, ANYWAY.
BUT IT'S GOT A COST. AND THE PEOPLE IN MY WAKE, THEY HAVE A HABIT OF BEARING THAT COST FOR ME.
AND EVEN IF I HAD OPPORTUNITY TO FORGET, THEY SHOW UP AND REMIND ME EVERY GODFORSAKEN DAY.
MY PRECIOUS GHOSTLY ENTOURAGE. THEY ONLY SHOW UP WHEN SOMETHING'S ABOUT TO GO TERRIBLY WRONG.
ALRIGHT, THEN. SOD OFF.

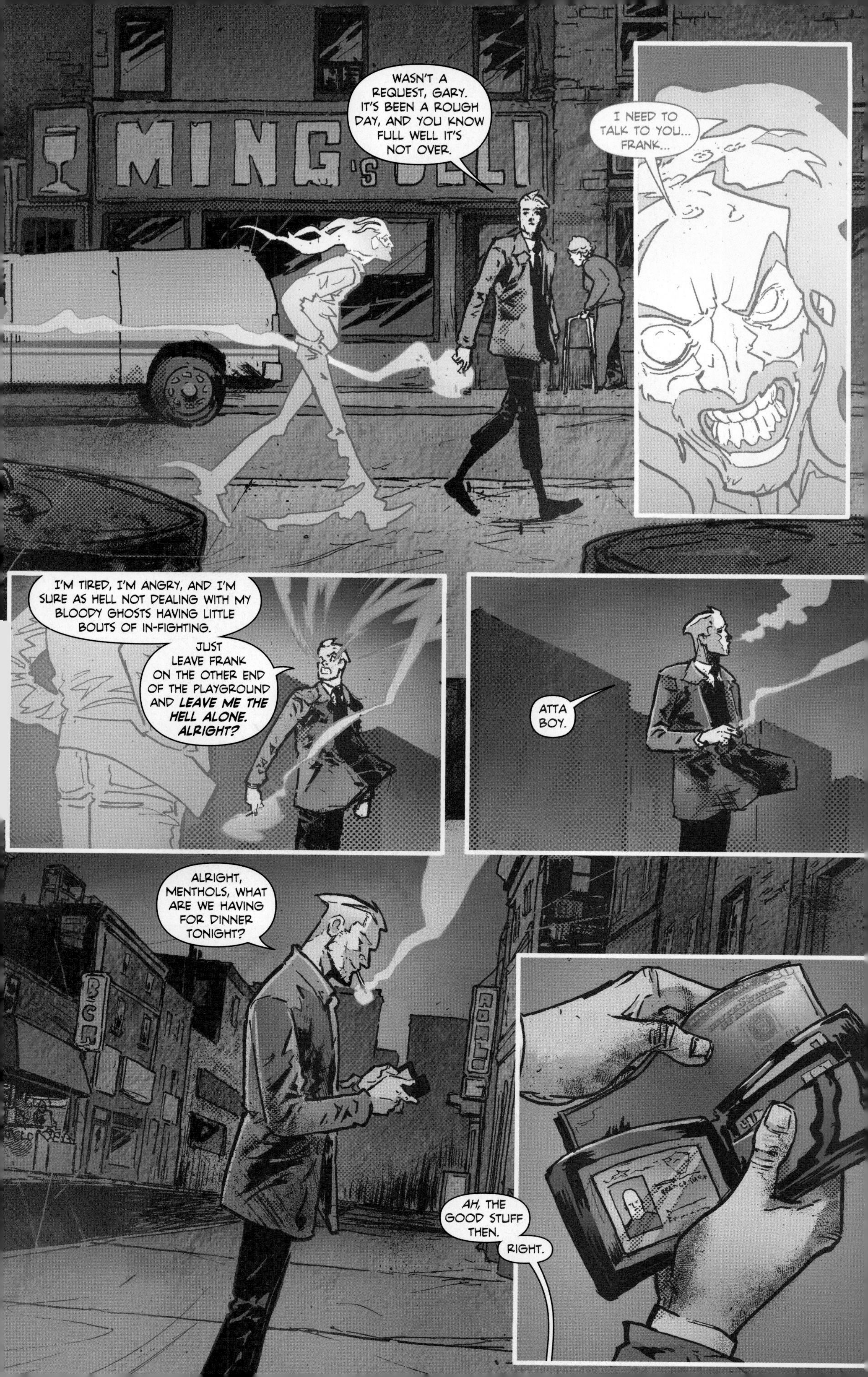

WASN'T A REQUEST, GARY. IT'S BEEN A ROUGH DAY, AND YOU KNOW FULL WELL IT'S NOT OVER.
MING'S DELI
I NEED TO TALK TO YOU... FRANK...
I'M TIRED, I'M ANGRY, AND I'M SURE AS HELL NOT DEALING WITH MY BLOODY GHOSTS HAVING LITTLE BOUTS OF IN-FIGHTING.
JUST LEAVE FRANK ON THE OTHER END OF THE PLAYGROUND AND *LEAVE ME THE HELL ALONE. ALRIGHT?*
ATTA BOY.
ALRIGHT, MENTHOLS, WHAT ARE WE HAVING FOR DINNER TONIGHT?
AH, THE GOOD STUFF THEN.
RIGHT.

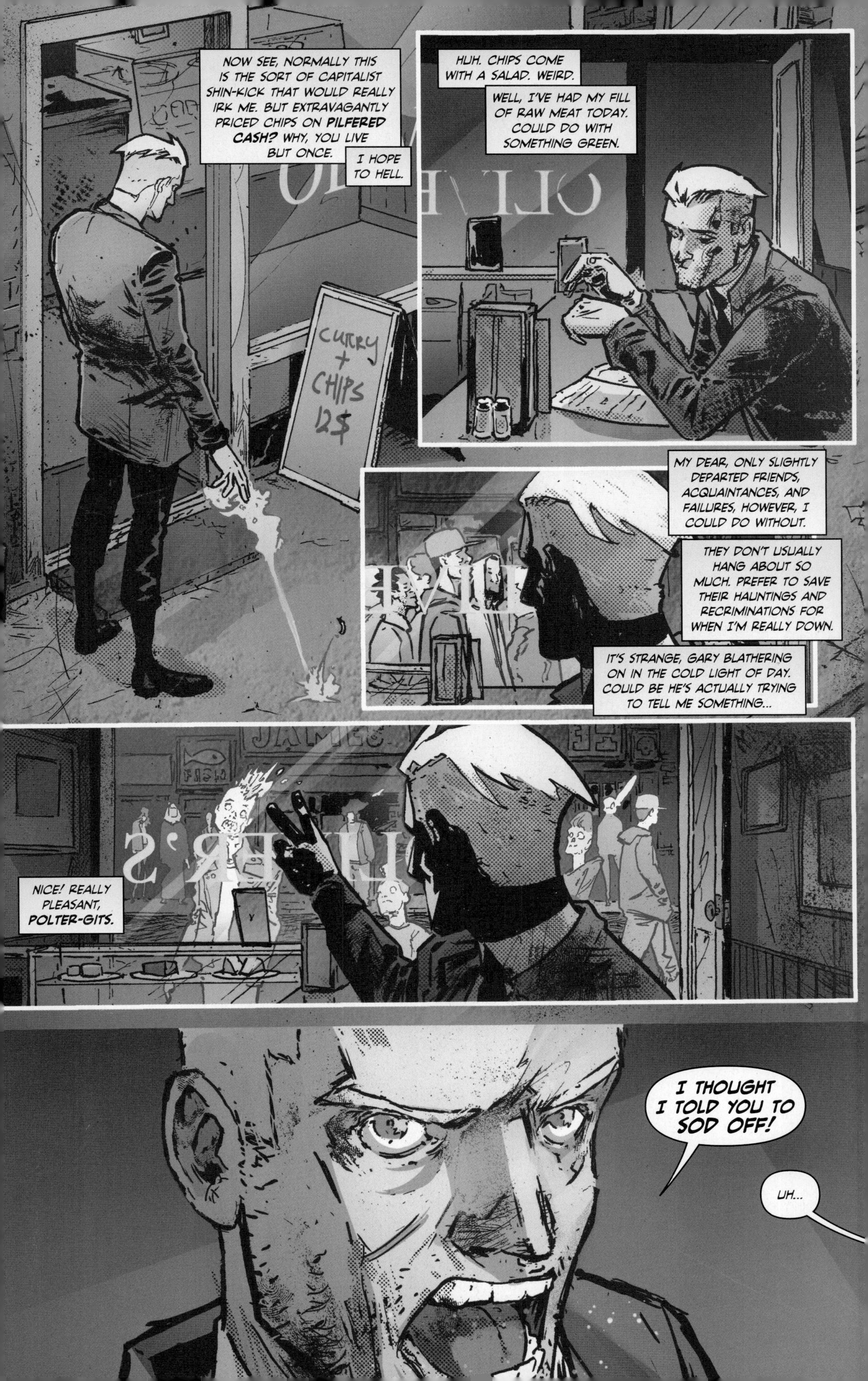
NOW SEE, NORMALLY THIS IS THE SORT OF CAPITALIST SHIN-KICK THAT WOULD REALLY IRK ME. BUT EXTRAVAGANTLY PRICED CHIPS ON **PILFERED CASH?** WHY, YOU LIVE BUT ONCE.
I HOPE TO HELL.
CURRY + CHIPS 12$
HUH. CHIPS COME WITH A SALAD. WEIRD.
WELL, I'VE HAD MY FILL OF RAW MEAT TODAY. COULD DO WITH SOMETHING GREEN.
MY DEAR, ONLY SLIGHTLY DEPARTED FRIENDS, ACQUAINTANCES, AND FAILURES, HOWEVER, I COULD DO WITHOUT.
THEY DON'T USUALLY HANG ABOUT SO MUCH. PREFER TO SAVE THEIR HAUNTINGS AND RECRIMINATIONS FOR WHEN I'M REALLY DOWN.
IT'S STRANGE, GARY BLATHERING ON IN THE COLD LIGHT OF DAY. COULD BE HE'S ACTUALLY TRYING TO TELL ME SOMETHING...
NICE! REALLY PLEASANT, **POLTER-GITS.**
I THOUGHT I TOLD YOU TO SOD OFF!
UH...

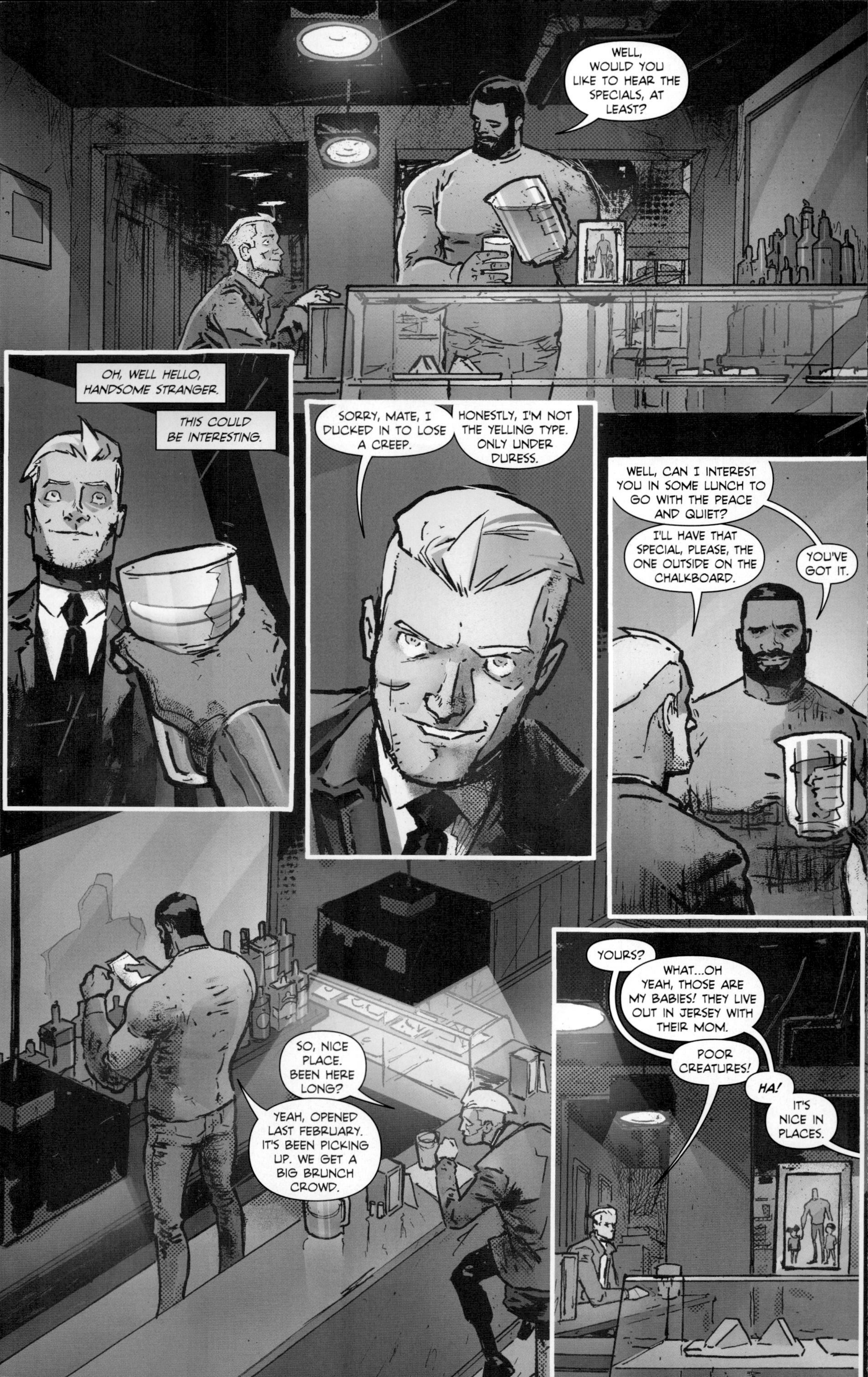
WELL, WOULD YOU LIKE TO HEAR THE SPECIALS, AT LEAST?
OH, WELL HELLO, HANDSOME STRANGER.
THIS COULD BE INTERESTING.
SORRY, MATE, I DUCKED IN TO LOSE A CREEP.
HONESTLY, I'M NOT THE YELLING TYPE. ONLY UNDER DURESS.
WELL, CAN I INTEREST YOU IN SOME LUNCH TO GO WITH THE PEACE AND QUIET?
I'LL HAVE THAT SPECIAL, PLEASE, THE ONE OUTSIDE ON THE CHALKBOARD.
YOU'VE GOT IT.
SO, NICE PLACE. BEEN HERE LONG?
YEAH, OPENED LAST FEBRUARY. IT'S BEEN PICKING UP. WE GET A BIG BRUNCH CROWD.
YOURS?
WHAT...OH YEAH, THOSE ARE MY BABIES! THEY LIVE OUT IN JERSEY WITH THEIR MOM.
POOR CREATURES!
HA!
IT'S NICE IN PLACES.

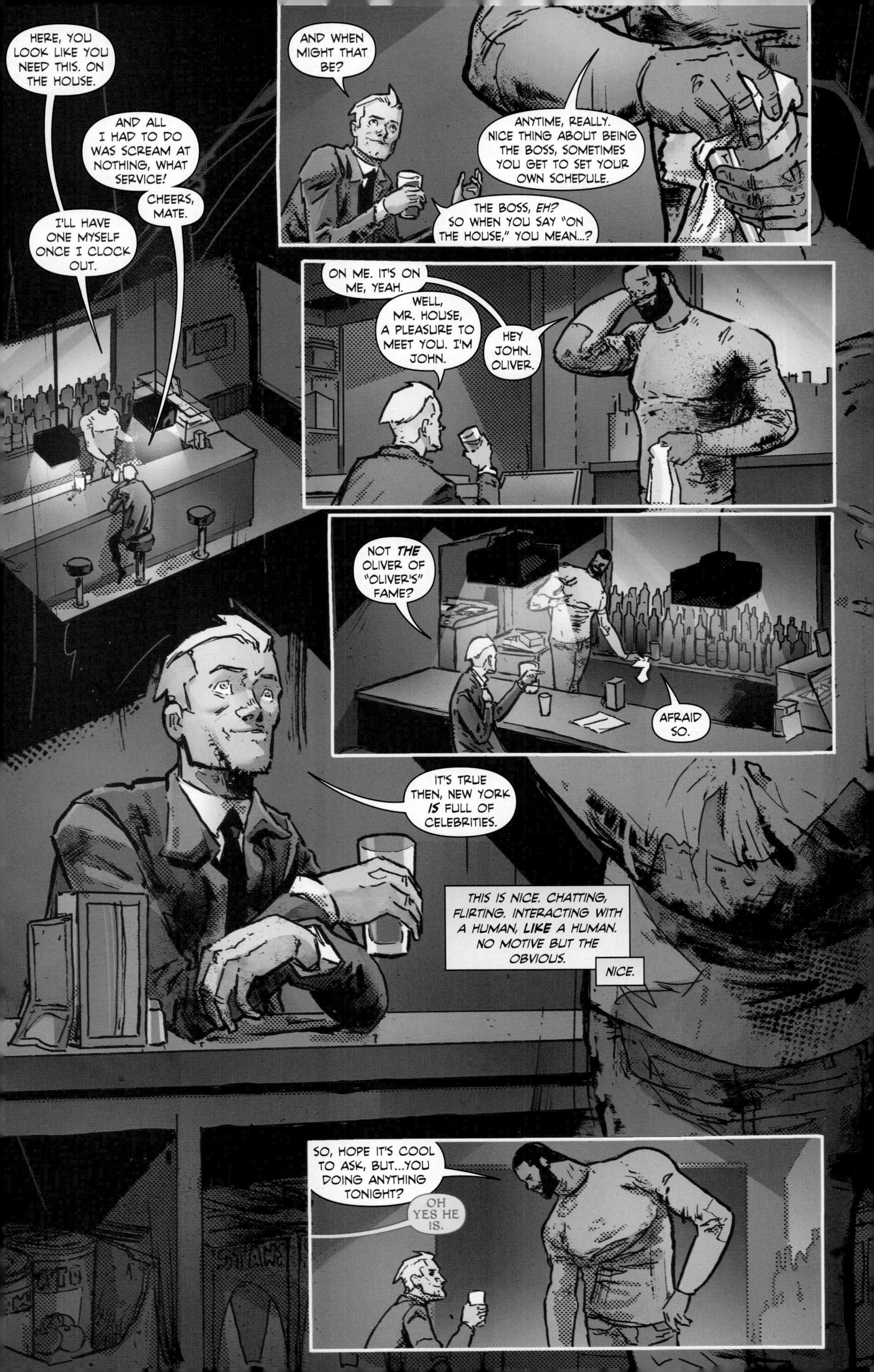
HERE, YOU LOOK LIKE YOU NEED THIS. ON THE HOUSE.
AND ALL I HAD TO DO WAS SCREAM AT NOTHING, WHAT SERVICE!
CHEERS, MATE.
I'LL HAVE ONE MYSELF ONCE I CLOCK OUT.
AND WHEN MIGHT THAT BE?
ANYTIME, REALLY. NICE THING ABOUT BEING THE BOSS, SOMETIMES YOU GET TO SET YOUR OWN SCHEDULE.
THE BOSS, EH? SO WHEN YOU SAY "ON THE HOUSE," YOU MEAN...?
ON ME. IT'S ON ME, YEAH.
WELL, MR. HOUSE, A PLEASURE TO MEET YOU. I'M JOHN.
HEY JOHN. OLIVER.
NOT THE OLIVER OF "OLIVER'S" FAME?
AFRAID SO.
IT'S TRUE THEN, NEW YORK IS FULL OF CELEBRITIES.
THIS IS NICE. CHATTING, FLIRTING. INTERACTING WITH A HUMAN, LIKE A HUMAN. NO MOTIVE BUT THE OBVIOUS.
NICE.
SO, HOPE IT'S COOL TO ASK, BUT...YOU DOING ANYTHING TONIGHT?
OH YES HE IS.

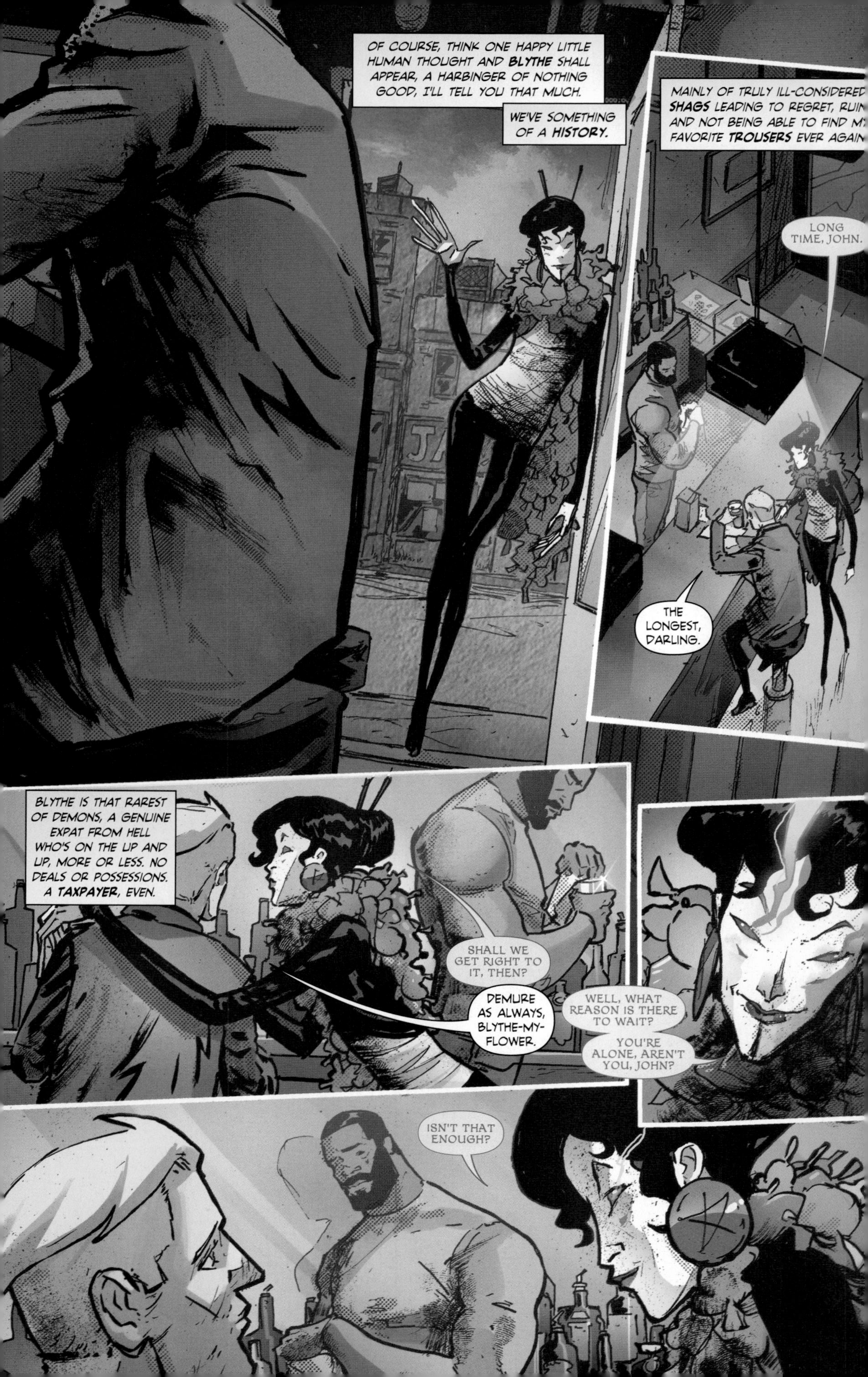
OF COURSE, THINK ONE HAPPY LITTLE HUMAN THOUGHT AND BLYTHE SHALL APPEAR, A HARBINGER OF NOTHING GOOD, I'LL TELL YOU THAT MUCH.
WE'VE SOMETHING OF A HISTORY.
MAINLY OF TRULY ILL-CONSIDERED SHAGS LEADING TO REGRET, RUIN AND NOT BEING ABLE TO FIND MY FAVORITE TROUSERS EVER AGAIN.
LONG TIME, JOHN.
THE LONGEST, DARLING.
BLYTHE IS THAT RAREST OF DEMONS, A GENUINE EXPAT FROM HELL WHO'S ON THE UP AND UP, MORE OR LESS. NO DEALS OR POSSESSIONS. A TAXPAYER, EVEN.
SHALL WE GET RIGHT TO IT, THEN?
DEMURE AS ALWAYS, BLYTHE-MY-FLOWER.
WELL, WHAT REASON IS THERE TO WAIT?
YOU'RE ALONE, AREN'T YOU, JOHN?
ISN'T THAT ENOUGH?

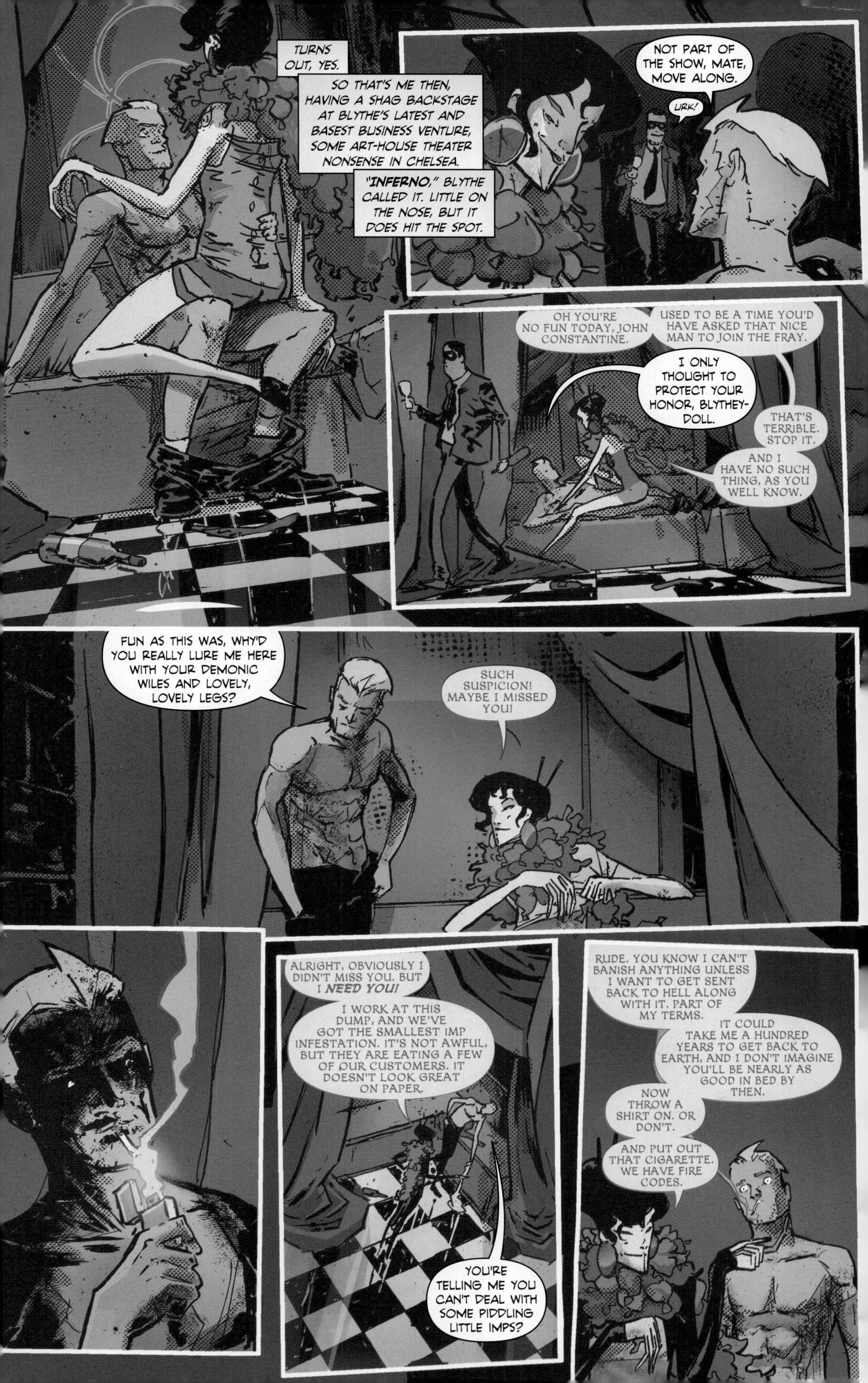
TURNS OUT, YES.
SO THAT'S ME THEN, HAVING A SHAG BACKSTAGE AT BLYTHE'S LATEST AND BASEST BUSINESS VENTURE, SOME ART-HOUSE THEATER NONSENSE IN CHELSEA.
"INFERNO," BLYTHE CALLED IT. LITTLE ON THE NOSE, BUT IT DOES HIT THE SPOT.
NOT PART OF THE SHOW, MATE, MOVE ALONG.
URK!
OH YOU'RE NO FUN TODAY, JOHN CONSTANTINE.
USED TO BE A TIME YOU'D HAVE ASKED THAT NICE MAN TO JOIN THE FRAY.
I ONLY THOUGHT TO PROTECT YOUR HONOR, BLYTHEY-DOLL.
THAT'S TERRIBLE. STOP IT.
AND I HAVE NO SUCH THING, AS YOU WELL KNOW.
FUN AS THIS WAS, WHY'D YOU REALLY LURE ME HERE WITH YOUR DEMONIC WILES AND LOVELY, LOVELY LEGS?
SUCH SUSPICION! MAYBE I MISSED YOU!
ALRIGHT, OBVIOUSLY I DIDN'T MISS YOU. BUT I NEED YOU!
I WORK AT THIS DUMP, AND WE'VE GOT THE SMALLEST IMP INFESTATION. IT'S NOT AWFUL, BUT THEY ARE EATING A FEW OF OUR CUSTOMERS. IT DOESN'T LOOK GREAT ON PAPER.
YOU'RE TELLING ME YOU CAN'T DEAL WITH SOME PIDDLING LITTLE IMPS?
RUDE. YOU KNOW I CAN'T BANISH ANYTHING UNLESS I WANT TO GET SENT BACK TO HELL ALONG WITH IT. PART OF MY TERMS.
IT COULD TAKE ME A HUNDRED YEARS TO GET BACK TO EARTH, AND I DON'T IMAGINE YOU'LL BE NEARLY AS GOOD IN BED BY THEN.
NOW THROW A SHIRT ON. OR DON'T.
AND PUT OUT THAT CIGARETTE. WE HAVE FIRE CODES.

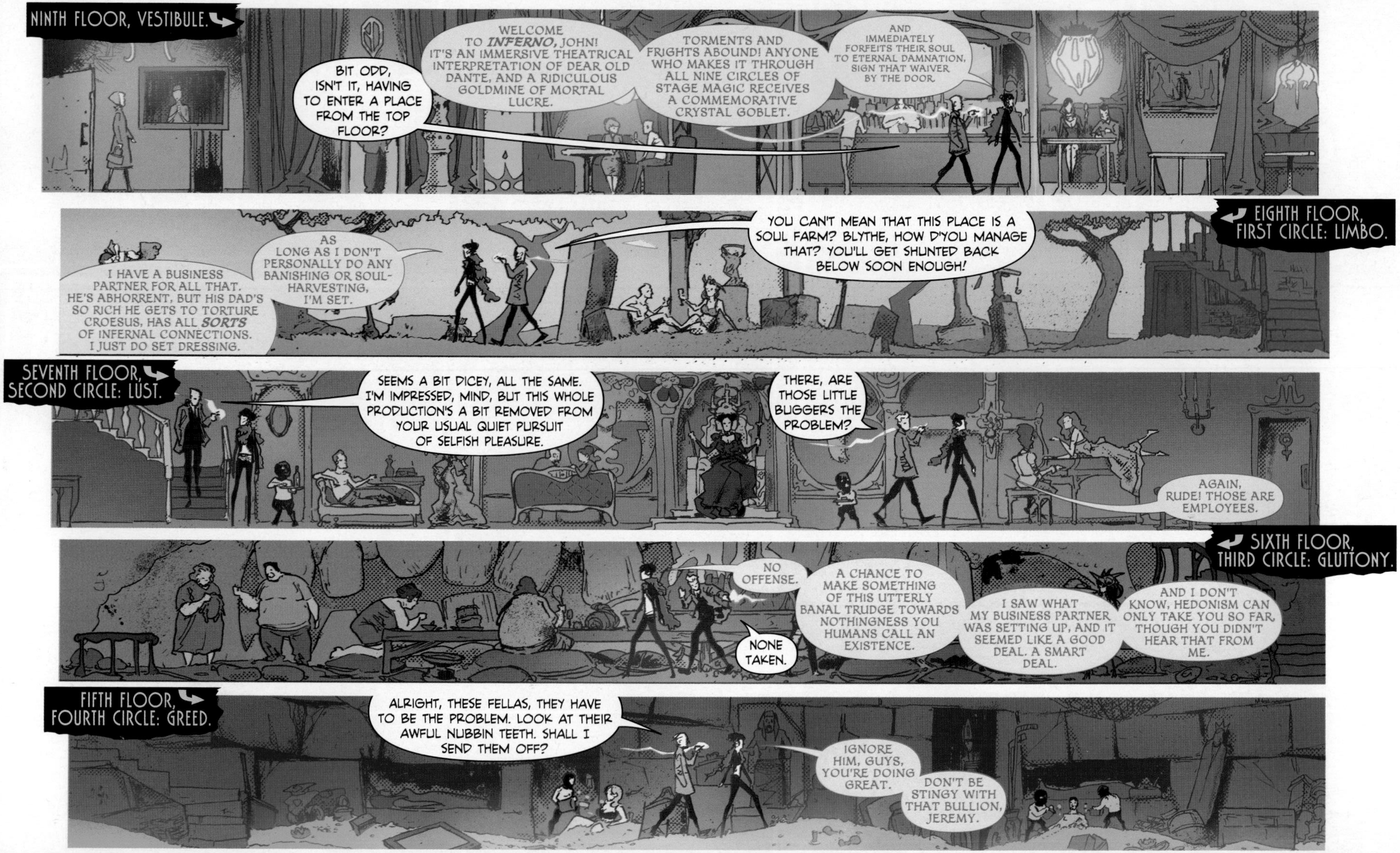

NINTH FLOOR, VESTIBULE.
BIT ODD, ISN'T IT, HAVING TO ENTER A PLACE FROM THE TOP FLOOR?
WELCOME TO *INFERNO*, JOHN! IT'S AN IMMERSIVE THEATRICAL INTERPRETATION OF DEAR OLD DANTE, AND A RIDICULOUS GOLDMINE OF MORTAL LUCRE.
TORMENTS AND FRIGHTS ABOUND! ANYONE WHO MAKES IT THROUGH ALL NINE CIRCLES OF STAGE MAGIC RECEIVES A COMMEMORATIVE CRYSTAL GOBLET.
AND IMMEDIATELY FORFEITS THEIR SOUL TO ETERNAL DAMNATION. SIGN THAT WAIVER BY THE DOOR.
EIGHTH FLOOR, FIRST CIRCLE: LIMBO.
YOU CAN'T MEAN THAT THIS PLACE IS A SOUL FARM? BLYTHE, HOW D'YOU MANAGE THAT? YOU'LL GET SHUNTED BACK BELOW SOON ENOUGH!
AS LONG AS I DON'T PERSONALLY DO ANY BANISHING OR SOUL-HARVESTING, I'M SET.
I HAVE A BUSINESS PARTNER FOR ALL THAT. HE'S ABHORRENT, BUT HIS DAD'S SO RICH HE GETS TO TORTURE CROESUS, HAS ALL *SORTS* OF INFERNAL CONNECTIONS. I JUST DO SET DRESSING.
SEVENTH FLOOR, SECOND CIRCLE: LUST.
SEEMS A BIT DICEY, ALL THE SAME. I'M IMPRESSED, MIND, BUT THIS WHOLE PRODUCTION'S A BIT REMOVED FROM YOUR USUAL QUIET PURSUIT OF SELFISH PLEASURE.
THERE, ARE THOSE LITTLE BUGGERS THE PROBLEM?
AGAIN, RUDE! THOSE ARE EMPLOYEES.
SIXTH FLOOR, THIRD CIRCLE: GLUTTONY.
NO OFFENSE.
NONE TAKEN.
A CHANCE TO MAKE SOMETHING OF THIS UTTERLY BANAL TRUDGE TOWARDS NOTHINGNESS YOU HUMANS CALL AN EXISTENCE.
I SAW WHAT MY BUSINESS PARTNER WAS SETTING UP, AND IT SEEMED LIKE A GOOD DEAL. A SMART DEAL.
AND I DON'T KNOW, HEDONISM CAN ONLY TAKE YOU SO FAR, THOUGH YOU DIDN'T HEAR THAT FROM ME.
FIFTH FLOOR, FOURTH CIRCLE: GREED.
ALRIGHT, THESE FELLAS, THEY HAVE TO BE THE PROBLEM. LOOK AT THEIR AWFUL NUBBIN TEETH. SHALL I SEND THEM OFF?
IGNORE HIM, GUYS, YOU'RE DOING GREAT.
DON'T BE STINGY WITH THAT BULLION, JEREMY.

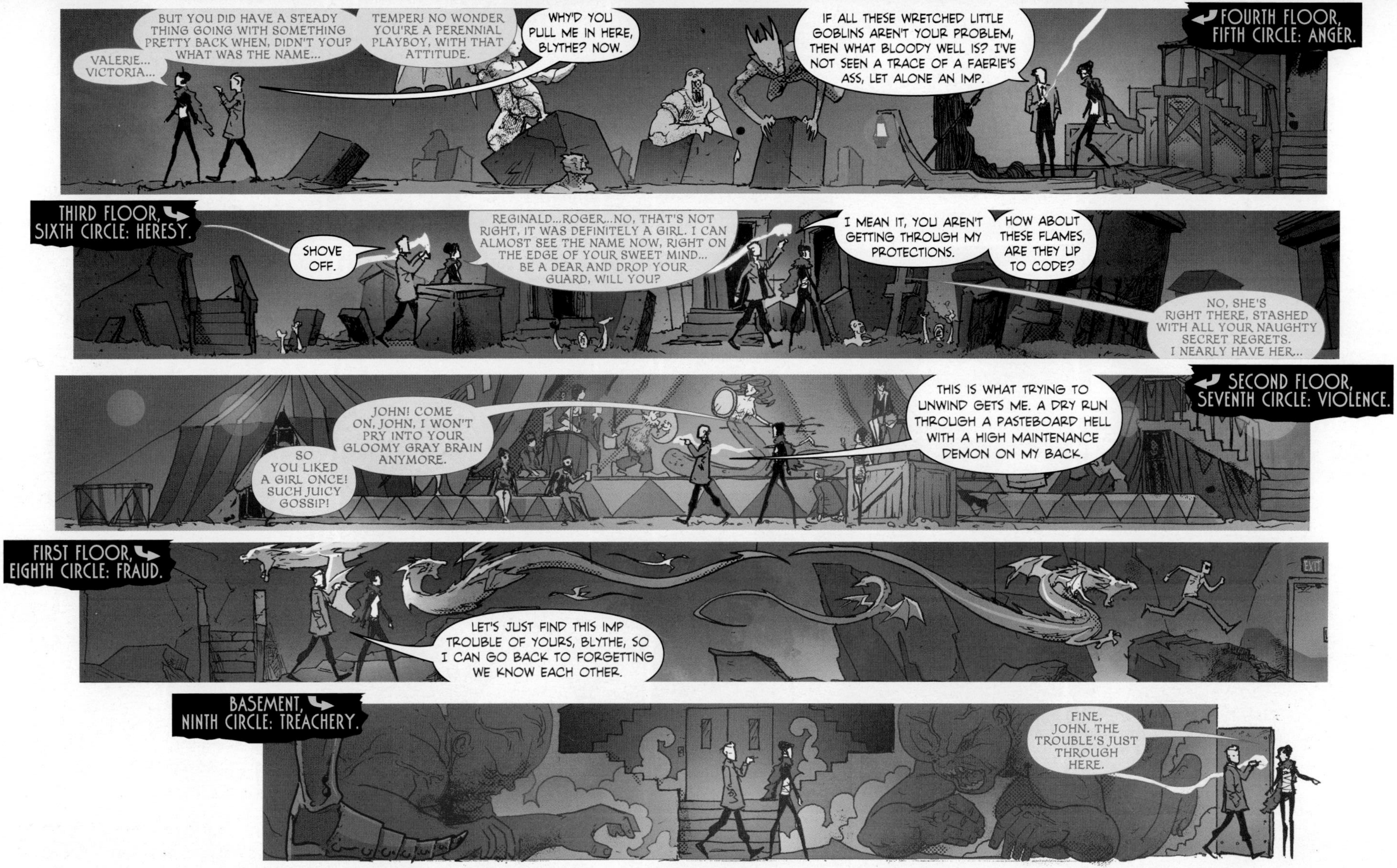
FOURTH FLOOR, FIFTH CIRCLE: ANGER.
IF ALL THESE WRETCHED LITTLE GOBLINS AREN'T YOUR PROBLEM, THEN WHAT BLOODY WELL IS? I'VE NOT SEEN A TRACE OF A FAERIE'S ASS, LET ALONE AN IMP.
WHY'D YOU PULL ME IN HERE, BLYTHE? NOW.
TEMPER! NO WONDER YOU'RE A PERENNIAL PLAYBOY, WITH THAT ATTITUDE.
BUT YOU DID HAVE A STEADY THING GOING WITH SOMETHING PRETTY BACK WHEN, DIDN'T YOU? WHAT WAS THE NAME...
VALERIE... VICTORIA...
THIRD FLOOR, SIXTH CIRCLE: HERESY.
SHOVE OFF.
REGINALD...ROGER...NO, THAT'S NOT RIGHT, IT WAS DEFINITELY A GIRL. I CAN ALMOST SEE THE NAME NOW, RIGHT ON THE EDGE OF YOUR SWEET MIND... BE A DEAR AND DROP YOUR GUARD, WILL YOU?
I MEAN IT, YOU AREN'T GETTING THROUGH MY PROTECTIONS.
HOW ABOUT THESE FLAMES, ARE THEY UP TO CODE?
NO, SHE'S RIGHT THERE, STASHED WITH ALL YOUR NAUGHTY SECRET REGRETS. I NEARLY HAVE HER...
SECOND FLOOR, SEVENTH CIRCLE: VIOLENCE.
THIS IS WHAT TRYING TO UNWIND GETS ME. A DRY RUN THROUGH A PASTEBOARD HELL WITH A HIGH MAINTENANCE DEMON ON MY BACK.
JOHN! COME ON, JOHN, I WON'T PRY INTO YOUR GLOOMY GRAY BRAIN ANYMORE.
SO YOU LIKED A GIRL ONCE! SUCH JUICY GOSSIP!
FIRST FLOOR, EIGHTH CIRCLE: FRAUD.
EXIT
LET'S JUST FIND THIS IMP TROUBLE OF YOURS, BLYTHE, SO I CAN GO BACK TO FORGETTING WE KNOW EACH OTHER.
BASEMENT, NINTH CIRCLE: TREACHERY.
FINE, JOHN. THE TROUBLE'S JUST THROUGH HERE.

SO WE'LL HAVE, WHAT, TEN DANCERS BROUGHT IN? FIFTEEN? WE'RE GETTING CATERING FROM MOMOFUKO, CASUAL. BUT WE'VE GOT THOSE SOUTH AFRICAN RAPPER KIDS AND DANGER MOUSE COMING BY, SO...

...THE HELL?

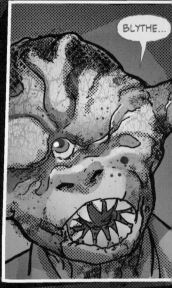

BLYTHE...

HALUK, HELLO. COME MEET A FRIEND.

JOHN CONSTANTINE, I'D LIKE YOU TO MEET MY BUSINESS PARTNER, HALUK. HE'S THE BIG SHOT BEHIND ALL THE UNDERHANDED SOUL-HARVESTING HERE.

HRRRRR...

RIGHT, SO THIS IS SOME KIND OF BACKSTABBING SOAP OPERA THING, THEN? NO THANKS.

SEE YOU TWO AGAIN NEVER.

SORRY, DARLING, BUT YOU KNOW I COULDN'T DO WITHOUT YOU HERE.

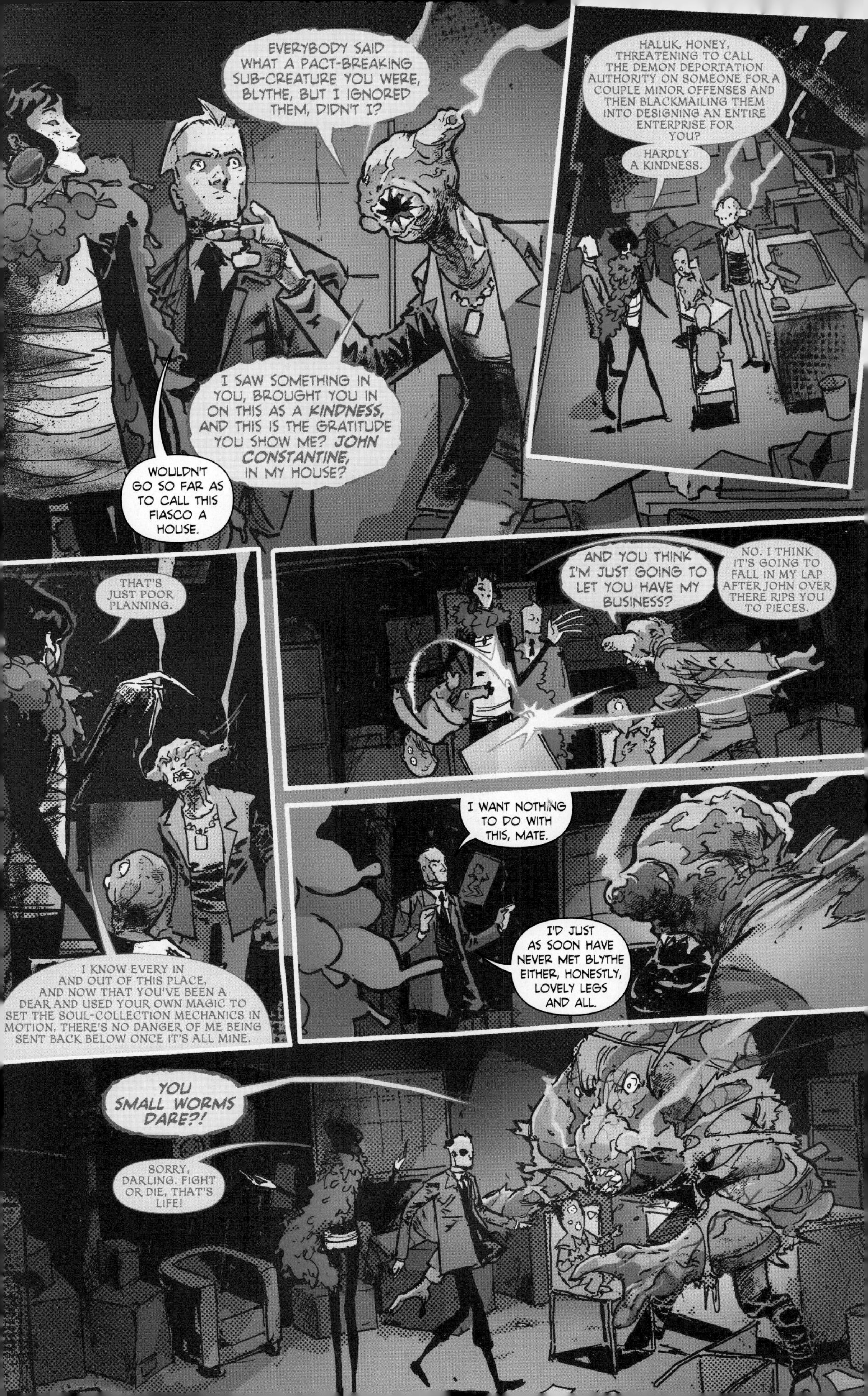
EVERYBODY SAID WHAT A PACT-BREAKING SUB-CREATURE YOU WERE, BLYTHE, BUT I IGNORED THEM, DIDN'T I?
I SAW SOMETHING IN YOU, BROUGHT YOU IN ON THIS AS A KINDNESS, AND THIS IS THE GRATITUDE YOU SHOW ME? JOHN CONSTANTINE, IN MY HOUSE?
WOULDN'T GO SO FAR AS TO CALL THIS FIASCO A HOUSE.
HALUK, HONEY, THREATENING TO CALL THE DEMON DEPORTATION AUTHORITY ON SOMEONE FOR A COUPLE MINOR OFFENSES AND THEN BLACKMAILING THEM INTO DESIGNING AN ENTIRE ENTERPRISE FOR YOU?
HARDLY A KINDNESS.
THAT'S JUST POOR PLANNING.
I KNOW EVERY IN AND OUT OF THIS PLACE, AND NOW THAT YOU'VE BEEN A DEAR AND USED YOUR OWN MAGIC TO SET THE SOUL-COLLECTION MECHANICS IN MOTION, THERE'S NO DANGER OF ME BEING SENT BACK BELOW ONCE IT'S ALL MINE.
AND YOU THINK I'M JUST GOING TO LET YOU HAVE MY BUSINESS?
NO. I THINK IT'S GOING TO FALL IN MY LAP AFTER JOHN OVER THERE RIPS YOU TO PIECES.
I WANT NOTHING TO DO WITH THIS, MATE.
I'D JUST AS SOON HAVE NEVER MET BLYTHE EITHER, HONESTLY, LOVELY LEGS AND ALL.
YOU SMALL WORMS DARE?!
SORRY, DARLING. FIGHT OR DIE, THAT'S LIFE!

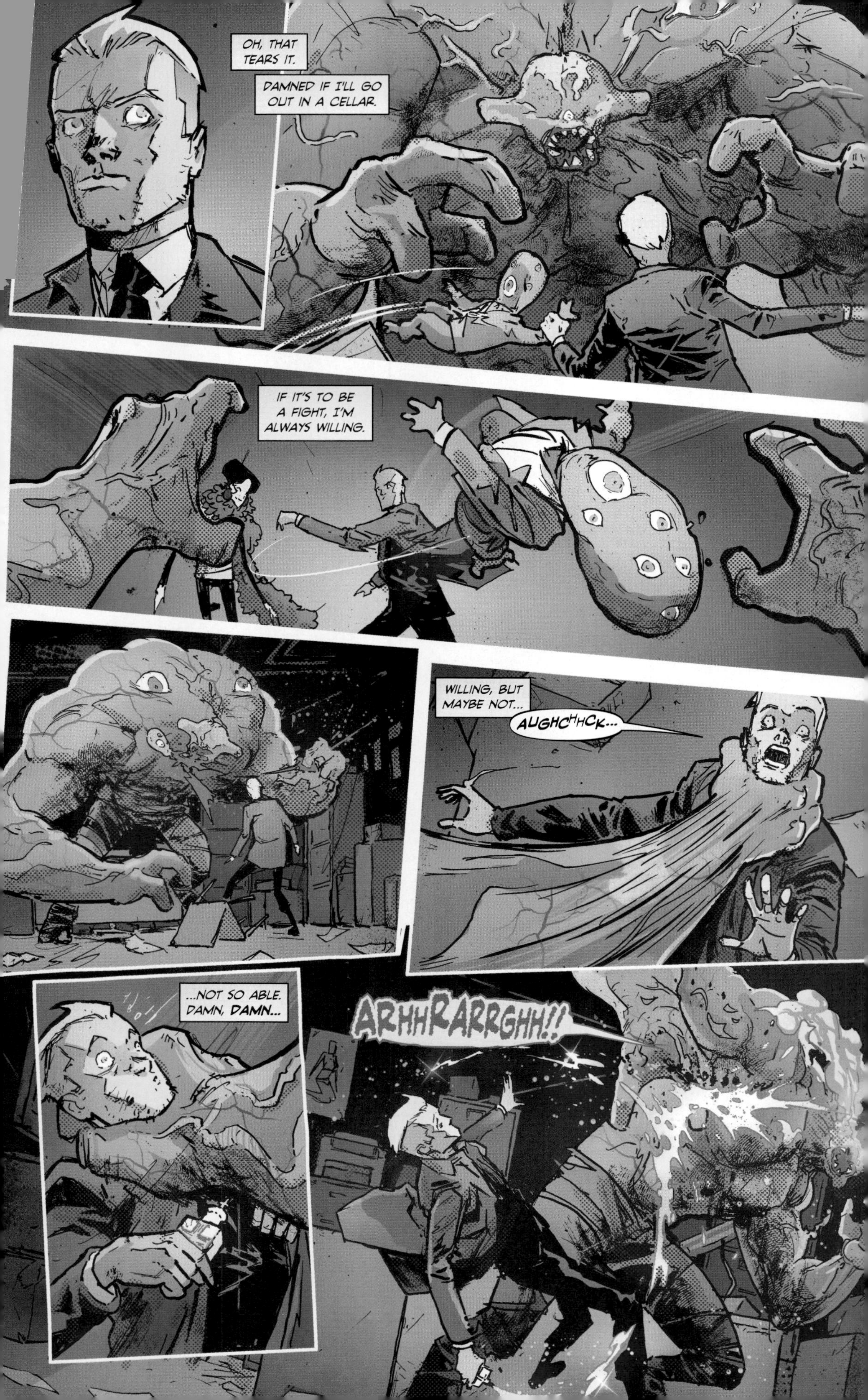
OH, THAT TEARS IT.
DAMNED IF I'LL GO OUT IN A CELLAR.
IF IT'S TO BE A FIGHT, I'M ALWAYS WILLING.
WILLING, BUT MAYBE NOT...
AUGHCHHCK...
...NOT SO ABLE. DAMN, DAMN...
ARHHRARRGHH!!

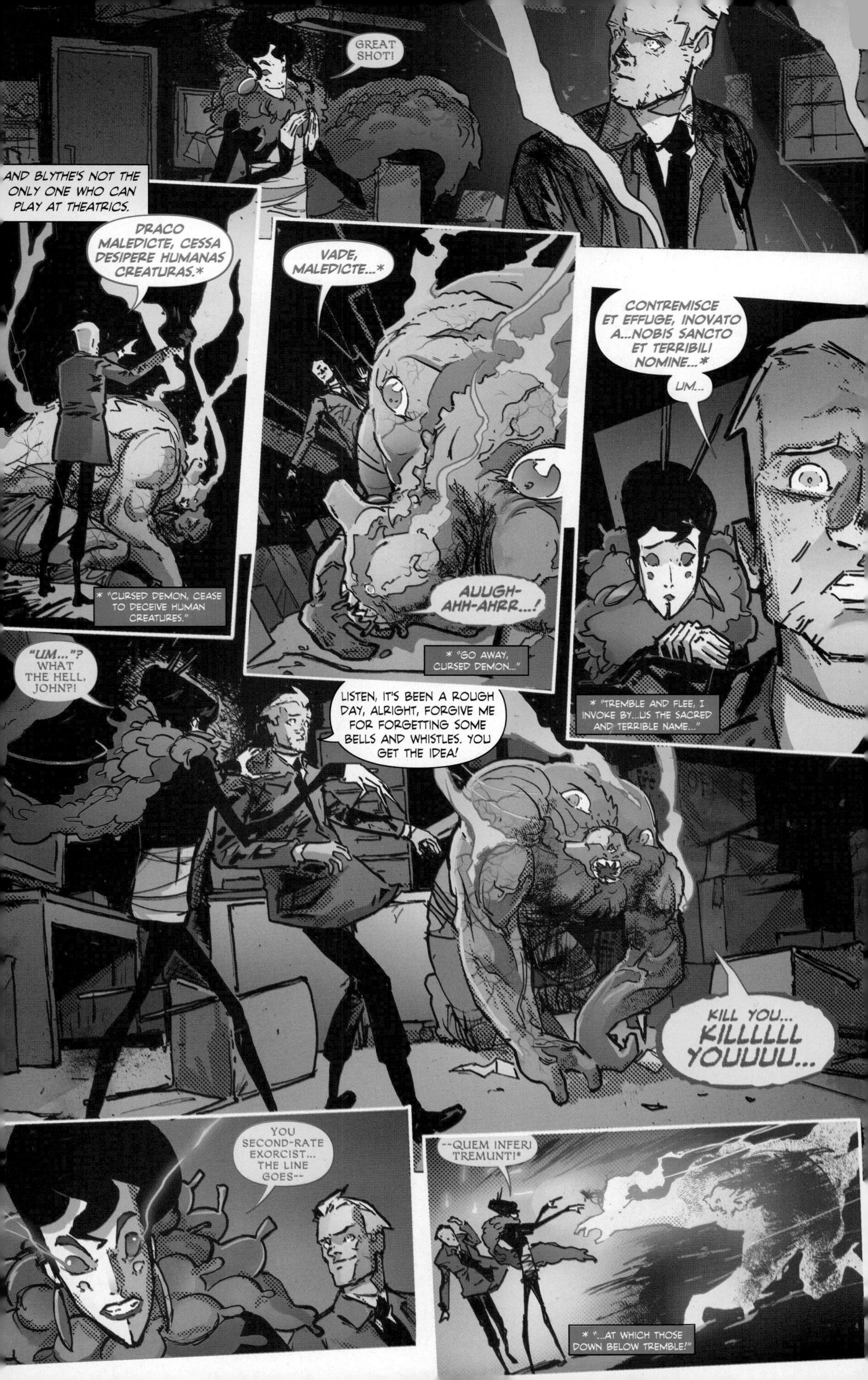
GREAT SHOT!
AND BLYTHE'S NOT THE ONLY ONE WHO CAN PLAY AT THEATRICS.
DRACO MALEDICTE, CESSA DESIPERE HUMANAS CREATURAS.*
* "CURSED DEMON, CEASE TO DECEIVE HUMAN CREATURES."
VADE, MALEDICTE...*
AUUGH-AHH-AHRR...!
* "GO AWAY, CURSED DEMON..."
CONTREMISCE ET EFFUGE, INOVATO A...NOBIS SANCTO ET TERRIBILI NOMINE...*
UM...
* "TREMBLE AND FLEE, I INVOKE BY...US THE SACRED AND TERRIBLE NAME..."
"UM..."? WHAT THE HELL, JOHN?!
LISTEN, IT'S BEEN A ROUGH DAY, ALRIGHT, FORGIVE ME FOR FORGETTING SOME BELLS AND WHISTLES. YOU GET THE IDEA!
KILL YOU... KILLLLLL YOUUUU...
YOU SECOND-RATE EXORCIST... THE LINE GOES--
--QUEM INFERI TREMUNT!*
* "...AT WHICH THOSE DOWN BELOW TREMBLE!"

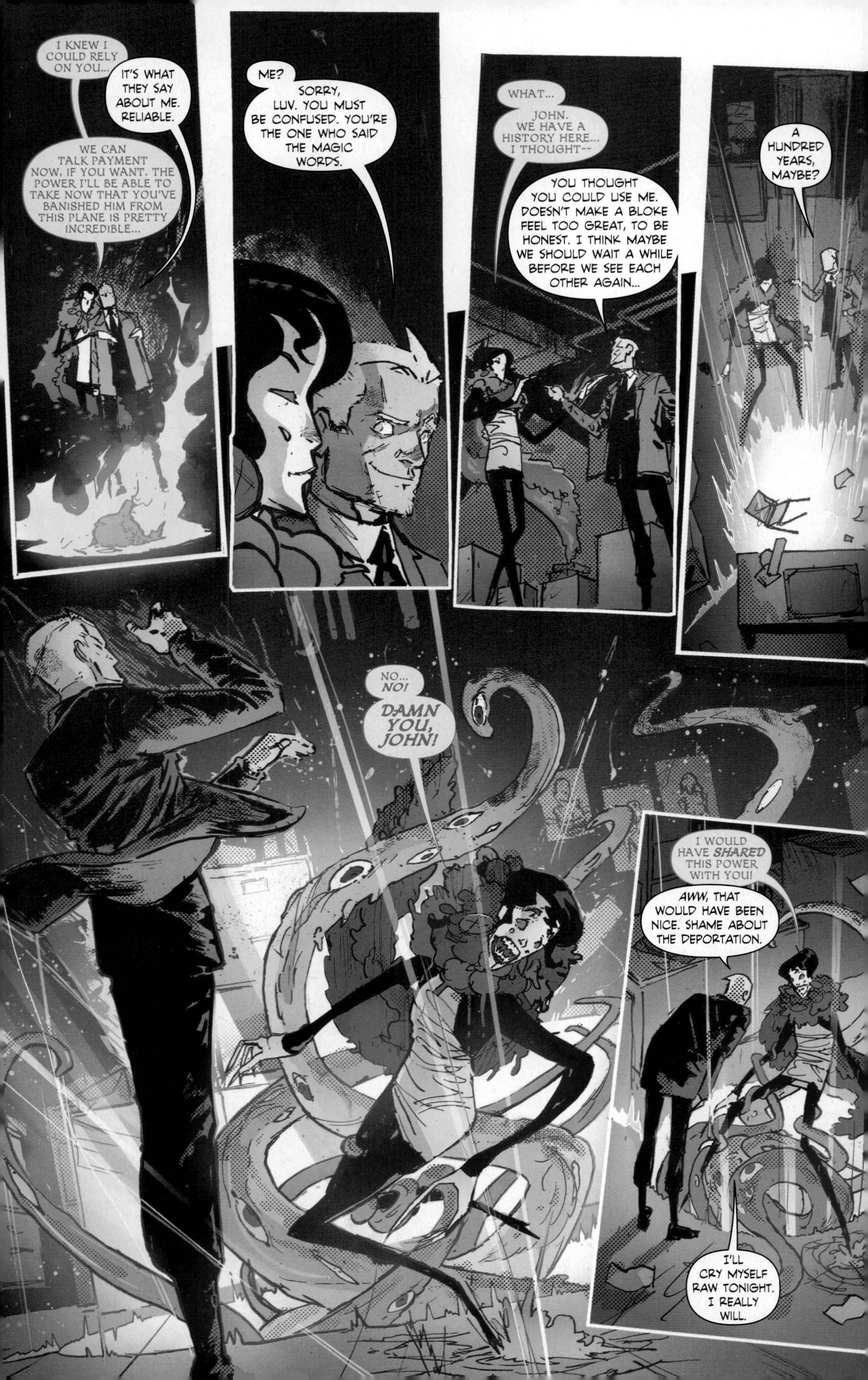
I KNEW I COULD RELY ON YOU...
IT'S WHAT THEY SAY ABOUT ME. RELIABLE.
WE CAN TALK PAYMENT NOW, IF YOU WANT. THE POWER I'LL BE ABLE TO TAKE NOW THAT YOU'VE BANISHED HIM FROM THIS PLANE IS PRETTY INCREDIBLE...
ME?
SORRY, LUV. YOU MUST BE CONFUSED. YOU'RE THE ONE WHO SAID THE MAGIC WORDS.
WHAT...
JOHN. WE HAVE A HISTORY HERE... I THOUGHT--
YOU THOUGHT YOU COULD USE ME. DOESN'T MAKE A BLOKE FEEL TOO GREAT, TO BE HONEST. I THINK MAYBE WE SHOULD WAIT A WHILE BEFORE WE SEE EACH OTHER AGAIN...
A HUNDRED YEARS, MAYBE?
NO... NO! DAMN YOU, JOHN!
I WOULD HAVE SHARED THIS POWER WITH YOU!
AWW, THAT WOULD HAVE BEEN NICE. SHAME ABOUT THE DEPORTATION.
I'LL CRY MYSELF RAW TONIGHT. I REALLY WILL.

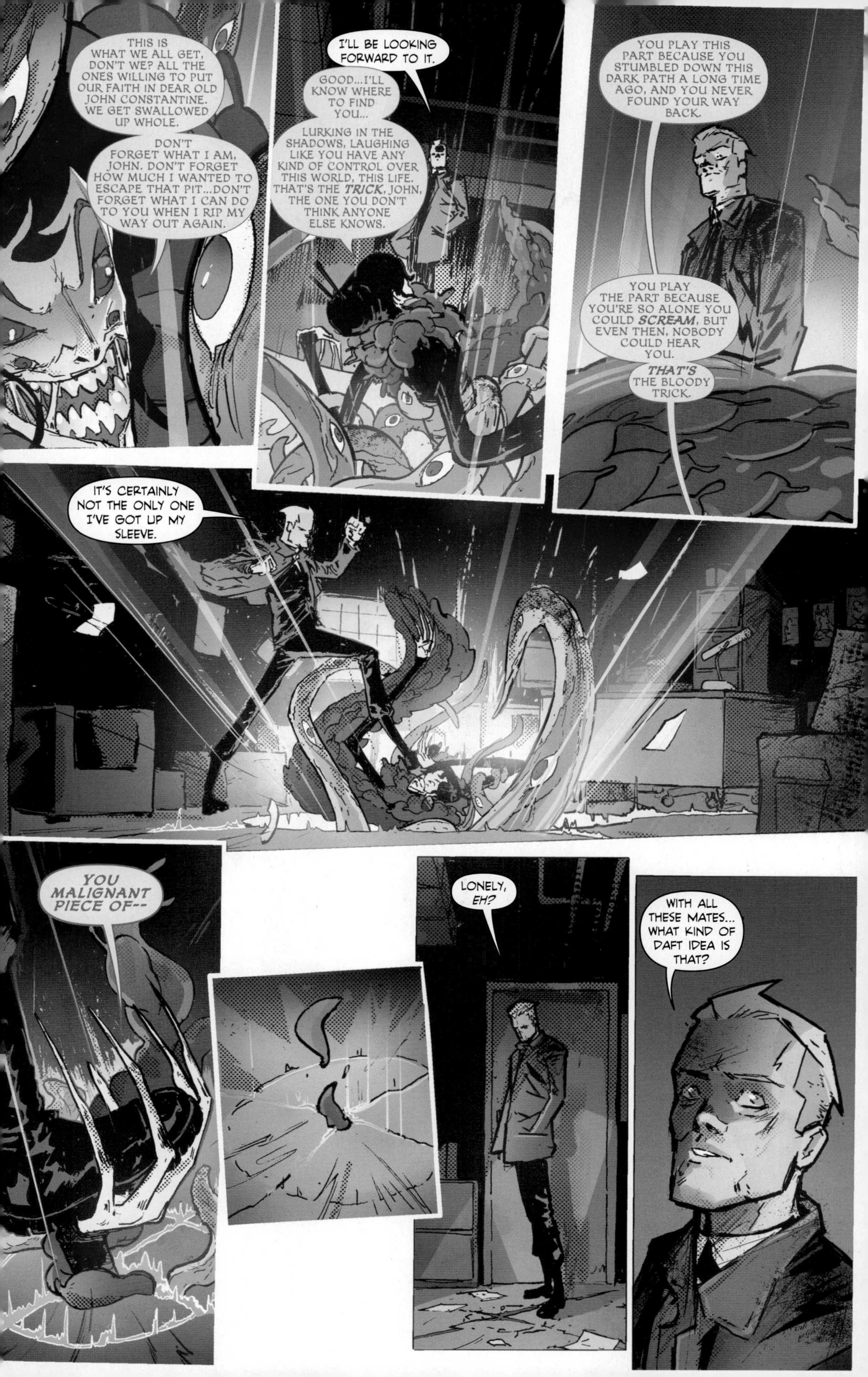
THIS IS WHAT WE ALL GET, DON'T WE? ALL THE ONES WILLING TO PUT OUR FAITH IN DEAR OLD JOHN CONSTANTINE. WE GET SWALLOWED UP WHOLE.
DON'T FORGET WHAT I AM, JOHN. DON'T FORGET HOW MUCH I WANTED TO ESCAPE THAT PIT...DON'T FORGET WHAT I CAN DO TO YOU WHEN I RIP MY WAY OUT AGAIN.
I'LL BE LOOKING FORWARD TO IT.
GOOD...I'LL KNOW WHERE TO FIND YOU...
LURKING IN THE SHADOWS, LAUGHING LIKE YOU HAVE ANY KIND OF CONTROL OVER THIS WORLD, THIS LIFE. THAT'S THE TRICK, JOHN, THE ONE YOU DON'T THINK ANYONE ELSE KNOWS.
YOU PLAY THIS PART BECAUSE YOU STUMBLED DOWN THIS DARK PATH A LONG TIME AGO, AND YOU NEVER FOUND YOUR WAY BACK.
YOU PLAY THE PART BECAUSE YOU'RE SO ALONE YOU COULD SCREAM, BUT EVEN THEN, NOBODY COULD HEAR YOU.
THAT'S THE BLOODY TRICK.
IT'S CERTAINLY NOT THE ONLY ONE I'VE GOT UP MY SLEEVE.
YOU MALIGNANT PIECE OF--
LONELY, EH?
WITH ALL THESE MATES... WHAT KIND OF DAFT IDEA IS THAT?

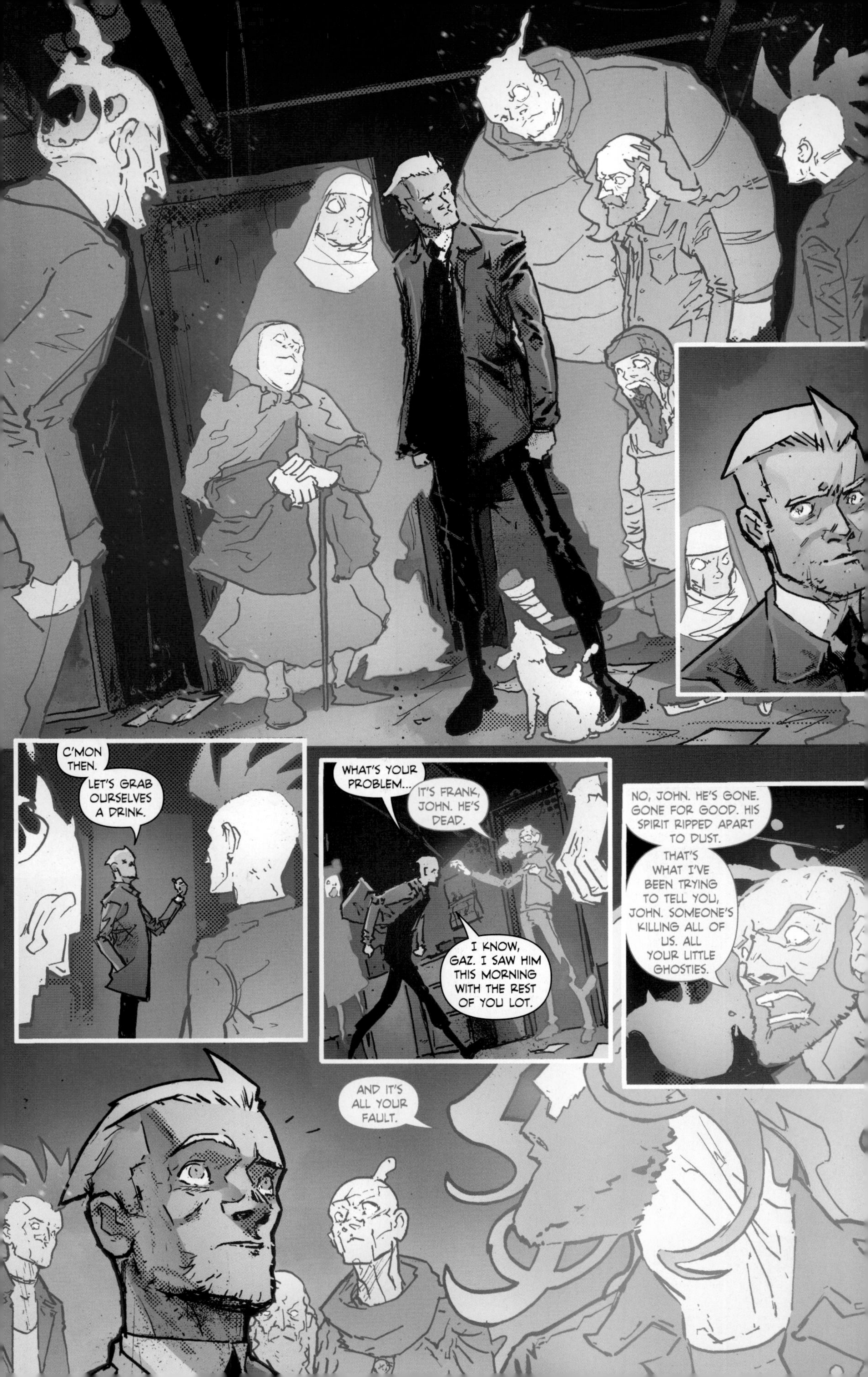
C'MON THEN.
LET'S GRAB OURSELVES A DRINK.
WHAT'S YOUR PROBLEM...
IT'S FRANK, JOHN. HE'S DEAD.
I KNOW, GAZ. I SAW HIM THIS MORNING WITH THE REST OF YOU LOT.
NO, JOHN. HE'S GONE. GONE FOR GOOD. HIS SPIRIT RIPPED APART TO DUST.
THAT'S WHAT I'VE BEEN TRYING TO TELL YOU, JOHN. SOMEONE'S KILLING ALL OF US. ALL YOUR LITTLE GHOSTIES.
AND IT'S ALL YOUR FAULT.

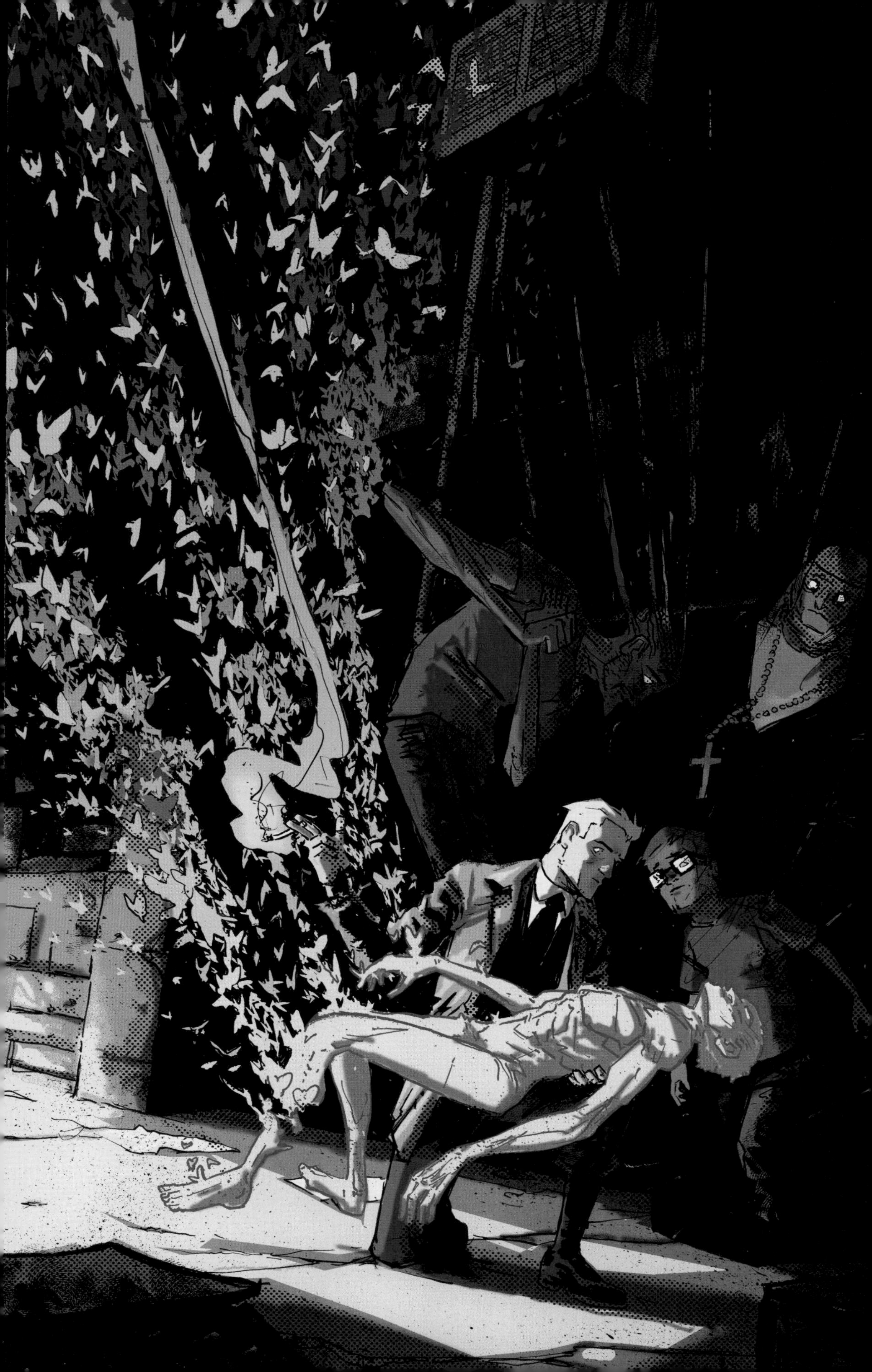

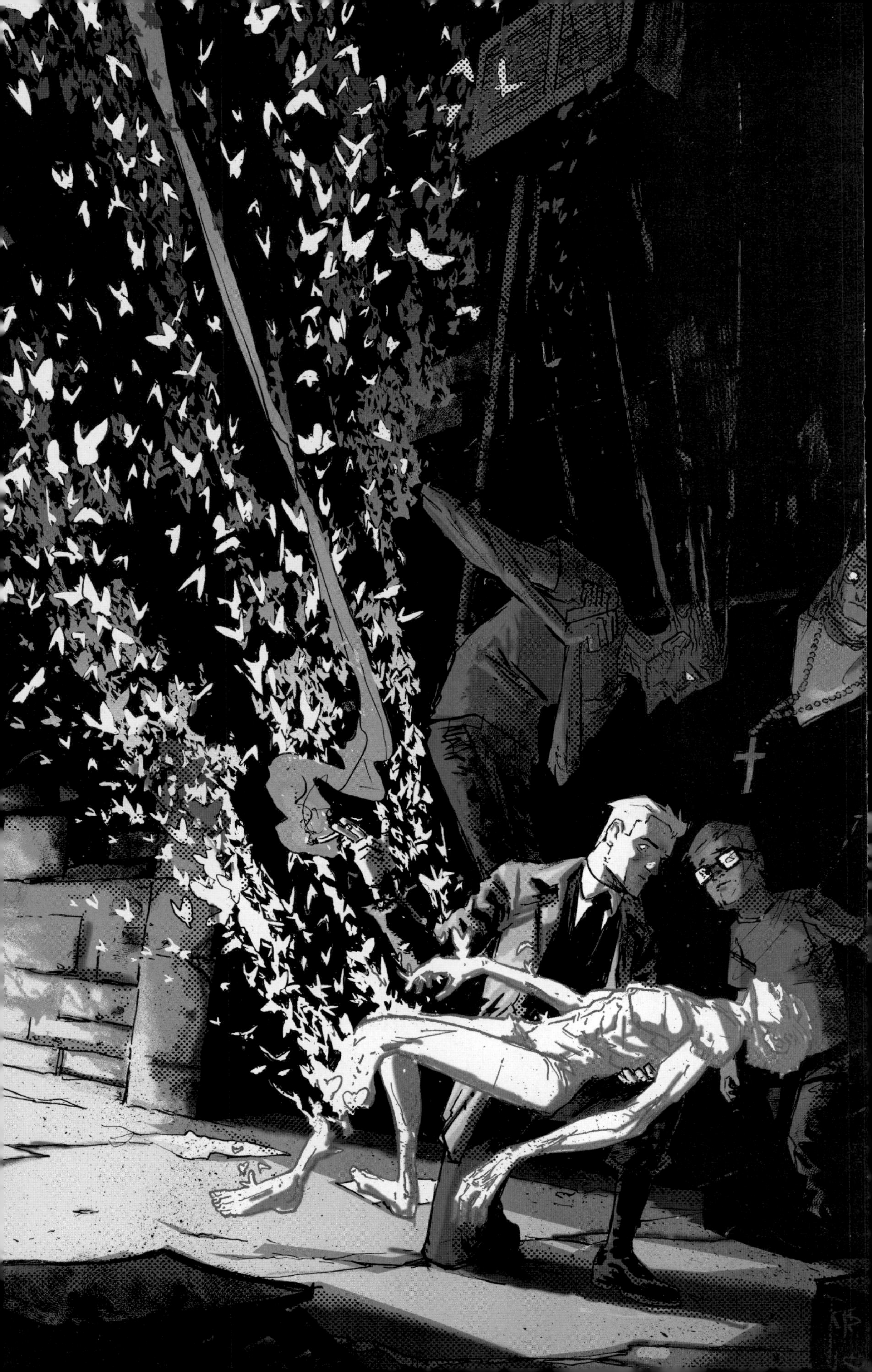

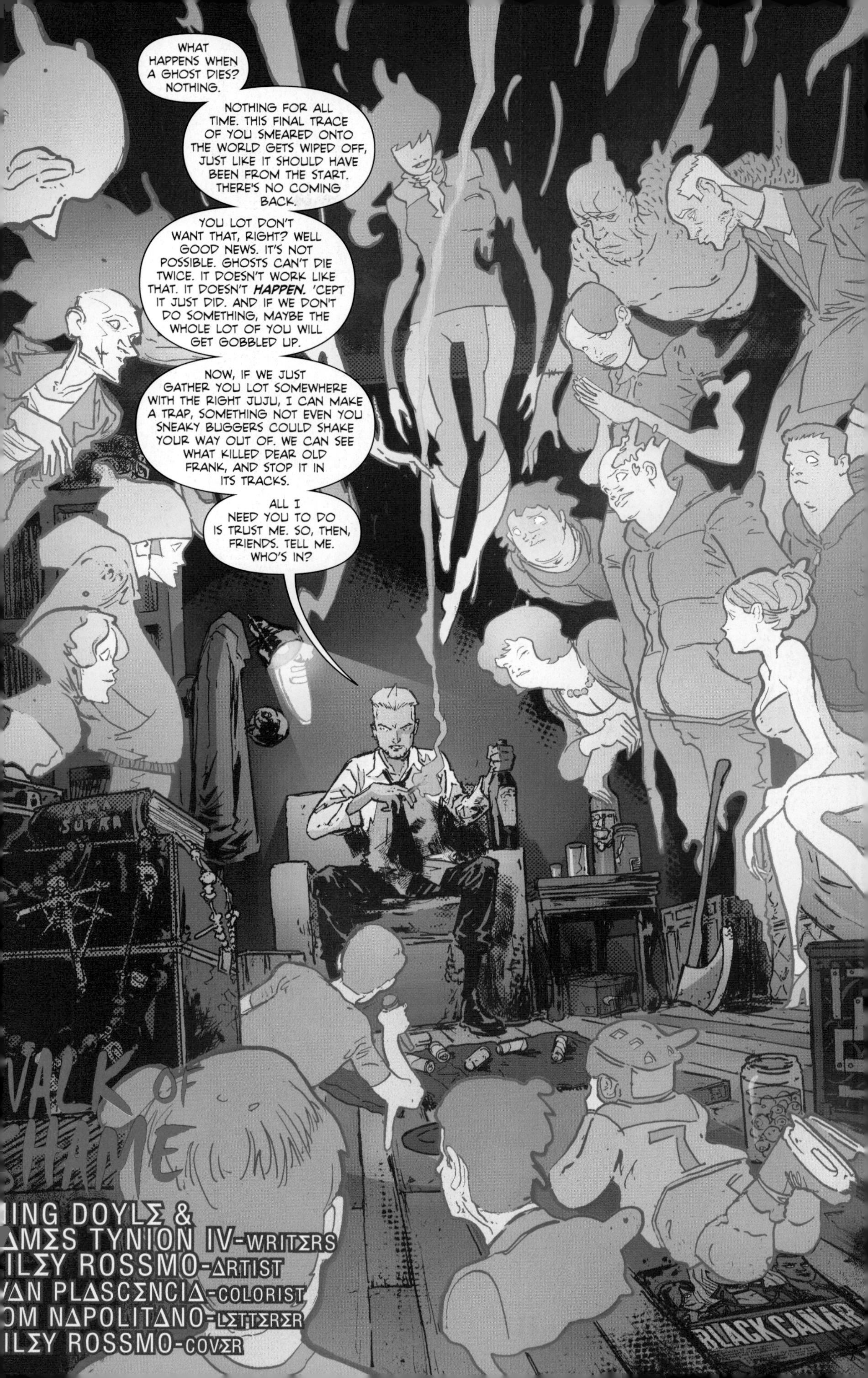
WHAT HAPPENS WHEN A GHOST DIES? NOTHING.
NOTHING FOR ALL TIME. THIS FINAL TRACE OF YOU SMEARED ONTO THE WORLD GETS WIPED OFF, JUST LIKE IT SHOULD HAVE BEEN FROM THE START. THERE'S NO COMING BACK.
YOU LOT DON'T WANT THAT, RIGHT? WELL GOOD NEWS. IT'S NOT POSSIBLE. GHOSTS CAN'T DIE TWICE. IT DOESN'T WORK LIKE THAT. IT DOESN'T ***HAPPEN.*** 'CEPT IT JUST DID. AND IF WE DON'T DO SOMETHING, MAYBE THE WHOLE LOT OF YOU WILL GET GOBBLED UP.
NOW, IF WE JUST GATHER YOU LOT SOMEWHERE WITH THE RIGHT JUJU, I CAN MAKE A TRAP, SOMETHING NOT EVEN YOU SNEAKY BUGGERS COULD SHAKE YOUR WAY OUT OF. WE CAN SEE WHAT KILLED DEAR OLD FRANK, AND STOP IT IN ITS TRACKS.
ALL I NEED YOU TO DO IS TRUST ME. SO, THEN, FRIENDS. TELL ME. WHO'S IN?
SUTRA
VALK OF
SHAME
IING DOYLE &
AMES TYNION IV-WRITERS
ILEY ROSSMO-ARTIST
VAN PLASCENCIA-COLORIST
OM NAPOLITANO-LETTERER
ILEY ROSSMO-COVER
BLACK CANAR

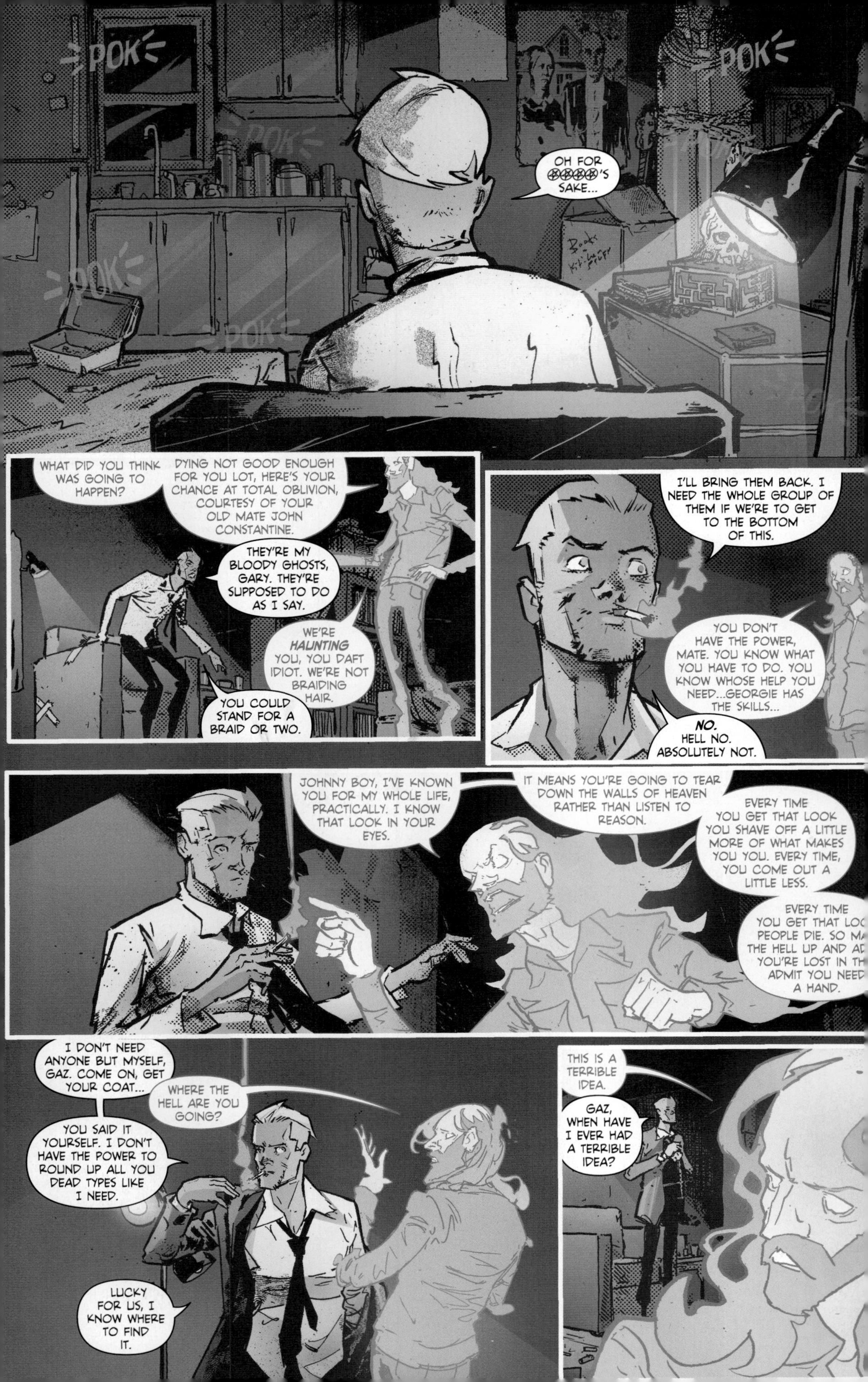
POK
POK
POK
POK
POK
OH FOR ****'S SAKE...
WHAT DID YOU THINK WAS GOING TO HAPPEN?
DYING NOT GOOD ENOUGH FOR YOU LOT, HERE'S YOUR CHANCE AT TOTAL OBLIVION, COURTESY OF YOUR OLD MATE JOHN CONSTANTINE.
THEY'RE MY BLOODY GHOSTS, GARY. THEY'RE SUPPOSED TO DO AS I SAY.
WE'RE *HAUNTING* YOU, YOU DAFT IDIOT. WE'RE NOT BRAIDING HAIR.
YOU COULD STAND FOR A BRAID OR TWO.
I'LL BRING THEM BACK. I NEED THE WHOLE GROUP OF THEM IF WE'RE TO GET TO THE BOTTOM OF THIS.
YOU DON'T HAVE THE POWER, MATE. YOU KNOW WHAT YOU HAVE TO DO. YOU KNOW WHOSE HELP YOU NEED...GEORGIE HAS THE SKILLS...
NO. HELL NO. ABSOLUTELY NOT.
JOHNNY BOY, I'VE KNOWN YOU FOR MY WHOLE LIFE, PRACTICALLY. I KNOW THAT LOOK IN YOUR EYES.
IT MEANS YOU'RE GOING TO TEAR DOWN THE WALLS OF HEAVEN RATHER THAN LISTEN TO REASON.
EVERY TIME YOU GET THAT LOOK YOU SHAVE OFF A LITTLE MORE OF WHAT MAKES YOU YOU. EVERY TIME, YOU COME OUT A LITTLE LESS.
EVERY TIME YOU GET THAT LOC PEOPLE DIE. SO MA THE HELL UP AND AD YOU'RE LOST IN TH ADMIT YOU NEED A HAND.
I DON'T NEED ANYONE BUT MYSELF, GAZ. COME ON, GET YOUR COAT...
WHERE THE HELL ARE YOU GOING?
YOU SAID IT YOURSELF. I DON'T HAVE THE POWER TO ROUND UP ALL YOU DEAD TYPES LIKE I NEED.
LUCKY FOR US, I KNOW WHERE TO FIND IT.
THIS IS A TERRIBLE IDEA.
GAZ, WHEN HAVE I EVER HAD A TERRIBLE IDEA?

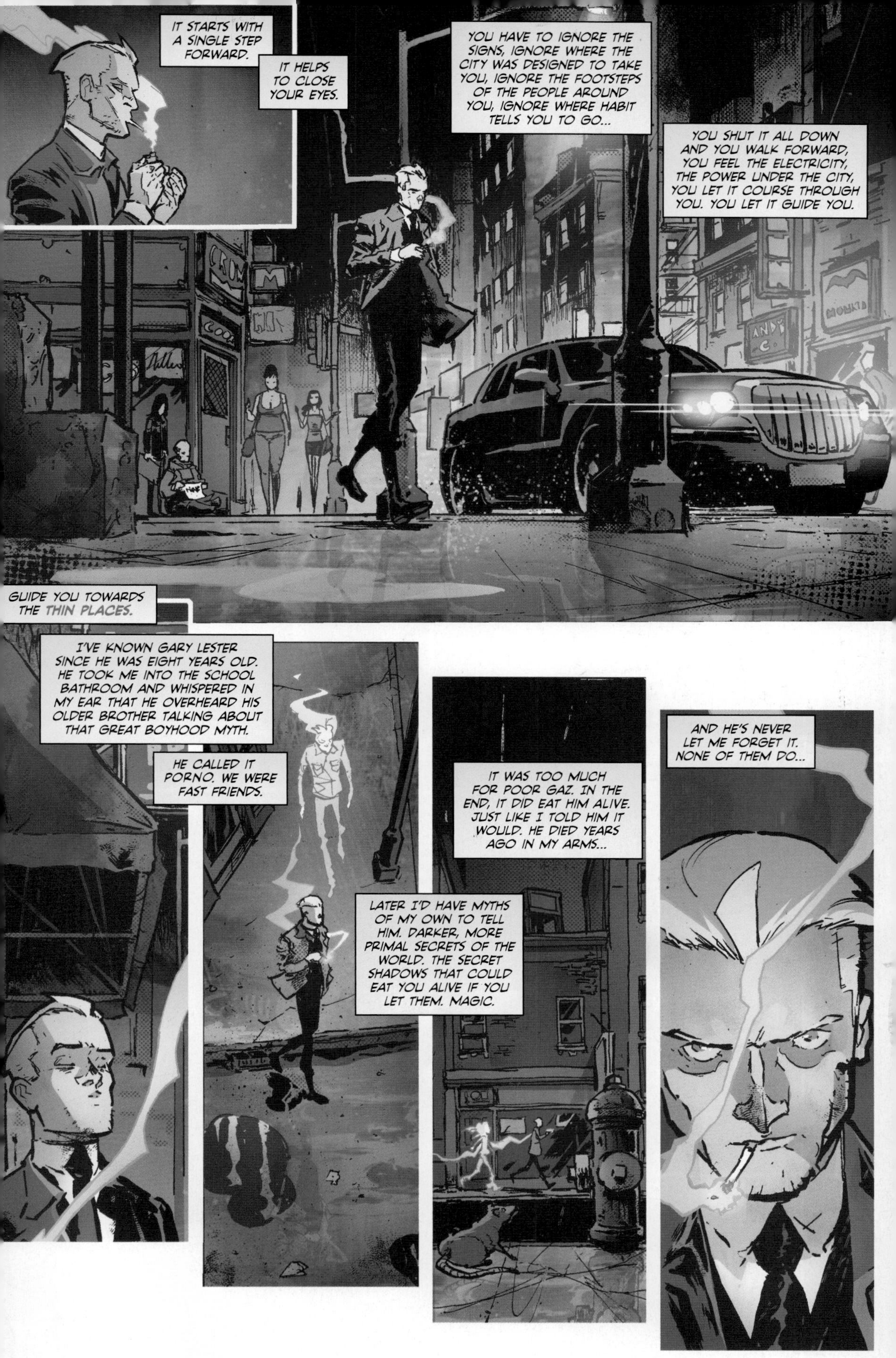
IT STARTS WITH A SINGLE STEP FORWARD.
IT HELPS TO CLOSE YOUR EYES.
YOU HAVE TO IGNORE THE SIGNS, IGNORE WHERE THE CITY WAS DESIGNED TO TAKE YOU, IGNORE THE FOOTSTEPS OF THE PEOPLE AROUND YOU, IGNORE WHERE HABIT TELLS YOU TO GO...
YOU SHUT IT ALL DOWN AND YOU WALK FORWARD, YOU FEEL THE ELECTRICITY, THE POWER UNDER THE CITY, YOU LET IT COURSE THROUGH YOU. YOU LET IT GUIDE YOU.
GUIDE YOU TOWARDS THE THIN PLACES.
I'VE KNOWN GARY LESTER SINCE HE WAS EIGHT YEARS OLD. HE TOOK ME INTO THE SCHOOL BATHROOM AND WHISPERED IN MY EAR THAT HE OVERHEARD HIS OLDER BROTHER TALKING ABOUT THAT GREAT BOYHOOD MYTH.
HE CALLED IT PORNO. WE WERE FAST FRIENDS.
LATER I'D HAVE MYTHS OF MY OWN TO TELL HIM. DARKER, MORE PRIMAL SECRETS OF THE WORLD. THE SECRET SHADOWS THAT COULD EAT YOU ALIVE IF YOU LET THEM. MAGIC.
IT WAS TOO MUCH FOR POOR GAZ. IN THE END, IT DID EAT HIM ALIVE. JUST LIKE I TOLD HIM IT WOULD. HE DIED YEARS AGO IN MY ARMS...
AND HE'S NEVER LET ME FORGET IT. NONE OF THEM DO...

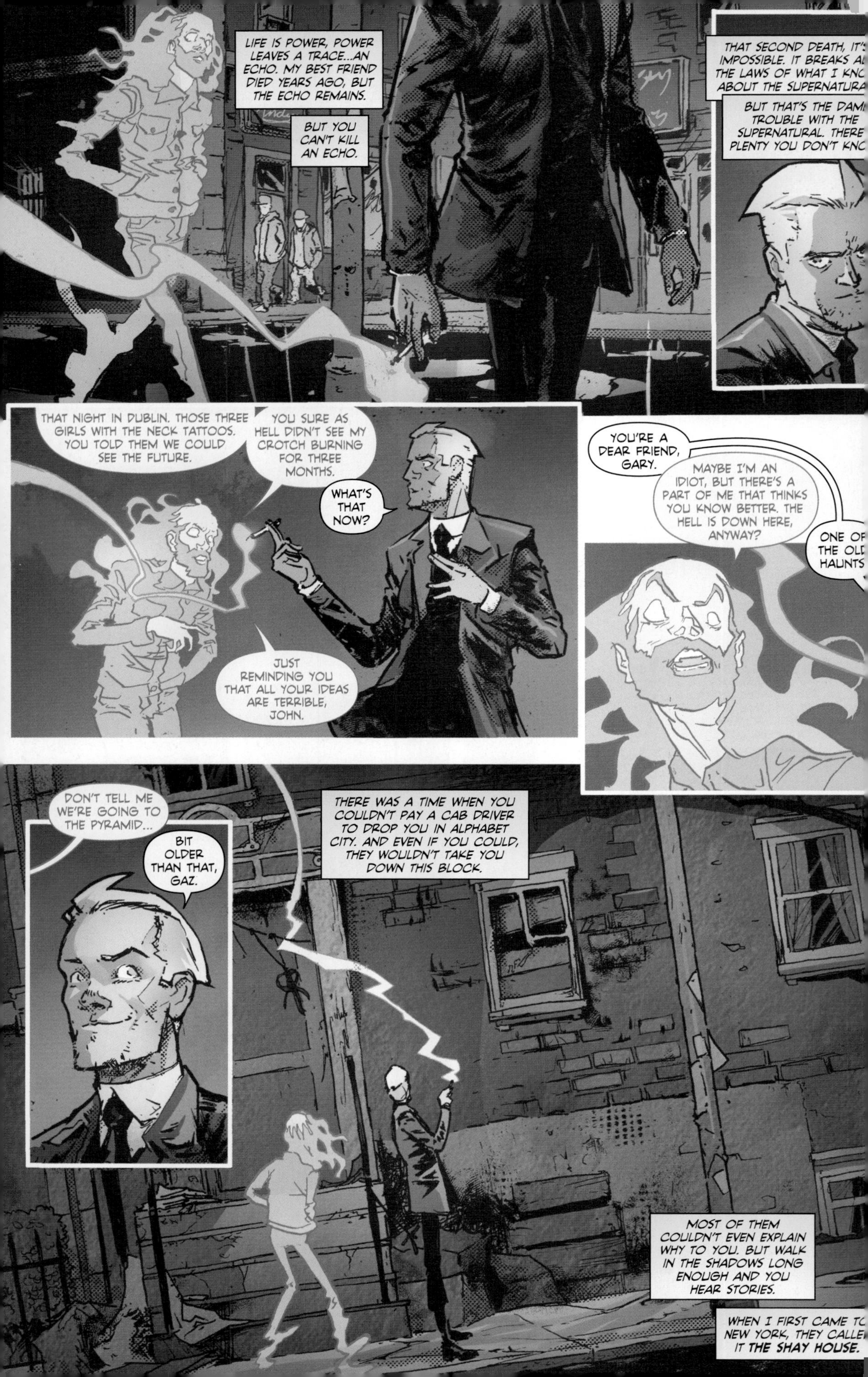

LIFE IS POWER, POWER LEAVES A TRACE...AN ECHO. MY BEST FRIEND DIED YEARS AGO, BUT THE ECHO REMAINS.
BUT YOU CAN'T KILL AN ECHO.
THAT SECOND DEATH, IT'S IMPOSSIBLE. IT BREAKS AL THE LAWS OF WHAT I KNO ABOUT THE SUPERNATURA
BUT THAT'S THE DAM TROUBLE WITH THE SUPERNATURAL. THERE PLENTY YOU DON'T KNO
THAT NIGHT IN DUBLIN. THOSE THREE GIRLS WITH THE NECK TATTOOS. YOU TOLD THEM WE COULD SEE THE FUTURE.
YOU SURE AS HELL DIDN'T SEE MY CROTCH BURNING FOR THREE MONTHS.
WHAT'S THAT NOW?
JUST REMINDING YOU THAT ALL YOUR IDEAS ARE TERRIBLE, JOHN.
YOU'RE A DEAR FRIEND, GARY.
MAYBE I'M AN IDIOT, BUT THERE'S A PART OF ME THAT THINKS YOU KNOW BETTER. THE HELL IS DOWN HERE, ANYWAY?
ONE OF THE OLD HAUNTS
DON'T TELL ME WE'RE GOING TO THE PYRAMID...
BIT OLDER THAN THAT, GAZ.
THERE WAS A TIME WHEN YOU COULDN'T PAY A CAB DRIVER TO DROP YOU IN ALPHABET CITY. AND EVEN IF YOU COULD, THEY WOULDN'T TAKE YOU DOWN THIS BLOCK.
MOST OF THEM COULDN'T EVEN EXPLAIN WHY TO YOU. BUT WALK IN THE SHADOWS LONG ENOUGH AND YOU HEAR STORIES.
WHEN I FIRST CAME TO NEW YORK, THEY CALLE IT THE SHAY HOUSE.

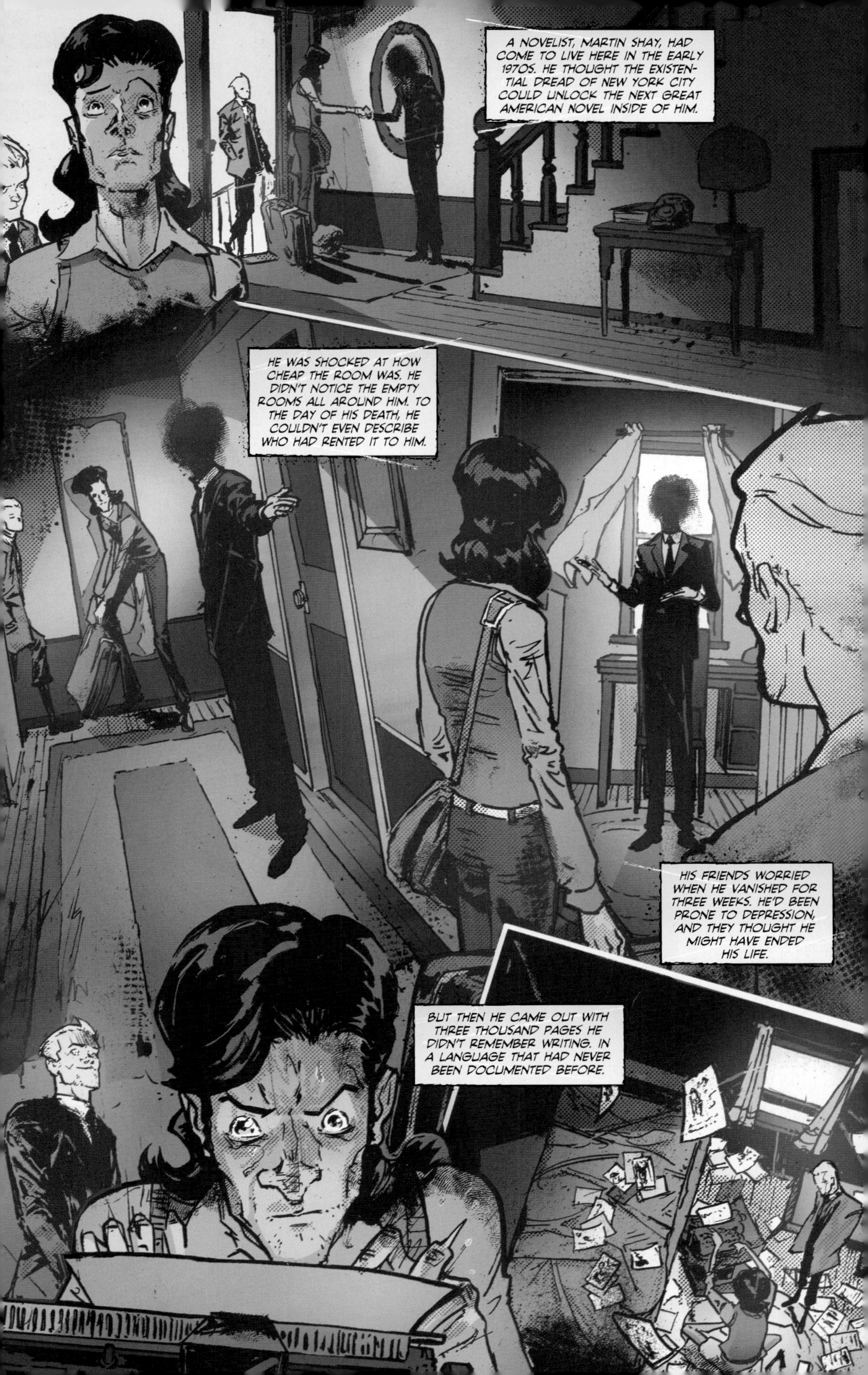

A NOVELIST, MARTIN SHAY, HAD COME TO LIVE HERE IN THE EARLY 1970S. HE THOUGHT THE EXISTENTIAL DREAD OF NEW YORK CITY COULD UNLOCK THE NEXT GREAT AMERICAN NOVEL INSIDE OF HIM.
HE WAS SHOCKED AT HOW CHEAP THE ROOM WAS. HE DIDN'T NOTICE THE EMPTY ROOMS ALL AROUND HIM. TO THE DAY OF HIS DEATH, HE COULDN'T EVEN DESCRIBE WHO HAD RENTED IT TO HIM.
HIS FRIENDS WORRIED WHEN HE VANISHED FOR THREE WEEKS. HE'D BEEN PRONE TO DEPRESSION, AND THEY THOUGHT HE MIGHT HAVE ENDED HIS LIFE.
BUT THEN HE CAME OUT WITH THREE THOUSAND PAGES HE DIDN'T REMEMBER WRITING. IN A LANGUAGE THAT HAD NEVER BEEN DOCUMENTED BEFORE.

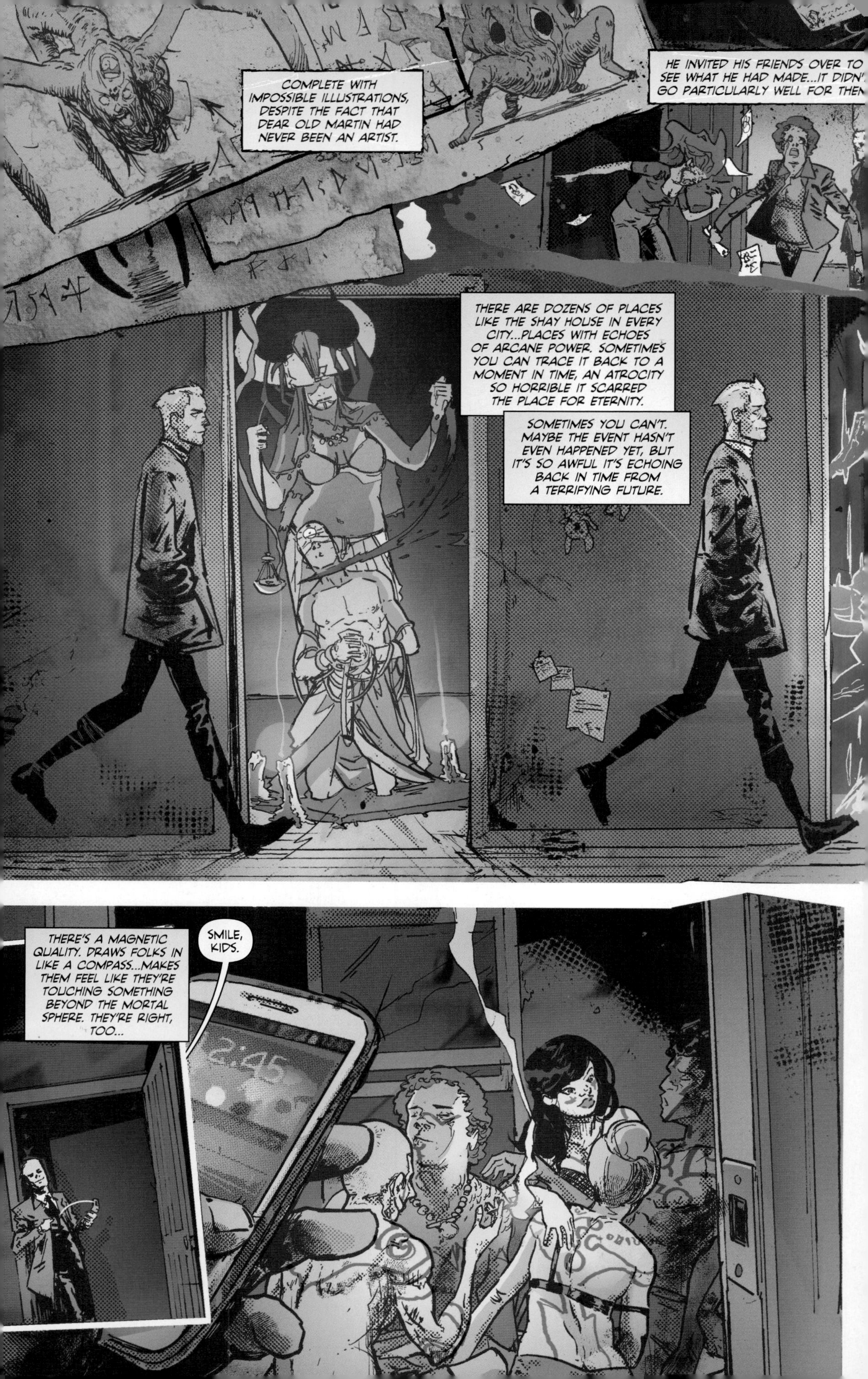
COMPLETE WITH IMPOSSIBLE ILLUSTRATIONS, DESPITE THE FACT THAT DEAR OLD MARTIN HAD NEVER BEEN AN ARTIST.
HE INVITED HIS FRIENDS OVER TO SEE WHAT HE HAD MADE...IT DIDN' GO PARTICULARLY WELL FOR THEN
THERE ARE DOZENS OF PLACES LIKE THE SHAY HOUSE IN EVERY CITY...PLACES WITH ECHOES OF ARCANE POWER. SOMETIMES YOU CAN TRACE IT BACK TO A MOMENT IN TIME, AN ATROCITY SO HORRIBLE IT SCARRED THE PLACE FOR ETERNITY.
SOMETIMES YOU CAN'T. MAYBE THE EVENT HASN'T EVEN HAPPENED YET, BUT IT'S SO AWFUL IT'S ECHOING BACK IN TIME FROM A TERRIFYING FUTURE.
THERE'S A MAGNETIC QUALITY. DRAWS FOLKS IN LIKE A COMPASS...MAKES THEM FEEL LIKE THEY'RE TOUCHING SOMETHING BEYOND THE MORTAL SPHERE. THEY'RE RIGHT, TOO...
SMILE, KIDS.
2:45

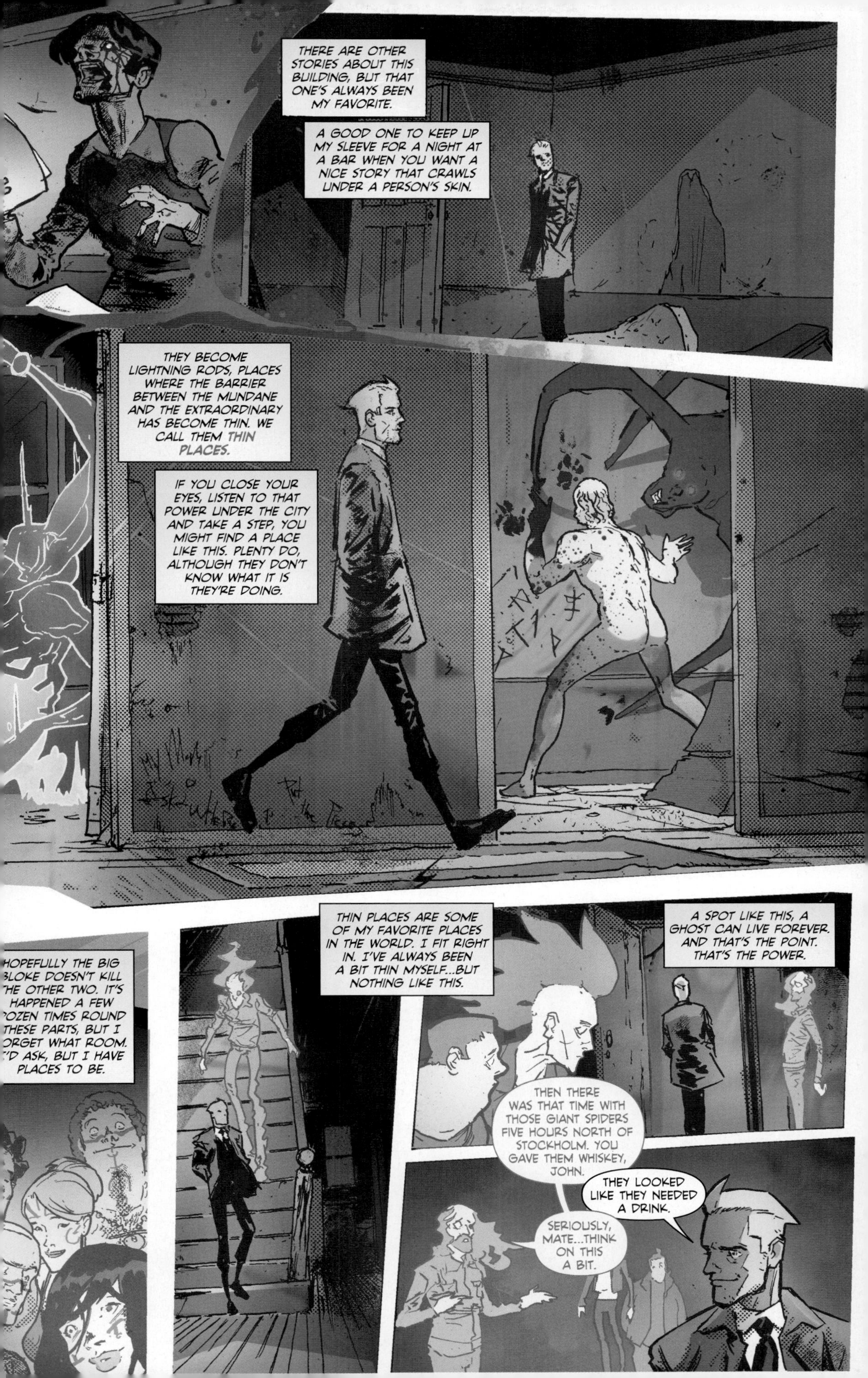
THERE ARE OTHER STORIES ABOUT THIS BUILDING, BUT THAT ONE'S ALWAYS BEEN MY FAVORITE.
A GOOD ONE TO KEEP UP MY SLEEVE FOR A NIGHT AT A BAR WHEN YOU WANT A NICE STORY THAT CRAWLS UNDER A PERSON'S SKIN.
THEY BECOME LIGHTNING RODS, PLACES WHERE THE BARRIER BETWEEN THE MUNDANE AND THE EXTRAORDINARY HAS BECOME THIN. WE CALL THEM THIN PLACES.
IF YOU CLOSE YOUR EYES, LISTEN TO THAT POWER UNDER THE CITY AND TAKE A STEP, YOU MIGHT FIND A PLACE LIKE THIS. PLENTY DO, ALTHOUGH THEY DON'T KNOW WHAT IT IS THEY'RE DOING.
HOPEFULLY THE BIG BLOKE DOESN'T KILL THE OTHER TWO. IT'S HAPPENED A FEW DOZEN TIMES ROUND THESE PARTS, BUT I FORGET WHAT ROOM. I'D ASK, BUT I HAVE PLACES TO BE.
THIN PLACES ARE SOME OF MY FAVORITE PLACES IN THE WORLD. I FIT RIGHT IN. I'VE ALWAYS BEEN A BIT THIN MYSELF...BUT NOTHING LIKE THIS.
A SPOT LIKE THIS, A GHOST CAN LIVE FOREVER. AND THAT'S THE POINT. THAT'S THE POWER.
THEN THERE WAS THAT TIME WITH THOSE GIANT SPIDERS FIVE HOURS NORTH OF STOCKHOLM. YOU GAVE THEM WHISKEY, JOHN.
THEY LOOKED LIKE THEY NEEDED A DRINK.
SERIOUSLY, MATE...THINK ON THIS A BIT.

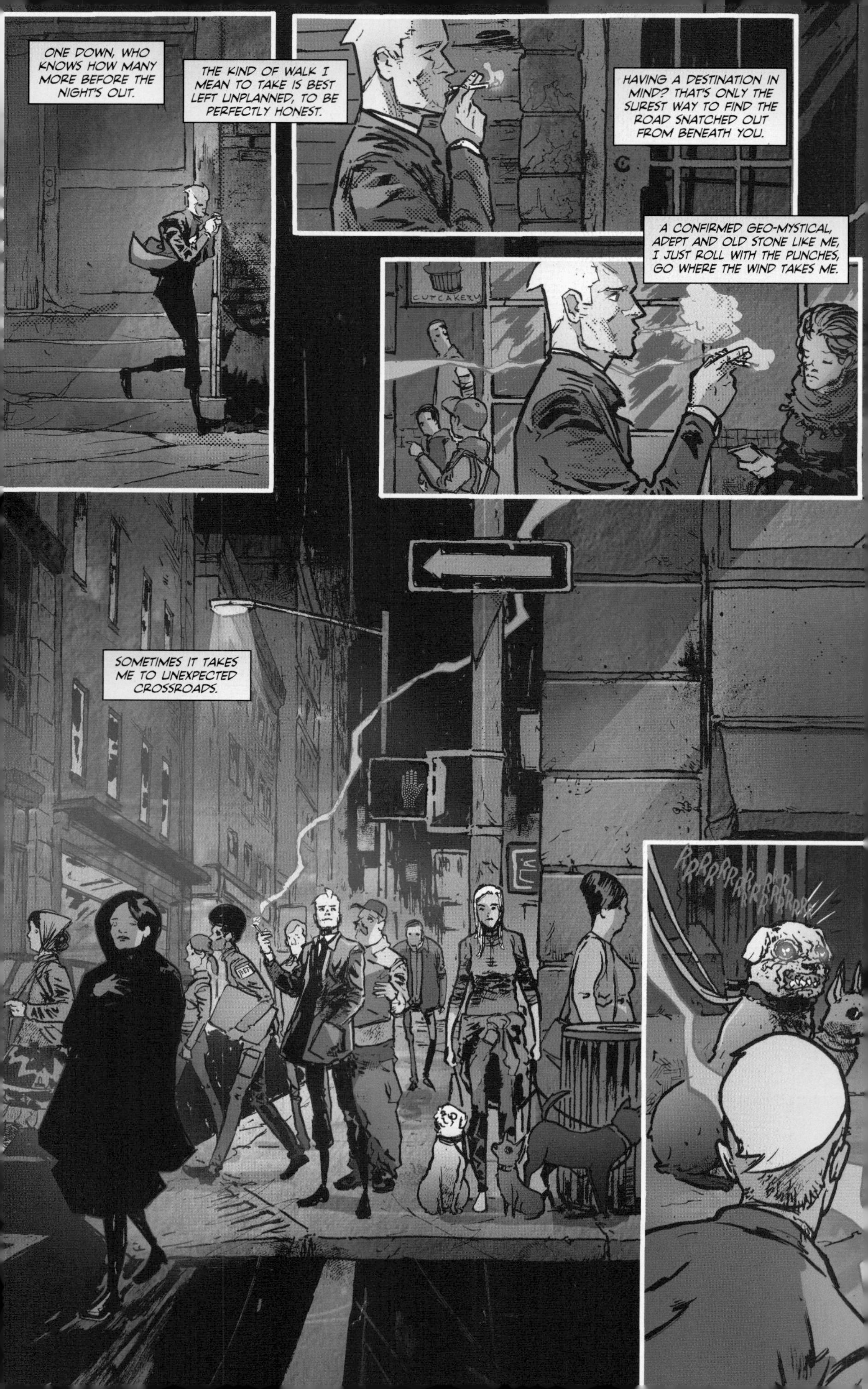
ONE DOWN, WHO KNOWS HOW MANY MORE BEFORE THE NIGHT'S OUT.
THE KIND OF WALK I MEAN TO TAKE IS BEST LEFT UNPLANNED, TO BE PERFECTLY HONEST.
HAVING A DESTINATION IN MIND? THAT'S ONLY THE SUREST WAY TO FIND THE ROAD SNATCHED OUT FROM BENEATH YOU.
A CONFIRMED GEO-MYSTICAL, ADEPT AND OLD STONE LIKE ME, I JUST ROLL WITH THE PUNCHES, GO WHERE THE WIND TAKES ME.
CUTCAKERY
SOMETIMES IT TAKES ME TO UNEXPECTED CROSSROADS.

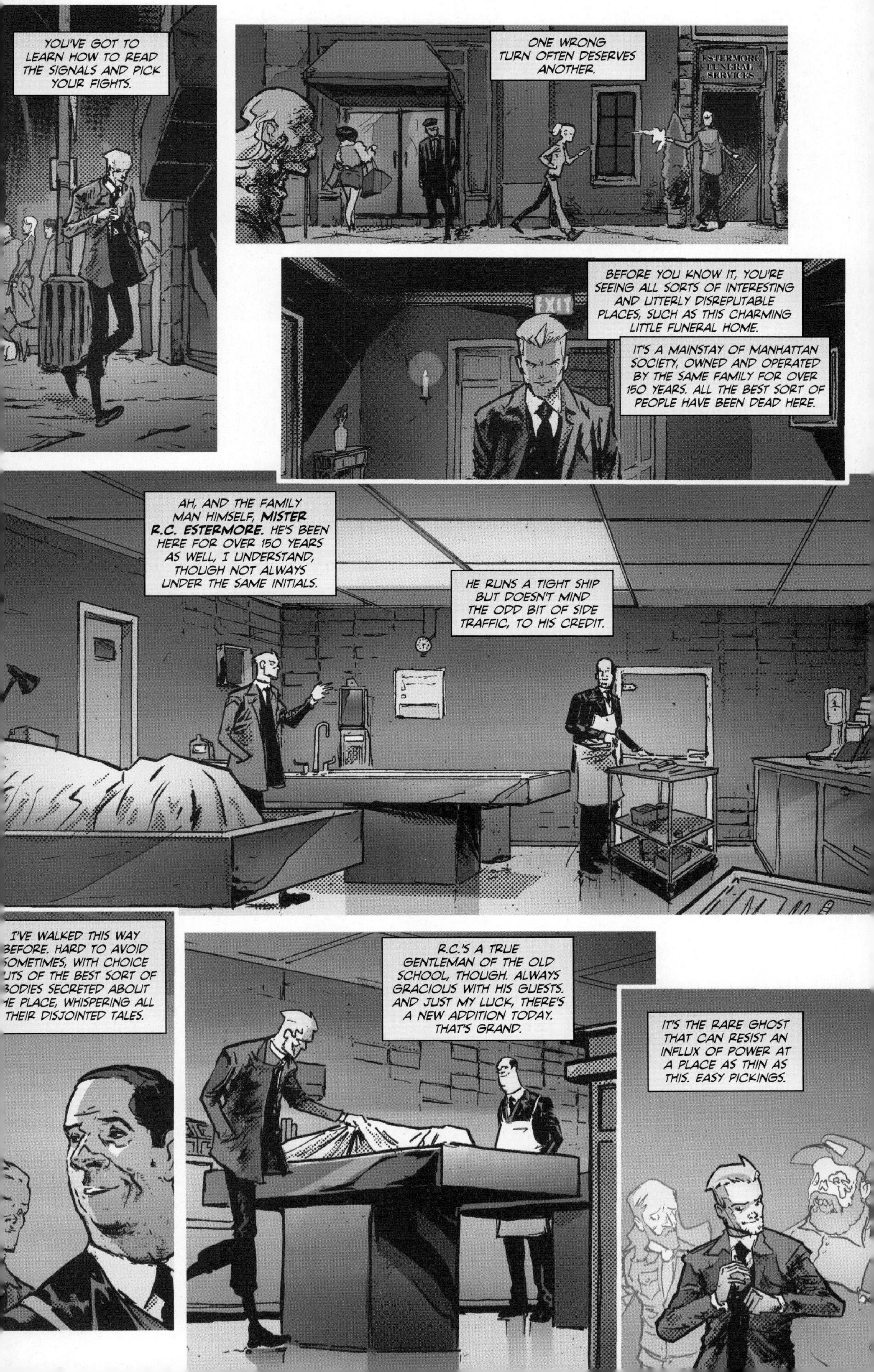
YOU'VE GOT TO LEARN HOW TO READ THE SIGNALS AND PICK YOUR FIGHTS.
ONE WRONG TURN OFTEN DESERVES ANOTHER.
ESTERMORE FUNERAL SERVICES
EXIT
BEFORE YOU KNOW IT, YOU'RE SEEING ALL SORTS OF INTERESTING AND UTTERLY DISREPUTABLE PLACES, SUCH AS THIS CHARMING LITTLE FUNERAL HOME.
IT'S A MAINSTAY OF MANHATTAN SOCIETY, OWNED AND OPERATED BY THE SAME FAMILY FOR OVER 150 YEARS. ALL THE BEST SORT OF PEOPLE HAVE BEEN DEAD HERE.
AH, AND THE FAMILY MAN HIMSELF, **MISTER R.C. ESTERMORE.** HE'S BEEN HERE FOR OVER 150 YEARS AS WELL, I UNDERSTAND, THOUGH NOT ALWAYS UNDER THE SAME INITIALS.
HE RUNS A TIGHT SHIP BUT DOESN'T MIND THE ODD BIT OF SIDE TRAFFIC, TO HIS CREDIT.
I'VE WALKED THIS WAY BEFORE. HARD TO AVOID SOMETIMES, WITH CHOICE UTS OF THE BEST SORT OF BODIES SECRETED ABOUT HE PLACE, WHISPERING ALL THEIR DISJOINTED TALES.
R.C.'S A TRUE GENTLEMAN OF THE OLD SCHOOL, THOUGH. ALWAYS GRACIOUS WITH HIS GUESTS. AND JUST MY LUCK, THERE'S A NEW ADDITION TODAY. THAT'S GRAND.
IT'S THE RARE GHOST THAT CAN RESIST AN INFLUX OF POWER AT A PLACE AS THIN AS THIS. EASY PICKINGS.

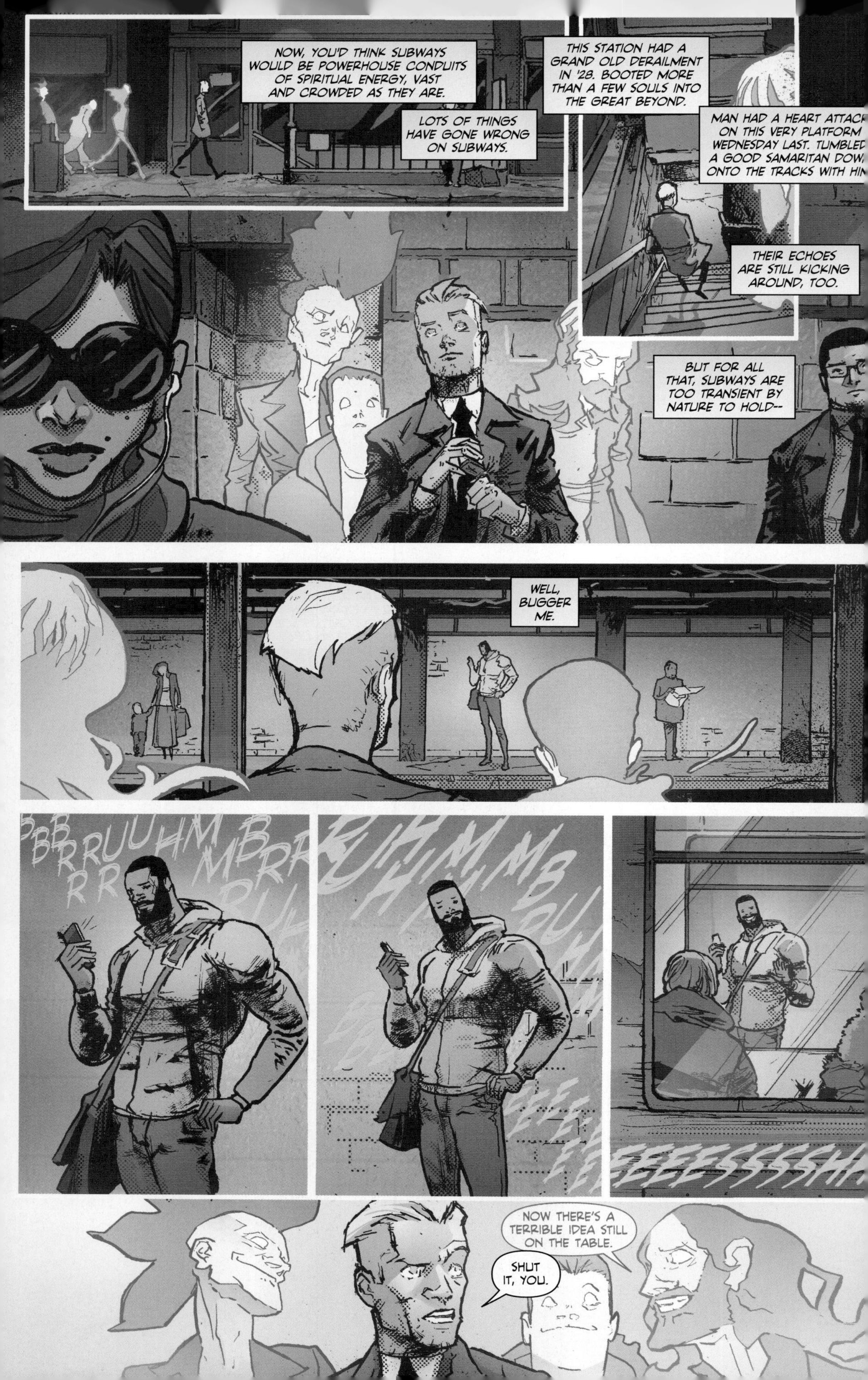
NOW, YOU'D THINK SUBWAYS WOULD BE POWERHOUSE CONDUITS OF SPIRITUAL ENERGY, VAST AND CROWDED AS THEY ARE.
LOTS OF THINGS HAVE GONE WRONG ON SUBWAYS.
THIS STATION HAD A GRAND OLD DERAILMENT IN '28. BOOTED MORE THAN A FEW SOULS INTO THE GREAT BEYOND.
MAN HAD A HEART ATTACK ON THIS VERY PLATFORM WEDNESDAY LAST. TUMBLED A GOOD SAMARITAN DOWN ONTO THE TRACKS WITH HIM.
THEIR ECHOES ARE STILL KICKING AROUND, TOO.
BUT FOR ALL THAT, SUBWAYS ARE TOO TRANSIENT BY NATURE TO HOLD--
WELL, BUGGER ME.
BBBRRUUHM RR MBRR
EEEEEEESSSSHH
NOW THERE'S A TERRIBLE IDEA STILL ON THE TABLE.
SHUT IT, YOU.

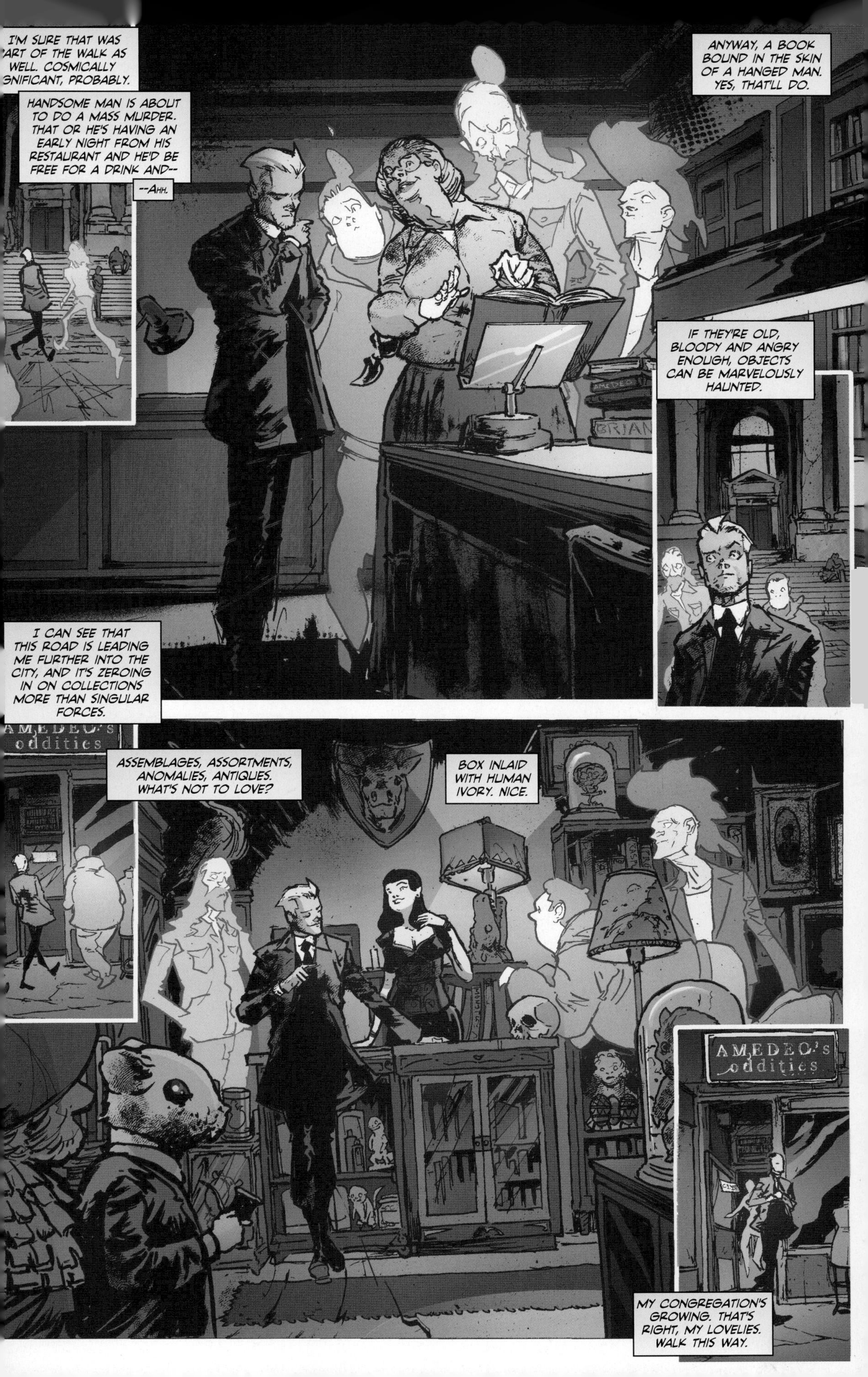
I'M SURE THAT WAS
ART OF THE WALK AS
WELL. COSMICALLY
GNIFICANT, PROBABLY.
HANDSOME MAN IS ABOUT TO DO A MASS MURDER. THAT OR HE'S HAVING AN EARLY NIGHT FROM HIS RESTAURANT AND HE'D BE FREE FOR A DRINK AND--
--AHH.
ANYWAY, A BOOK BOUND IN THE SKIN OF A HANGED MAN. YES, THAT'LL DO.
AMEDEO
BRIAN
IF THEY'RE OLD, BLOODY AND ANGRY ENOUGH, OBJECTS CAN BE MARVELOUSLY HAUNTED.
I CAN SEE THAT THIS ROAD IS LEADING ME FURTHER INTO THE CITY, AND IT'S ZEROING IN ON COLLECTIONS MORE THAN SINGULAR FORCES.
AMEDEO's oddities
ASSEMBLAGES, ASSORTMENTS, ANOMALIES, ANTIQUES. WHAT'S NOT TO LOVE?
BOX INLAID WITH HUMAN IVORY. NICE.
AMEDEO's oddities
MY CONGREGATION'S GROWING. THAT'S RIGHT, MY LOVELIES. WALK THIS WAY.

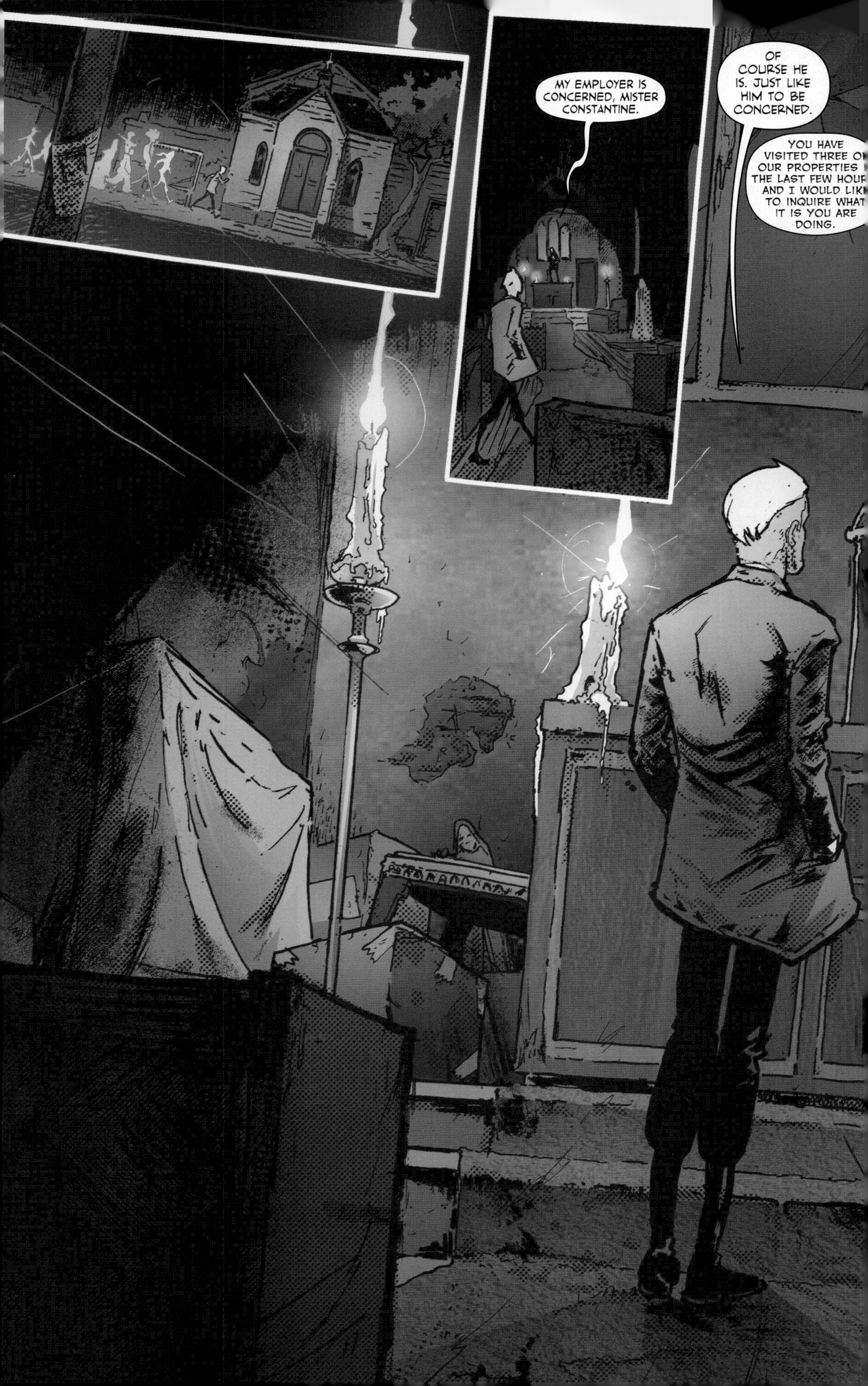
MY EMPLOYER IS CONCERNED, MISTER CONSTANTINE.
OF COURSE HE IS. JUST LIKE HIM TO BE CONCERNED.
YOU HAVE VISITED THREE O OUR PROPERTIES THE LAST FEW HOUR AND I WOULD LIK TO INQUIRE WHAT IT IS YOU ARE DOING.

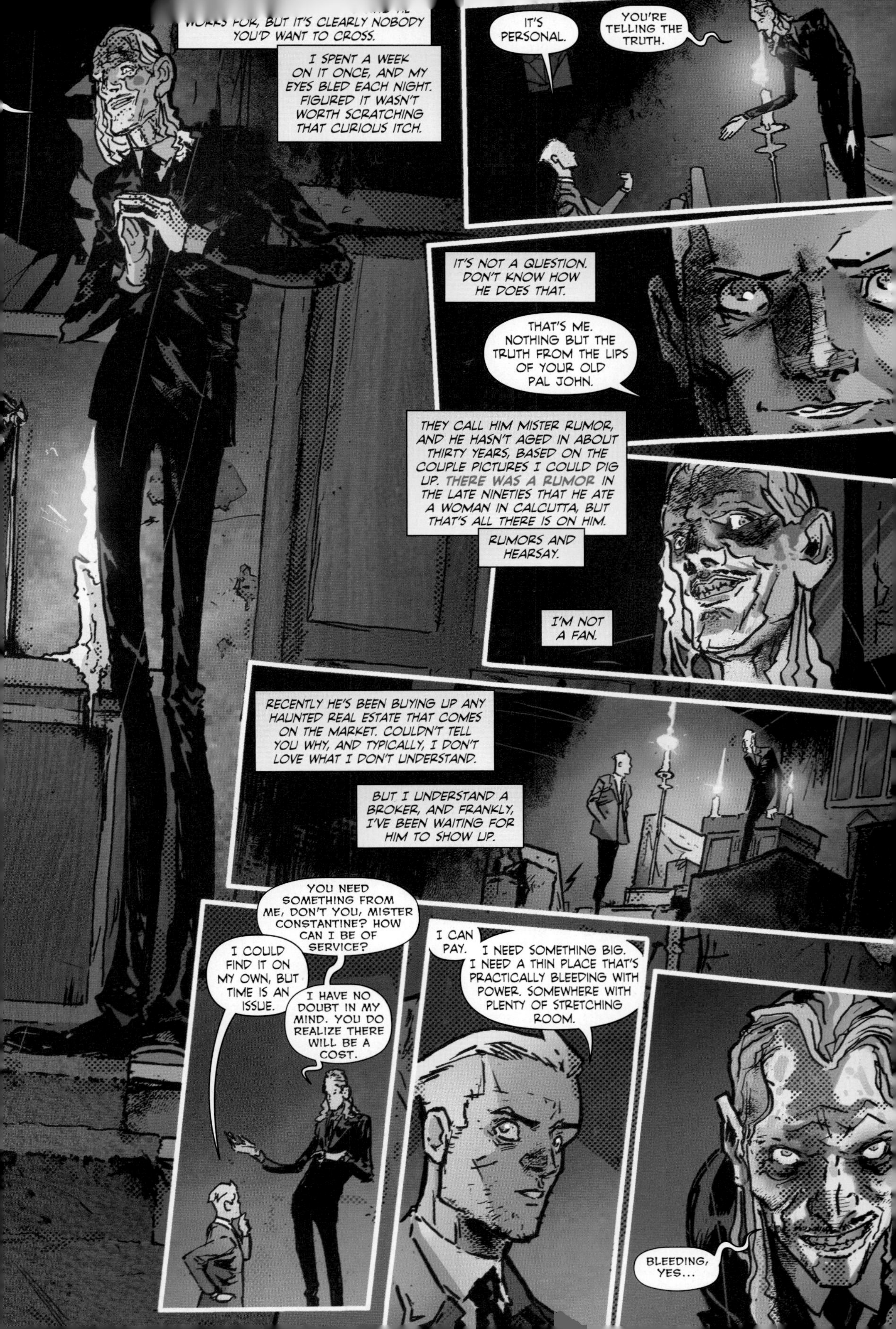
WORKS FOR, BUT IT'S CLEARLY NOBODY YOU'D WANT TO CROSS.
I SPENT A WEEK ON IT ONCE, AND MY EYES BLED EACH NIGHT. FIGURED IT WASN'T WORTH SCRATCHING THAT CURIOUS ITCH.
IT'S PERSONAL.
YOU'RE TELLING THE TRUTH.
IT'S NOT A QUESTION. DON'T KNOW HOW HE DOES THAT.
THAT'S ME. NOTHING BUT THE TRUTH FROM THE LIPS OF YOUR OLD PAL JOHN.
THEY CALL HIM MISTER RUMOR, AND HE HASN'T AGED IN ABOUT THIRTY YEARS, BASED ON THE COUPLE PICTURES I COULD DIG UP. THERE WAS A RUMOR IN THE LATE NINETIES THAT HE ATE A WOMAN IN CALCUTTA, BUT THAT'S ALL THERE IS ON HIM.
RUMORS AND HEARSAY.
I'M NOT A FAN.
RECENTLY HE'S BEEN BUYING UP ANY HAUNTED REAL ESTATE THAT COMES ON THE MARKET. COULDN'T TELL YOU WHY, AND TYPICALLY, I DON'T LOVE WHAT I DON'T UNDERSTAND.
BUT I UNDERSTAND A BROKER, AND FRANKLY, I'VE BEEN WAITING FOR HIM TO SHOW UP.
YOU NEED SOMETHING FROM ME, DON'T YOU, MISTER CONSTANTINE? HOW CAN I BE OF SERVICE?
I COULD FIND IT ON MY OWN, BUT TIME IS AN ISSUE.
I HAVE NO DOUBT IN MY MIND. YOU DO REALIZE THERE WILL BE A COST.
I CAN PAY.
I NEED SOMETHING BIG. I NEED A THIN PLACE THAT'S PRACTICALLY BLEEDING WITH POWER. SOMEWHERE WITH PLENTY OF STRETCHING ROOM.
BLEEDING, YES...

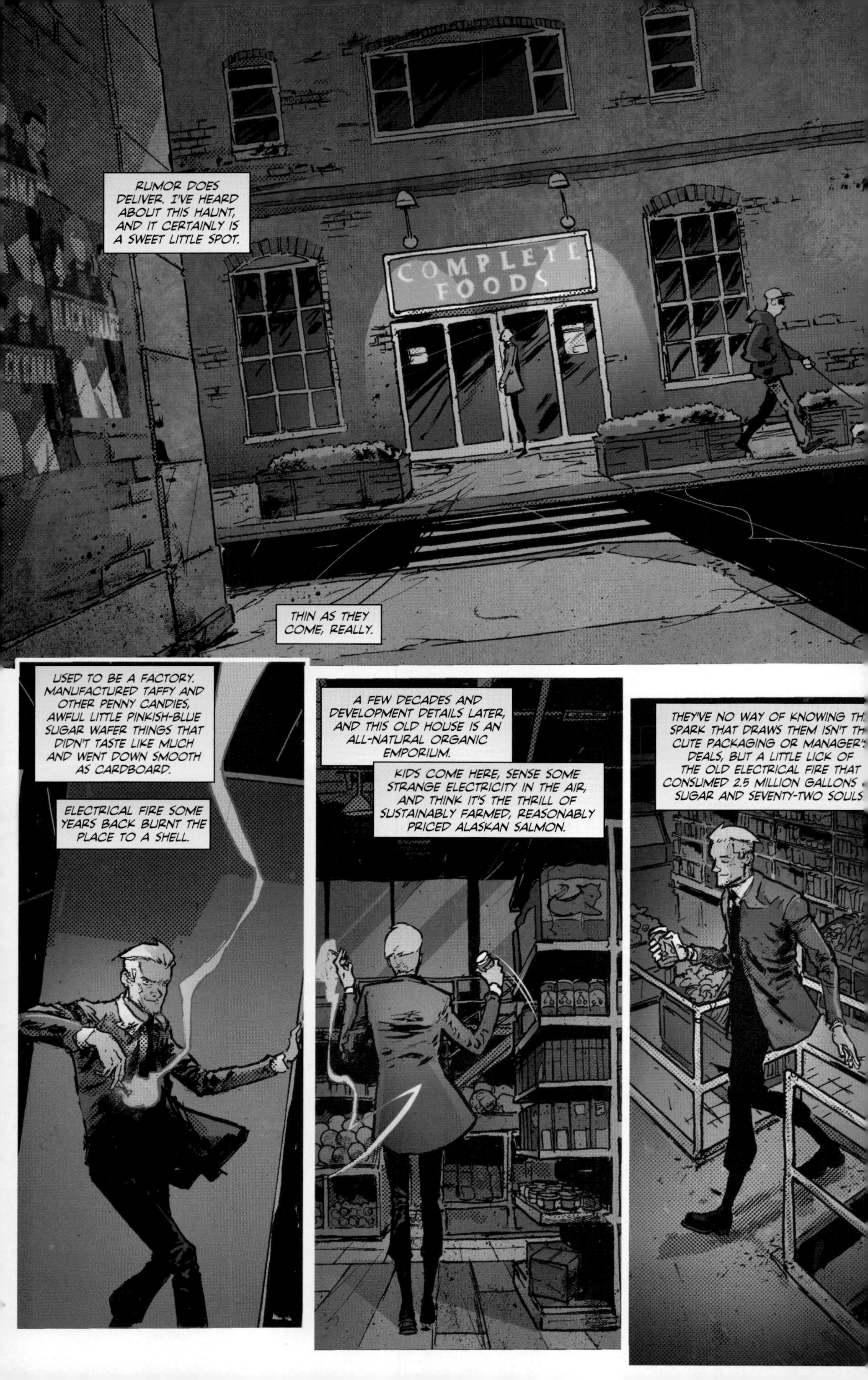
RUMOR DOES DELIVER. I'VE HEARD ABOUT THIS HAUNT, AND IT CERTAINLY IS A SWEET LITTLE SPOT.
COMPLETE FOODS
THIN AS THEY COME, REALLY.
USED TO BE A FACTORY. MANUFACTURED TAFFY AND OTHER PENNY CANDIES, AWFUL LITTLE PINKISH-BLUE SUGAR WAFER THINGS THAT DIDN'T TASTE LIKE MUCH AND WENT DOWN SMOOTH AS CARDBOARD.
ELECTRICAL FIRE SOME YEARS BACK BURNT THE PLACE TO A SHELL.
A FEW DECADES AND DEVELOPMENT DETAILS LATER, AND THIS OLD HOUSE IS AN ALL-NATURAL ORGANIC EMPORIUM.
KIDS COME HERE, SENSE SOME STRANGE ELECTRICITY IN THE AIR, AND THINK IT'S THE THRILL OF SUSTAINABLY FARMED, REASONABLY PRICED ALASKAN SALMON.
THEY'VE NO WAY OF KNOWING TH SPARK THAT DRAWS THEM ISN'T TH CUTE PACKAGING OR MANAGER' DEALS, BUT A LITTLE LICK OF THE OLD ELECTRICAL FIRE THAT CONSUMED 2.5 MILLION GALLONS SUGAR AND SEVENTY-TWO SOULS.

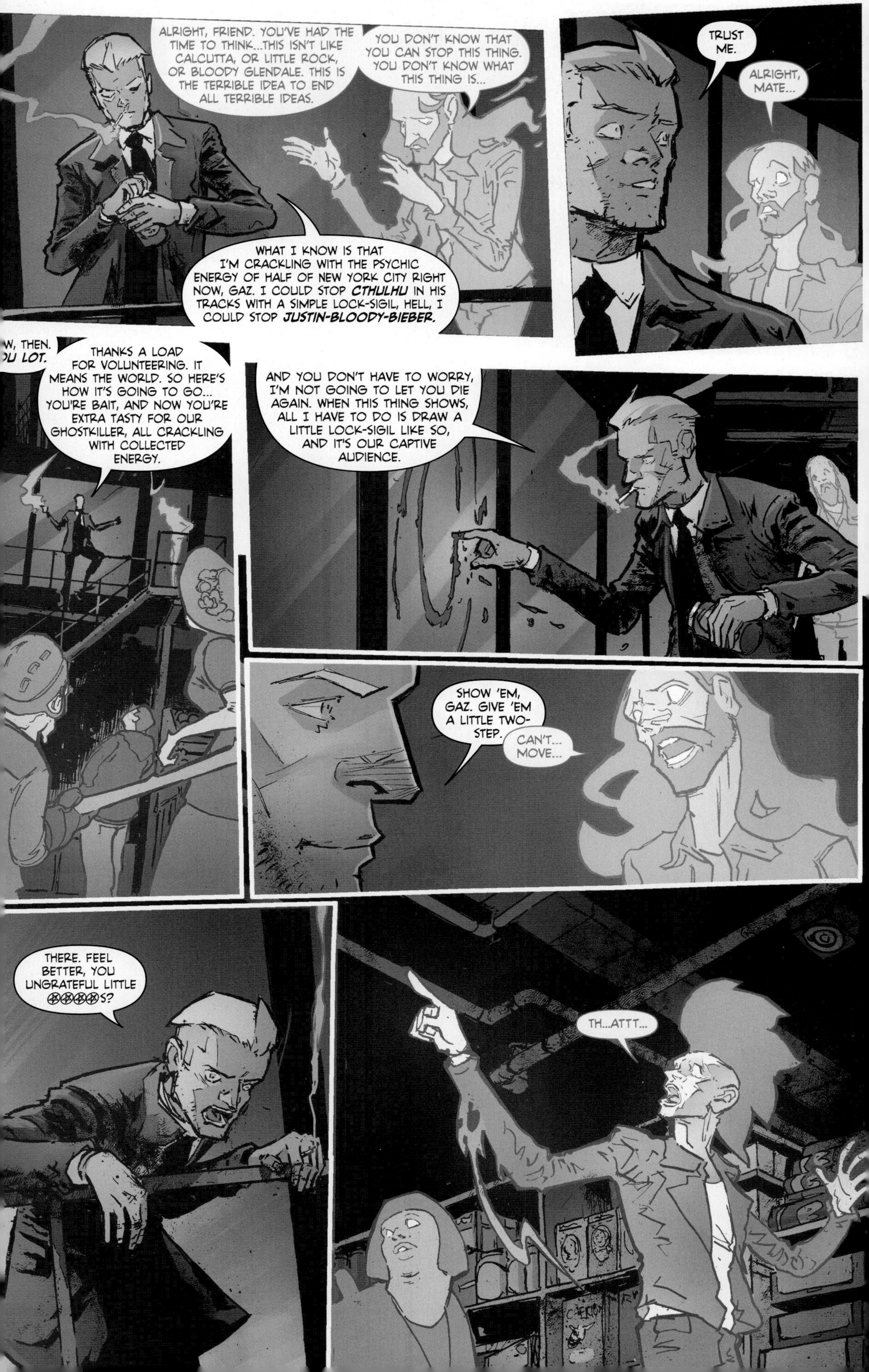
ALRIGHT, FRIEND. YOU'VE HAD THE TIME TO THINK...THIS ISN'T LIKE CALCUTTA, OR LITTLE ROCK, OR BLOODY GLENDALE. THIS IS THE TERRIBLE IDEA TO END ALL TERRIBLE IDEAS.
YOU DON'T KNOW THAT YOU CAN STOP THIS THING. YOU DON'T KNOW WHAT THIS THING IS...
WHAT I KNOW IS THAT I'M CRACKLING WITH THE PSYCHIC ENERGY OF HALF OF NEW YORK CITY RIGHT NOW, GAZ. I COULD STOP ***CTHULHU*** IN HIS TRACKS WITH A SIMPLE LOCK-SIGIL, HELL, I COULD STOP ***JUSTIN-BLOODY-BIEBER.***
TRUST ME.
ALRIGHT, MATE...
THANKS A LOAD FOR VOLUNTEERING. IT MEANS THE WORLD. SO HERE'S HOW IT'S GOING TO GO... YOU'RE BAIT, AND NOW YOU'RE EXTRA TASTY FOR OUR GHOSTKILLER, ALL CRACKLING WITH COLLECTED ENERGY.
AND YOU DON'T HAVE TO WORRY, I'M NOT GOING TO LET YOU DIE AGAIN. WHEN THIS THING SHOWS, ALL I HAVE TO DO IS DRAW A LITTLE LOCK-SIGIL LIKE SO, AND IT'S OUR CAPTIVE AUDIENCE.
SHOW 'EM, GAZ. GIVE 'EM A LITTLE TWO-STEP.
CAN'T... MOVE...
THERE. FEEL BETTER, YOU UNGRATEFUL LITTLE ⛤⛤⛤⛤S?
TH...ATTT...

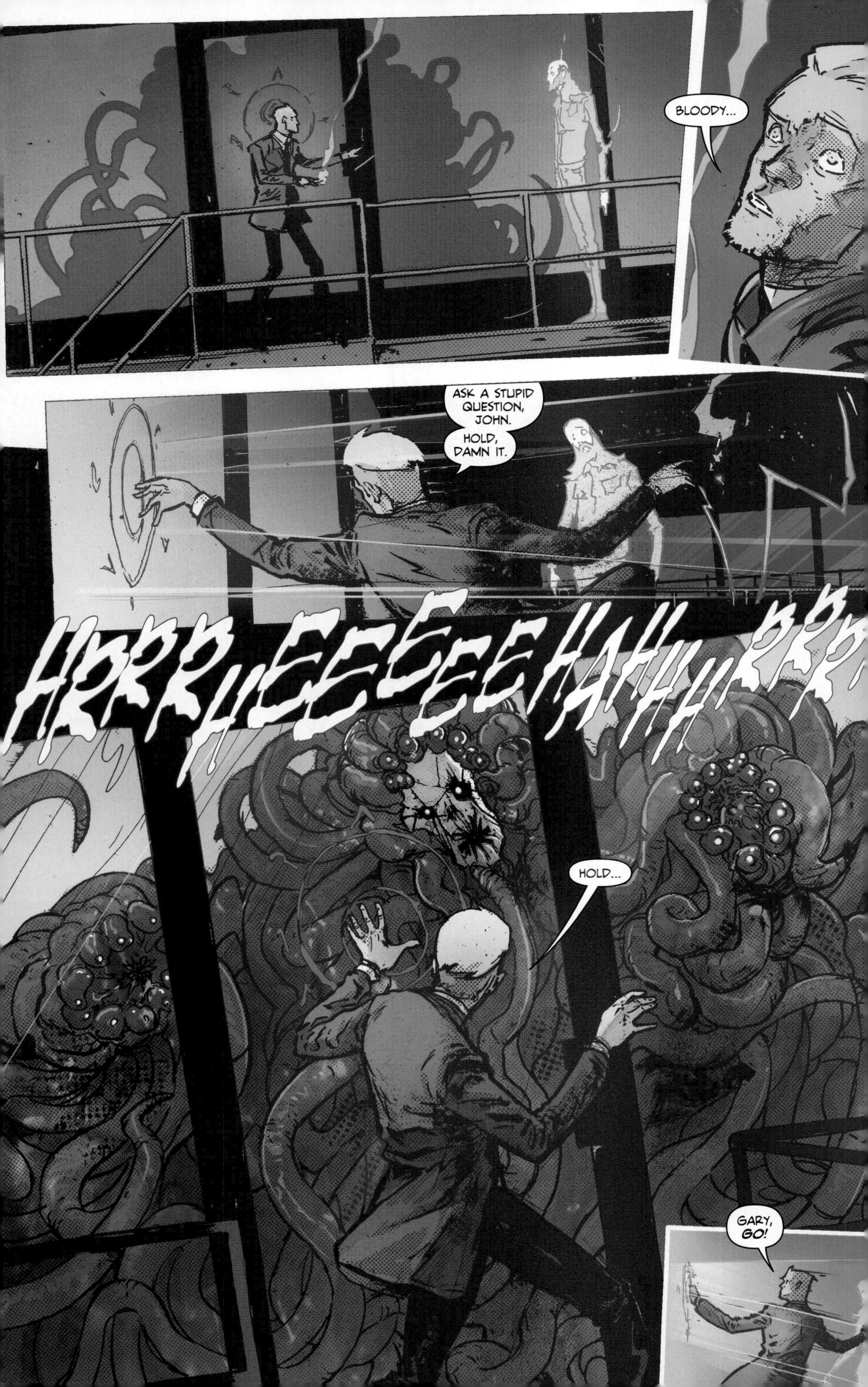
BLOODY...
ASK A STUPID QUESTION, JOHN.
HOLD, DAMN IT.
HRRRHEEEEEEHAHHHRRR
HOLD...
GARY, GO!

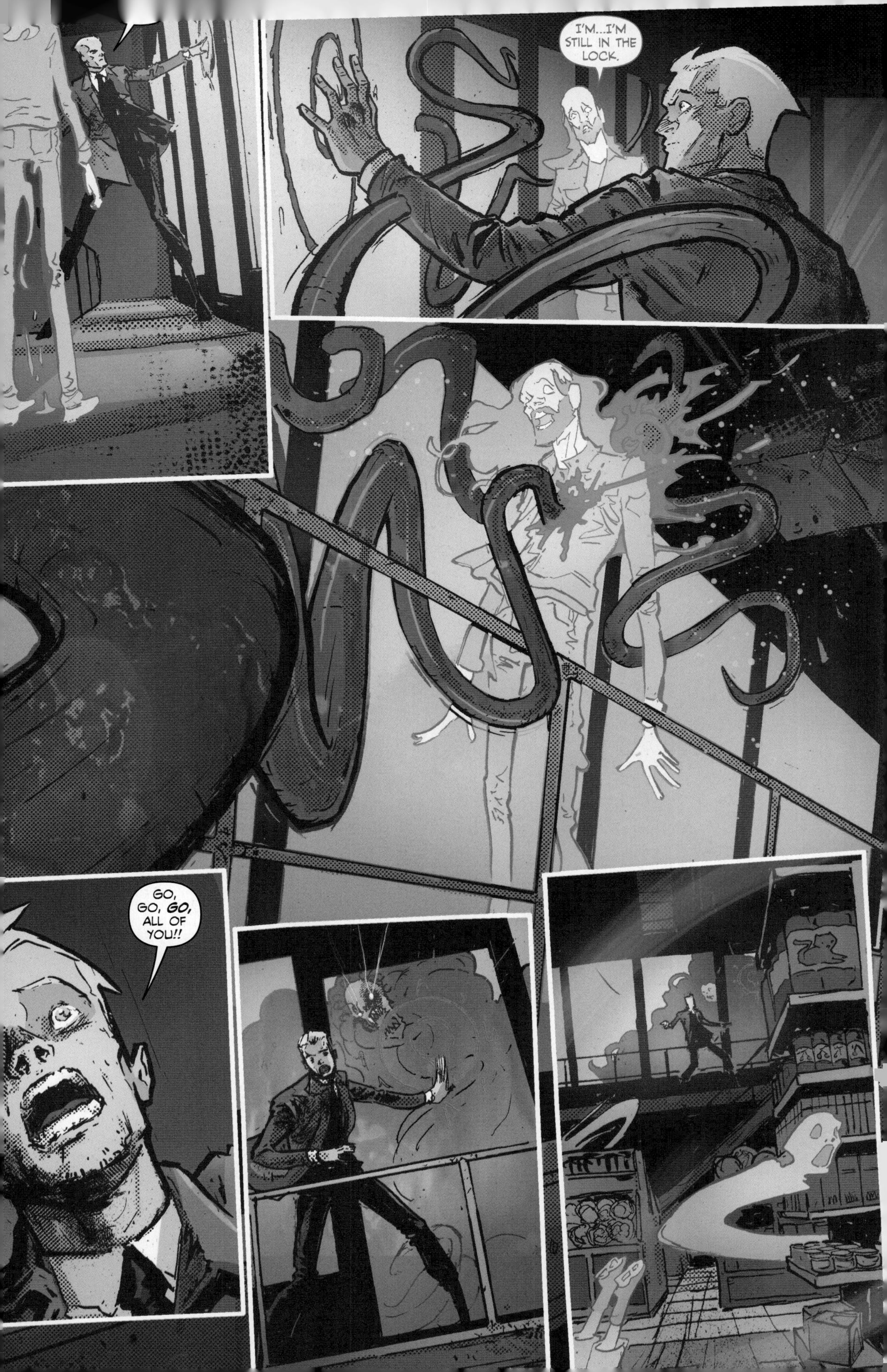
I'M...I'M STILL IN THE LOCK.
GO, GO, **GO,** ALL OF YOU!!

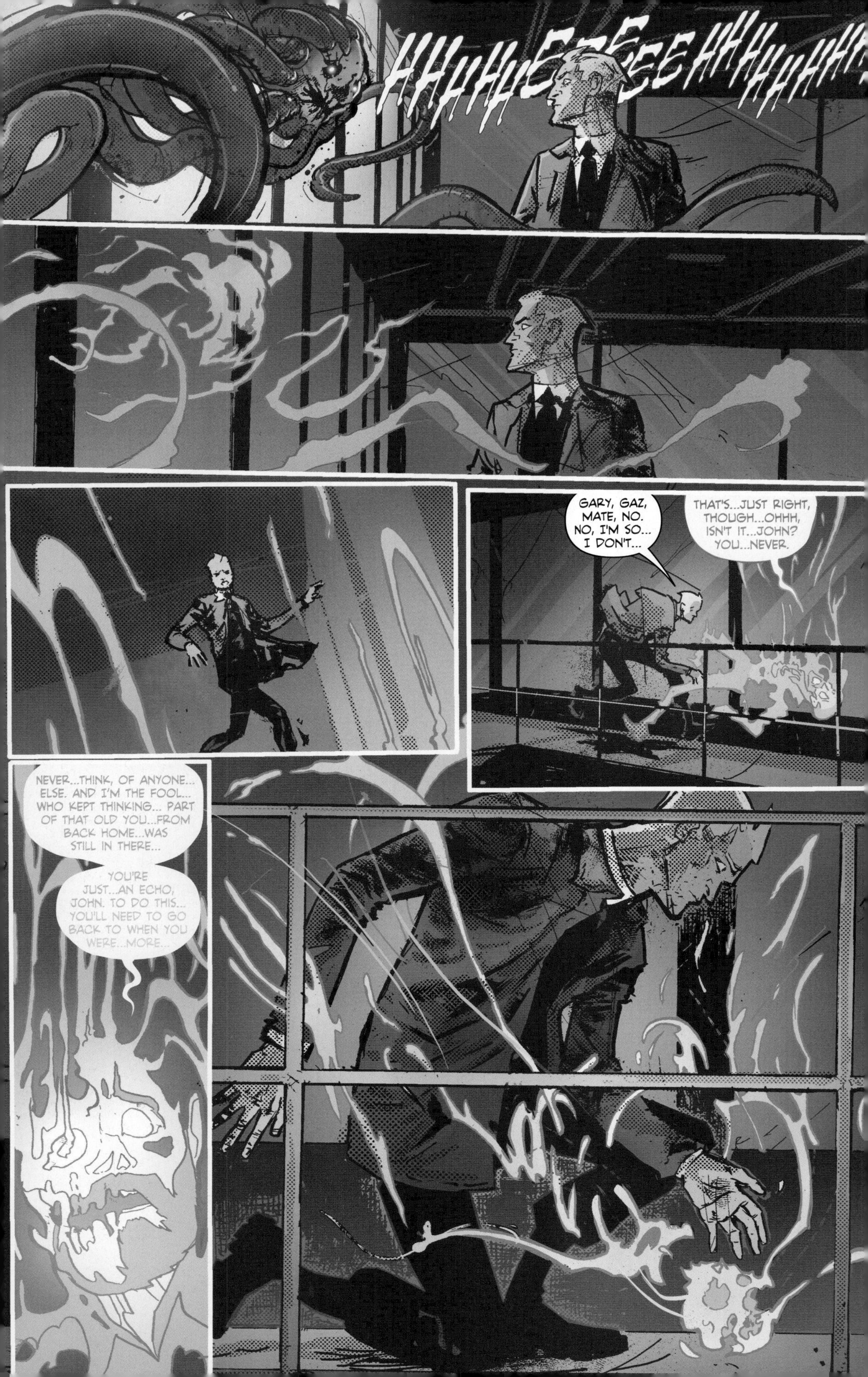
HHHHHEEEEEEHHHHHHHH
GARY, GAZ, MATE, NO. NO, I'M SO... I DON'T...
THAT'S...JUST RIGHT, THOUGH...OHHH, ISN'T IT...JOHN? YOU...NEVER.
NEVER...THINK, OF ANYONE... ELSE. AND I'M THE FOOL... WHO KEPT THINKING... PART OF THAT OLD YOU...FROM BACK HOME...WAS STILL IN THERE...
YOU'RE JUST...AN ECHO, JOHN. TO DO THIS... YOU'LL NEED TO GO BACK TO WHEN YOU WERE...MORE...

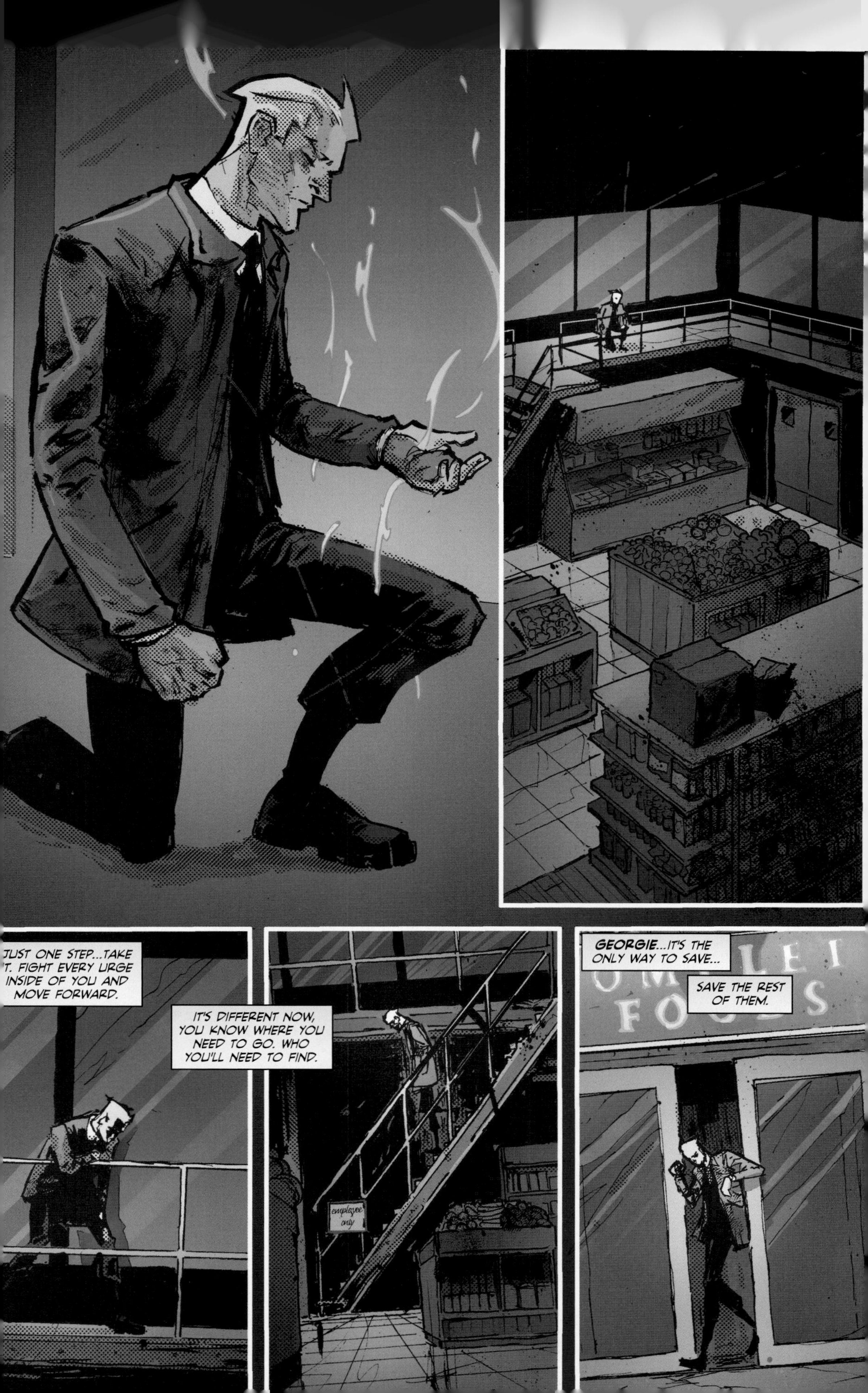
JUST ONE STEP...TAKE T. FIGHT EVERY URGE INSIDE OF YOU AND MOVE FORWARD.
IT'S DIFFERENT NOW, YOU KNOW WHERE YOU NEED TO GO. WHO YOU'LL NEED TO FIND.
employee only
GEORGIE...IT'S THE ONLY WAY TO SAVE...
SAVE THE REST OF THEM.

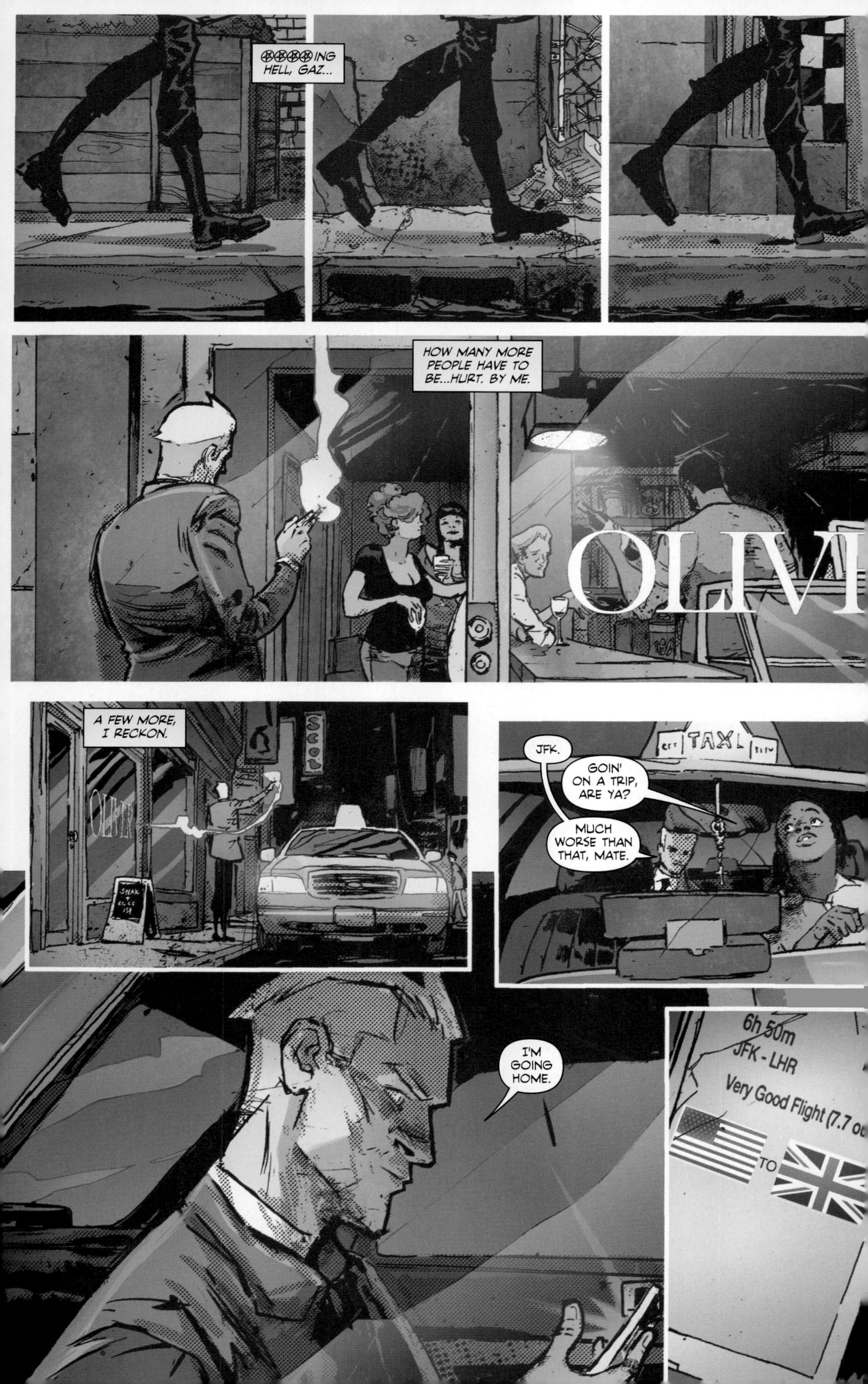
⊗⊗⊗⊗ING HELL, GAZ...
HOW MANY MORE PEOPLE HAVE TO BE...HURT. BY ME.
OLIVE
A FEW MORE, I RECKON.
OLIVER
TAXI
JFK.
GOIN' ON A TRIP, ARE YA?
MUCH WORSE THAN THAT, MATE.
I'M GOING HOME.
6h 50m
JFK - LHR
Very Good Flight (7.7 o
TO

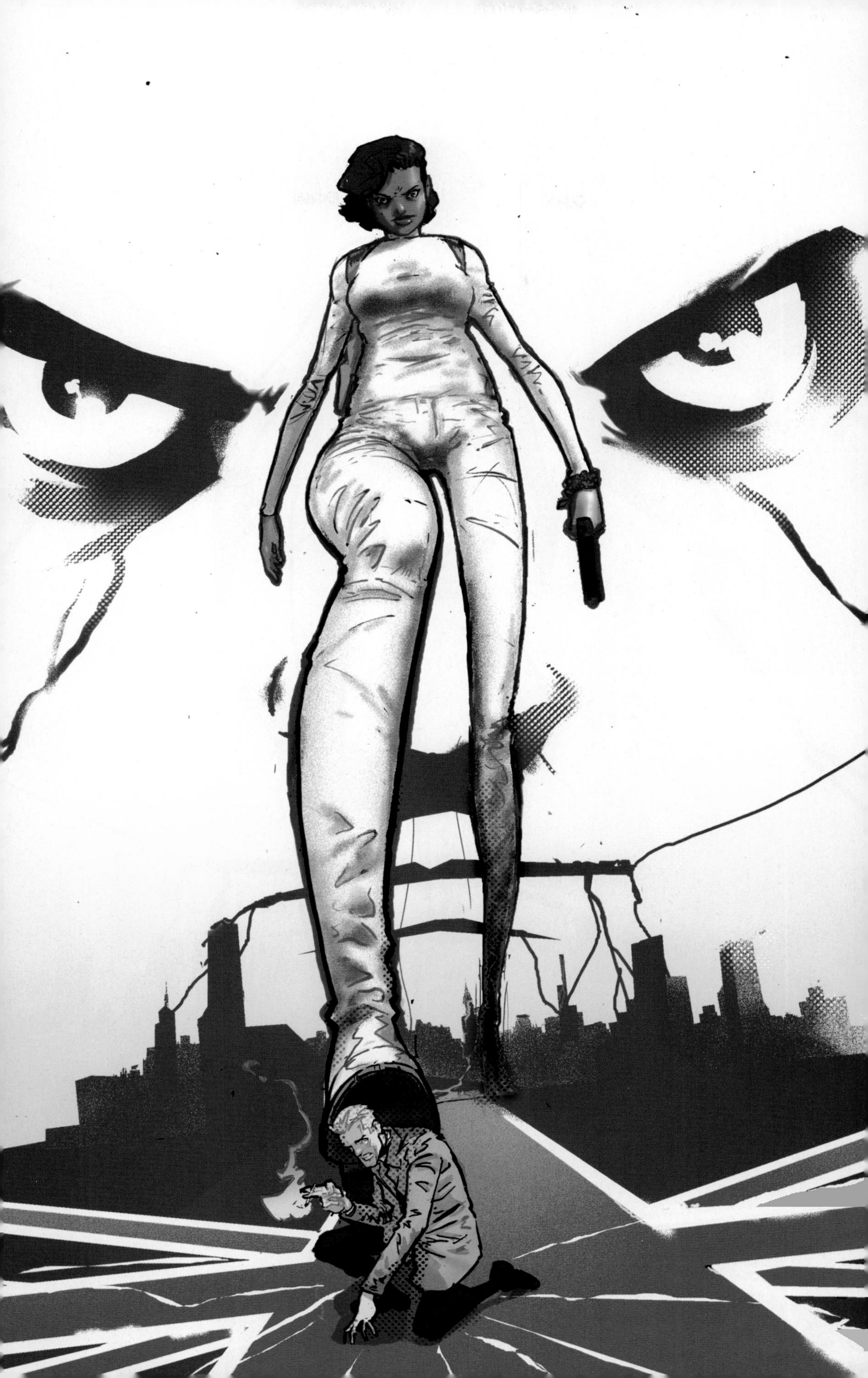

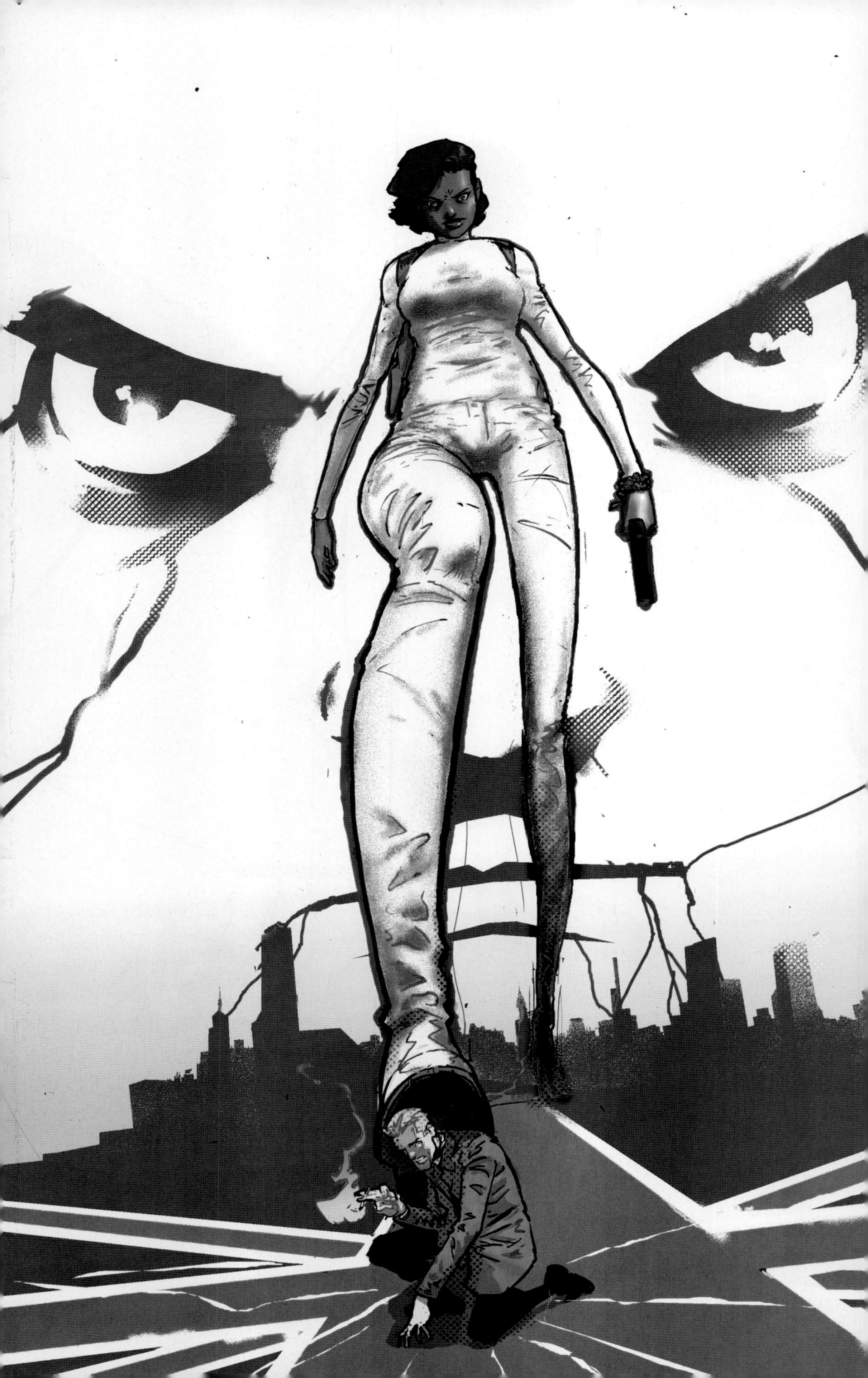

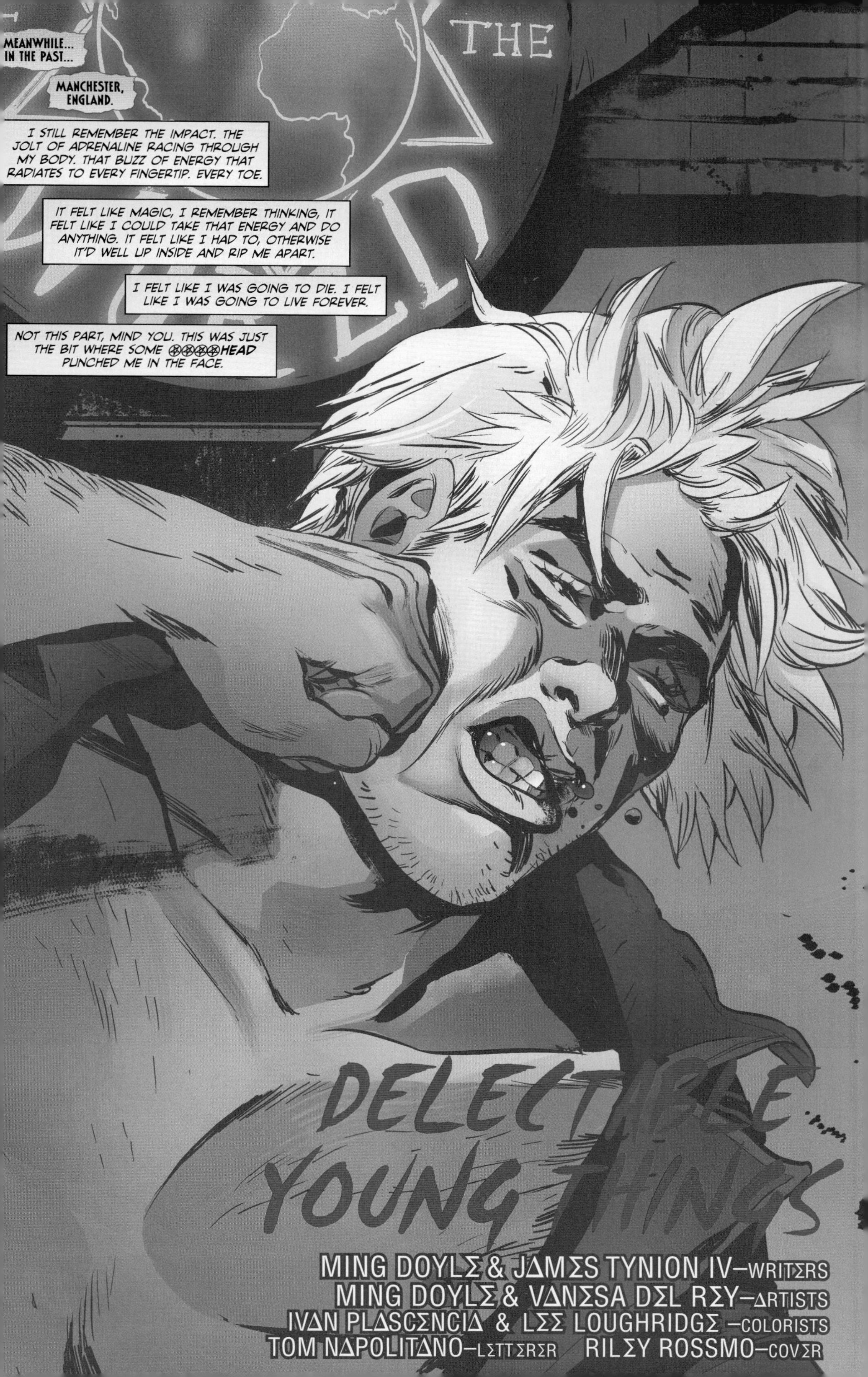
MEANWHILE... IN THE PAST...
MANCHESTER, ENGLAND.
THE
I STILL REMEMBER THE IMPACT. THE JOLT OF ADRENALINE RACING THROUGH MY BODY. THAT BUZZ OF ENERGY THAT RADIATES TO EVERY FINGERTIP. EVERY TOE.
IT FELT LIKE MAGIC, I REMEMBER THINKING, IT FELT LIKE I COULD TAKE THAT ENERGY AND DO ANYTHING. IT FELT LIKE I HAD TO, OTHERWISE IT'D WELL UP INSIDE AND RIP ME APART.
I FELT LIKE I WAS GOING TO DIE. I FELT LIKE I WAS GOING TO LIVE FOREVER.
NOT THIS PART, MIND YOU. THIS WAS JUST THE BIT WHERE SOME ⊗⊗⊗⊗HEAD PUNCHED ME IN THE FACE.
DELECTABLE YOUNG THINGS
MING DOYLE & JAMES TYNION IV—WRITERS
MING DOYLE & VANESA DEL REY—ARTISTS
IVAN PLASCENCIA & LEE LOUGHRIDGE —COLORISTS
TOM NAPOLITANO—LETTERER RILEY ROSSMO—COVER

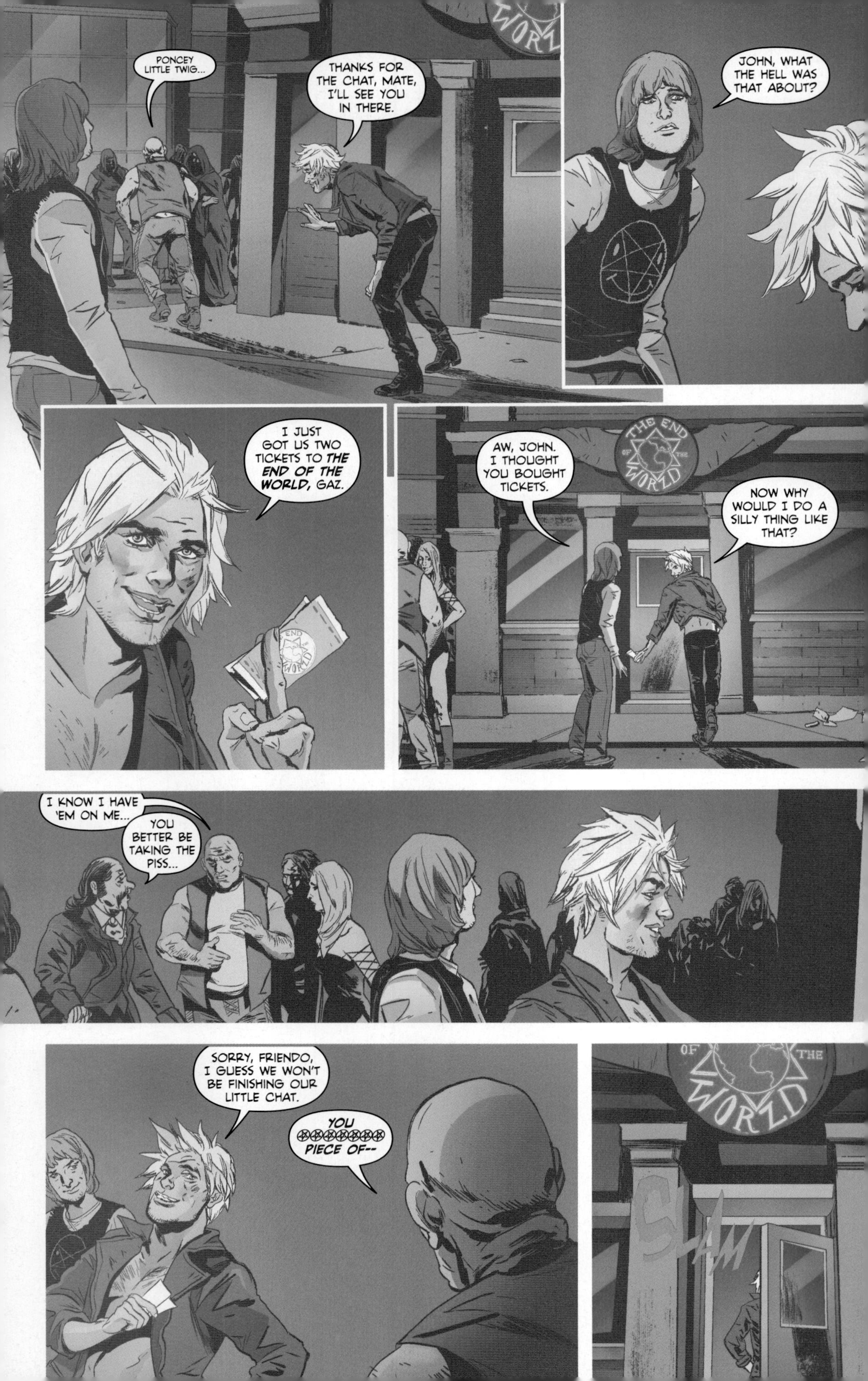
PONCEY LITTLE TWIG...
THANKS FOR THE CHAT, MATE, I'LL SEE YOU IN THERE.
JOHN, WHAT THE HELL WAS THAT ABOUT?
I JUST GOT US TWO TICKETS TO THE END OF THE WORLD, GAZ.
END WORLD
THE END OF THE WORLD
AW, JOHN. I THOUGHT YOU BOUGHT TICKETS.
NOW WHY WOULD I DO A SILLY THING LIKE THAT?
I KNOW I HAVE 'EM ON ME...
YOU BETTER BE TAKING THE PISS...
SORRY, FRIENDO, I GUESS WE WON'T BE FINISHING OUR LITTLE CHAT.
YOU ✡✡✡✡✡✡✡ PIECE OF--
OF THE WORLD
SLAM

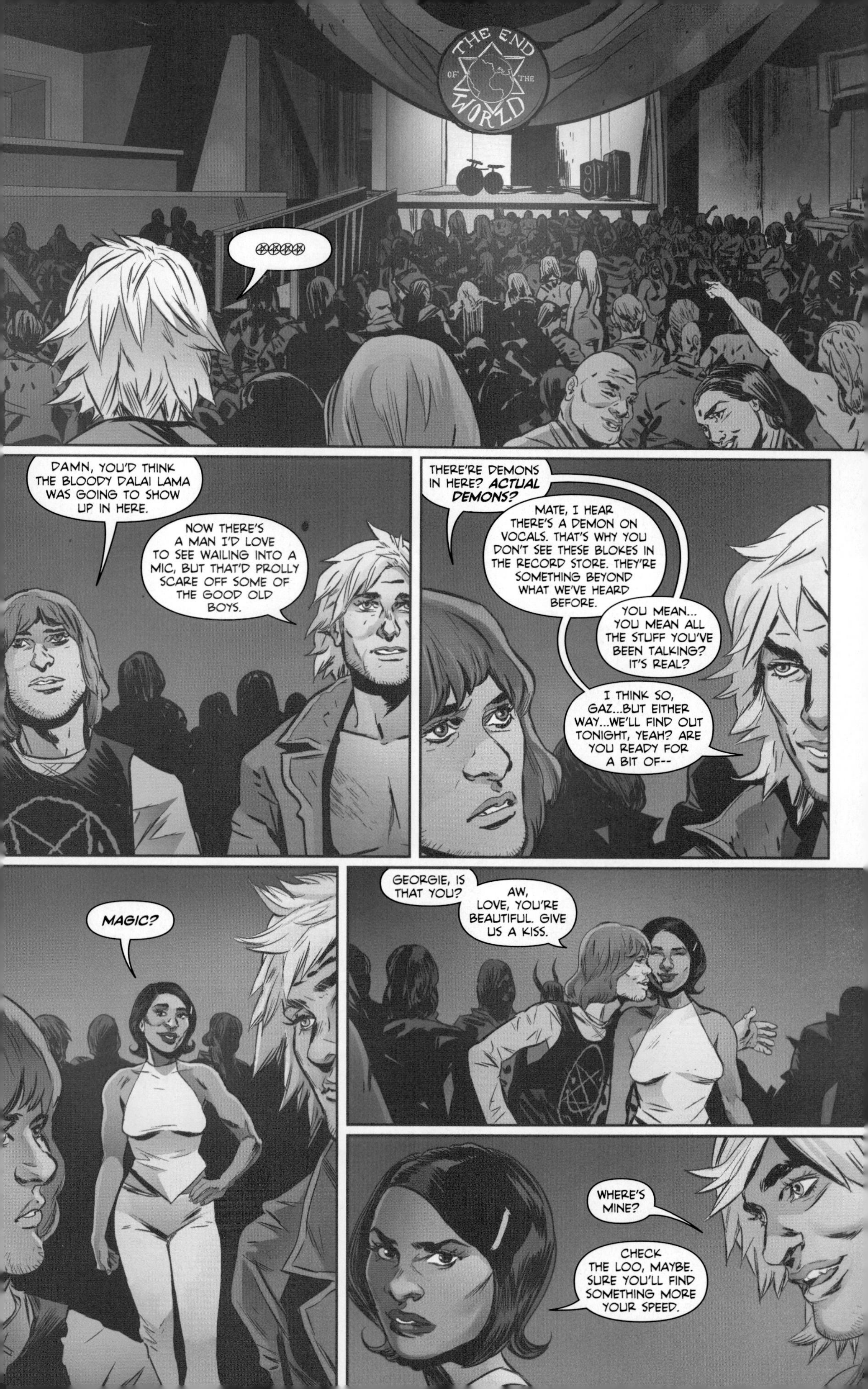
THE END OF THE WORLD
DAMN, YOU'D THINK THE BLOODY DALAI LAMA WAS GOING TO SHOW UP IN HERE.
NOW THERE'S A MAN I'D LOVE TO SEE WAILING INTO A MIC, BUT THAT'D PROLLY SCARE OFF SOME OF THE GOOD OLD BOYS.
THERE'RE DEMONS IN HERE? ACTUAL DEMONS?
MATE, I HEAR THERE'S A DEMON ON VOCALS. THAT'S WHY YOU DON'T SEE THESE BLOKES IN THE RECORD STORE. THEY'RE SOMETHING BEYOND WHAT WE'VE HEARD BEFORE.
YOU MEAN... YOU MEAN ALL THE STUFF YOU'VE BEEN TALKING? IT'S REAL?
I THINK SO, GAZ...BUT EITHER WAY...WE'LL FIND OUT TONIGHT, YEAH? ARE YOU READY FOR A BIT OF--
MAGIC?
GEORGIE, IS THAT YOU?
AW, LOVE, YOU'RE BEAUTIFUL. GIVE US A KISS.
WHERE'S MINE?
CHECK THE LOO, MAYBE. SURE YOU'LL FIND SOMETHING MORE YOUR SPEED.

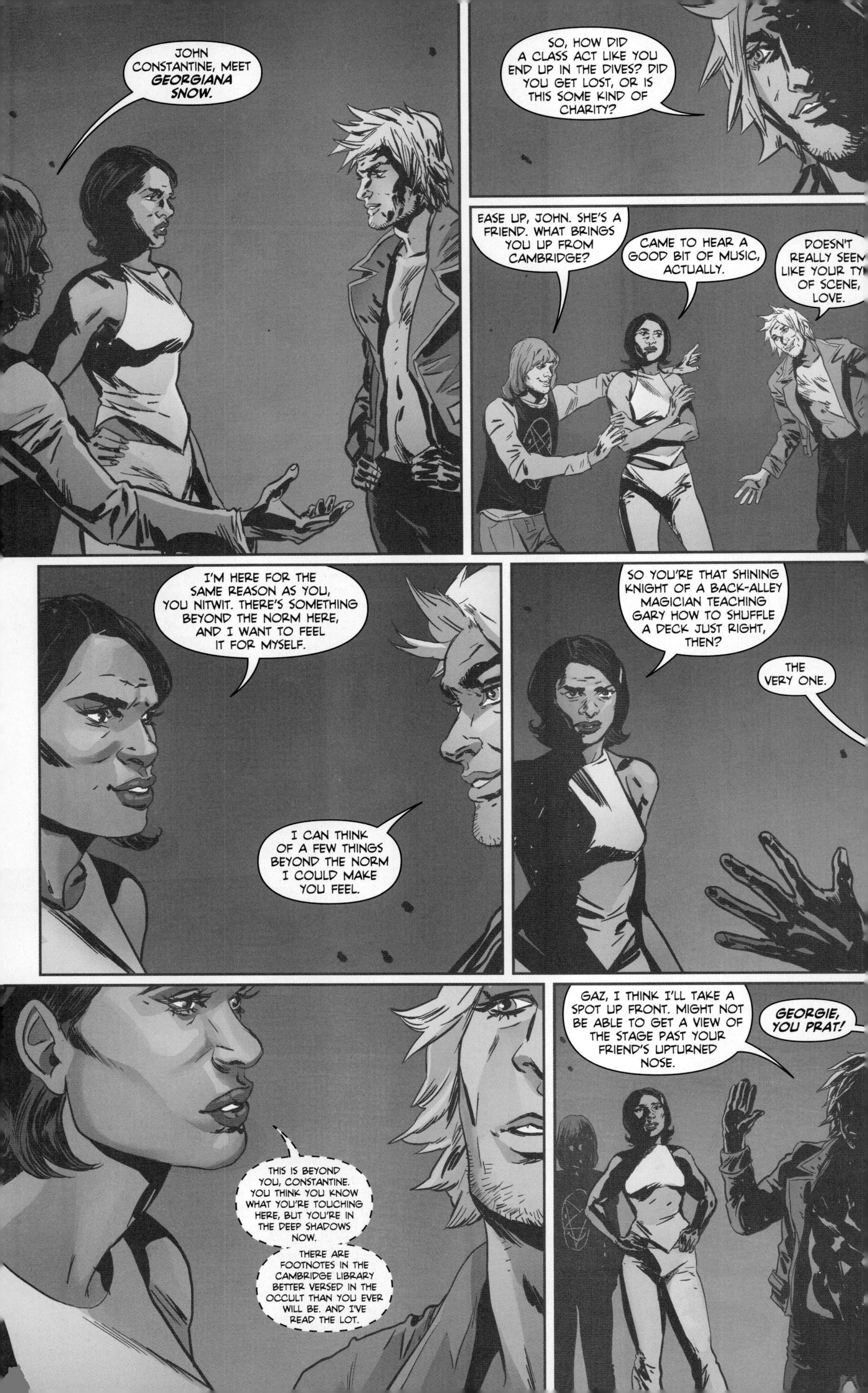
JOHN CONSTANTINE, MEET *GEORGIANA SNOW.*
SO, HOW DID A CLASS ACT LIKE YOU END UP IN THE DIVES? DID YOU GET LOST, OR IS THIS SOME KIND OF CHARITY?
EASE UP, JOHN. SHE'S A FRIEND. WHAT BRINGS YOU UP FROM CAMBRIDGE?
CAME TO HEAR A GOOD BIT OF MUSIC, ACTUALLY.
DOESN'T REALLY SEEM LIKE YOUR TY OF SCENE, LOVE.
I'M HERE FOR THE SAME REASON AS YOU, YOU NITWIT. THERE'S SOMETHING BEYOND THE NORM HERE, AND I WANT TO FEEL IT FOR MYSELF.
I CAN THINK OF A FEW THINGS BEYOND THE NORM I COULD MAKE YOU FEEL.
SO YOU'RE THAT SHINING KNIGHT OF A BACK-ALLEY MAGICIAN TEACHING GARY HOW TO SHUFFLE A DECK JUST RIGHT, THEN?
THE VERY ONE.
THIS IS BEYOND YOU, CONSTANTINE. YOU THINK YOU KNOW WHAT YOU'RE TOUCHING HERE, BUT YOU'RE IN THE DEEP SHADOWS NOW.
THERE ARE FOOTNOTES IN THE CAMBRIDGE LIBRARY BETTER VERSED IN THE OCCULT THAN YOU EVER WILL BE. AND I'VE READ THE LOT.
GAZ, I THINK I'LL TAKE A SPOT UP FRONT. MIGHT NOT BE ABLE TO GET A VIEW OF THE STAGE PAST YOUR FRIEND'S UPTURNED NOSE.
GEORGIE, YOU PRAT!

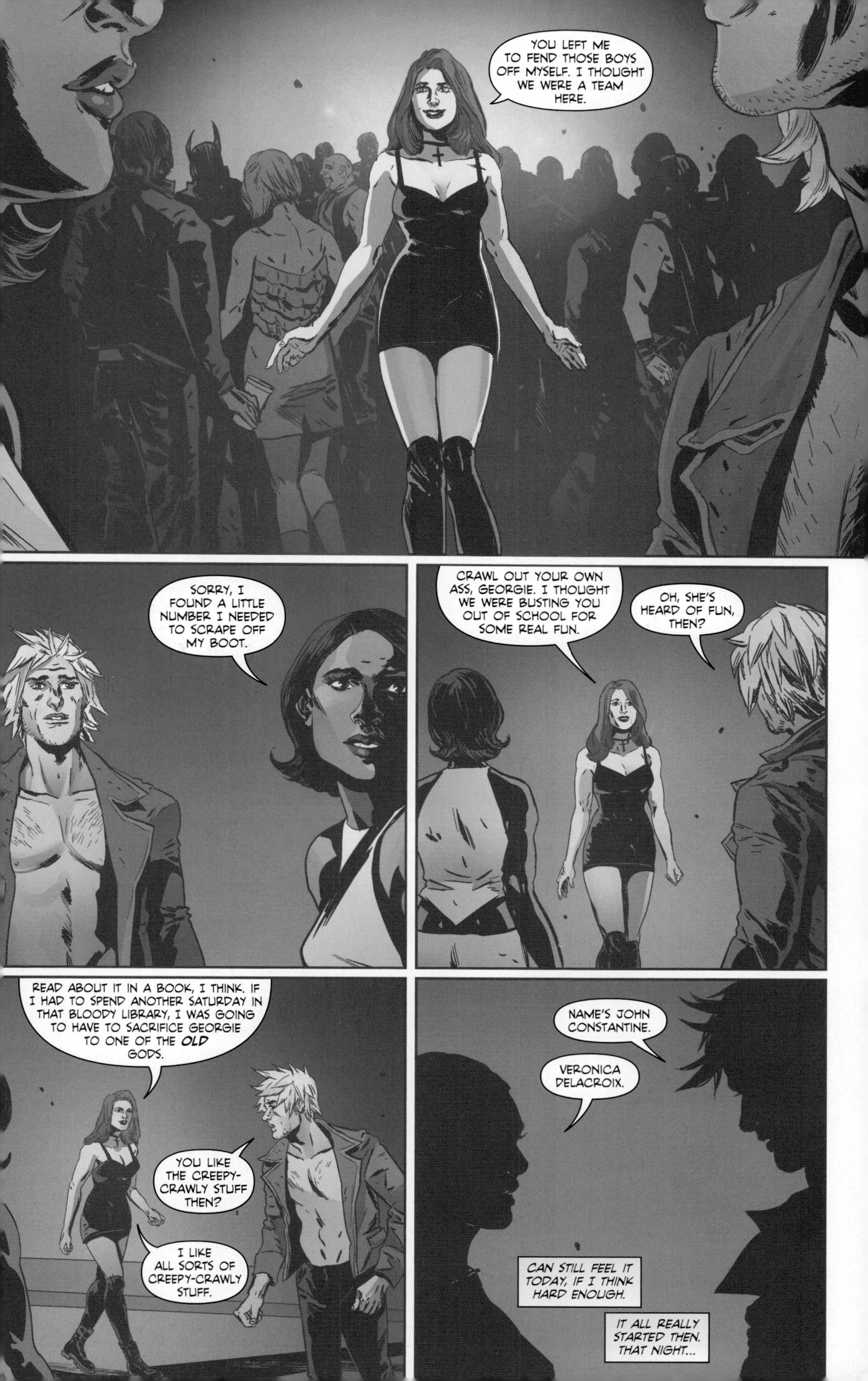
YOU LEFT ME TO FEND THOSE BOYS OFF MYSELF. I THOUGHT WE WERE A TEAM HERE.
SORRY, I FOUND A LITTLE NUMBER I NEEDED TO SCRAPE OFF MY BOOT.
CRAWL OUT YOUR OWN ASS, GEORGIE. I THOUGHT WE WERE BUSTING YOU OUT OF SCHOOL FOR SOME REAL FUN.
OH, SHE'S HEARD OF FUN, THEN?
READ ABOUT IT IN A BOOK, I THINK. IF I HAD TO SPEND ANOTHER SATURDAY IN THAT BLOODY LIBRARY, I WAS GOING TO HAVE TO SACRIFICE GEORGIE TO ONE OF THE OLD GODS.
YOU LIKE THE CREEPY-CRAWLY STUFF THEN?
I LIKE ALL SORTS OF CREEPY-CRAWLY STUFF.
NAME'S JOHN CONSTANTINE.
VERONICA DELACROIX.
CAN STILL FEEL IT TODAY, IF I THINK HARD ENOUGH.
IT ALL REALLY STARTED THEN. THAT NIGHT...

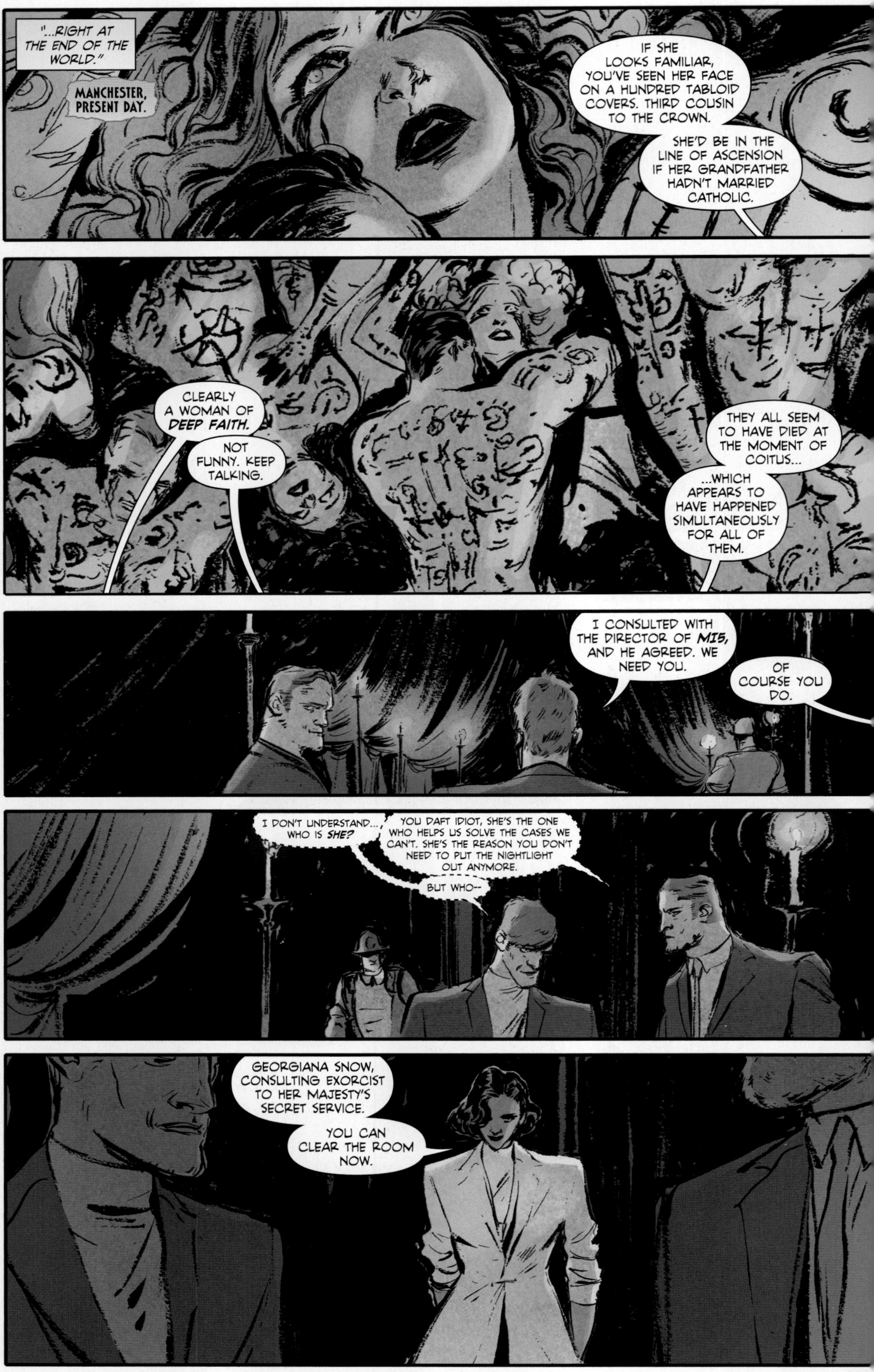
"...RIGHT AT THE END OF THE WORLD."
MANCHESTER, PRESENT DAY.
IF SHE LOOKS FAMILIAR, YOU'VE SEEN HER FACE ON A HUNDRED TABLOID COVERS. THIRD COUSIN TO THE CROWN.
SHE'D BE IN THE LINE OF ASCENSION IF HER GRANDFATHER HADN'T MARRIED CATHOLIC.
CLEARLY A WOMAN OF DEEP FAITH.
NOT FUNNY. KEEP TALKING.
THEY ALL SEEM TO HAVE DIED AT THE MOMENT OF COITUS...
...WHICH APPEARS TO HAVE HAPPENED SIMULTANEOUSLY FOR ALL OF THEM.
I CONSULTED WITH THE DIRECTOR OF MI5, AND HE AGREED. WE NEED YOU.
OF COURSE YOU DO.
I DON'T UNDERSTAND... WHO IS SHE?
YOU DAFT IDIOT, SHE'S THE ONE WHO HELPS US SOLVE THE CASES WE CAN'T. SHE'S THE REASON YOU DON'T NEED TO PUT THE NIGHTLIGHT OUT ANYMORE.
BUT WHO--
GEORGIANA SNOW, CONSULTING EXORCIST TO HER MAJESTY'S SECRET SERVICE.
YOU CAN CLEAR THE ROOM NOW.

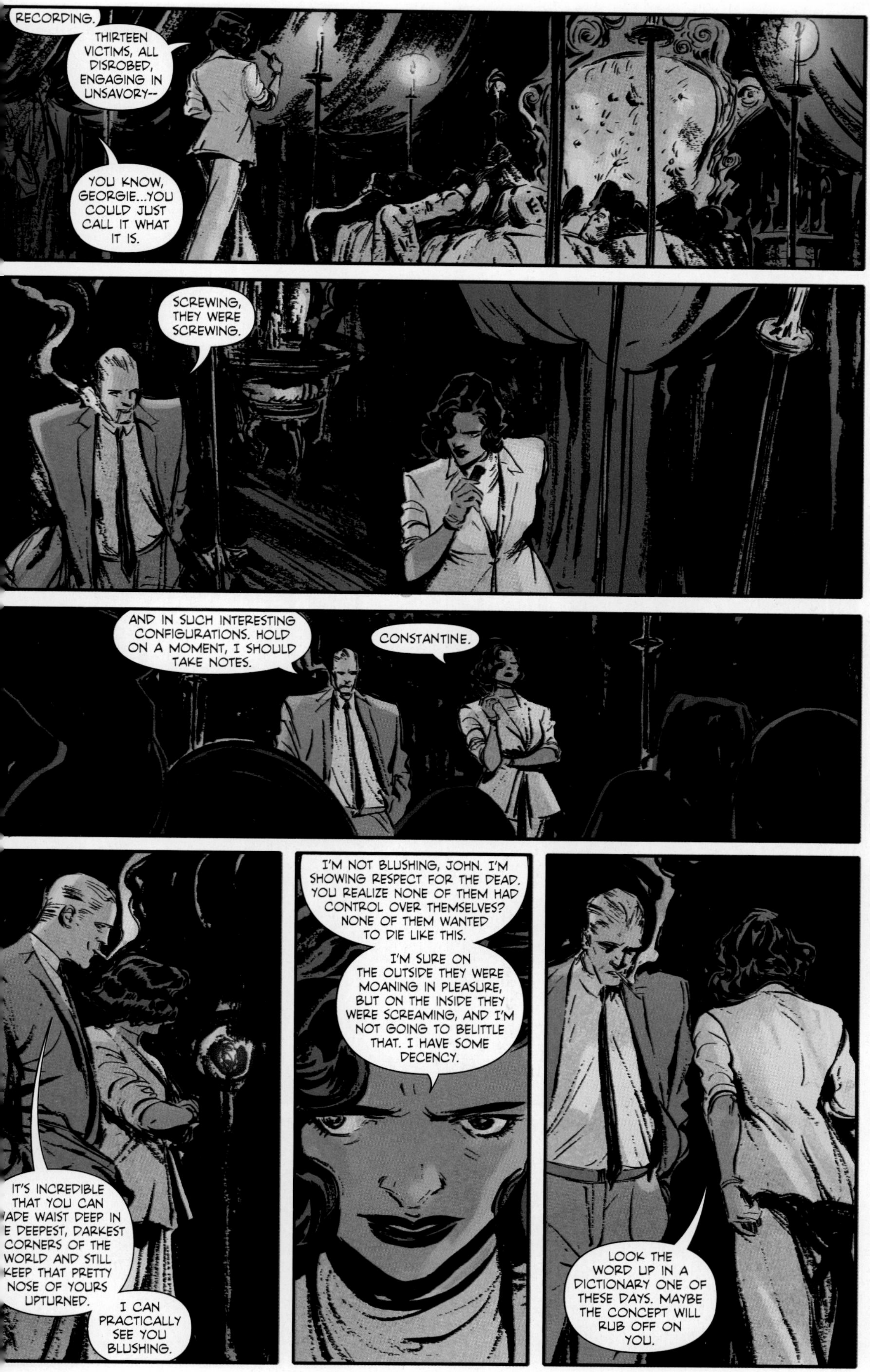
RECORDING.
THIRTEEN VICTIMS, ALL DISROBED, ENGAGING IN UNSAVORY--
YOU KNOW, GEORGIE...YOU COULD JUST CALL IT WHAT IT IS.
SCREWING, THEY WERE SCREWING.
AND IN SUCH INTERESTING CONFIGURATIONS. HOLD ON A MOMENT, I SHOULD TAKE NOTES.
CONSTANTINE.
IT'S INCREDIBLE THAT YOU CAN ADE WAIST DEEP IN E DEEPEST, DARKEST CORNERS OF THE WORLD AND STILL KEEP THAT PRETTY NOSE OF YOURS UPTURNED.
I CAN PRACTICALLY SEE YOU BLUSHING.
I'M NOT BLUSHING, JOHN. I'M SHOWING RESPECT FOR THE DEAD. YOU REALIZE NONE OF THEM HAD CONTROL OVER THEMSELVES? NONE OF THEM WANTED TO DIE LIKE THIS.
I'M SURE ON THE OUTSIDE THEY WERE MOANING IN PLEASURE, BUT ON THE INSIDE THEY WERE SCREAMING, AND I'M NOT GOING TO BELITTLE THAT. I HAVE SOME DECENCY.
LOOK THE WORD UP IN A DICTIONARY ONE OF THESE DAYS. MAYBE THE CONCEPT WILL RUB OFF ON YOU.

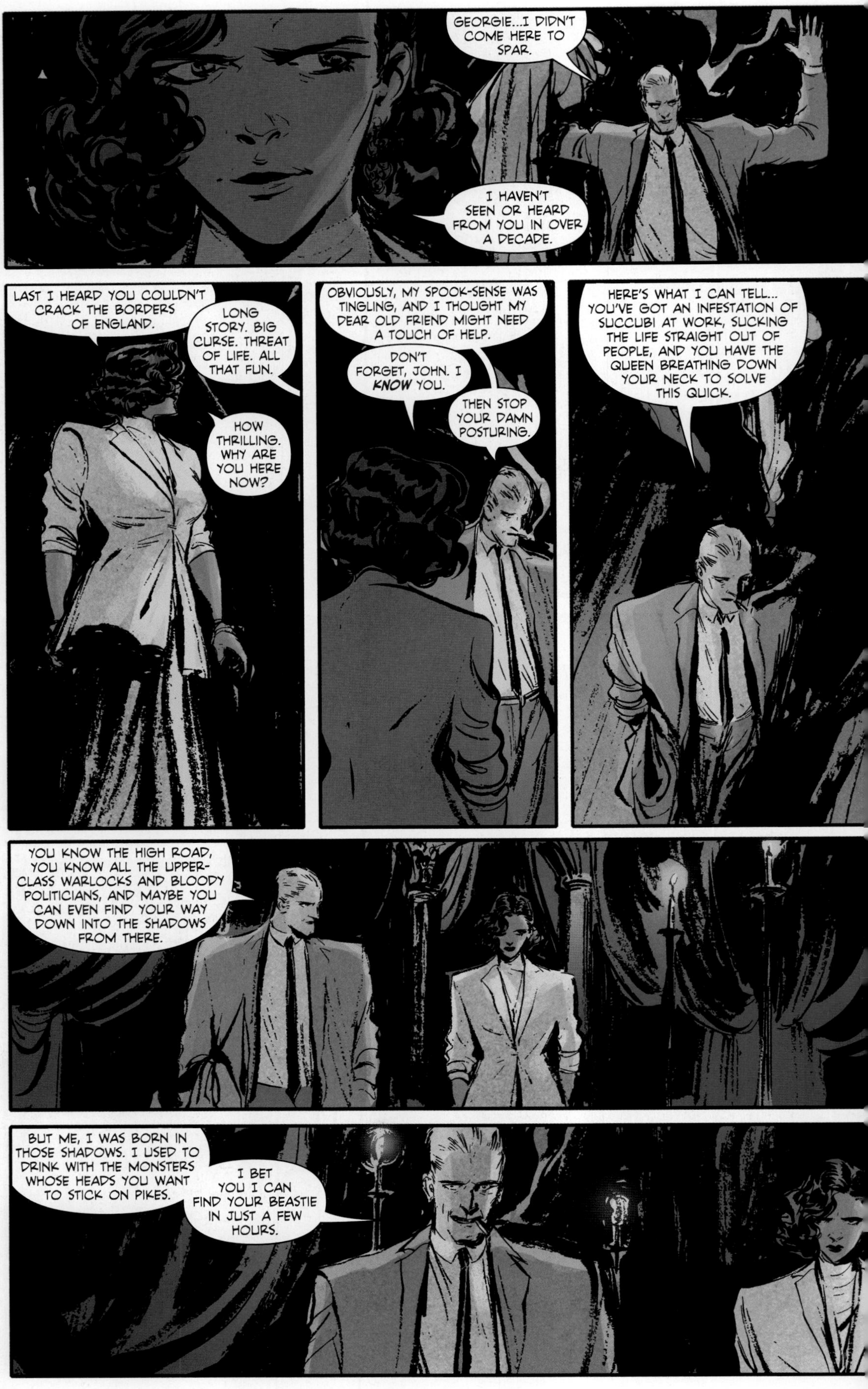
GEORGIE...I DIDN'T COME HERE TO SPAR.
I HAVEN'T SEEN OR HEARD FROM YOU IN OVER A DECADE.
LAST I HEARD YOU COULDN'T CRACK THE BORDERS OF ENGLAND.
LONG STORY. BIG CURSE. THREAT OF LIFE. ALL THAT FUN.
HOW THRILLING. WHY ARE YOU HERE NOW?
OBVIOUSLY, MY SPOOK-SENSE WAS TINGLING, AND I THOUGHT MY DEAR OLD FRIEND MIGHT NEED A TOUCH OF HELP.
DON'T FORGET, JOHN. I KNOW YOU.
THEN STOP YOUR DAMN POSTURING.
HERE'S WHAT I CAN TELL... YOU'VE GOT AN INFESTATION OF SUCCUBI AT WORK, SUCKING THE LIFE STRAIGHT OUT OF PEOPLE, AND YOU HAVE THE QUEEN BREATHING DOWN YOUR NECK TO SOLVE THIS QUICK.
YOU KNOW THE HIGH ROAD, YOU KNOW ALL THE UPPER-CLASS WARLOCKS AND BLOODY POLITICIANS, AND MAYBE YOU CAN EVEN FIND YOUR WAY DOWN INTO THE SHADOWS FROM THERE.
BUT ME, I WAS BORN IN THOSE SHADOWS. I USED TO DRINK WITH THE MONSTERS WHOSE HEADS YOU WANT TO STICK ON PIKES.
I BET YOU I CAN FIND YOUR BEASTIE IN JUST A FEW HOURS.

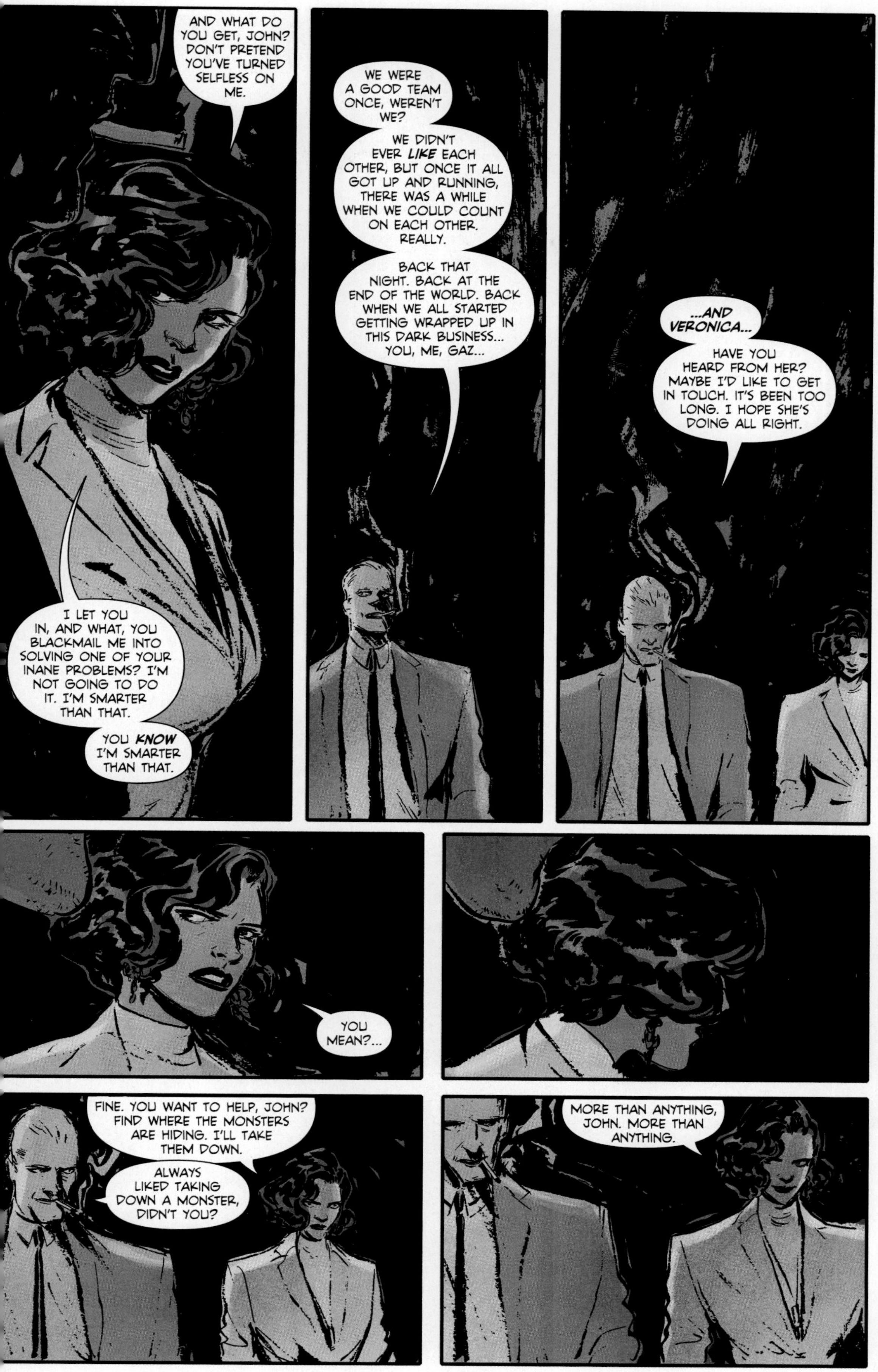
AND WHAT DO YOU GET, JOHN? DON'T PRETEND YOU'VE TURNED SELFLESS ON ME.
I LET YOU IN, AND WHAT, YOU BLACKMAIL ME INTO SOLVING ONE OF YOUR INANE PROBLEMS? I'M NOT GOING TO DO IT. I'M SMARTER THAN THAT.
YOU KNOW I'M SMARTER THAN THAT.
WE WERE A GOOD TEAM ONCE, WEREN'T WE?
WE DIDN'T EVER LIKE EACH OTHER, BUT ONCE IT ALL GOT UP AND RUNNING, THERE WAS A WHILE WHEN WE COULD COUNT ON EACH OTHER. REALLY.
BACK THAT NIGHT. BACK AT THE END OF THE WORLD. BACK WHEN WE ALL STARTED GETTING WRAPPED UP IN THIS DARK BUSINESS... YOU, ME, GAZ...
...AND VERONICA...
HAVE YOU HEARD FROM HER? MAYBE I'D LIKE TO GET IN TOUCH. IT'S BEEN TOO LONG. I HOPE SHE'S DOING ALL RIGHT.
YOU MEAN?...
FINE. YOU WANT TO HELP, JOHN? FIND WHERE THE MONSTERS ARE HIDING. I'LL TAKE THEM DOWN.
ALWAYS LIKED TAKING DOWN A MONSTER, DIDN'T YOU?
MORE THAN ANYTHING, JOHN. MORE THAN ANYTHING.

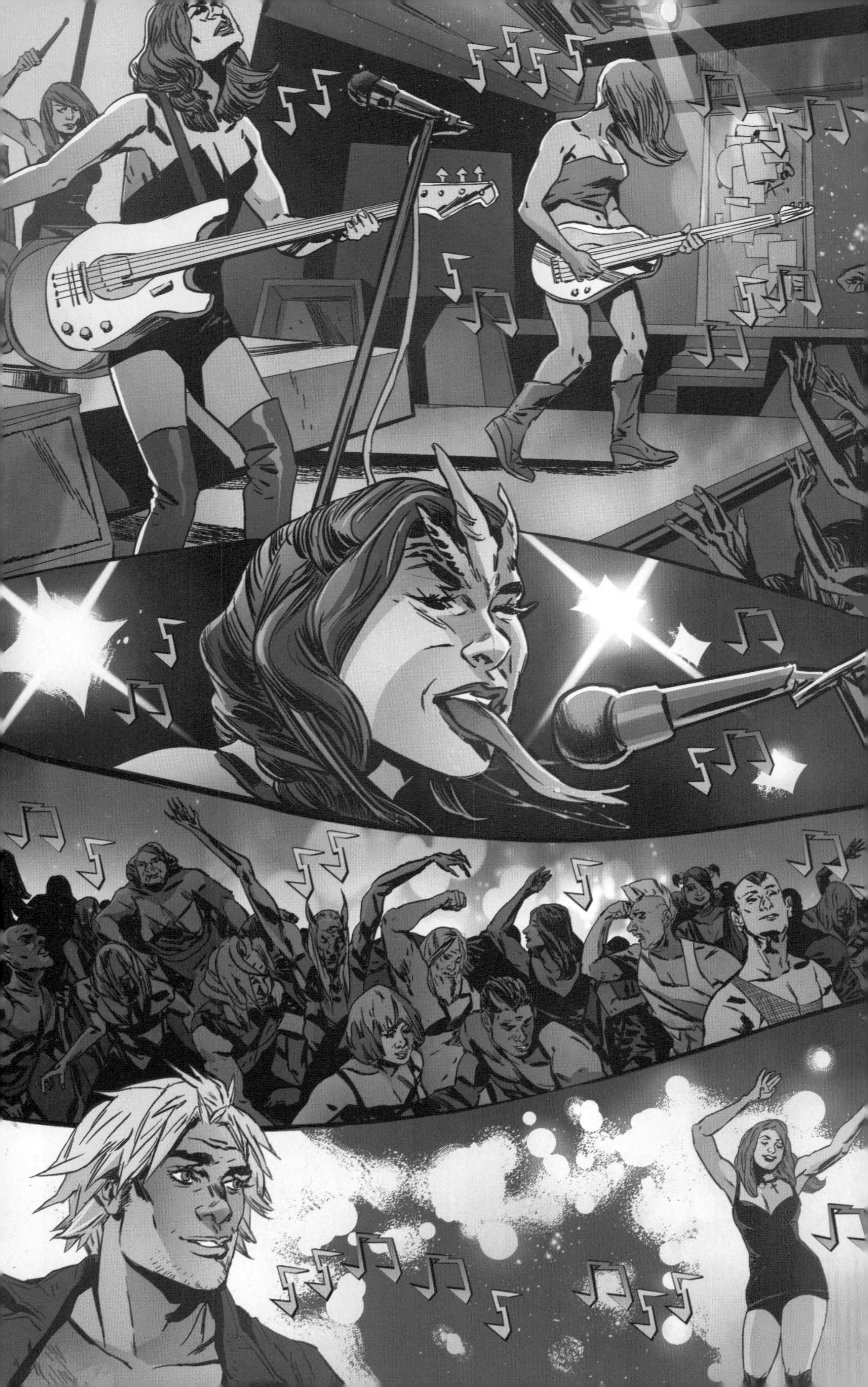

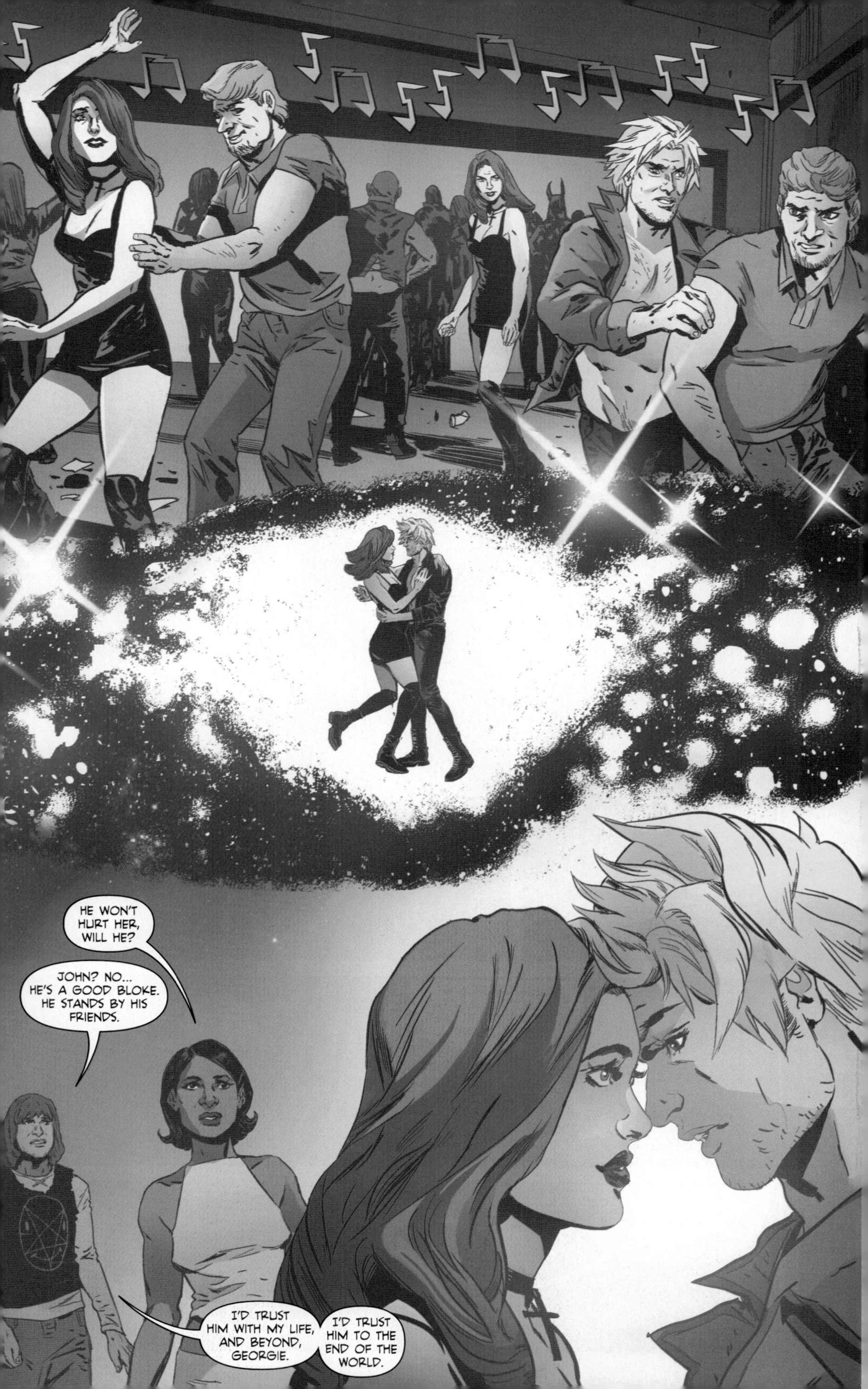
HE WON'T HURT HER, WILL HE?
JOHN? NO... HE'S A GOOD BLOKE. HE STANDS BY HIS FRIENDS.
I'D TRUST HIM WITH MY LIFE, AND BEYOND, GEORGIE.
I'D TRUST HIM TO THE END OF THE WORLD.

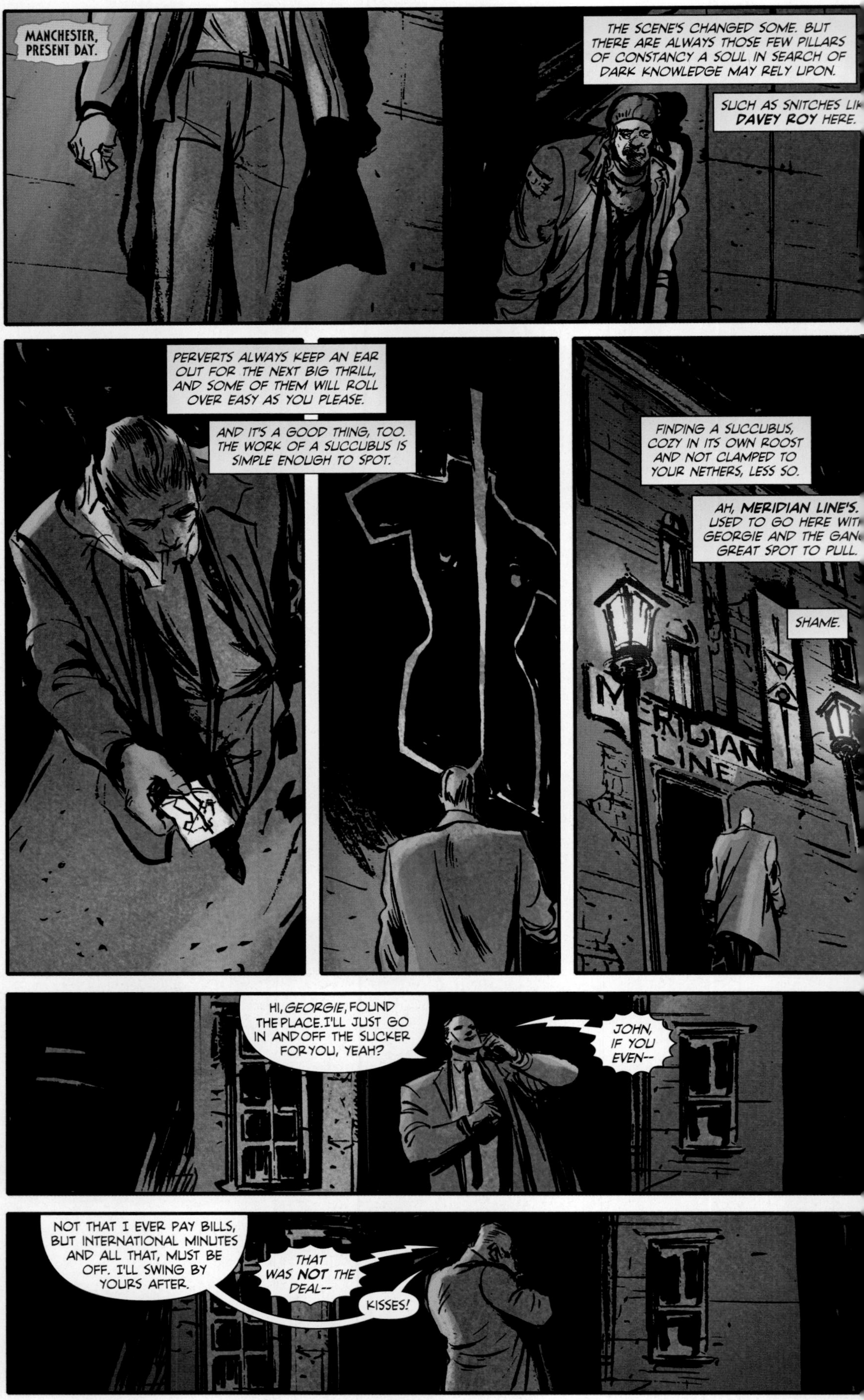
MANCHESTER, PRESENT DAY.
THE SCENE'S CHANGED SOME. BUT THERE ARE ALWAYS THOSE FEW PILLARS OF CONSTANCY A SOUL IN SEARCH OF DARK KNOWLEDGE MAY RELY UPON.
SUCH AS SNITCHES LIK
DAVEY ROY HERE.
PERVERTS ALWAYS KEEP AN EAR OUT FOR THE NEXT BIG THRILL, AND SOME OF THEM WILL ROLL OVER EASY AS YOU PLEASE.
AND IT'S A GOOD THING, TOO. THE WORK OF A SUCCUBUS IS SIMPLE ENOUGH TO SPOT.
FINDING A SUCCUBUS, COZY IN ITS OWN ROOST AND NOT CLAMPED TO YOUR NETHERS, LESS SO.
AH, MERIDIAN LINE'S. USED TO GO HERE WIT GEORGIE AND THE GAN GREAT SPOT TO PULL.
SHAME.
MERIDIAN LINE
HI, GEORGIE, FOUND THE PLACE. I'LL JUST GO IN AND OFF THE SUCKER FOR YOU, YEAH?
JOHN, IF YOU EVEN--
NOT THAT I EVER PAY BILLS, BUT INTERNATIONAL MINUTES AND ALL THAT, MUST BE OFF. I'LL SWING BY YOURS AFTER.
THAT WAS NOT THE DEAL--
KISSES!

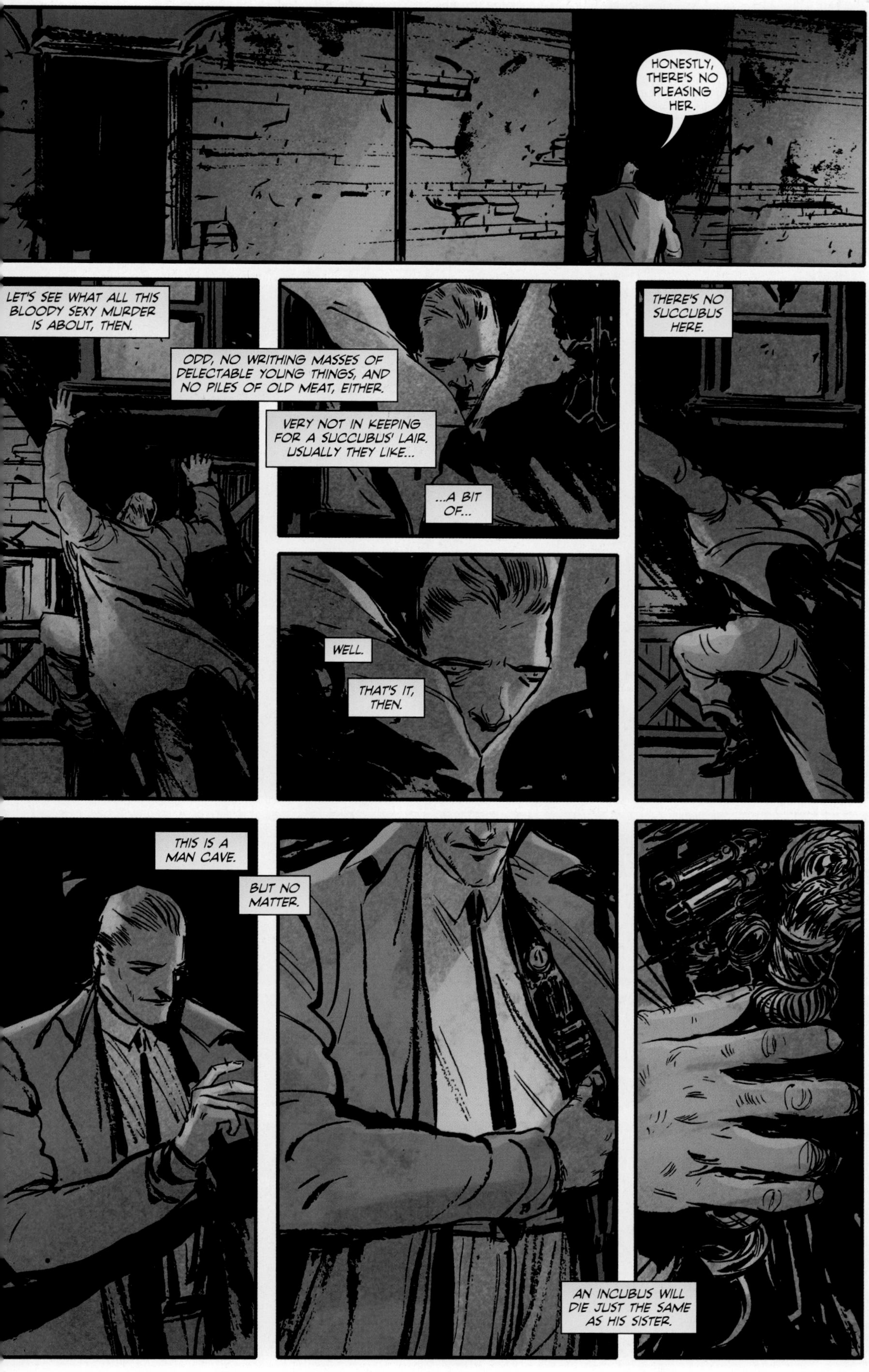
HONESTLY, THERE'S NO PLEASING HER.
LET'S SEE WHAT ALL THIS BLOODY SEXY MURDER IS ABOUT, THEN.
ODD, NO WRITHING MASSES OF DELECTABLE YOUNG THINGS, AND NO PILES OF OLD MEAT, EITHER.
VERY NOT IN KEEPING FOR A SUCCUBUS' LAIR. USUALLY THEY LIKE...
...A BIT OF...
WELL.
THAT'S IT, THEN.
THERE'S NO SUCCUBUS HERE.
THIS IS A MAN CAVE.
BUT NO MATTER.
AN INCUBUS WILL DIE JUST THE SAME AS HIS SISTER.

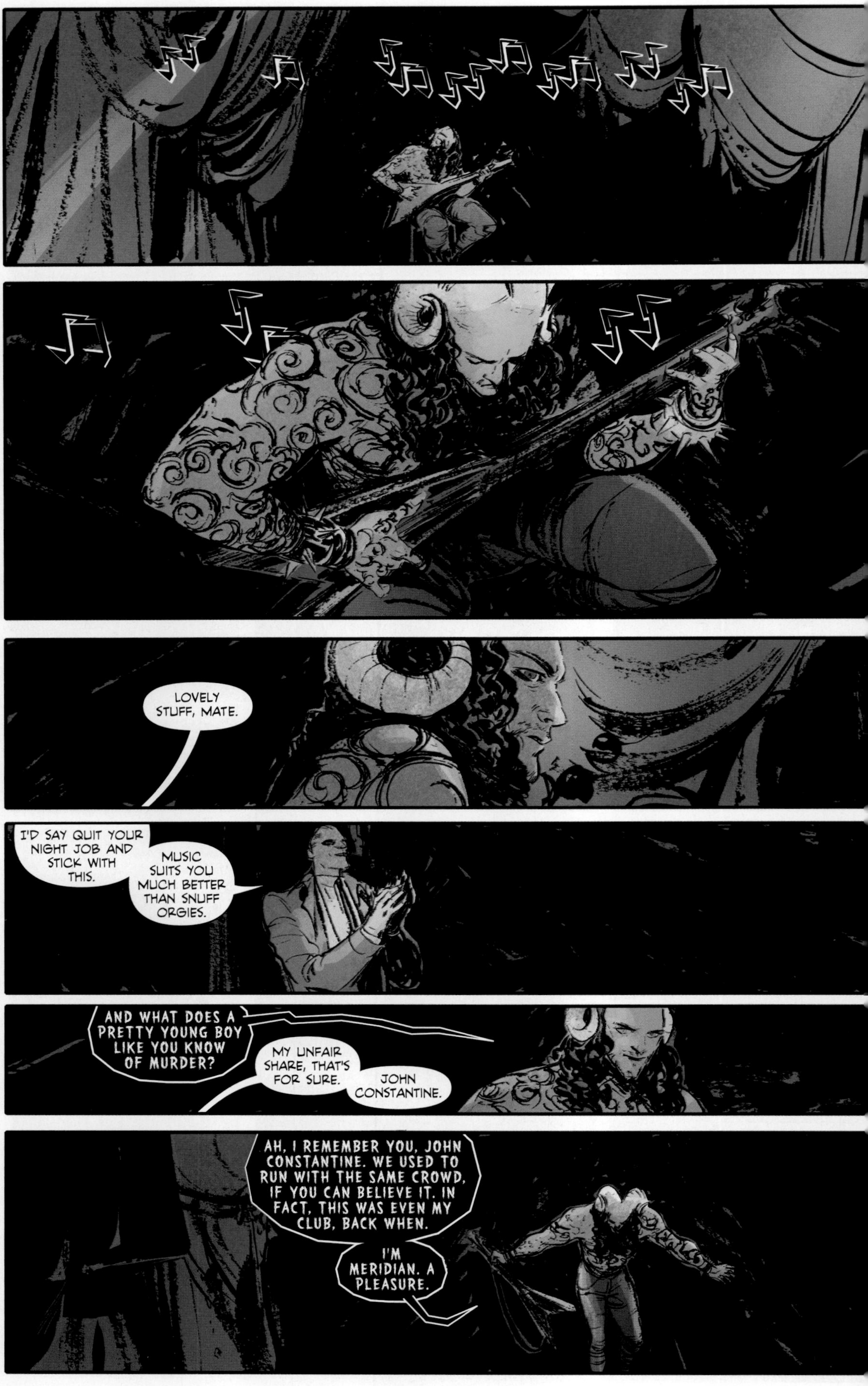
LOVELY STUFF, MATE.
I'D SAY QUIT YOUR NIGHT JOB AND STICK WITH THIS.
MUSIC SUITS YOU MUCH BETTER THAN SNUFF ORGIES.
AND WHAT DOES A PRETTY YOUNG BOY LIKE YOU KNOW OF MURDER?
MY UNFAIR SHARE, THAT'S FOR SURE.
JOHN CONSTANTINE.
AH, I REMEMBER YOU, JOHN CONSTANTINE. WE USED TO RUN WITH THE SAME CROWD, IF YOU CAN BELIEVE IT. IN FACT, THIS WAS EVEN MY CLUB, BACK WHEN.
I'M MERIDIAN. A PLEASURE.

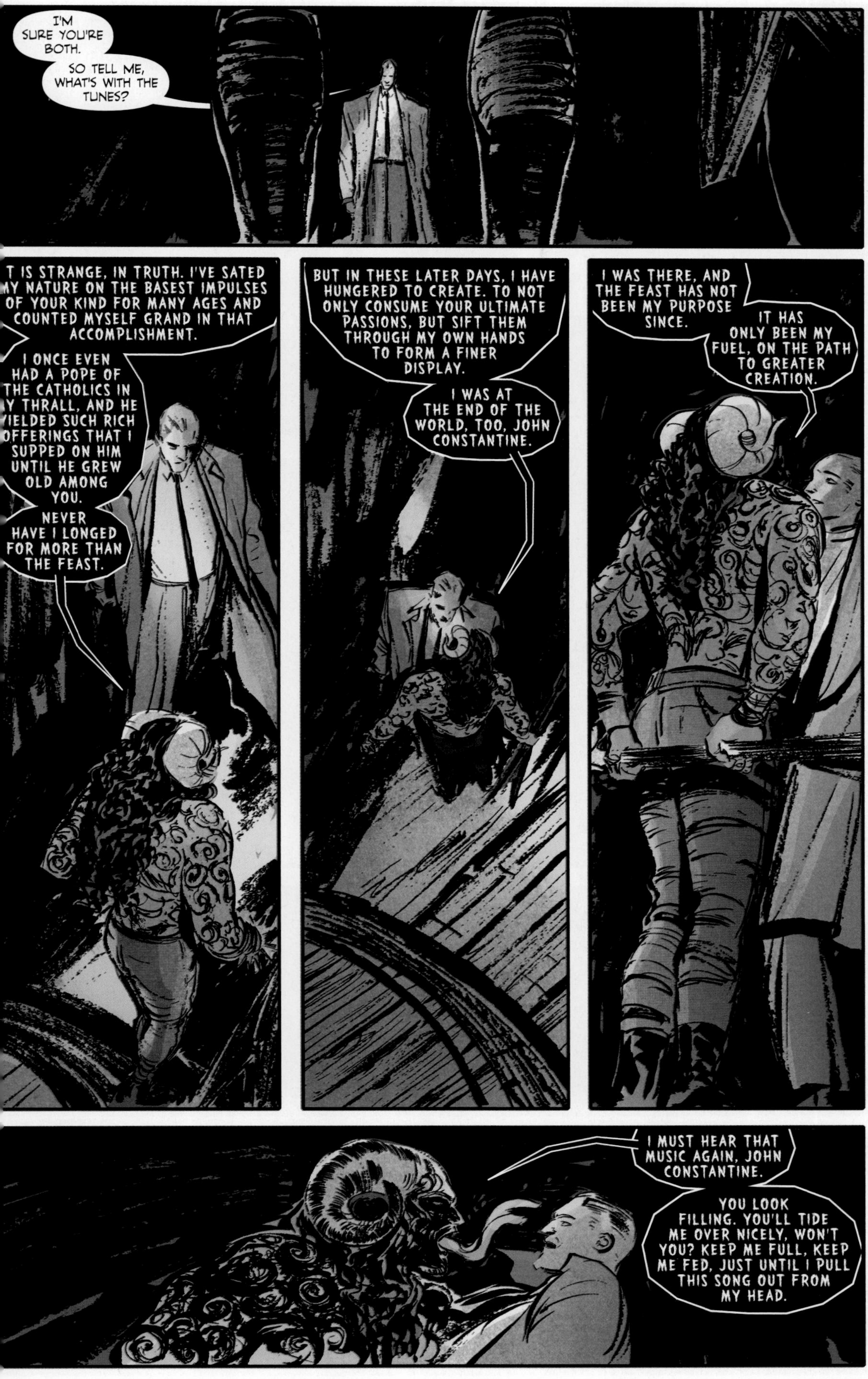
I'M SURE YOU'RE BOTH.
SO TELL ME, WHAT'S WITH THE TUNES?
T IS STRANGE, IN TRUTH. I'VE SATED MY NATURE ON THE BASEST IMPULSES OF YOUR KIND FOR MANY AGES AND COUNTED MYSELF GRAND IN THAT ACCOMPLISHMENT.
I ONCE EVEN HAD A POPE OF THE CATHOLICS IN Y THRALL, AND HE IELDED SUCH RICH OFFERINGS THAT I SUPPED ON HIM UNTIL HE GREW OLD AMONG YOU.
NEVER HAVE I LONGED FOR MORE THAN THE FEAST.
BUT IN THESE LATER DAYS, I HAVE HUNGERED TO CREATE. TO NOT ONLY CONSUME YOUR ULTIMATE PASSIONS, BUT SIFT THEM THROUGH MY OWN HANDS TO FORM A FINER DISPLAY.
I WAS AT THE END OF THE WORLD, TOO, JOHN CONSTANTINE.
I WAS THERE, AND THE FEAST HAS NOT BEEN MY PURPOSE SINCE.
IT HAS ONLY BEEN MY FUEL, ON THE PATH TO GREATER CREATION.
I MUST HEAR THAT MUSIC AGAIN, JOHN CONSTANTINE.
YOU LOOK FILLING. YOU'LL TIDE ME OVER NICELY, WON'T YOU? KEEP ME FULL, KEEP ME FED, JUST UNTIL I PULL THIS SONG OUT FROM MY HEAD.

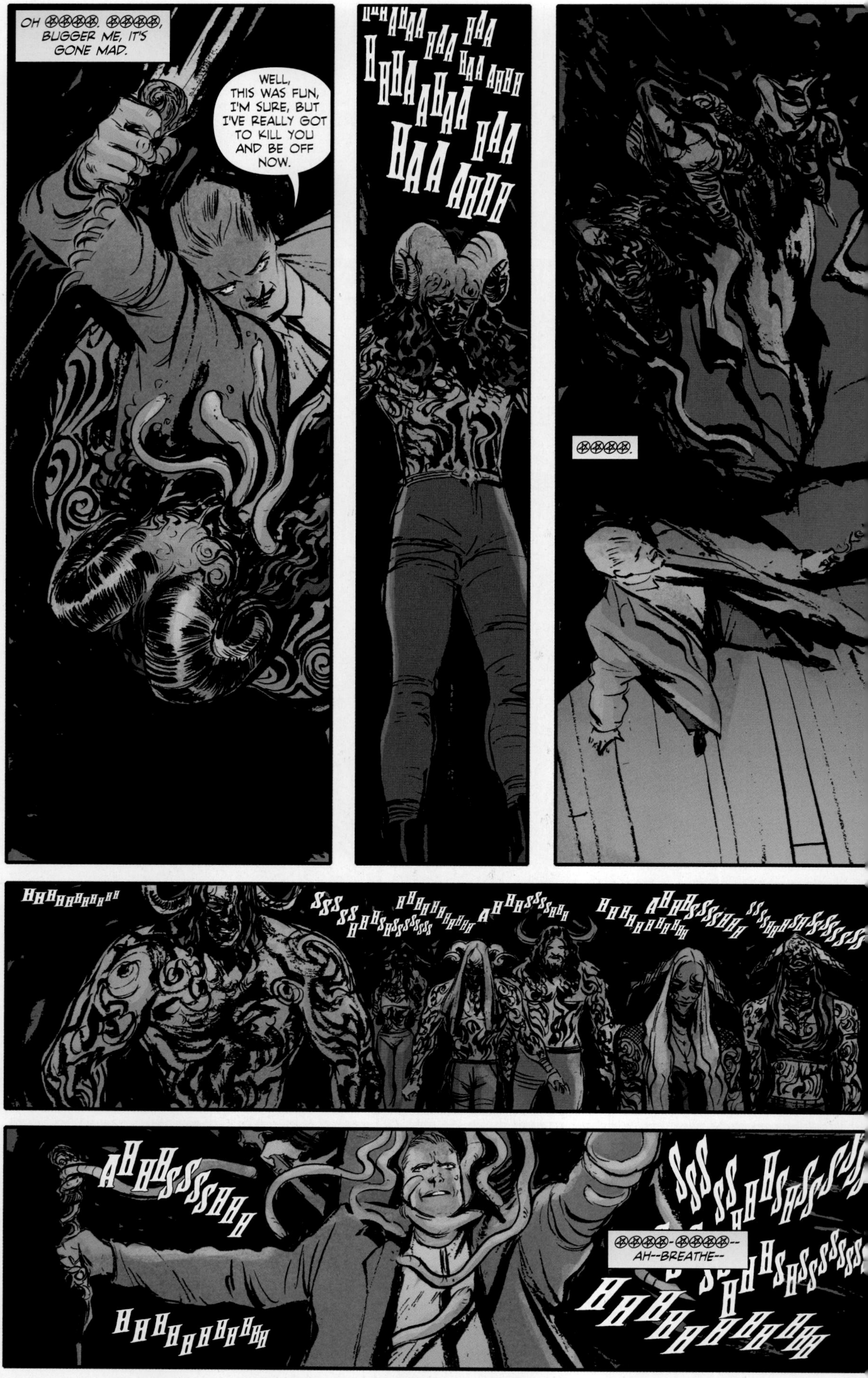
OH ⛤⛤⛤⛤. ⛤⛤⛤⛤, BUGGER ME, IT'S GONE MAD.
WELL, THIS WAS FUN, I'M SURE, BUT I'VE REALLY GOT TO KILL YOU AND BE OFF NOW.
⛤⛤⛤⛤.
⛤⛤⛤⛤-⛤⛤⛤⛤-- AH--BREATHE--

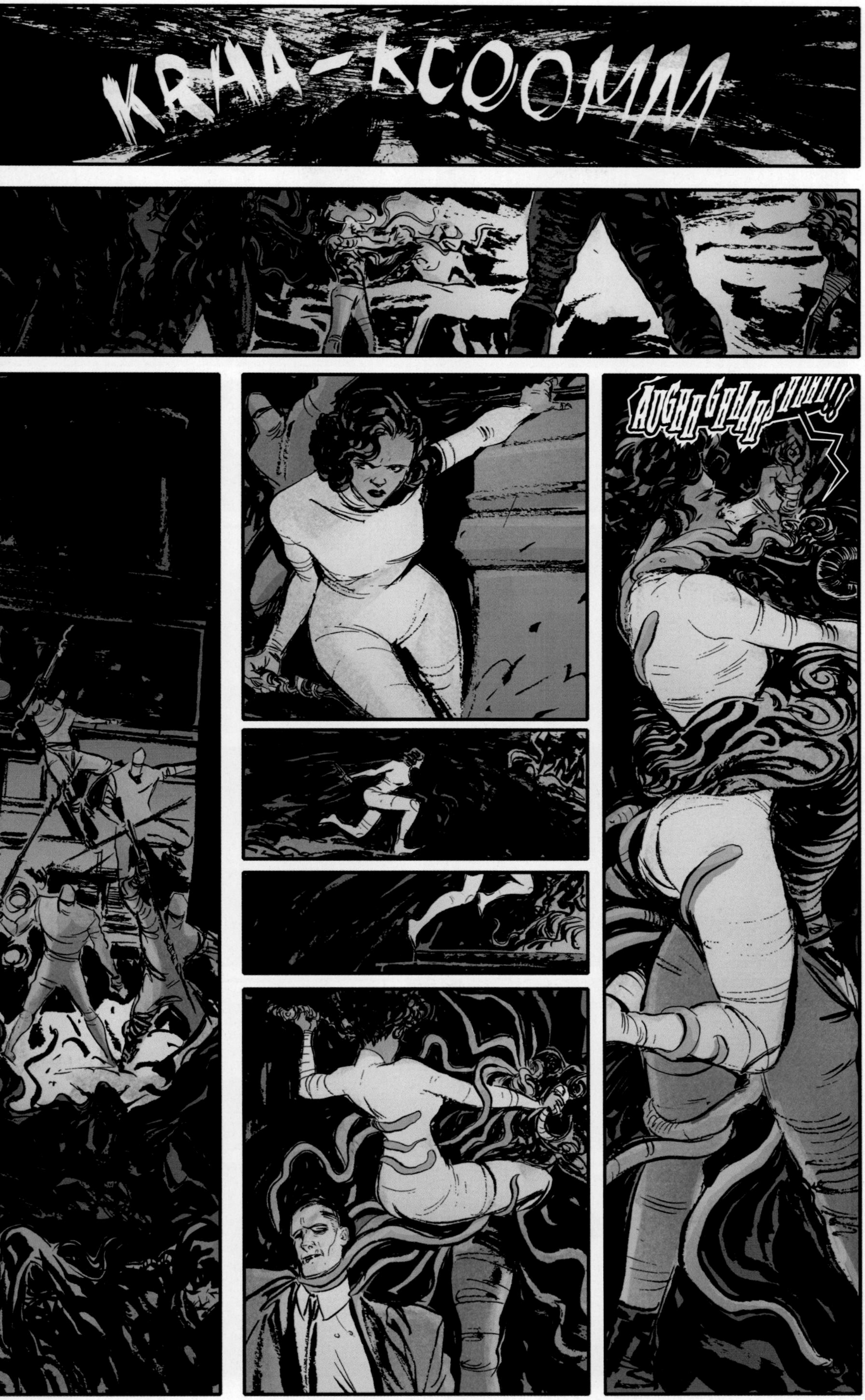
KRHA-KOOMM
AUGHH GHHARSHHHH!!

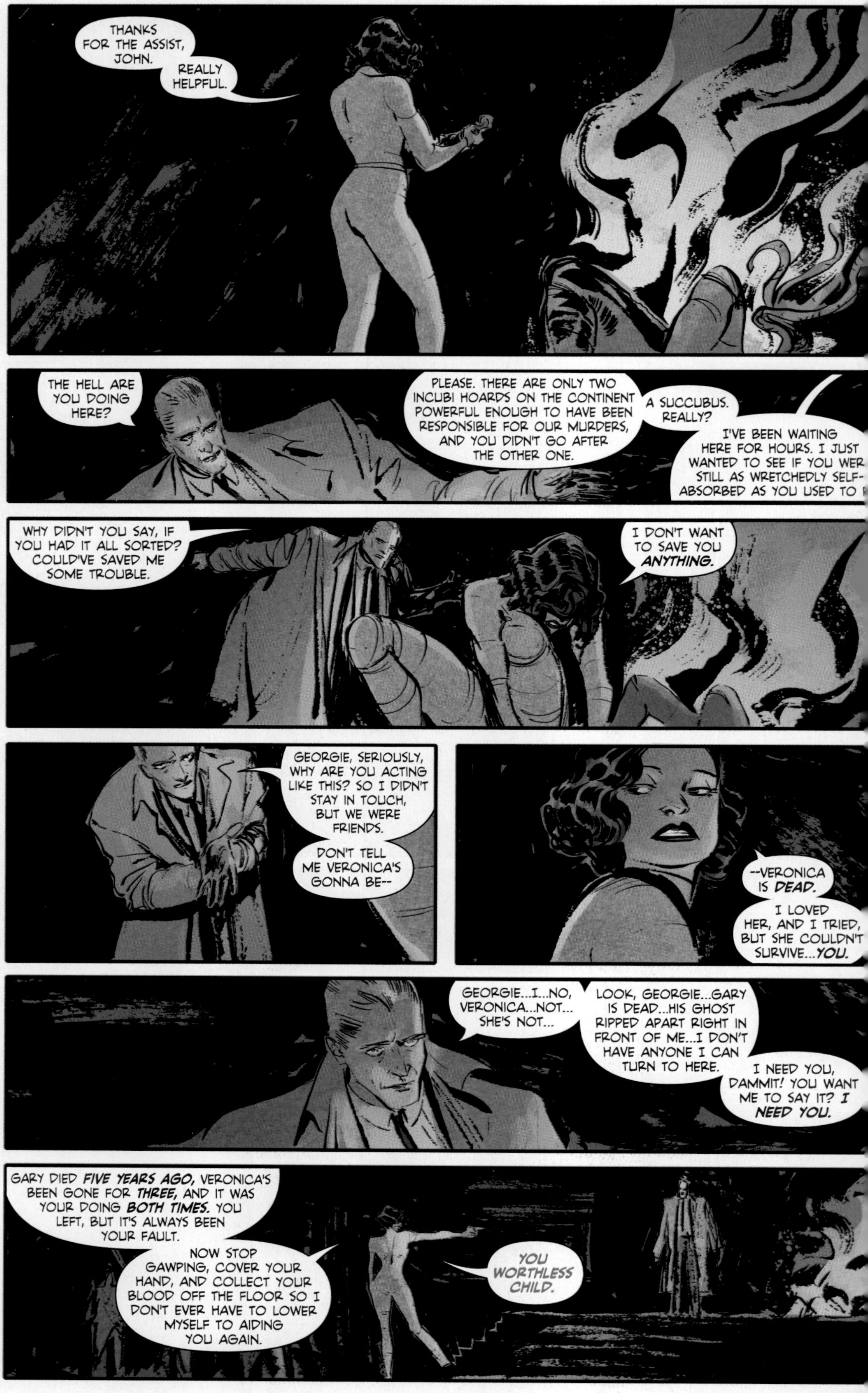

THANKS FOR THE ASSIST, JOHN.
REALLY HELPFUL.
THE HELL ARE YOU DOING HERE?
PLEASE. THERE ARE ONLY TWO INCUBI HOARDS ON THE CONTINENT POWERFUL ENOUGH TO HAVE BEEN RESPONSIBLE FOR OUR MURDERS, AND YOU DIDN'T GO AFTER THE OTHER ONE.
A SUCCUBUS. REALLY?
I'VE BEEN WAITING HERE FOR HOURS. I JUST WANTED TO SEE IF YOU WER STILL AS WRETCHEDLY SELF-ABSORBED AS YOU USED TO
WHY DIDN'T YOU SAY, IF YOU HAD IT ALL SORTED? COULD'VE SAVED ME SOME TROUBLE.
I DON'T WANT TO SAVE YOU ANYTHING.
GEORGIE, SERIOUSLY, WHY ARE YOU ACTING LIKE THIS? SO I DIDN'T STAY IN TOUCH, BUT WE WERE FRIENDS.
DON'T TELL ME VERONICA'S GONNA BE--
--VERONICA IS DEAD.
I LOVED HER, AND I TRIED, BUT SHE COULDN'T SURVIVE...YOU.
GEORGIE...I...NO, VERONICA...NOT... SHE'S NOT...
LOOK, GEORGIE...GARY IS DEAD...HIS GHOST RIPPED APART RIGHT IN FRONT OF ME...I DON'T HAVE ANYONE I CAN TURN TO HERE.
I NEED YOU, DAMMIT! YOU WANT ME TO SAY IT? I NEED YOU.
GARY DIED FIVE YEARS AGO, VERONICA'S BEEN GONE FOR THREE, AND IT WAS YOUR DOING BOTH TIMES. YOU LEFT, BUT IT'S ALWAYS BEEN YOUR FAULT.
NOW STOP GAWPING, COVER YOUR HAND, AND COLLECT YOUR BLOOD OFF THE FLOOR SO I DON'T EVER HAVE TO LOWER MYSELF TO AIDING YOU AGAIN.
YOU WORTHLESS CHILD.

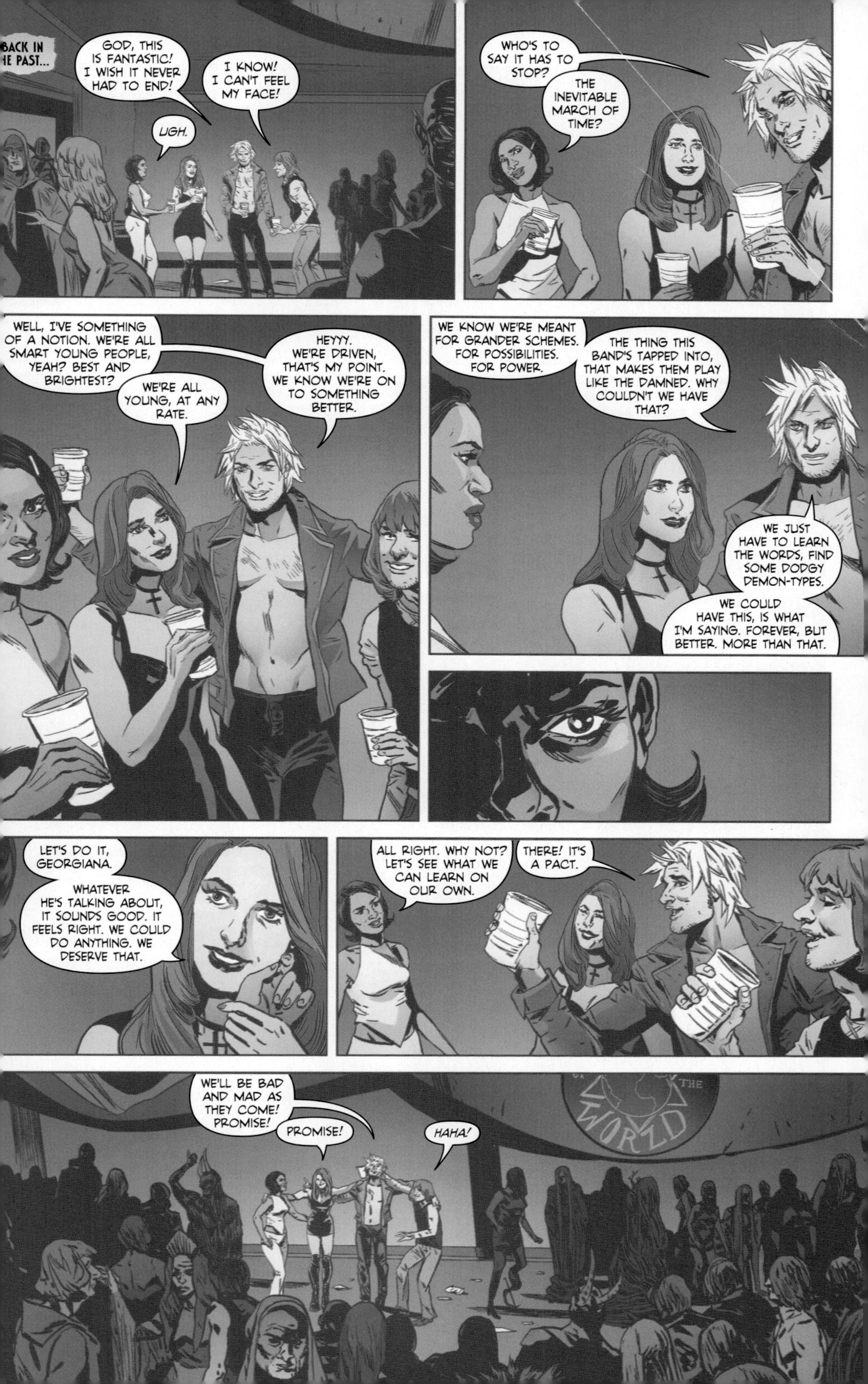
BACK IN THE PAST...
GOD, THIS IS FANTASTIC! I WISH IT NEVER HAD TO END!
I KNOW! I CAN'T FEEL MY FACE!
UGH.
WHO'S TO SAY IT HAS TO STOP?
THE INEVITABLE MARCH OF TIME?
WELL, I'VE SOMETHING OF A NOTION. WE'RE ALL SMART YOUNG PEOPLE, YEAH? BEST AND BRIGHTEST?
WE'RE ALL YOUNG, AT ANY RATE.
HEYYY. WE'RE DRIVEN, THAT'S MY POINT. WE KNOW WE'RE ON TO SOMETHING BETTER.
WE KNOW WE'RE MEANT FOR GRANDER SCHEMES. FOR POSSIBILITIES. FOR POWER.
THE THING THIS BAND'S TAPPED INTO, THAT MAKES THEM PLAY LIKE THE DAMNED. WHY COULDN'T WE HAVE THAT?
WE JUST HAVE TO LEARN THE WORDS, FIND SOME DODGY DEMON-TYPES.
WE COULD HAVE THIS, IS WHAT I'M SAYING. FOREVER, BUT BETTER. MORE THAN THAT.
LET'S DO IT, GEORGIANA.
WHATEVER HE'S TALKING ABOUT, IT SOUNDS GOOD. IT FEELS RIGHT. WE COULD DO ANYTHING. WE DESERVE THAT.
ALL RIGHT. WHY NOT? LET'S SEE WHAT WE CAN LEARN ON OUR OWN.
THERE! IT'S A PACT.
WE'LL BE BAD AND MAD AS THEY COME! PROMISE!
PROMISE!
HAHA!
THE WORLD

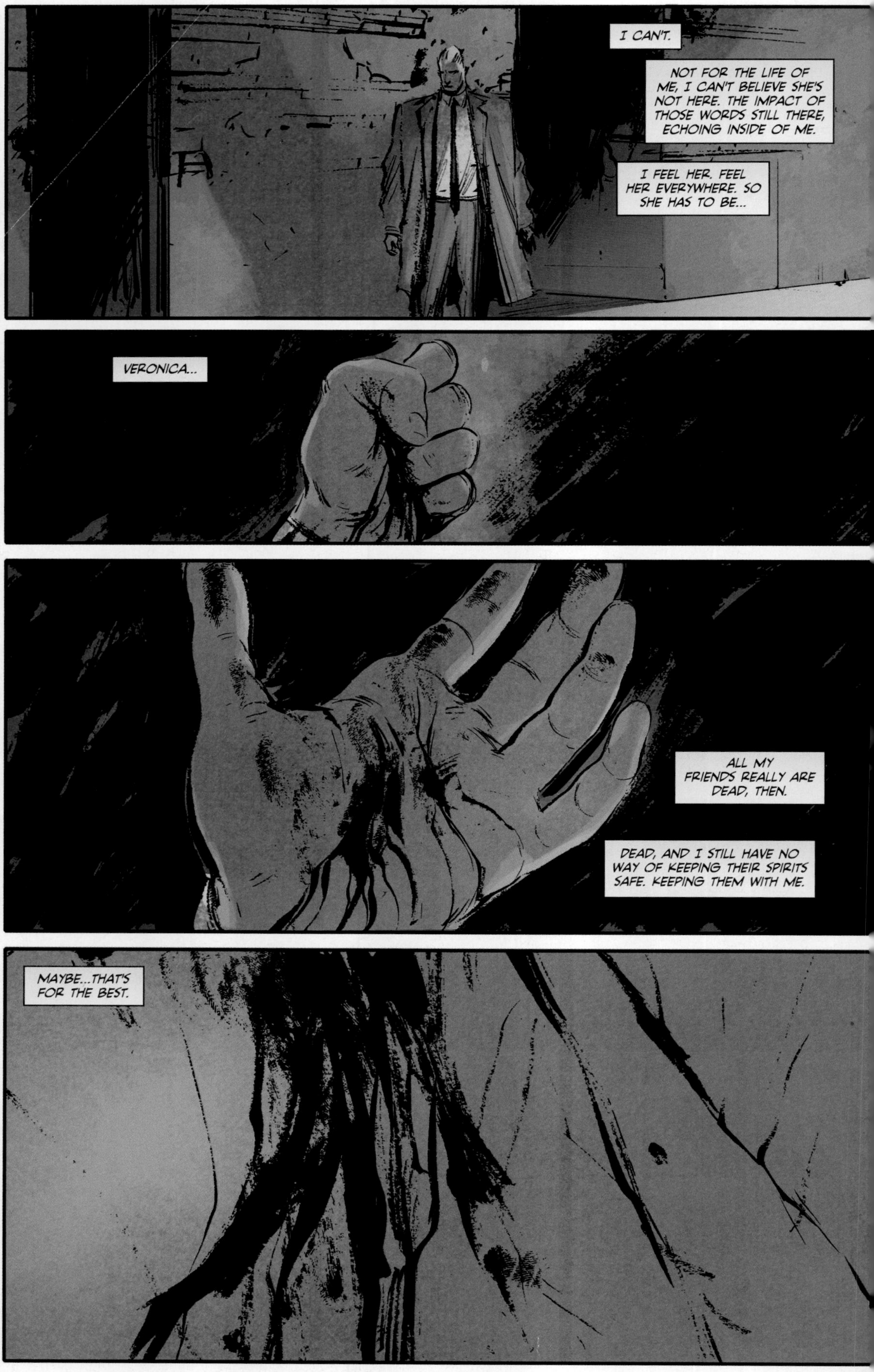
I CAN'T.
NOT FOR THE LIFE OF ME, I CAN'T BELIEVE SHE'S NOT HERE. THE IMPACT OF THOSE WORDS STILL THERE, ECHOING INSIDE OF ME.
I FEEL HER. FEEL HER EVERYWHERE. SO SHE HAS TO BE...
VERONICA...
ALL MY FRIENDS REALLY ARE DEAD, THEN.
DEAD, AND I STILL HAVE NO WAY OF KEEPING THEIR SPIRITS SAFE. KEEPING THEM WITH ME.
MAYBE...THAT'S FOR THE BEST.

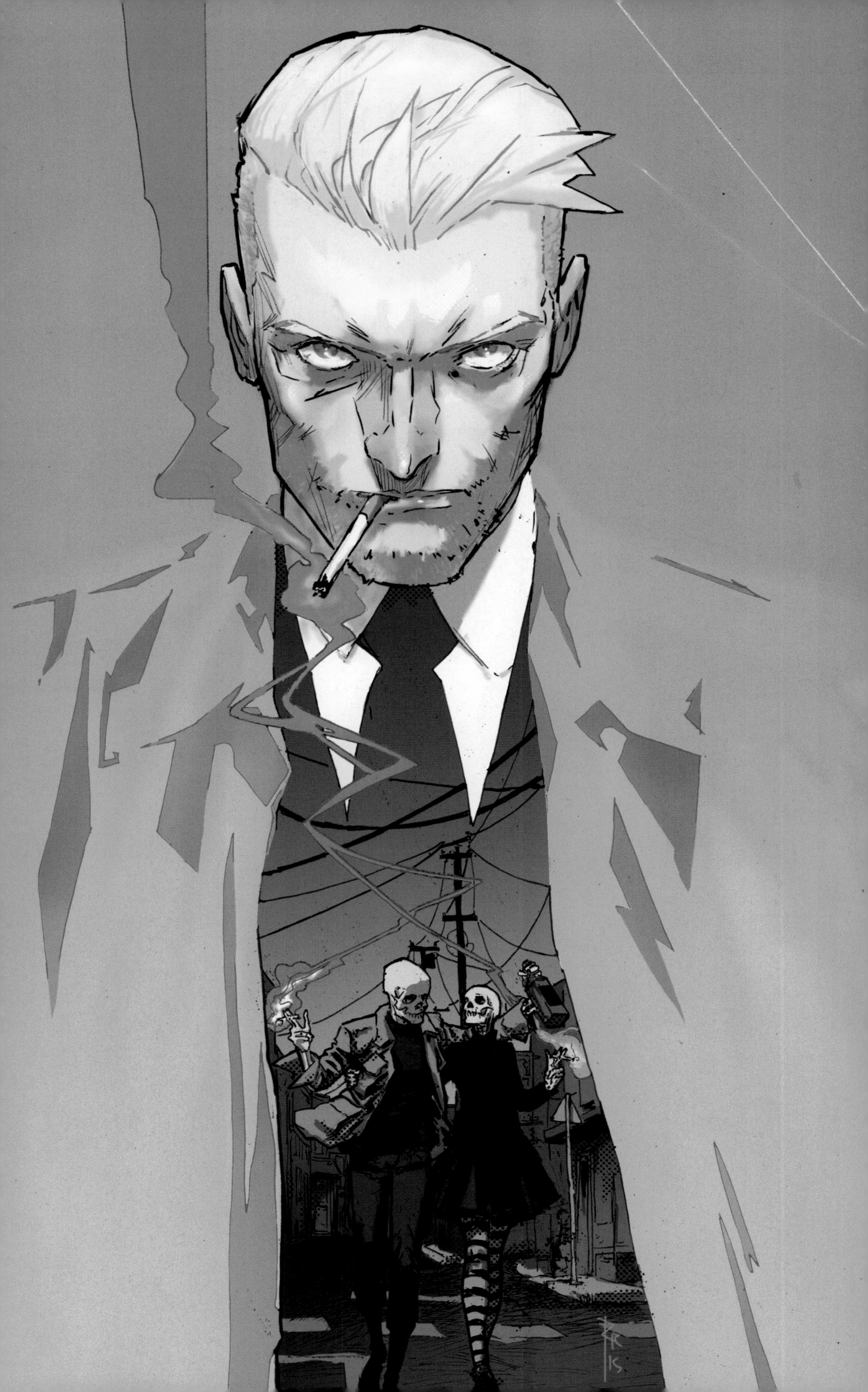

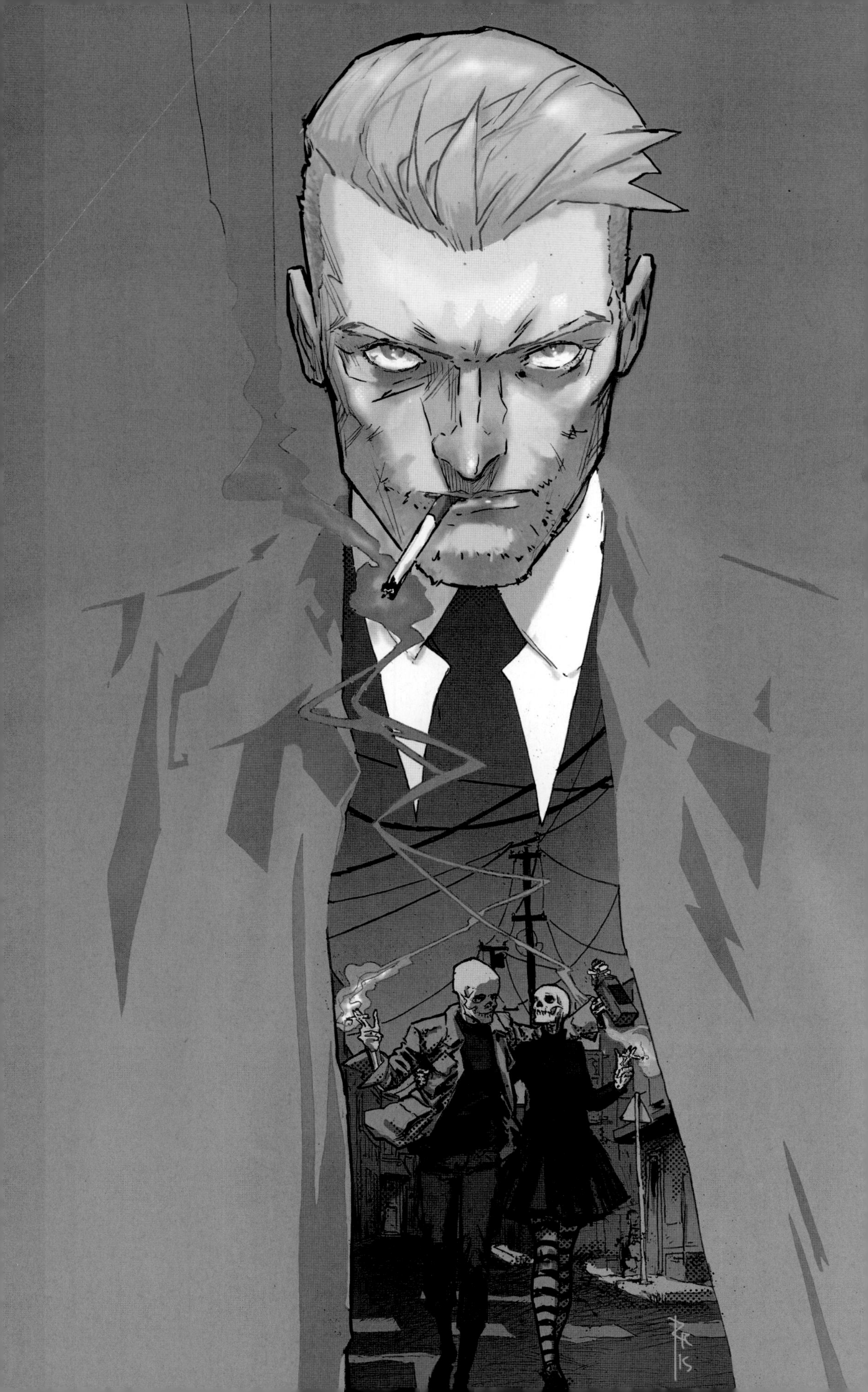

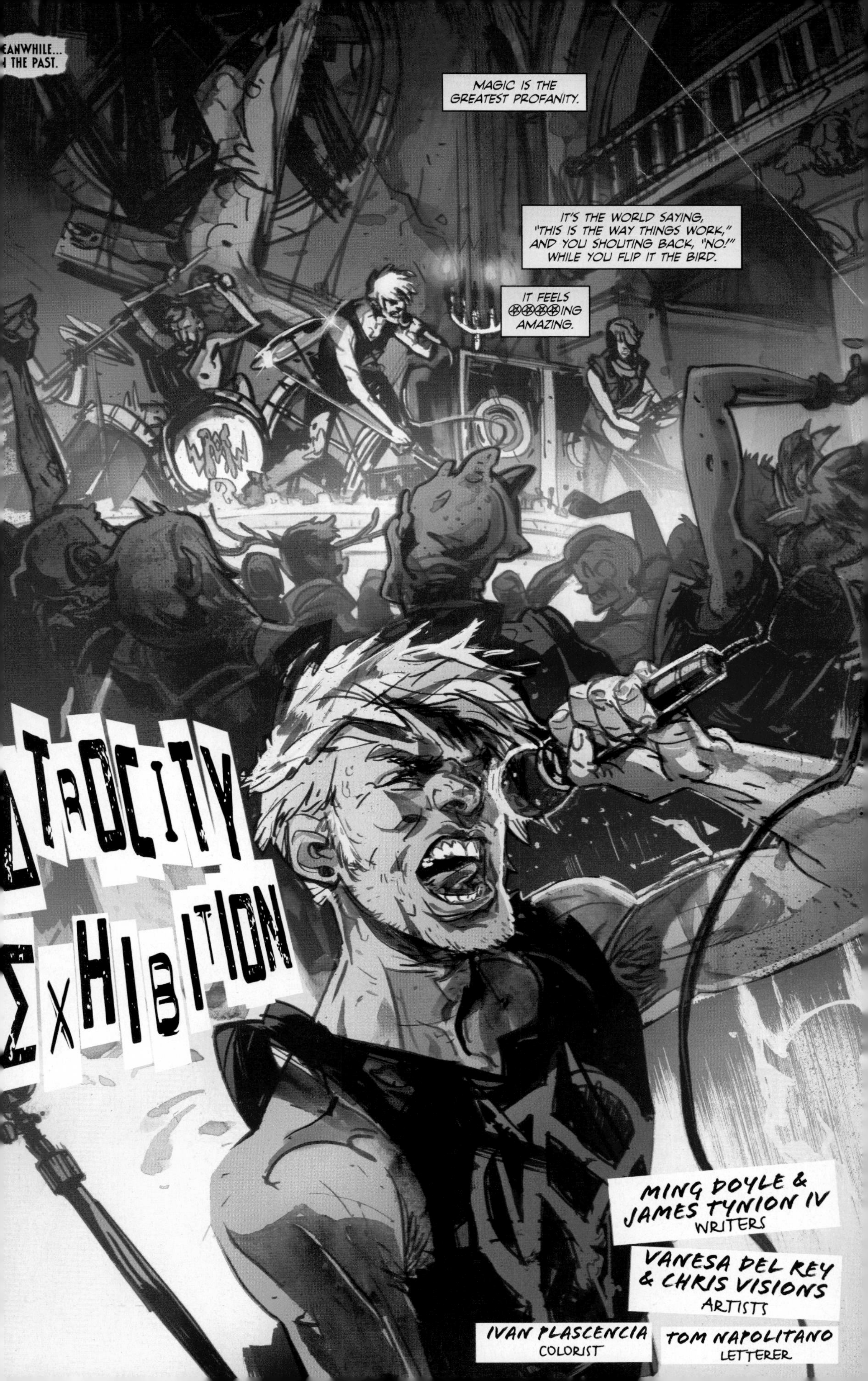
EANWHILE...
N THE PAST.
MAGIC IS THE GREATEST PROFANITY.
IT'S THE WORLD SAYING, "THIS IS THE WAY THINGS WORK," AND YOU SHOUTING BACK, "NO!" WHILE YOU FLIP IT THE BIRD.
IT FEELS ⊗⊗⊗⊗ING AMAZING.
ATROCITY EXHIBITION
MING DOYLE & JAMES TYNION IV
WRITERS
VANESA DEL REY & CHRIS VISIONS
ARTISTS
IVAN PLASCENCIA
COLORIST
TOM NAPOLITANO
LETTERER

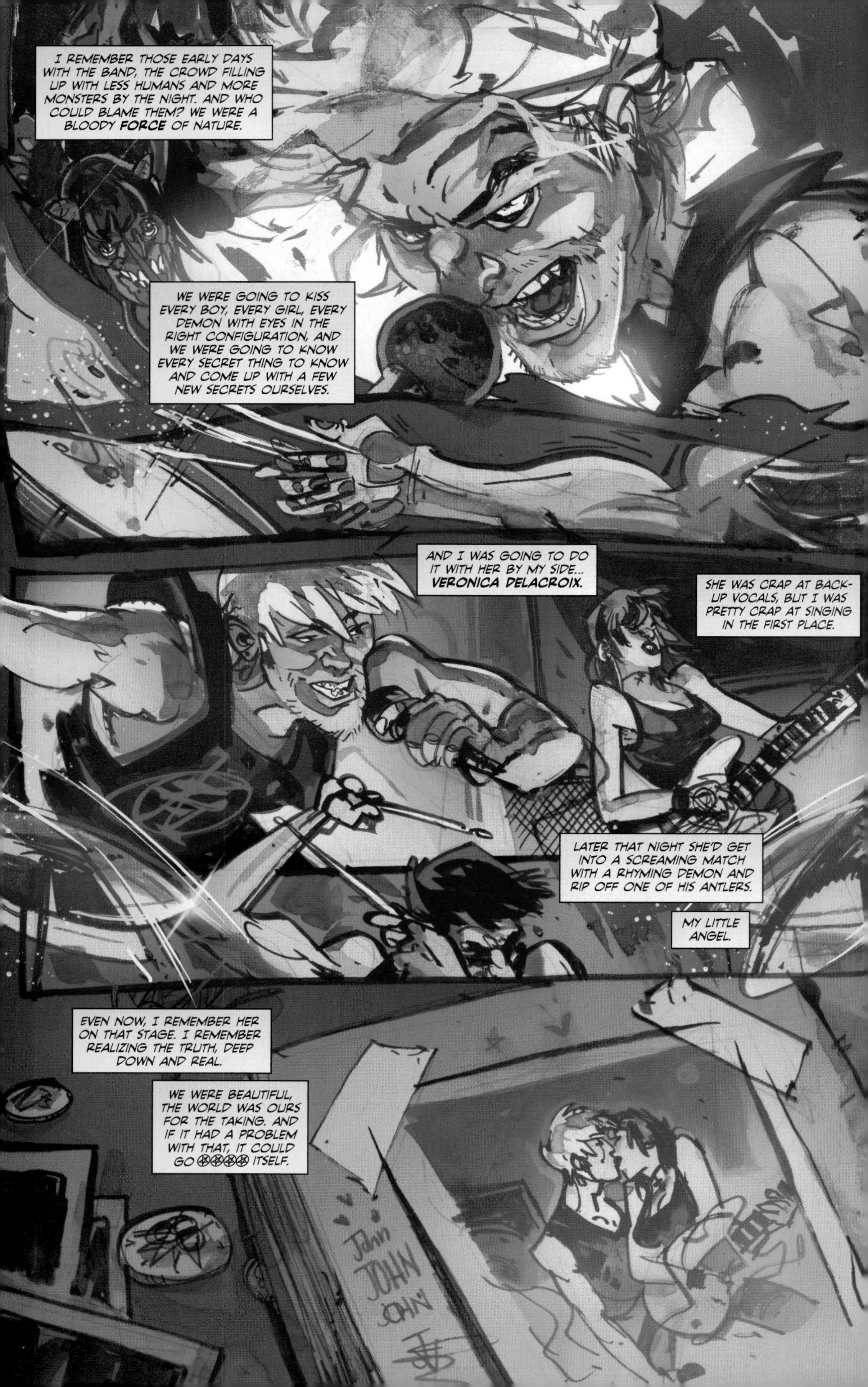
I REMEMBER THOSE EARLY DAYS WITH THE BAND, THE CROWD FILLING UP WITH LESS HUMANS AND MORE MONSTERS BY THE NIGHT. AND WHO COULD BLAME THEM? WE WERE A BLOODY **FORCE** OF NATURE.
WE WERE GOING TO KISS EVERY BOY, EVERY GIRL, EVERY DEMON WITH EYES IN THE RIGHT CONFIGURATION, AND WE WERE GOING TO KNOW EVERY SECRET THING TO KNOW AND COME UP WITH A FEW NEW SECRETS OURSELVES.
AND I WAS GOING TO DO IT WITH HER BY MY SIDE... **VERONICA DELACROIX.**
SHE WAS CRAP AT BACK-UP VOCALS, BUT I WAS PRETTY CRAP AT SINGING IN THE FIRST PLACE.
LATER THAT NIGHT SHE'D GET INTO A SCREAMING MATCH WITH A RHYMING DEMON AND RIP OFF ONE OF HIS ANTLERS.
MY LITTLE ANGEL.
EVEN NOW, I REMEMBER HER ON THAT STAGE. I REMEMBER REALIZING THE TRUTH, DEEP DOWN AND REAL.
WE WERE BEAUTIFUL, THE WORLD WAS OURS FOR THE TAKING. AND IF IT HAD A PROBLEM WITH THAT, IT COULD GO ⛧⛧⛧⛧ ITSELF.
John
JOHN
JOHN

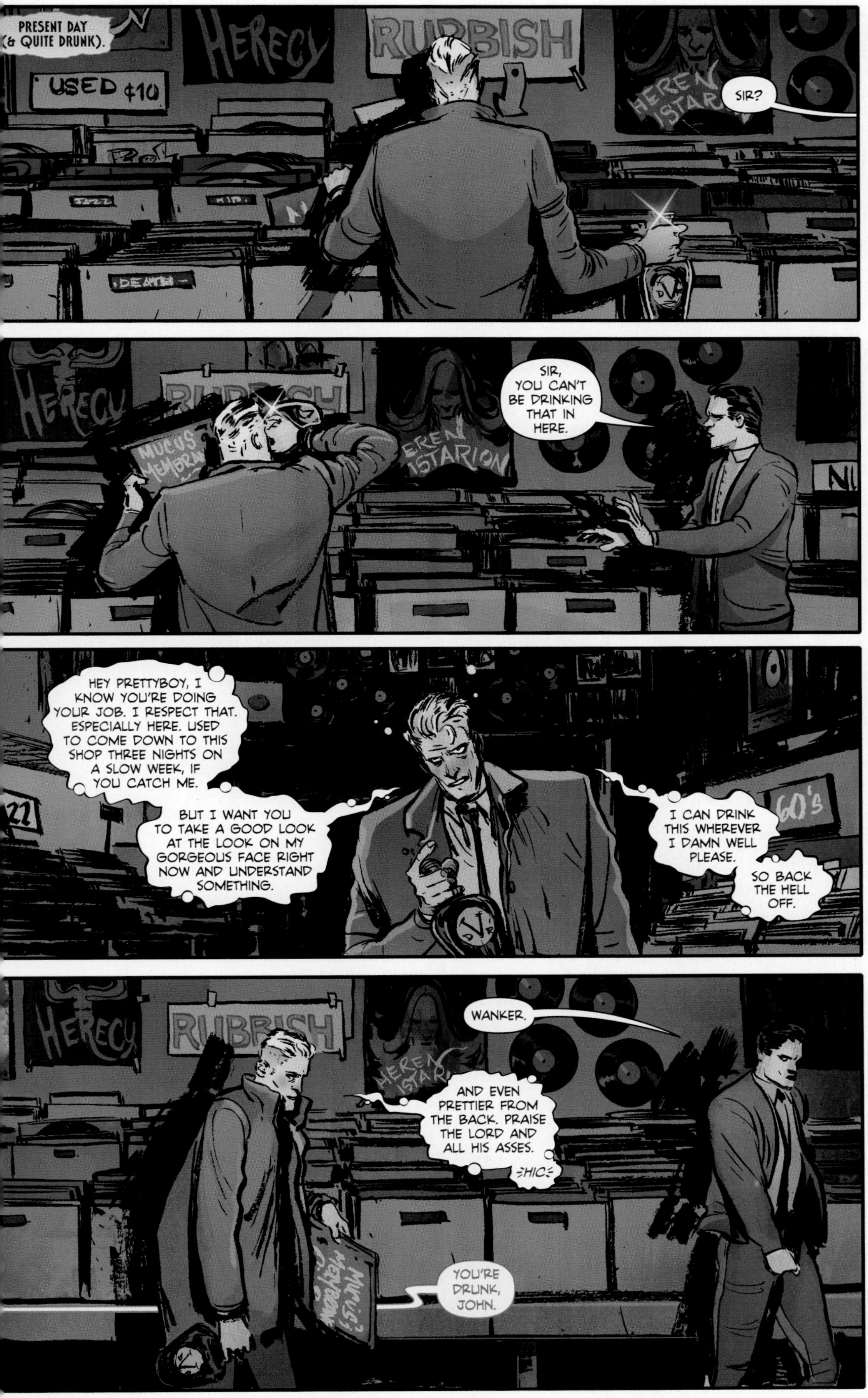
PRESENT DAY (& QUITE DRUNK).
HERECY
RUBBISH
USED $10
SIR?
SIR, YOU CAN'T BE DRINKING THAT IN HERE.
HEY PRETTYBOY, I KNOW YOU'RE DOING YOUR JOB. I RESPECT THAT. ESPECIALLY HERE. USED TO COME DOWN TO THIS SHOP THREE NIGHTS ON A SLOW WEEK, IF YOU CATCH ME.
BUT I WANT YOU TO TAKE A GOOD LOOK AT THE LOOK ON MY GORGEOUS FACE RIGHT NOW AND UNDERSTAND SOMETHING.
I CAN DRINK THIS WHEREVER I DAMN WELL PLEASE.
SO BACK THE HELL OFF.
WANKER.
AND EVEN PRETTIER FROM THE BACK. PRAISE THE LORD AND ALL HIS ASSES.
=HIC=
YOU'RE DRUNK, JOHN.

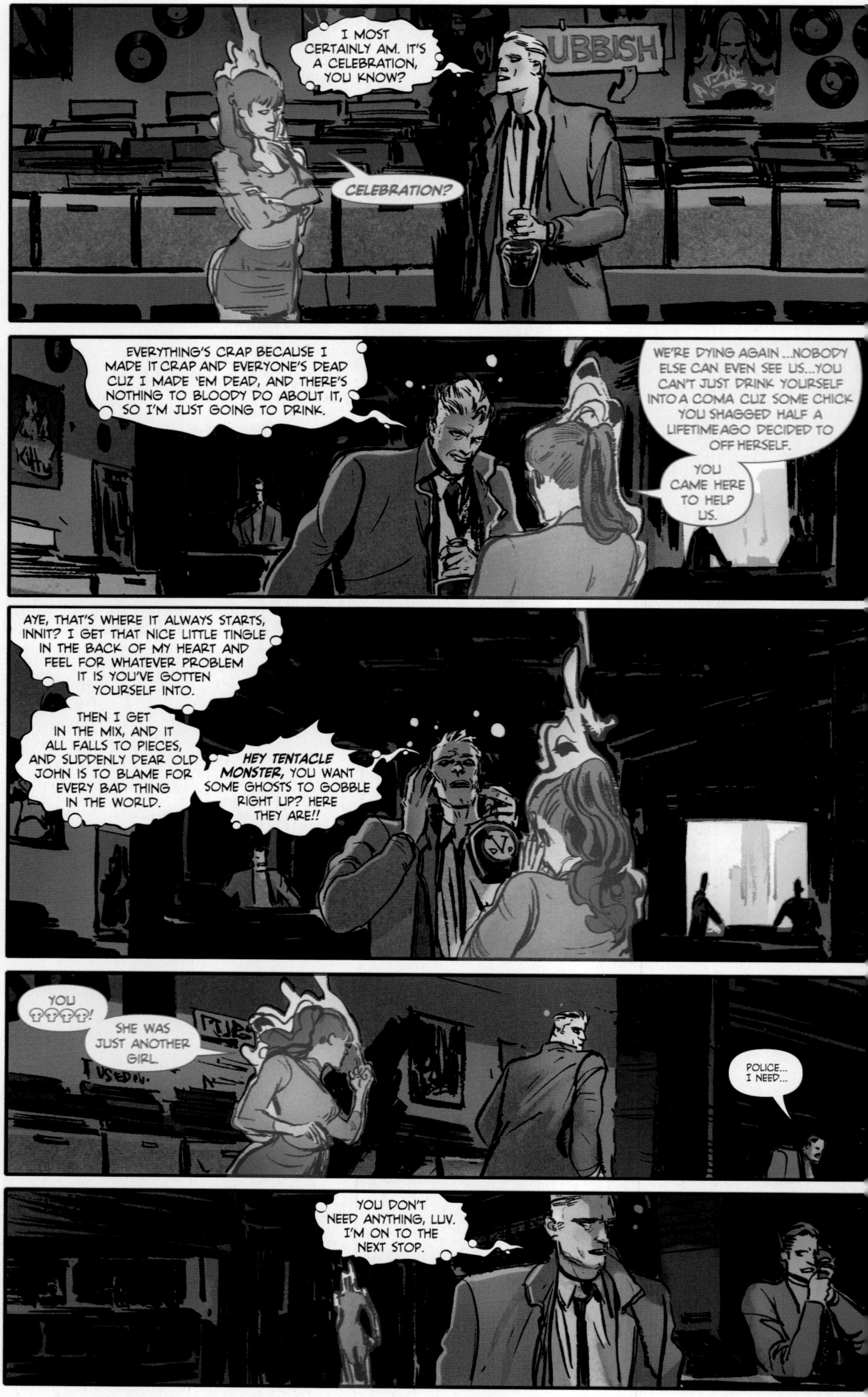

I MOST CERTAINLY AM. IT'S A CELEBRATION, YOU KNOW?
CELEBRATION?
EVERYTHING'S CRAP BECAUSE I MADE IT CRAP AND EVERYONE'S DEAD CUZ I MADE 'EM DEAD, AND THERE'S NOTHING TO BLOODY DO ABOUT IT, SO I'M JUST GOING TO DRINK.
WE'RE DYING AGAIN ...NOBODY ELSE CAN EVEN SEE US...YOU CAN'T JUST DRINK YOURSELF INTO A COMA CUZ SOME CHICK YOU SHAGGED HALF A LIFETIME AGO DECIDED TO OFF HERSELF.
YOU CAME HERE TO HELP US.
AYE, THAT'S WHERE IT ALWAYS STARTS, INNIT? I GET THAT NICE LITTLE TINGLE IN THE BACK OF MY HEART AND FEEL FOR WHATEVER PROBLEM IT IS YOU'VE GOTTEN YOURSELF INTO.
THEN I GET IN THE MIX, AND IT ALL FALLS TO PIECES, AND SUDDENLY DEAR OLD JOHN IS TO BLAME FOR EVERY BAD THING IN THE WORLD.
HEY TENTACLE MONSTER, YOU WANT SOME GHOSTS TO GOBBLE RIGHT UP? HERE THEY ARE!!
YOU ☠☠☠☠!
SHE WAS JUST ANOTHER GIRL.
POLICE... I NEED...
YOU DON'T NEED ANYTHING, LUV. I'M ON TO THE NEXT STOP.

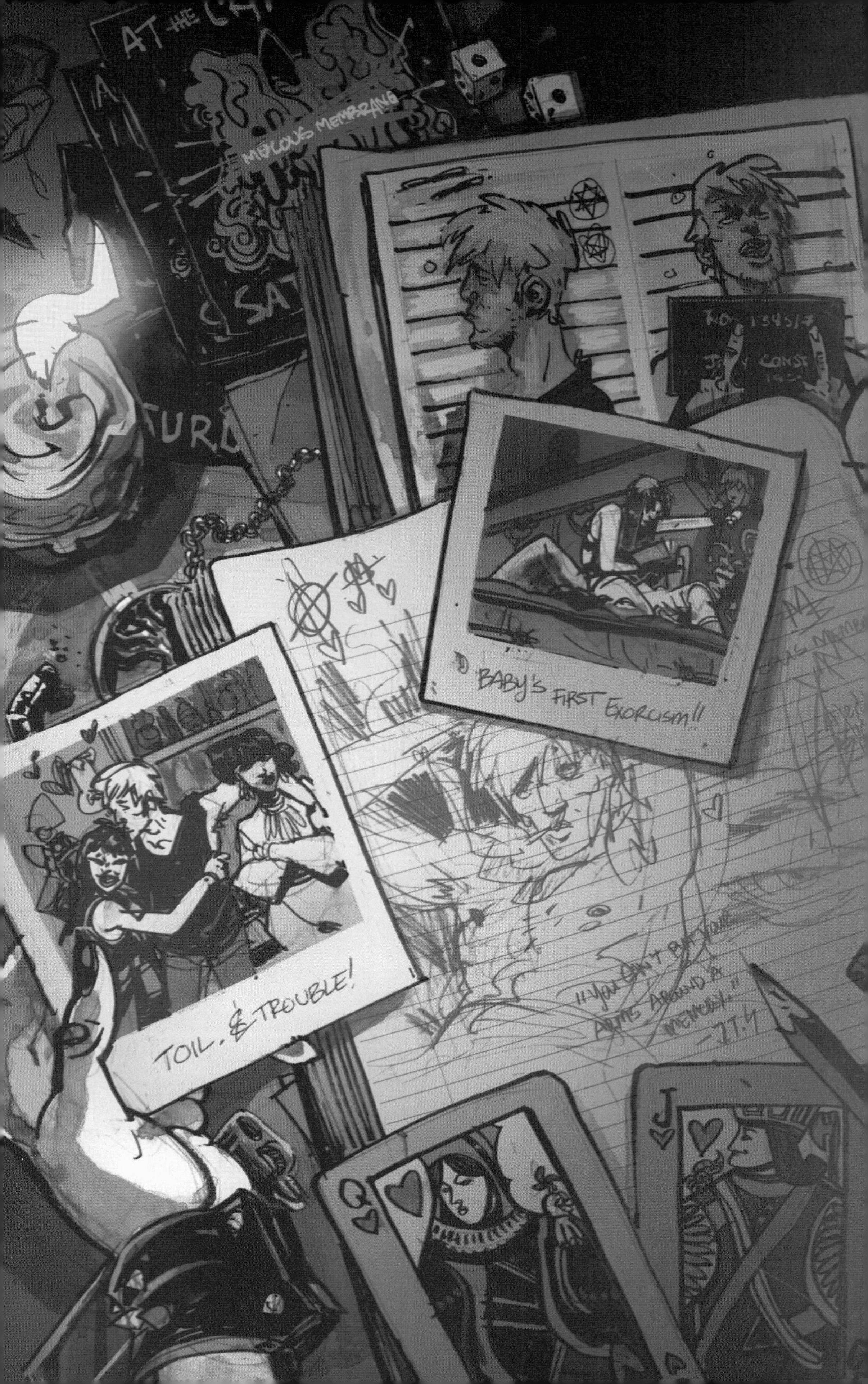

BABY'S FIRST EXORCISM!!
TOIL. & TROUBLE!

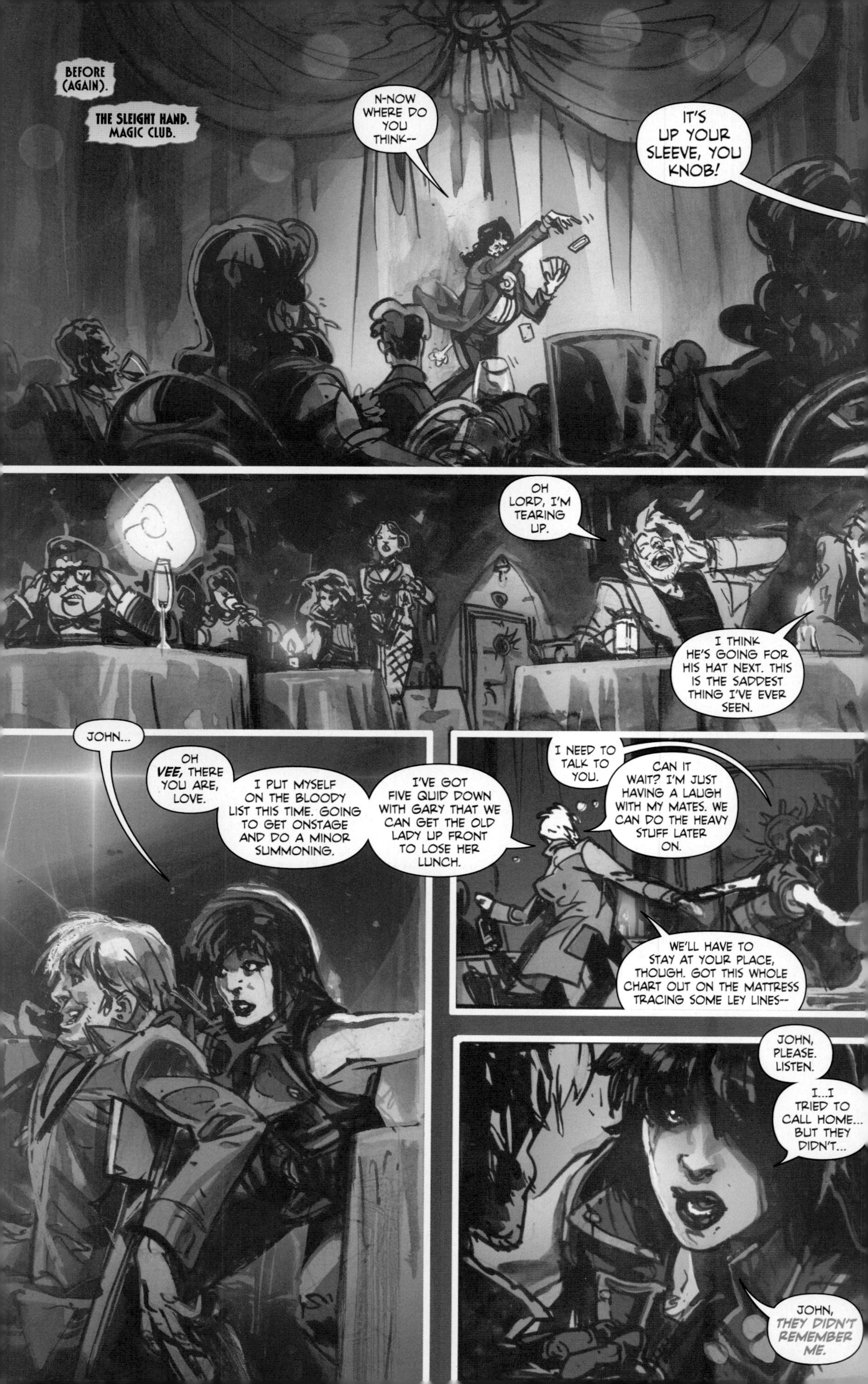
BEFORE (AGAIN).
THE SLEIGHT HAND. MAGIC CLUB.
N-NOW WHERE DO YOU THINK--
IT'S UP YOUR SLEEVE, YOU KNOB!
OH LORD, I'M TEARING UP.
I THINK HE'S GOING FOR HIS HAT NEXT. THIS IS THE SADDEST THING I'VE EVER SEEN.
JOHN...
OH *VEE,* THERE YOU ARE, LOVE.
I PUT MYSELF ON THE BLOODY LIST THIS TIME. GOING TO GET ONSTAGE AND DO A MINOR SUMMONING.
I'VE GOT FIVE QUID DOWN WITH GARY THAT WE CAN GET THE OLD LADY UP FRONT TO LOSE HER LUNCH.
I NEED TO TALK TO YOU.
CAN IT WAIT? I'M JUST HAVING A LAUGH WITH MY MATES. WE CAN DO THE HEAVY STUFF LATER ON.
WE'LL HAVE TO STAY AT YOUR PLACE, THOUGH. GOT THIS WHOLE CHART OUT ON THE MATTRESS TRACING SOME LEY LINES--
JOHN, PLEASE. LISTEN.
I...I TRIED TO CALL HOME... BUT THEY DIDN'T...
JOHN, *THEY DIDN'T REMEMBER ME.*

...WE'RE GETTING INTO THIS TOO DEEP... MAKING MAGIC PART OF THE MUSIC ACT...

...YOU REALIZE WE'RE NOT EVEN PERFORMING FOR *PEOPLE* ANYMORE...

IT'S LIKE WE'RE FALLING OUT OF THE CRACKS OF THE WORLD. DOESN'T THAT SCARE YOU?

TOO DEEP? VERONICA, WE'RE JUST GETTING STARTED.

LOOK, THOSE PEOPLE OUT THERE, THEY THINK THIS GARBAGE IS WHAT MAGIC IS. WE'VE BARELY JUST SCRATCHED THE SURFACE OF WHAT WE CAN DO.

I CAN'T DO IT... I THINK I NEED TO STOP.

NEVER TOOK YOU AS THE BORING TYPE.

JOHN...

IF YOU'RE NOT IN, THEN JUST GET OUT.

AND NEXT ON OUR LIST, ALL THE WAY IN FROM THE STATES, THE BEAUTIFUL, ZATANNA!

NOW.

OI, YOU. GET OFF.

WHO THE HELL--

GET OFF THE BLOODY STAGE.

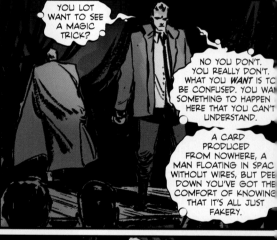

YOU LOT WANT TO SEE A MAGIC TRICK?

NO YOU DON'T. YOU REALLY DON'T. WHAT YOU *WANT* IS TO BE CONFUSED. YOU WANT SOMETHING TO HAPPEN HERE THAT YOU CAN'T UNDERSTAND.

A CARD PRODUCED FROM NOWHERE, A MAN FLOATING IN SPACE WITHOUT WIRES, BUT DEEP DOWN YOU'VE GOT THE COMFORT OF KNOWING THAT IT'S ALL JUST FAKERY.

IF YOU SAW SOMETHING *REAL*, YOUR BRAIN WOULDN'T EVEN KNOW HOW TO PROCESS IT. EVERYTHING YOU BELIEVE IN WOULD BE CALLED INTO QUESTION.

ALL OF A SUDDEN, THE WORLD WOULD BECOME A LOT SCARIER AND YOU'D JUST HAVE TO BLOODY LIVE WITH IT, NOW, WOULDN'T YOU?

AND THE MORE YOU'D LIVE WITH IT, THE LESS YOU COULD LIVE WITH THE LITTLE THINGS AROUND YOU. YOUR PRECIOUS LIFE WOULD START FALLING APART.

SO LET ME ASK YOU AGAIN...DO YOU WANT TO *SEE* SOME MAGIC?

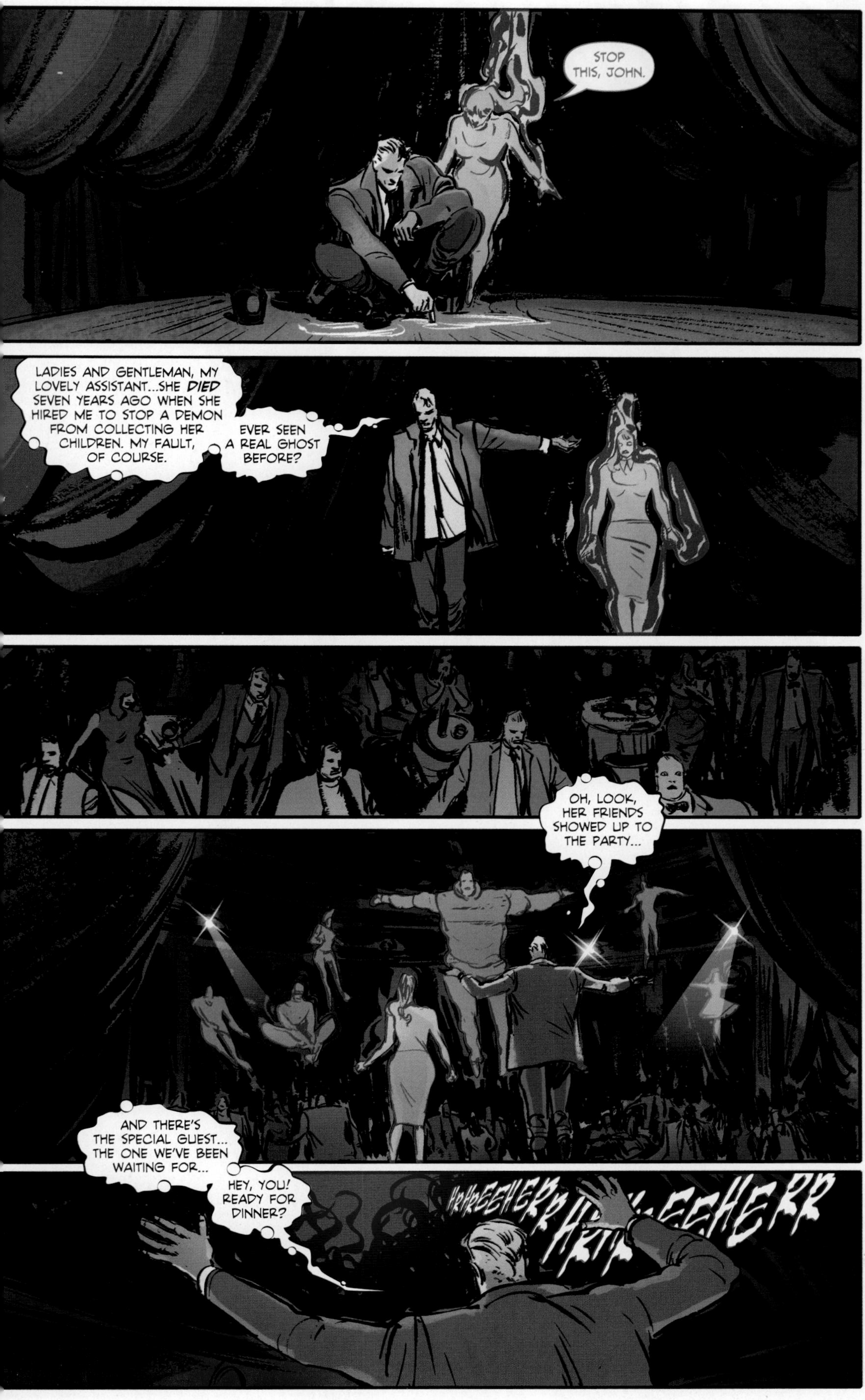
STOP THIS, JOHN.
LADIES AND GENTLEMAN, MY LOVELY ASSISTANT...SHE *DIED* SEVEN YEARS AGO WHEN SHE HIRED ME TO STOP A DEMON FROM COLLECTING HER CHILDREN. MY FAULT, OF COURSE.
EVER SEEN A REAL GHOST BEFORE?
OH, LOOK, HER FRIENDS SHOWED UP TO THE PARTY...
AND THERE'S THE SPECIAL GUEST... THE ONE WE'VE BEEN WAITING FOR...
HEY, YOU! READY FOR DINNER?

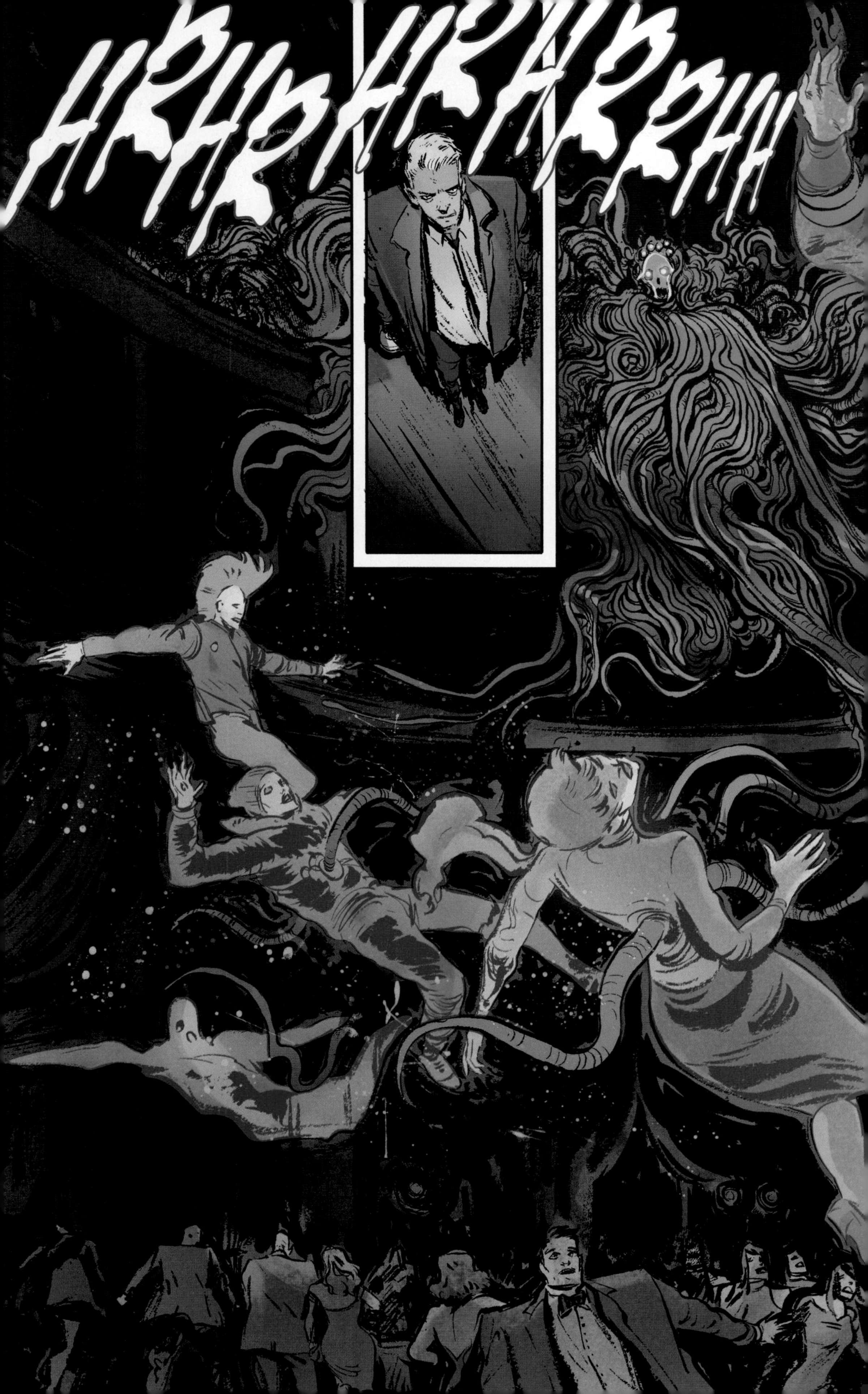

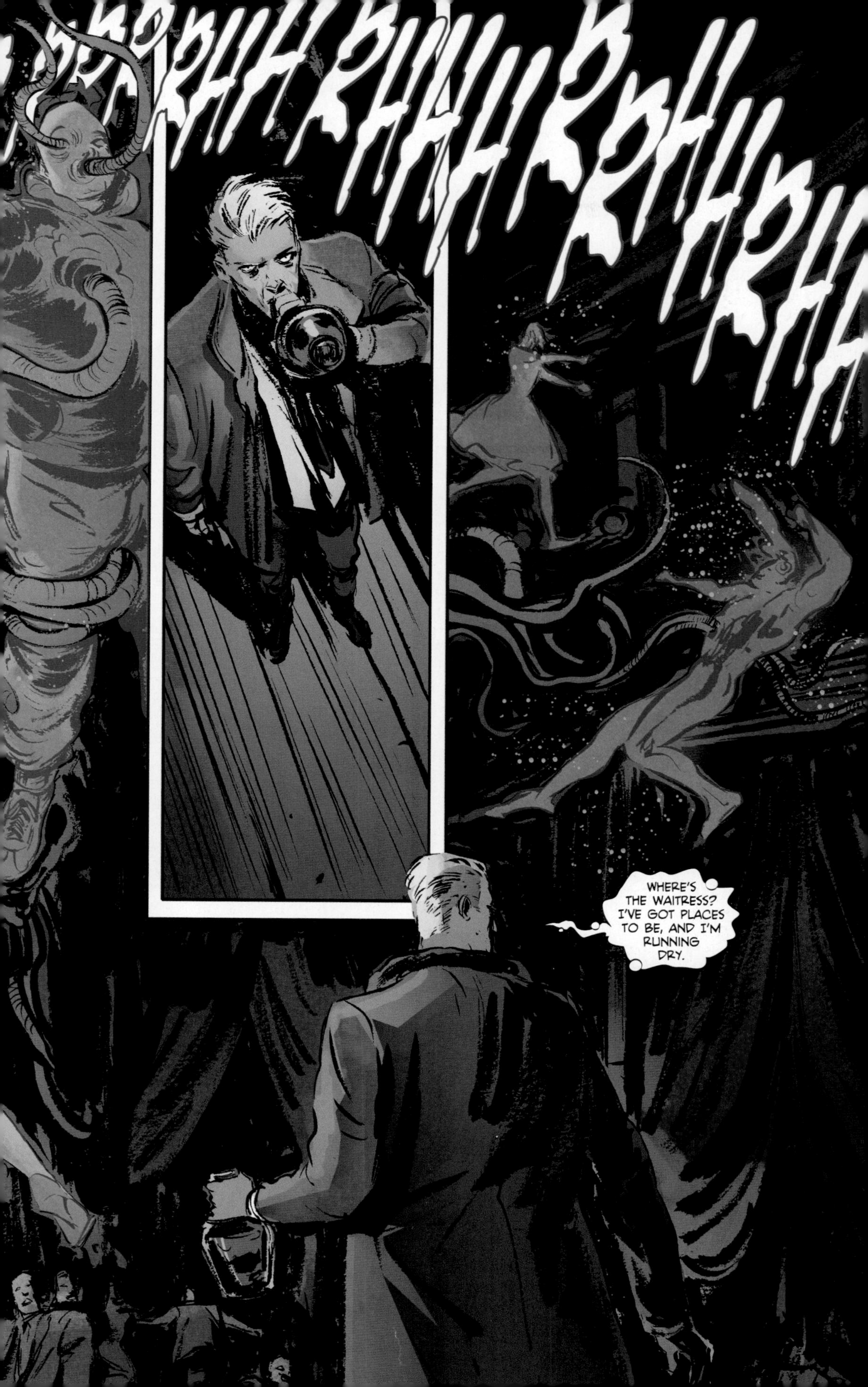
WHERE'S THE WAITRESS? I'VE GOT PLACES TO BE, AND I'M RUNNING DRY.

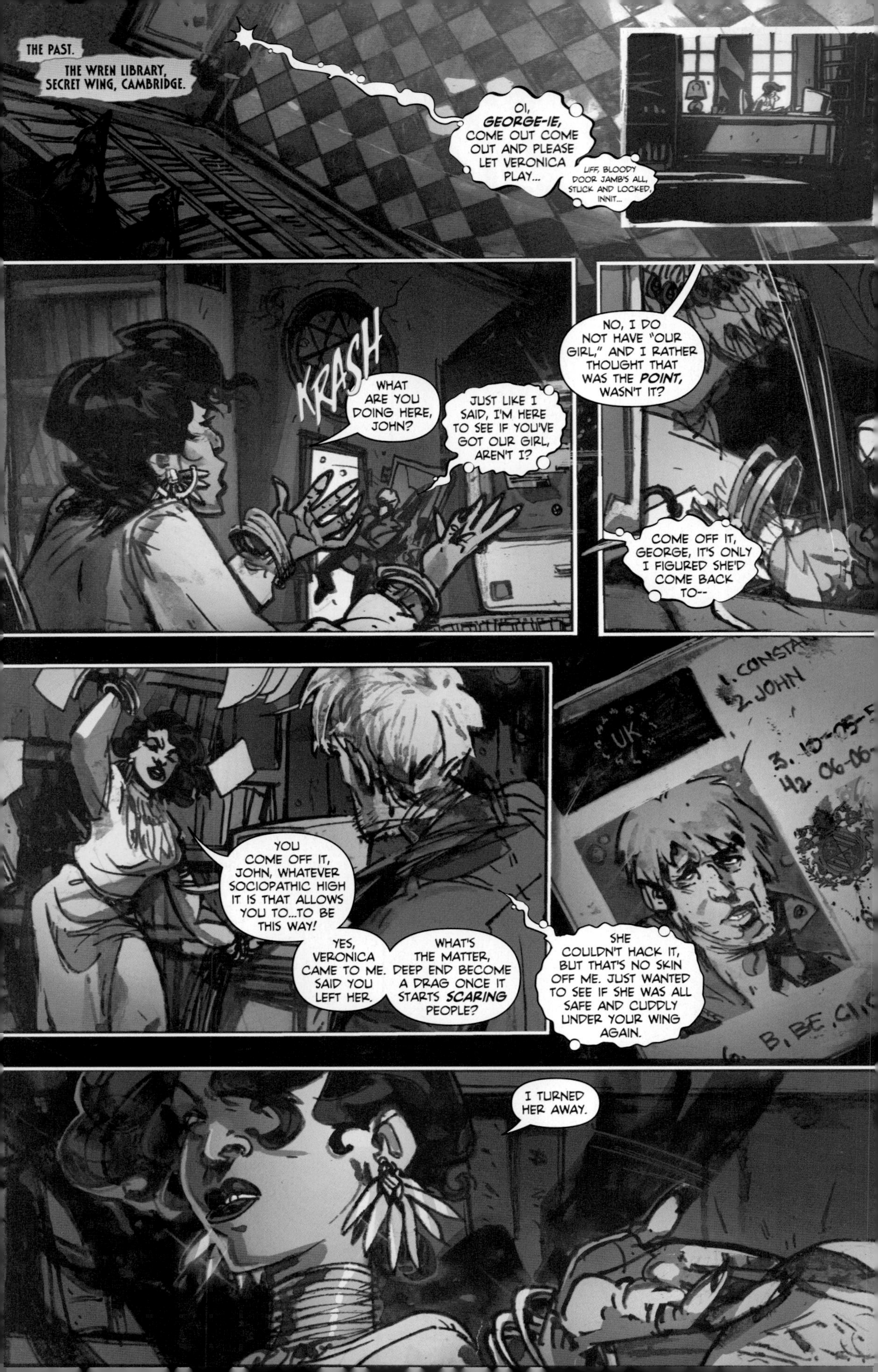
THE PAST.
THE WREN LIBRARY, SECRET WING, CAMBRIDGE.
OI, GEORGE-IE, COME OUT COME OUT AND PLEASE LET VERONICA PLAY...
UFF, BLOODY DOOR JAMB'S ALL, STUCK AND LOCKED, INNIT...
KRASH
WHAT ARE YOU DOING HERE, JOHN?
JUST LIKE I SAID, I'M HERE TO SEE IF YOU'VE GOT OUR GIRL, AREN'T I?
NO, I DO NOT HAVE "OUR GIRL," AND I RATHER THOUGHT THAT WAS THE POINT, WASN'T IT?
COME OFF IT, GEORGE, IT'S ONLY I FIGURED SHE'D COME BACK TO--
YOU COME OFF IT, JOHN, WHATEVER SOCIOPATHIC HIGH IT IS THAT ALLOWS YOU TO...TO BE THIS WAY!
YES, VERONICA CAME TO ME. SAID YOU LEFT HER.
WHAT'S THE MATTER, DEEP END BECOME A DRAG ONCE IT STARTS SCARING PEOPLE?
SHE COULDN'T HACK IT, BUT THAT'S NO SKIN OFF ME. JUST WANTED TO SEE IF SHE WAS ALL SAFE AND CUDDLY UNDER YOUR WING AGAIN.
I TURNED HER AWAY.

WHAT?

I'VE HAD IT, JOHN. HAD IT FROM *BOTH* OF YOU.

ALWAYS THINKING YOU CAN RELY ON ME TO SORT YOUR BLOODY MESSES. WELL, I'M NOT YOUR NURSEMAID.

I WON'T HAVE ANYONE TREATING ME AS A BACKUP PLAN OR SECOND BEST.

SHE WAS SO FAR GONE, I COULD HARDLY SEE HER. SHE'S BARELY A PART OF THIS WORLD, ANYMORE. EITHER INDUCT HER FULLY OR FIND A MAGICIAN WHO CAN.

NOW GET OUT, FIX THIS MESS, AND NEVER DARKEN MY DOOR AGAIN.

GEORGIANA...?

⊗⊗⊗⊗!

HE'S JUST LEAVING, *AHMES.*

WHAT, SNEAKY OLD MAN? NEVER SEEN HANDSOME BEFORE?

'M SO SORRY, SIR. NO IDEA HOW HE T IN, HE SHOULDN'T OW THE KNOCK. I'LL LOOK INTO IT.

IT WON'T HAPPEN AGAIN.

HE WON'T BE BACK.

NOW.

NEVER PAID MUCH ATTENTION IN MY YOUNGER DAYS. NOT TO A LOT OF THINGS.

I WAS MORE INTERESTED IN HOW MUCH I COULD GET DONE ON MY OWN.

SEEMED MORE IMPRESSIVE, BEING A NATURAL AT THE SUPERNATURAL.

ALL THAT ACADEMIC NONSENSE, THAT WAS GEORGIE. RULES AND REGULATIONS, THIS AND THAT, HALLS OF LEARNING.

HANG IT. IT'S ALWAYS BEEN A REBEL'S LIFE FOR ME.

TAP

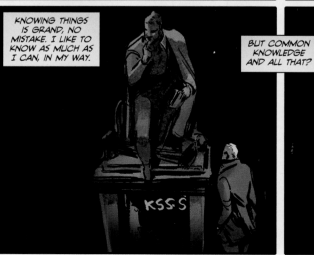

KNOWING THINGS IS GRAND, NO MISTAKE. I LIKE TO KNOW AS MUCH AS I CAN, IN MY WAY.

BUT COMMON KNOWLEDGE AND ALL THAT?

KSS-S

JUST ANOTHER ROAD TO HELL.

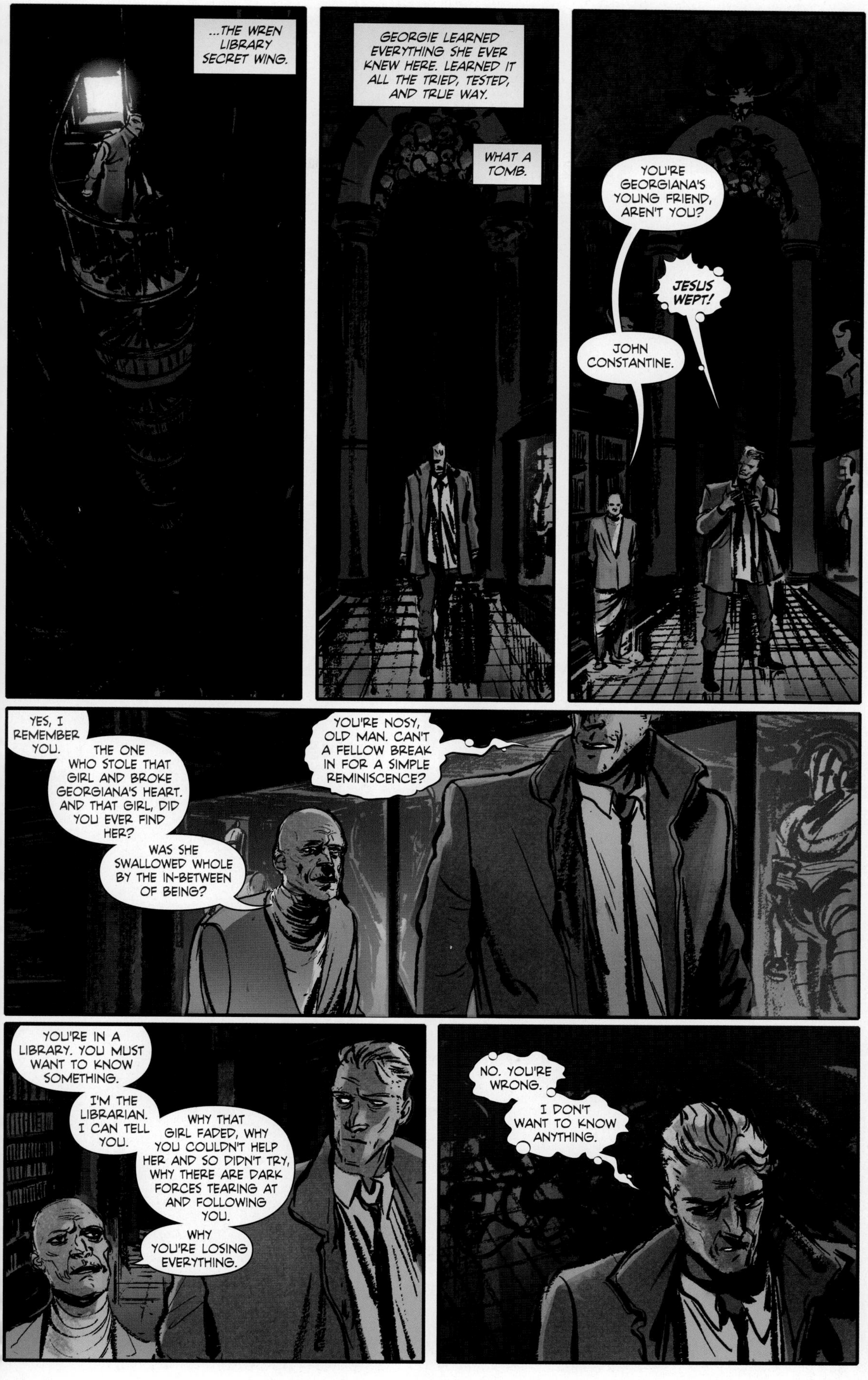
...THE WREN LIBRARY SECRET WING.
GEORGIE LEARNED EVERYTHING SHE EVER KNEW HERE. LEARNED IT ALL THE TRIED, TESTED, AND TRUE WAY.
WHAT A TOMB.
YOU'RE GEORGIANA'S YOUNG FRIEND, AREN'T YOU?
JESUS WEPT!
JOHN CONSTANTINE.
YES, I REMEMBER YOU.
THE ONE WHO STOLE THAT GIRL AND BROKE GEORGIANA'S HEART. AND THAT GIRL, DID YOU EVER FIND HER?
WAS SHE SWALLOWED WHOLE BY THE IN-BETWEEN OF BEING?
YOU'RE NOSY, OLD MAN. CAN'T A FELLOW BREAK IN FOR A SIMPLE REMINISCENCE?
YOU'RE IN A LIBRARY. YOU MUST WANT TO KNOW SOMETHING.
I'M THE LIBRARIAN. I CAN TELL YOU.
WHY THAT GIRL FADED, WHY YOU COULDN'T HELP HER AND SO DIDN'T TRY, WHY THERE ARE DARK FORCES TEARING AT AND FOLLOWING YOU.
WHY YOU'RE LOSING EVERYTHING.
NO. YOU'RE WRONG.
I DON'T WANT TO KNOW ANYTHING.

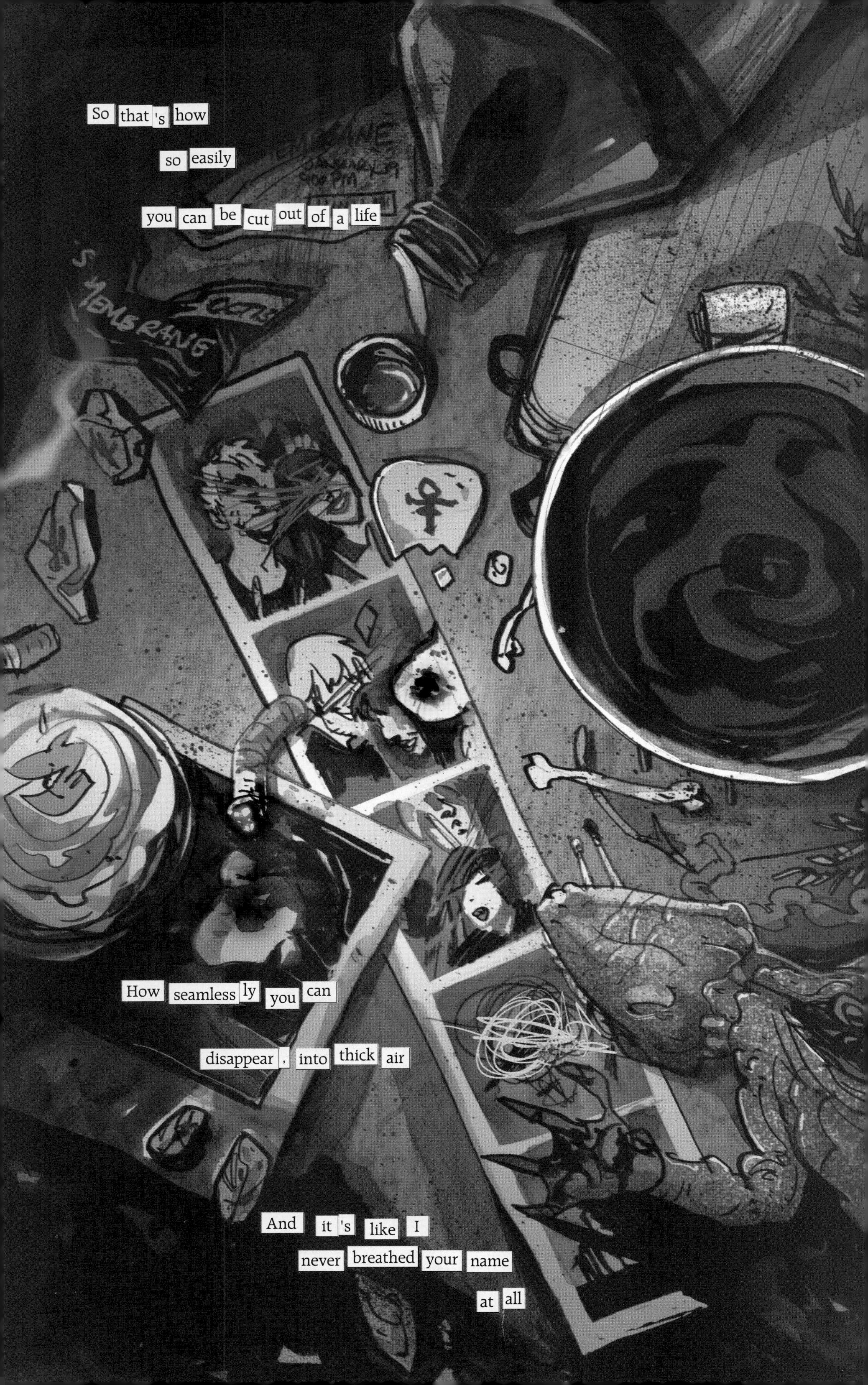
So that 's how
so easily
you can be cut out of a life
How seamless ly you can
disappear , into thick air
And it 's like I
never breathed your name
at all

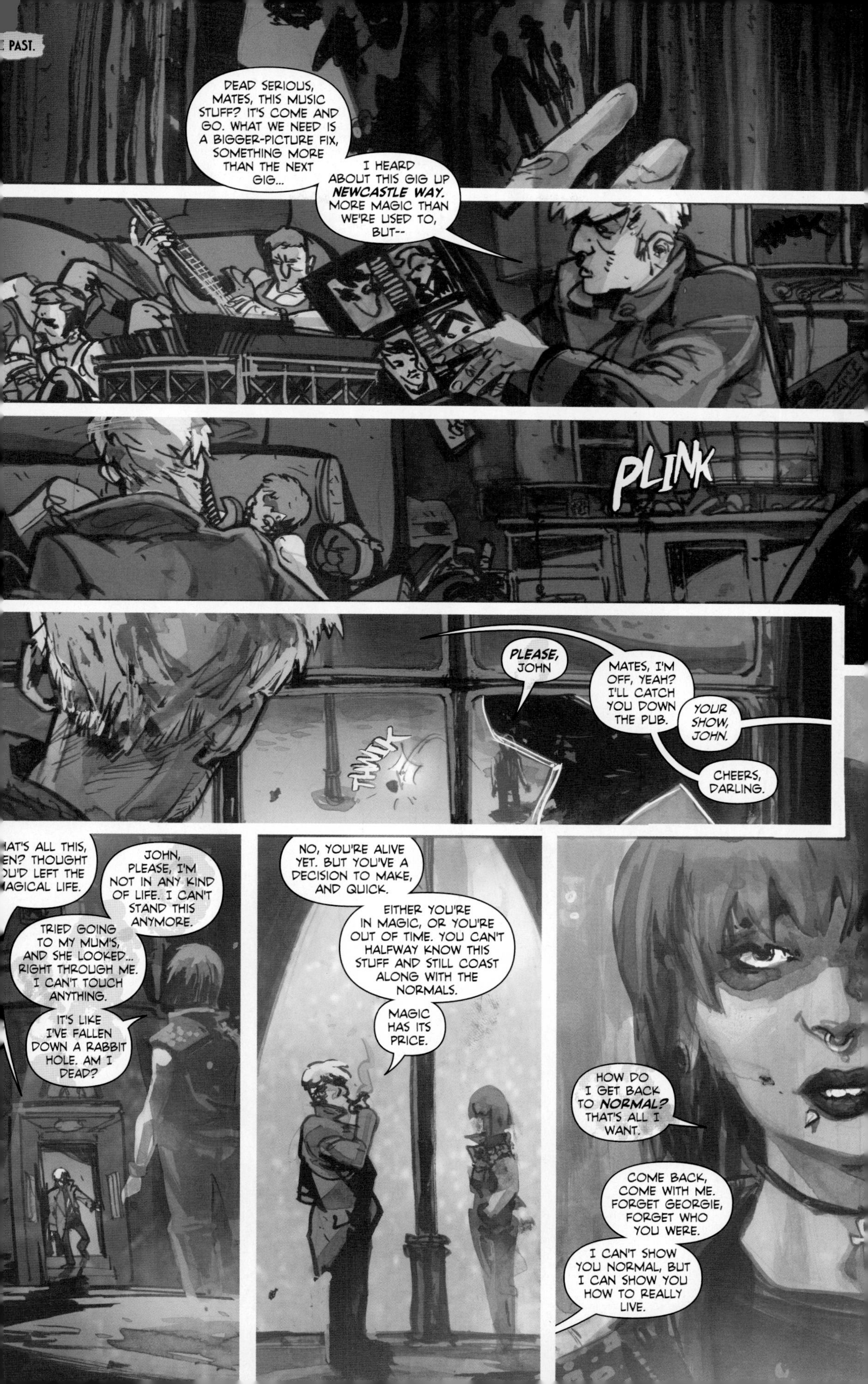
PAST.
DEAD SERIOUS, MATES, THIS MUSIC STUFF? IT'S COME AND GO. WHAT WE NEED IS A BIGGER-PICTURE FIX, SOMETHING MORE THAN THE NEXT GIG...
I HEARD ABOUT THIS GIG UP NEWCASTLE WAY. MORE MAGIC THAN WE'RE USED TO, BUT--
PLINK
PLEASE, JOHN
MATES, I'M OFF, YEAH? I'LL CATCH YOU DOWN THE PUB.
YOUR SHOW, JOHN.
CHEERS, DARLING.
THWIK
HAT'S ALL THIS, EN? THOUGHT U'D LEFT THE AGICAL LIFE.
JOHN, PLEASE, I'M NOT IN ANY KIND OF LIFE. I CAN'T STAND THIS ANYMORE.
TRIED GOING TO MY MUM'S, AND SHE LOOKED... RIGHT THROUGH ME. I CAN'T TOUCH ANYTHING.
IT'S LIKE I'VE FALLEN DOWN A RABBIT HOLE. AM I DEAD?
NO, YOU'RE ALIVE YET. BUT YOU'VE A DECISION TO MAKE, AND QUICK.
EITHER YOU'RE IN MAGIC, OR YOU'RE OUT OF TIME. YOU CAN'T HALFWAY KNOW THIS STUFF AND STILL COAST ALONG WITH THE NORMALS.
MAGIC HAS ITS PRICE.
HOW DO I GET BACK TO NORMAL? THAT'S ALL I WANT.
COME BACK, COME WITH ME. FORGET GEORGIE, FORGET WHO YOU WERE.
I CAN'T SHOW YOU NORMAL, BUT I CAN SHOW YOU HOW TO REALLY LIVE.

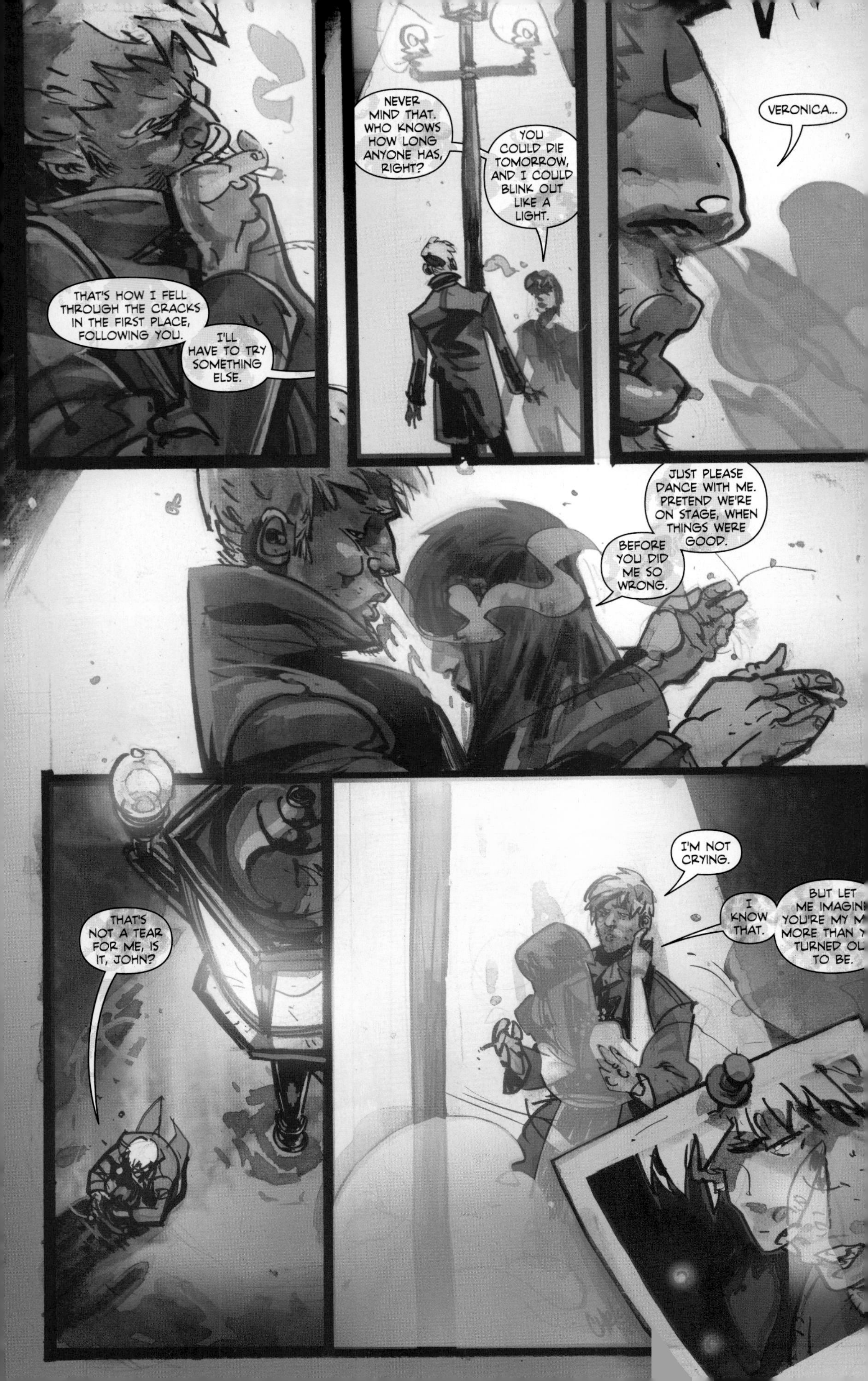
THAT'S HOW I FELL THROUGH THE CRACKS IN THE FIRST PLACE, FOLLOWING YOU.
I'LL HAVE TO TRY SOMETHING ELSE.
NEVER MIND THAT. WHO KNOWS HOW LONG ANYONE HAS, RIGHT?
YOU COULD DIE TOMORROW, AND I COULD BLINK OUT LIKE A LIGHT.
VERONICA...
JUST PLEASE DANCE WITH ME. PRETEND WE'RE ON STAGE, WHEN THINGS WERE GOOD.
BEFORE YOU DID ME SO WRONG.
THAT'S NOT A TEAR FOR ME, IS IT, JOHN?
I'M NOT CRYING.
I KNOW THAT.
BUT LET ME IMAGIN YOU'RE MY M MORE THAN Y TURNED OU TO BE.

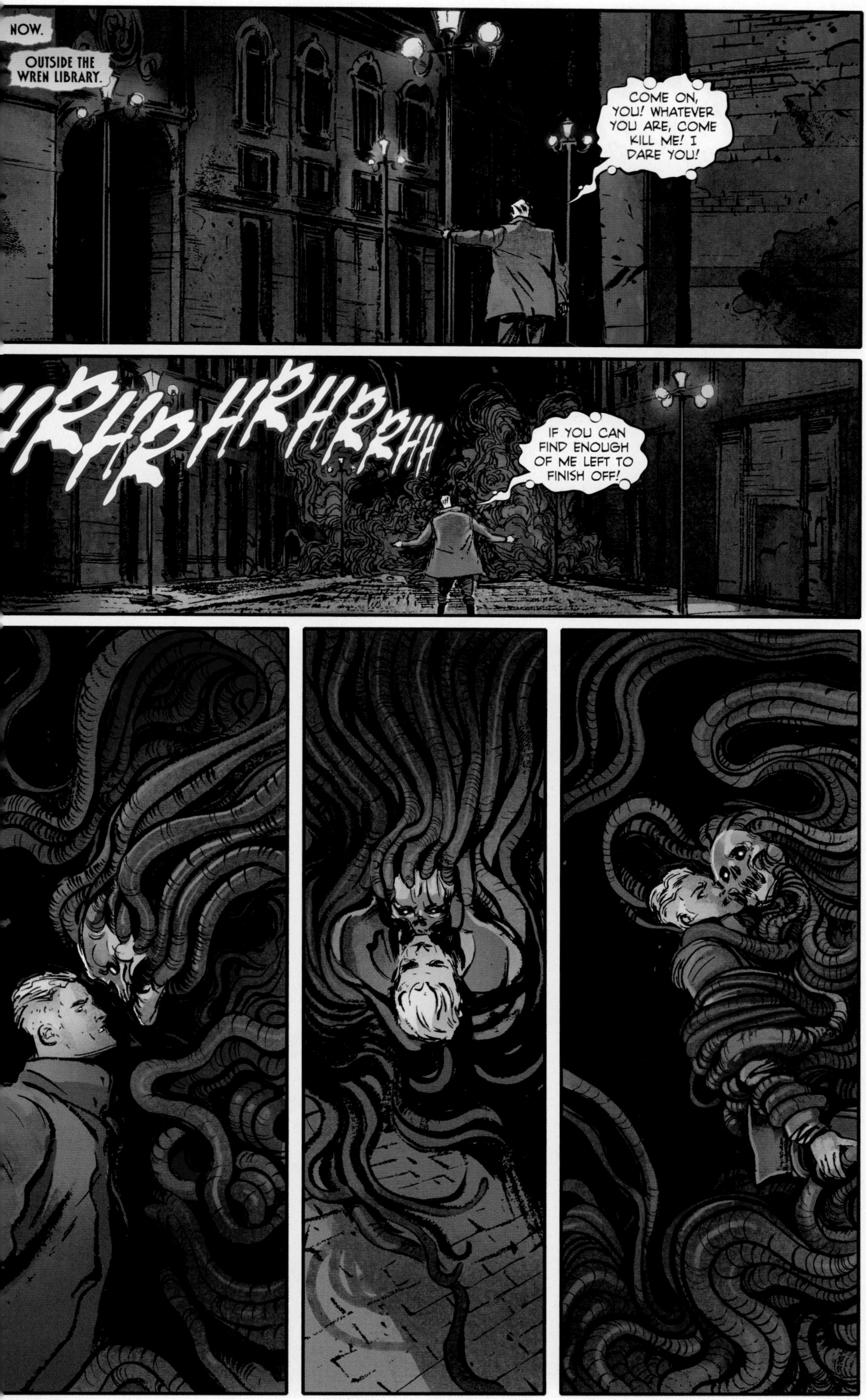
NOW.
OUTSIDE THE WREN LIBRARY.
COME ON, YOU! WHATEVER YOU ARE, COME KILL ME! I DARE YOU!
HRHRHRHRHRRRAH
IF YOU CAN FIND ENOUGH OF ME LEFT TO FINISH OFF!

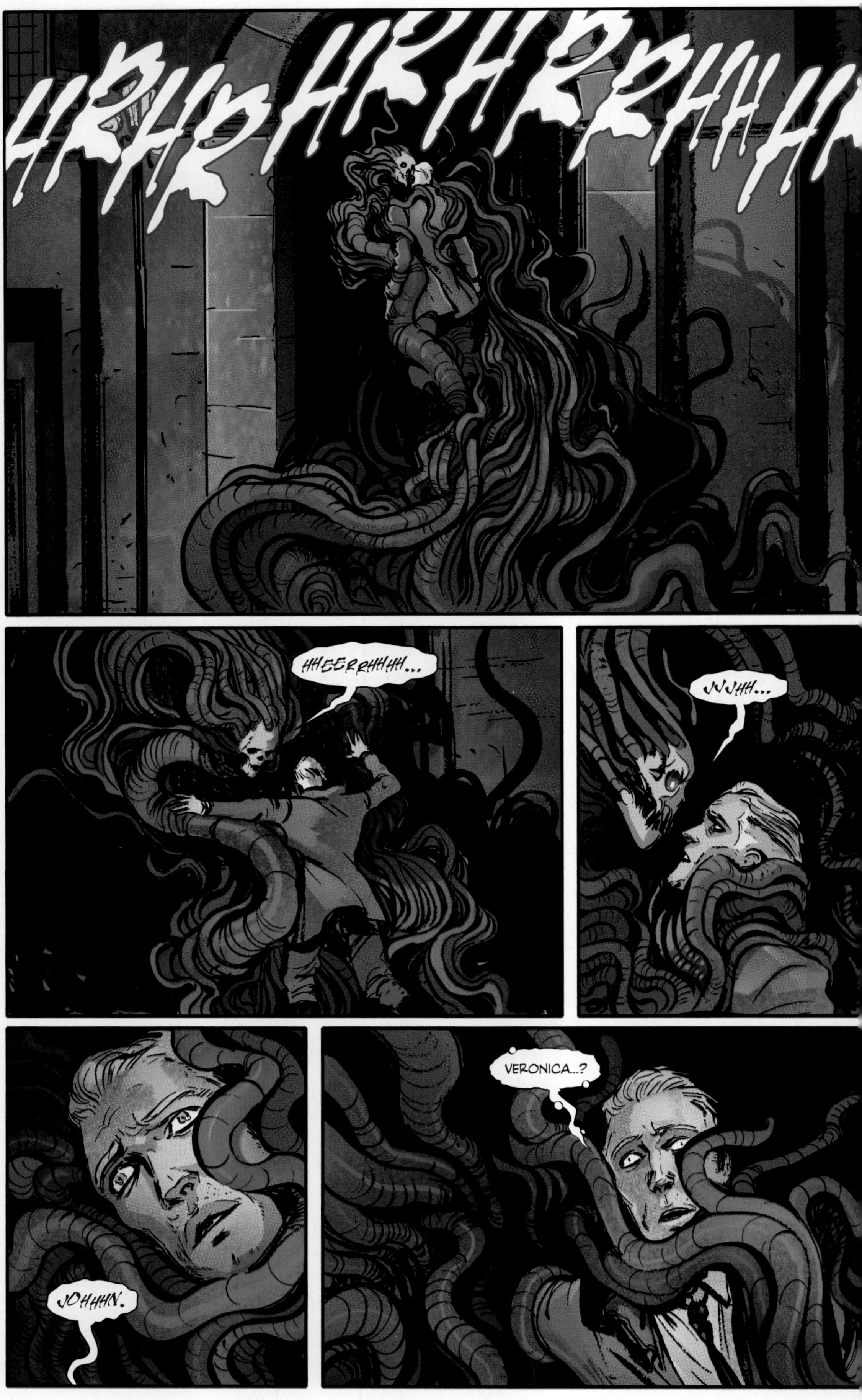
HRHRHRHRHRRHHHH
HHEERRHHHH...
JJJHH...
JOHHHN.
VERONICA...?

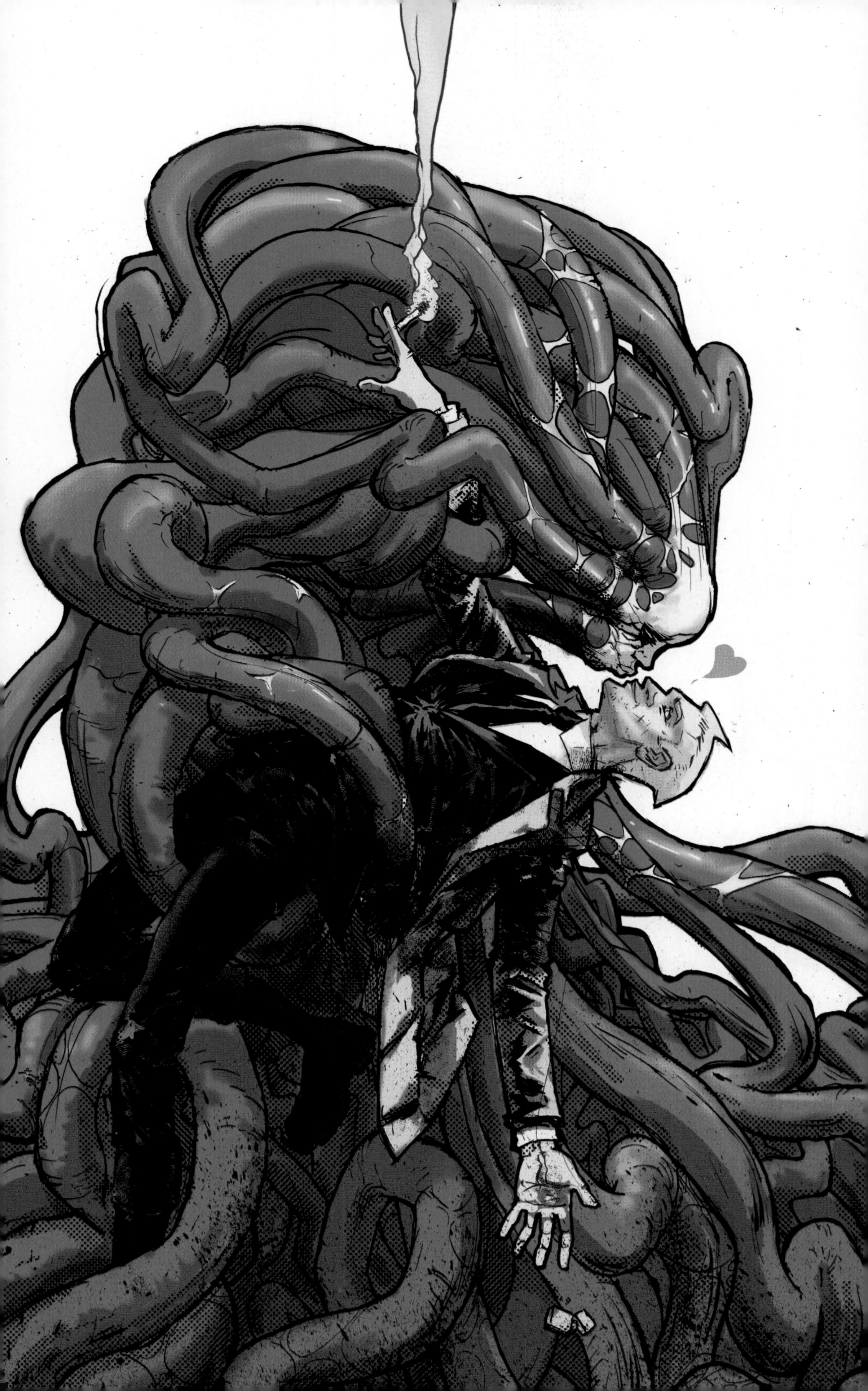

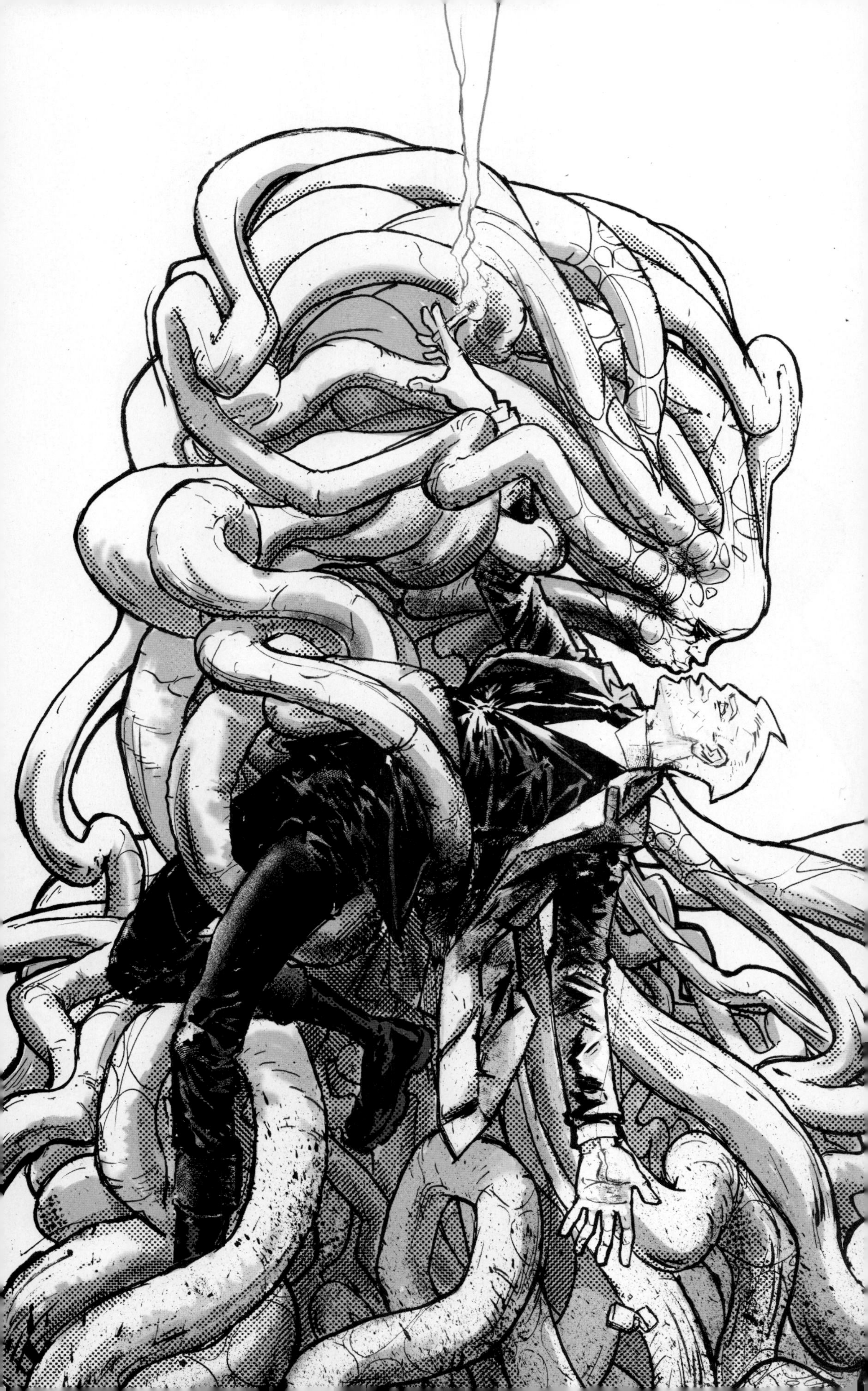

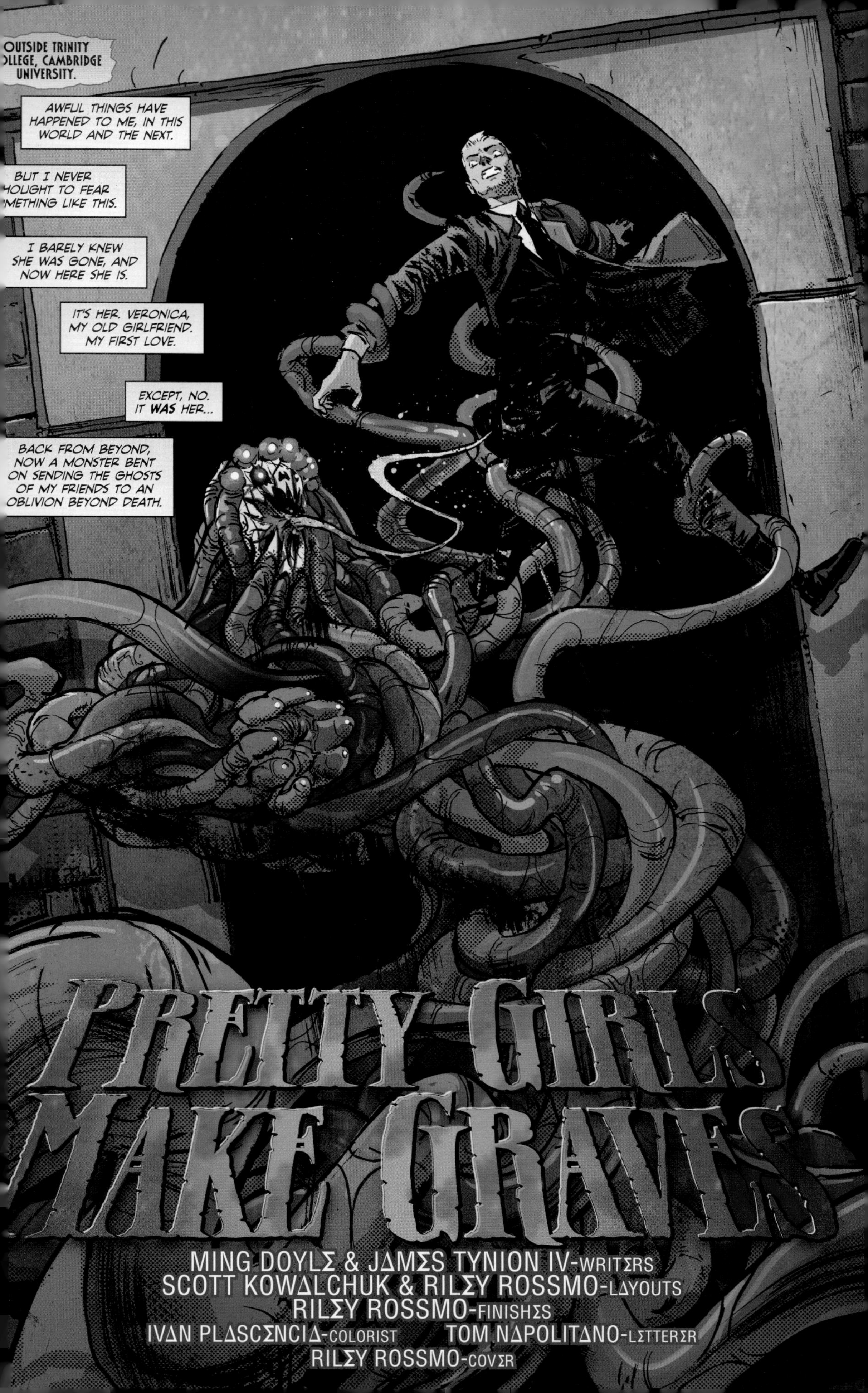
OUTSIDE TRINITY
OLLEGE, CAMBRIDGE
UNIVERSITY.
AWFUL THINGS HAVE HAPPENED TO ME, IN THIS WORLD AND THE NEXT.
BUT I NEVER HOUGHT TO FEAR METHING LIKE THIS.
I BARELY KNEW SHE WAS GONE, AND NOW HERE SHE IS.
IT'S HER. VERONICA, MY OLD GIRLFRIEND. MY FIRST LOVE.
EXCEPT, NO. IT WAS HER...
BACK FROM BEYOND, NOW A MONSTER BENT ON SENDING THE GHOSTS OF MY FRIENDS TO AN OBLIVION BEYOND DEATH.
PRETTY GIRLS MAKE GRAVES
MING DOYLE & JAMES TYNION IV-WRITERS
SCOTT KOWALCHUK & RILEY ROSSMO-LAYOUTS
RILEY ROSSMO-FINISHES
IVAN PLASCENCIA-COLORIST
TOM NAPOLITANO-LETTERER
RILEY ROSSMO-COVER

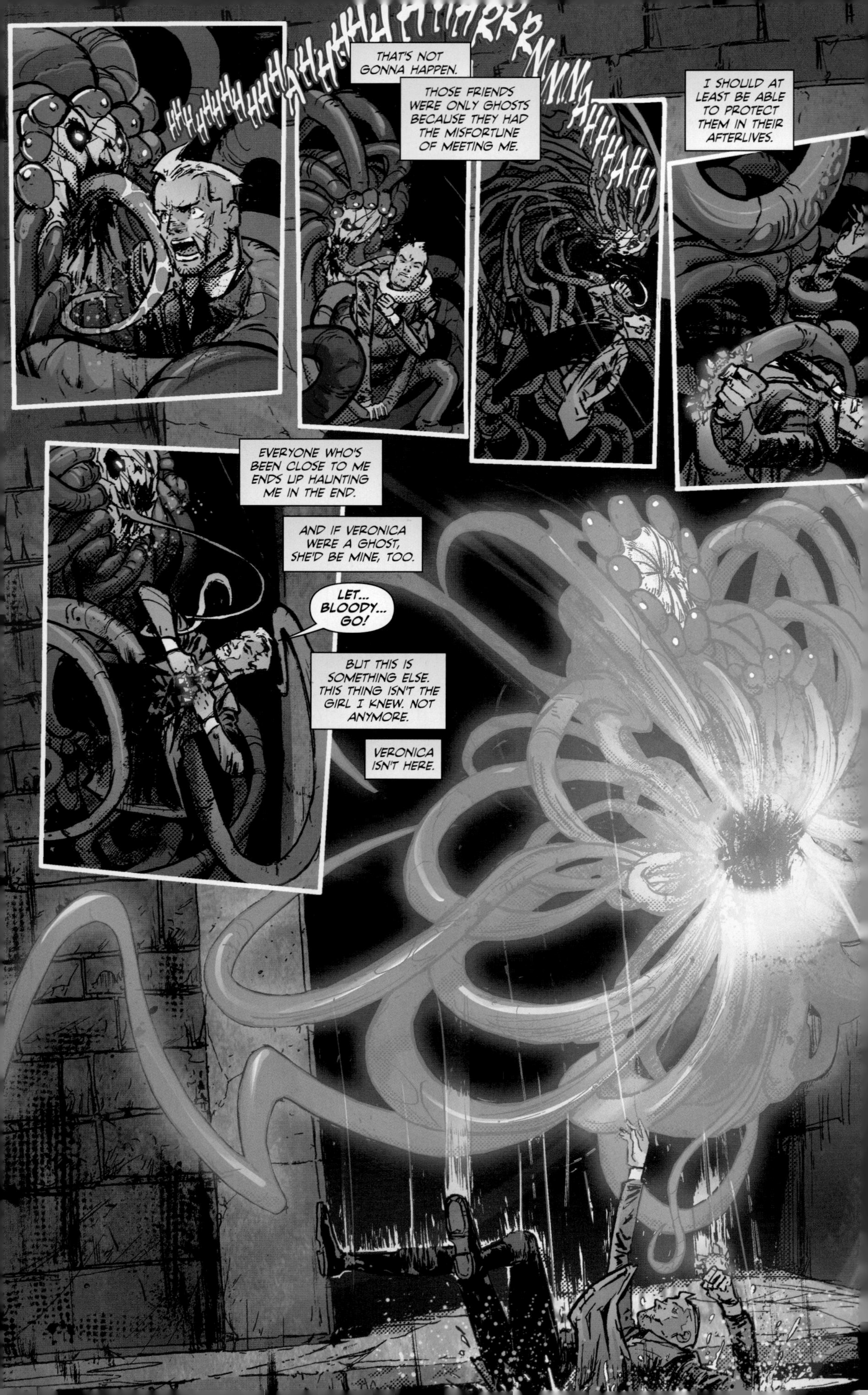
THAT'S NOT GONNA HAPPEN.
THOSE FRIENDS WERE ONLY GHOSTS BECAUSE THEY HAD THE MISFORTUNE OF MEETING ME.
I SHOULD AT LEAST BE ABLE TO PROTECT THEM IN THEIR AFTERLIVES.
EVERYONE WHO'S BEEN CLOSE TO ME ENDS UP HAUNTING ME IN THE END.
AND IF VERONICA WERE A GHOST, SHE'D BE MINE, TOO.
LET... BLOODY... GO!
BUT THIS IS SOMETHING ELSE. THIS THING ISN'T THE GIRL I KNEW. NOT ANYMORE.
VERONICA ISN'T HERE.

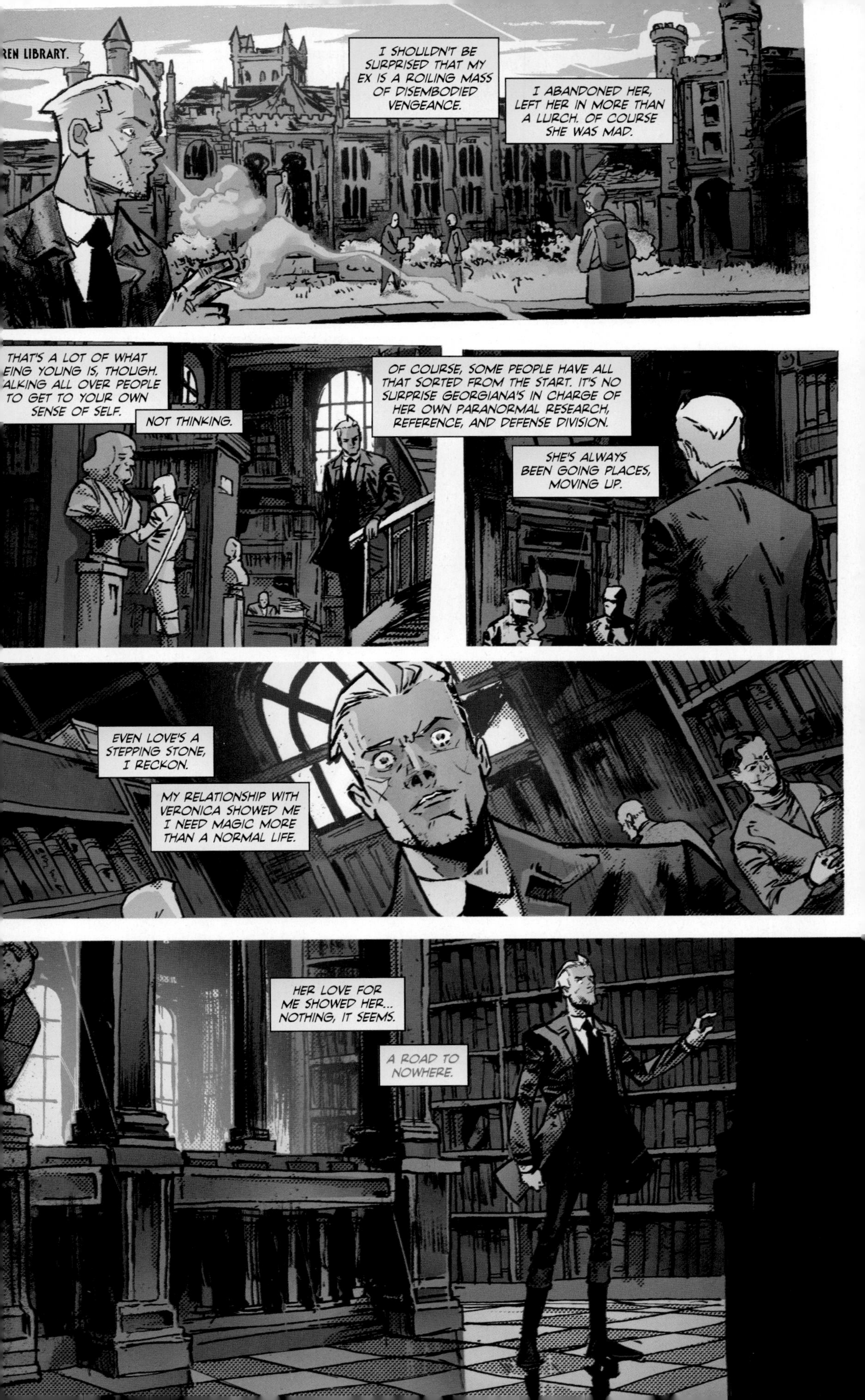
REN LIBRARY.
I SHOULDN'T BE SURPRISED THAT MY EX IS A ROILING MASS OF DISEMBODIED VENGEANCE.
I ABANDONED HER, LEFT HER IN MORE THAN A LURCH. OF COURSE SHE WAS MAD.
THAT'S A LOT OF WHAT EING YOUNG IS, THOUGH. ALKING ALL OVER PEOPLE TO GET TO YOUR OWN SENSE OF SELF.
NOT THINKING.
OF COURSE, SOME PEOPLE HAVE ALL THAT SORTED FROM THE START. IT'S NO SURPRISE GEORGIANA'S IN CHARGE OF HER OWN PARANORMAL RESEARCH, REFERENCE, AND DEFENSE DIVISION.
SHE'S ALWAYS BEEN GOING PLACES, MOVING UP.
EVEN LOVE'S A STEPPING STONE, I RECKON.
MY RELATIONSHIP WITH VERONICA SHOWED ME I NEED MAGIC MORE THAN A NORMAL LIFE.
HER LOVE FOR ME SHOWED HER... NOTHING, IT SEEMS.
A ROAD TO NOWHERE.

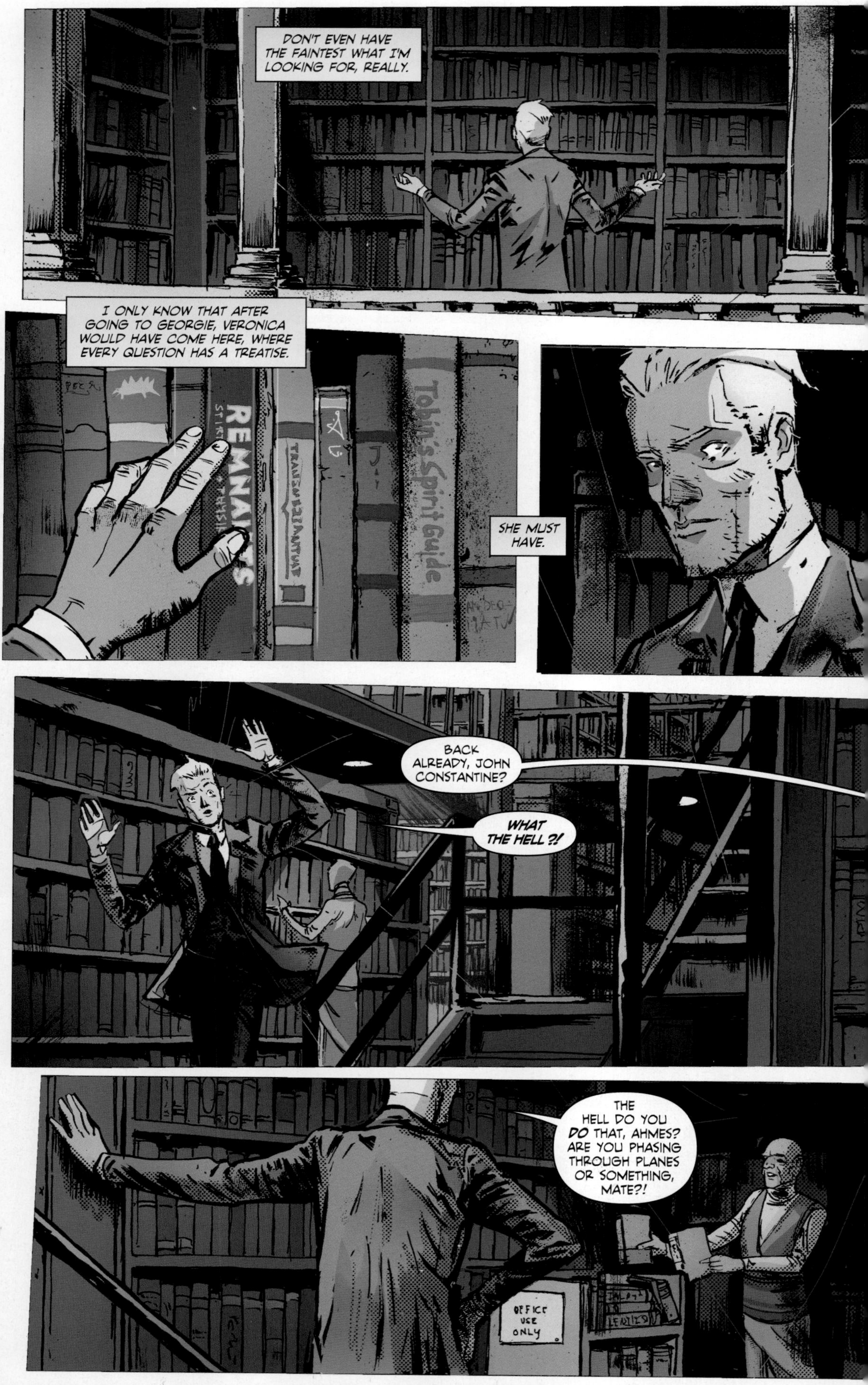
DON'T EVEN HAVE THE FAINTEST WHAT I'M LOOKING FOR, REALLY.
I ONLY KNOW THAT AFTER GOING TO GEORGIE, VERONICA WOULD HAVE COME HERE, WHERE EVERY QUESTION HAS A TREATISE.
REMNANTS
Tobin's Spirit Guide
SHE MUST HAVE.
BACK ALREADY, JOHN CONSTANTINE?
WHAT THE HELL ?!
THE HELL DO YOU DO THAT, AHMES? ARE YOU PHASING THROUGH PLANES OR SOMETHING, MATE?!
OFFICE USE ONLY

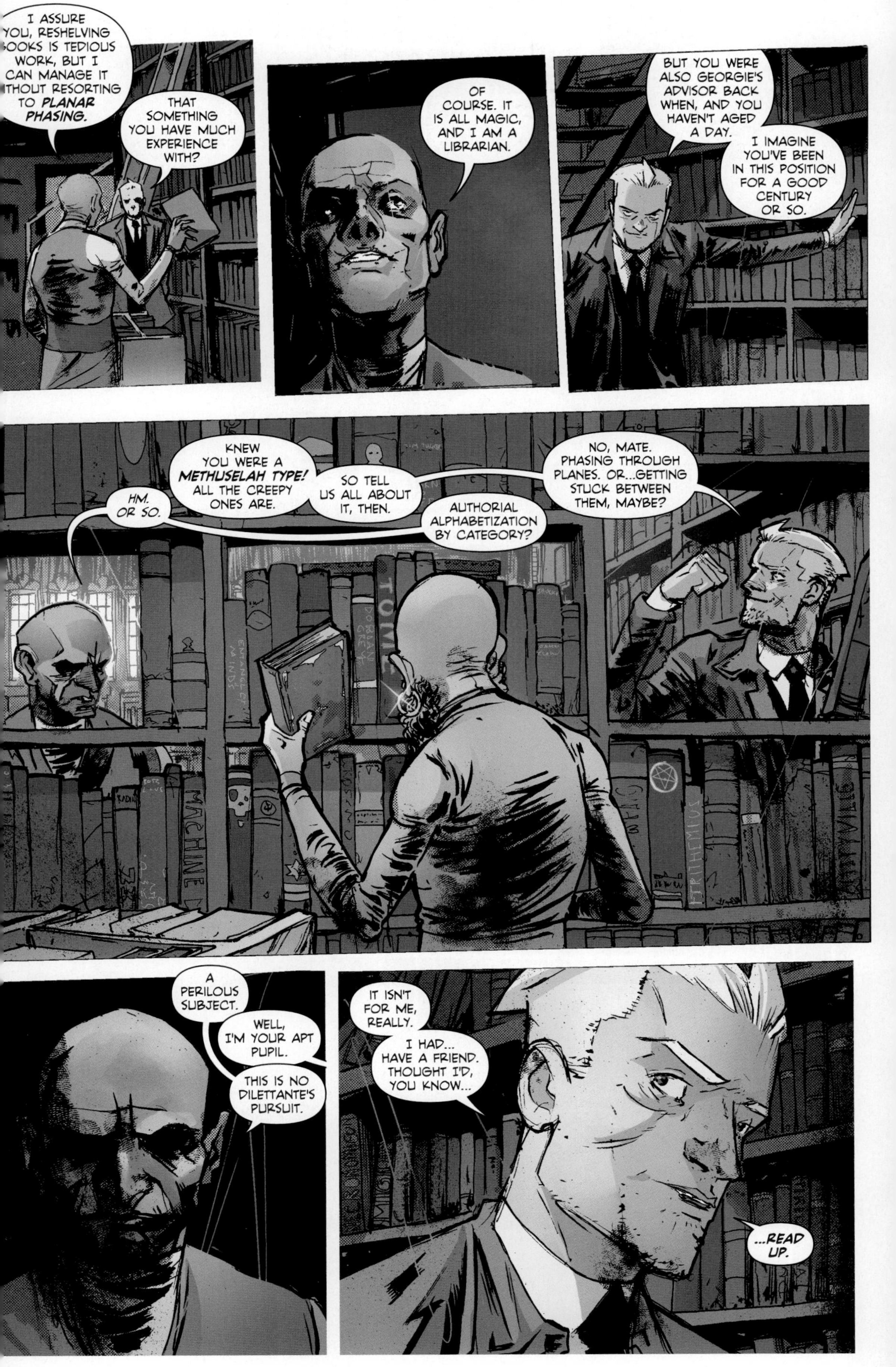
I ASSURE YOU, RESHELVING BOOKS IS TEDIOUS WORK, BUT I CAN MANAGE IT WITHOUT RESORTING TO *PLANAR PHASING.*
THAT SOMETHING YOU HAVE MUCH EXPERIENCE WITH?
OF COURSE. IT IS ALL MAGIC, AND I AM A LIBRARIAN.
BUT YOU WERE ALSO GEORGIE'S ADVISOR BACK WHEN, AND YOU HAVEN'T AGED A DAY.
I IMAGINE YOU'VE BEEN IN THIS POSITION FOR A GOOD CENTURY OR SO.
HM. OR SO.
KNEW YOU WERE A *METHUSELAH TYPE!* ALL THE CREEPY ONES ARE.
SO TELL US ALL ABOUT IT, THEN.
AUTHORIAL ALPHABETIZATION BY CATEGORY?
NO, MATE. PHASING THROUGH PLANES. OR...GETTING STUCK BETWEEN THEM, MAYBE?
TOME
MACHINE
TRITHEMIUS
A PERILOUS SUBJECT.
WELL, I'M YOUR APT PUPIL.
THIS IS NO DILETTANTE'S PURSUIT.
IT ISN'T FOR ME, REALLY.
I HAD... HAVE A FRIEND. THOUGHT I'D, YOU KNOW...
...READ UP.

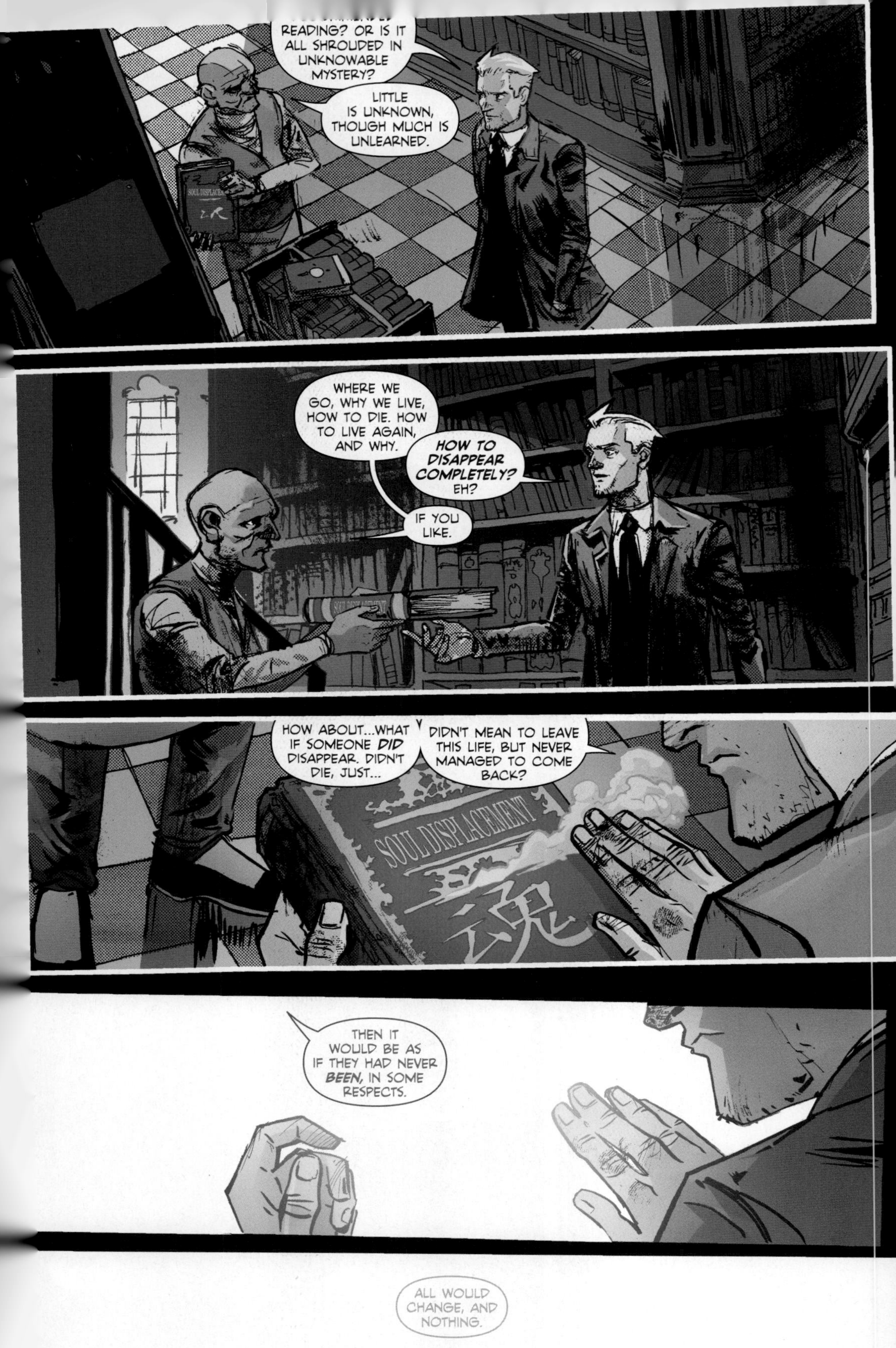
READING? OR IS IT ALL SHROUDED IN UNKNOWABLE MYSTERY?
LITTLE IS UNKNOWN, THOUGH MUCH IS UNLEARNED.
WHERE WE GO, WHY WE LIVE, HOW TO DIE. HOW TO LIVE AGAIN, AND WHY.
HOW TO DISAPPEAR COMPLETELY? EH?
IF YOU LIKE.
HOW ABOUT...WHAT IF SOMEONE DID DISAPPEAR. DIDN'T DIE, JUST...
DIDN'T MEAN TO LEAVE THIS LIFE, BUT NEVER MANAGED TO COME BACK?
SOUL DISPLACEMENT
魂
THEN IT WOULD BE AS IF THEY HAD NEVER BEEN, IN SOME RESPECTS.
ALL WOULD CHANGE, AND NOTHING.

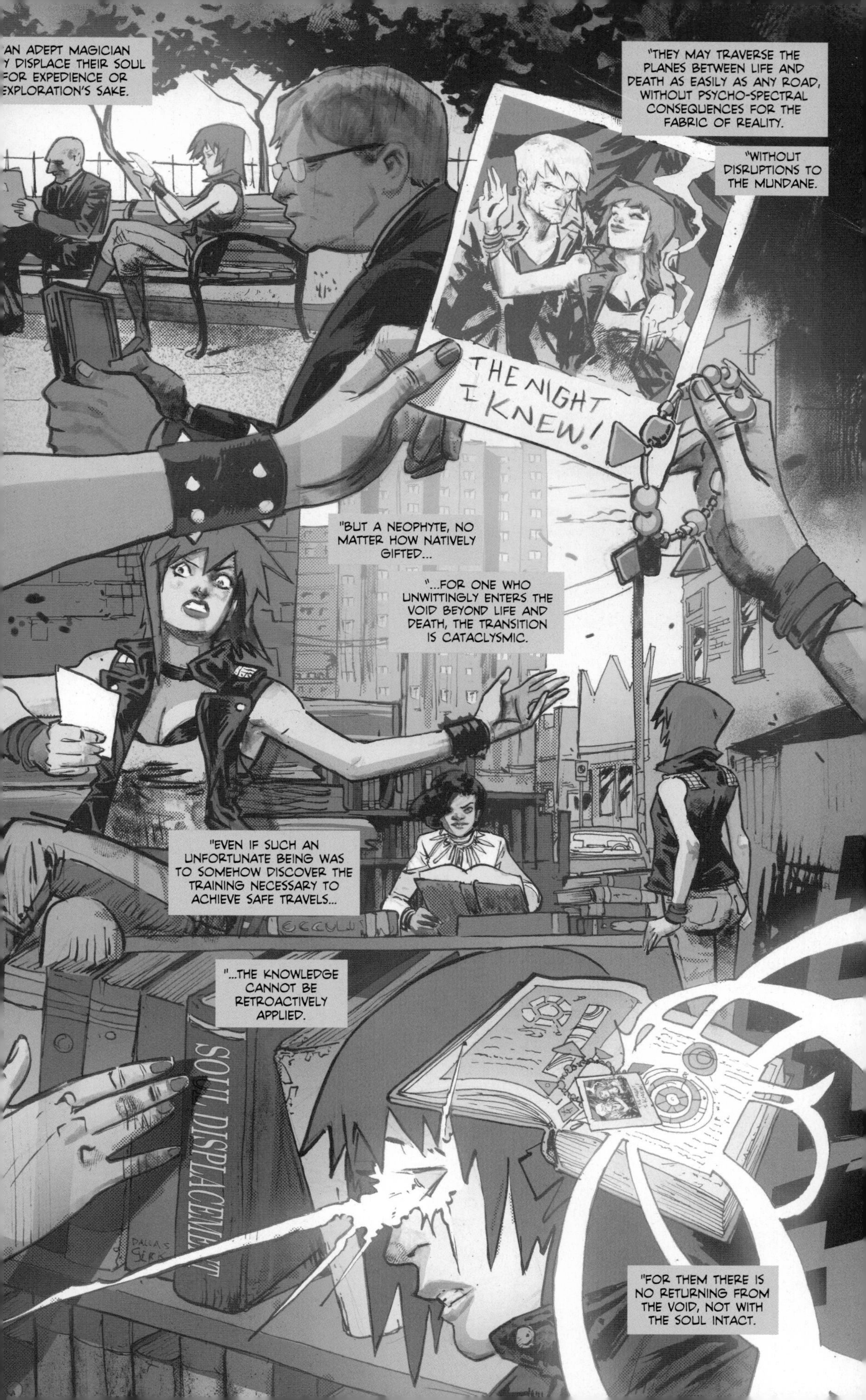
"AN ADEPT MAGICIAN
Y DISPLACE THEIR SOUL
FOR EXPEDIENCE OR
EXPLORATION'S SAKE.
"THEY MAY TRAVERSE THE PLANES BETWEEN LIFE AND DEATH AS EASILY AS ANY ROAD, WITHOUT PSYCHO-SPECTRAL CONSEQUENCES FOR THE FABRIC OF REALITY.
"WITHOUT DISRUPTIONS TO THE MUNDANE.
THE NIGHT I KNEW!
"BUT A NEOPHYTE, NO MATTER HOW NATIVELY GIFTED...
"...FOR ONE WHO UNWITTINGLY ENTERS THE VOID BEYOND LIFE AND DEATH, THE TRANSITION IS CATACLYSMIC.
"EVEN IF SUCH AN UNFORTUNATE BEING WAS TO SOMEHOW DISCOVER THE TRAINING NECESSARY TO ACHIEVE SAFE TRAVELS...
OCCULT
"...THE KNOWLEDGE CANNOT BE RETROACTIVELY APPLIED.
SOUL DISPLACEMENT
"FOR THEM THERE IS NO RETURNING FROM THE VOID, NOT WITH THE SOUL INTACT.

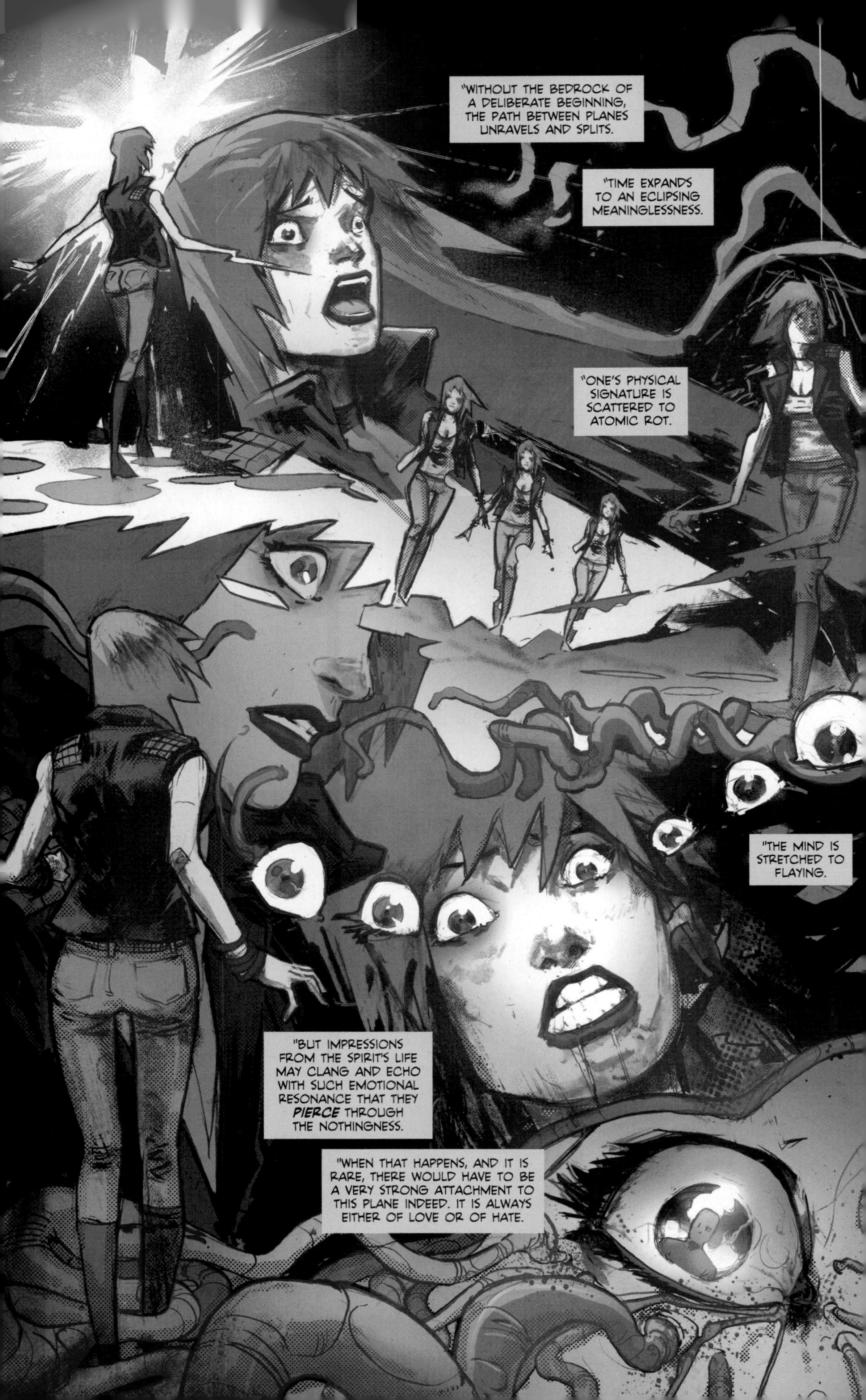
"WITHOUT THE BEDROCK OF A DELIBERATE BEGINNING, THE PATH BETWEEN PLANES UNRAVELS AND SPLITS.
"TIME EXPANDS TO AN ECLIPSING MEANINGLESSNESS.
"ONE'S PHYSICAL SIGNATURE IS SCATTERED TO ATOMIC ROT.
"THE MIND IS STRETCHED TO FLAYING.
"BUT IMPRESSIONS FROM THE SPIRIT'S LIFE MAY CLANG AND ECHO WITH SUCH EMOTIONAL RESONANCE THAT THEY *PIERCE* THROUGH THE NOTHINGNESS.
"WHEN THAT HAPPENS, AND IT IS RARE, THERE WOULD HAVE TO BE A VERY STRONG ATTACHMENT TO THIS PLANE INDEED. IT IS ALWAYS EITHER OF LOVE OR OF HATE.

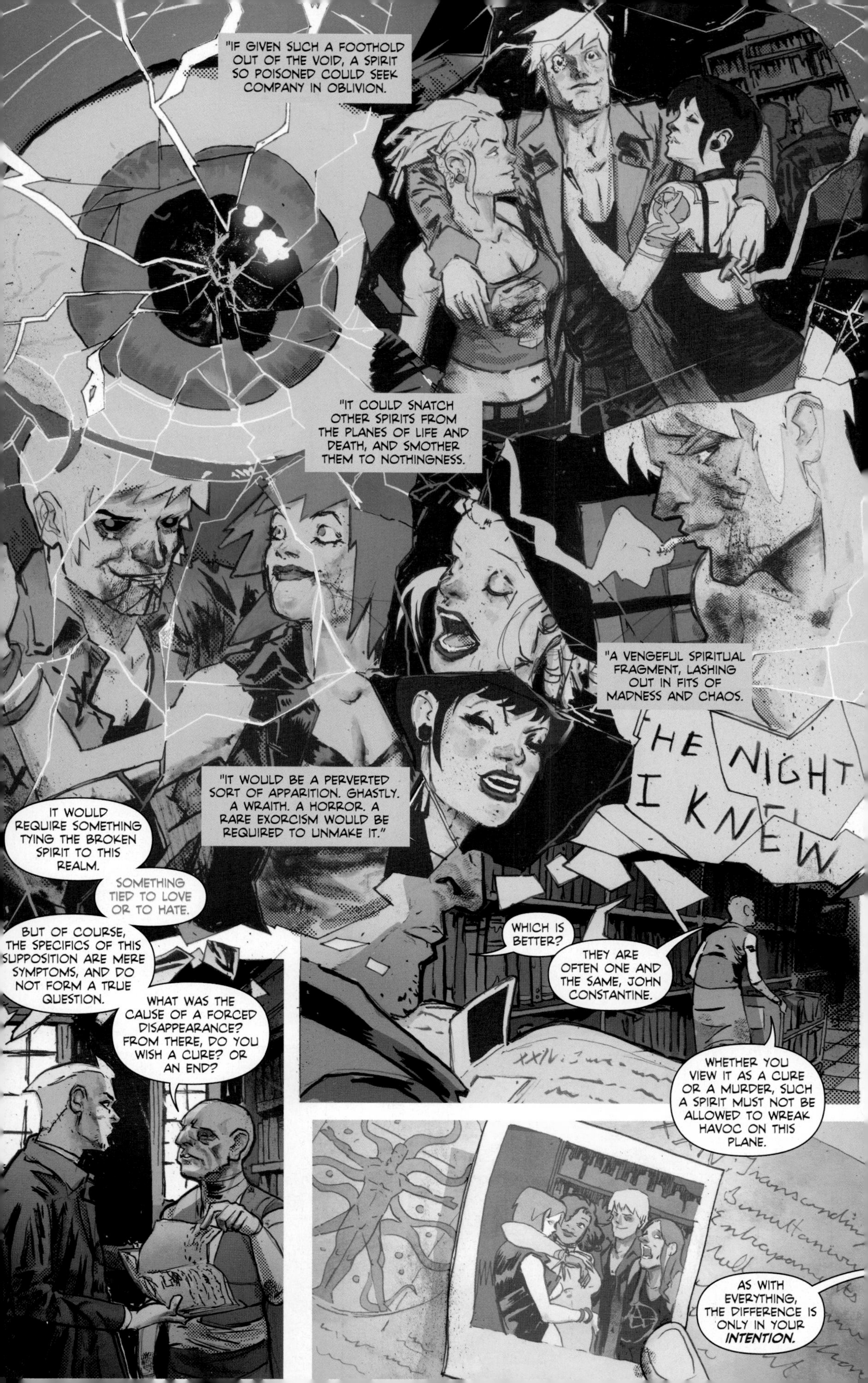
"IF GIVEN SUCH A FOOTHOLD OUT OF THE VOID, A SPIRIT SO POISONED COULD SEEK COMPANY IN OBLIVION.
"IT COULD SNATCH OTHER SPIRITS FROM THE PLANES OF LIFE AND DEATH, AND SMOTHER THEM TO NOTHINGNESS.
"A VENGEFUL SPIRITUAL FRAGMENT, LASHING OUT IN FITS OF MADNESS AND CHAOS.
THE NIGHT I KNEW
"IT WOULD BE A PERVERTED SORT OF APPARITION. GHASTLY. A WRAITH. A HORROR. A RARE EXORCISM WOULD BE REQUIRED TO UNMAKE IT."
IT WOULD REQUIRE SOMETHING TYING THE BROKEN SPIRIT TO THIS REALM.
SOMETHING TIED TO LOVE OR TO HATE.
WHICH IS BETTER?
THEY ARE OFTEN ONE AND THE SAME, JOHN CONSTANTINE.
BUT OF COURSE, THE SPECIFICS OF THIS SUPPOSITION ARE MERE SYMPTOMS, AND DO NOT FORM A TRUE QUESTION.
WHAT WAS THE CAUSE OF A FORCED DISAPPEARANCE? FROM THERE, DO YOU WISH A CURE? OR AN END?
WHETHER YOU VIEW IT AS A CURE OR A MURDER, SUCH A SPIRIT MUST NOT BE ALLOWED TO WREAK HAVOC ON THIS PLANE.
AS WITH EVERYTHING, THE DIFFERENCE IS ONLY IN YOUR ***INTENTION.***

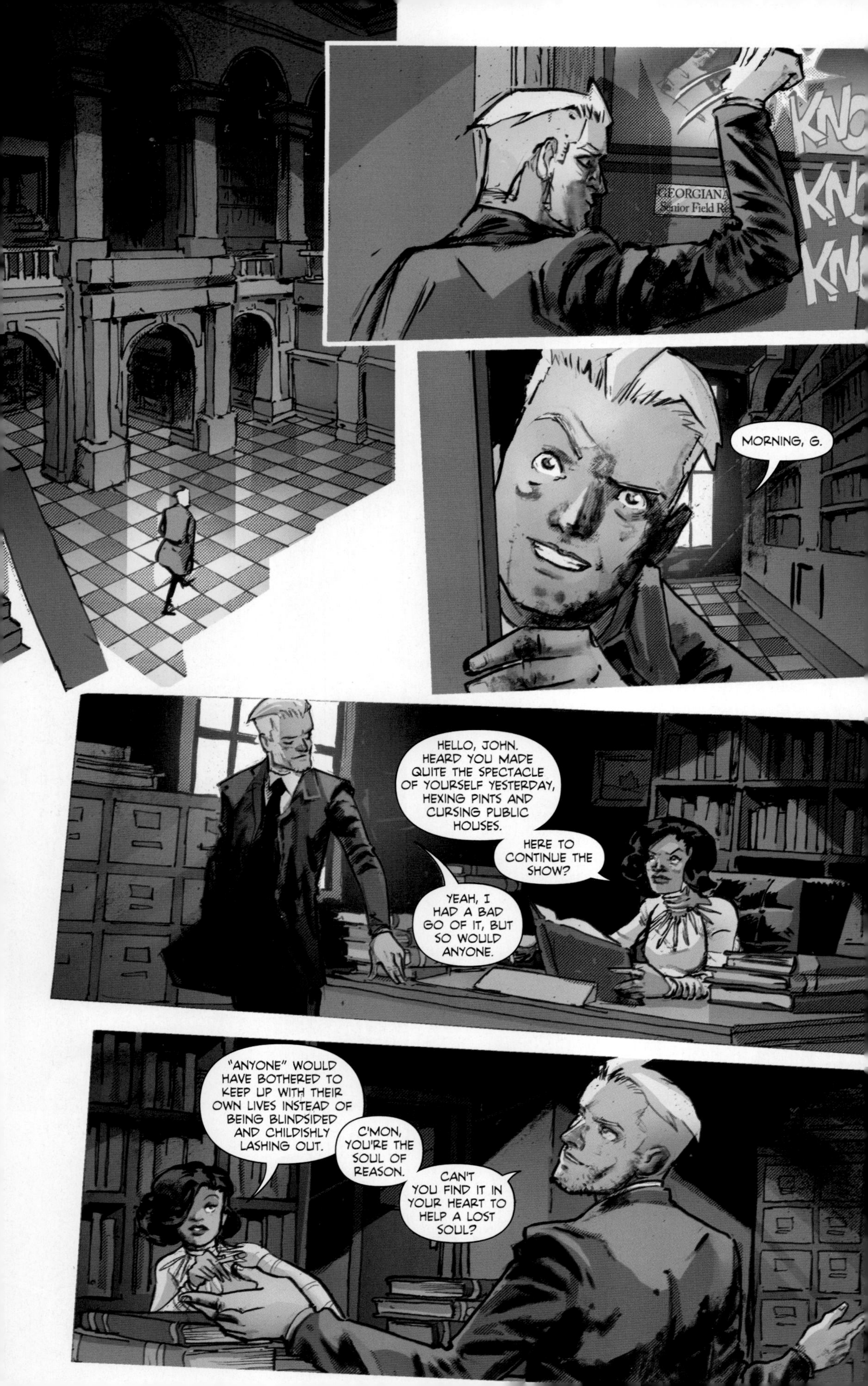
GEORGIANA
Senior Field Re
KNO
KNO
KNO
MORNING, G.
HELLO, JOHN. HEARD YOU MADE QUITE THE SPECTACLE OF YOURSELF YESTERDAY, HEXING PINTS AND CURSING PUBLIC HOUSES.
HERE TO CONTINUE THE SHOW?
YEAH, I HAD A BAD GO OF IT, BUT SO WOULD ANYONE.
"ANYONE" WOULD HAVE BOTHERED TO KEEP UP WITH THEIR OWN LIVES INSTEAD OF BEING BLINDSIDED AND CHILDISHLY LASHING OUT.
C'MON, YOU'RE THE SOUL OF REASON.
CAN'T YOU FIND IT IN YOUR HEART TO HELP A LOST SOUL?

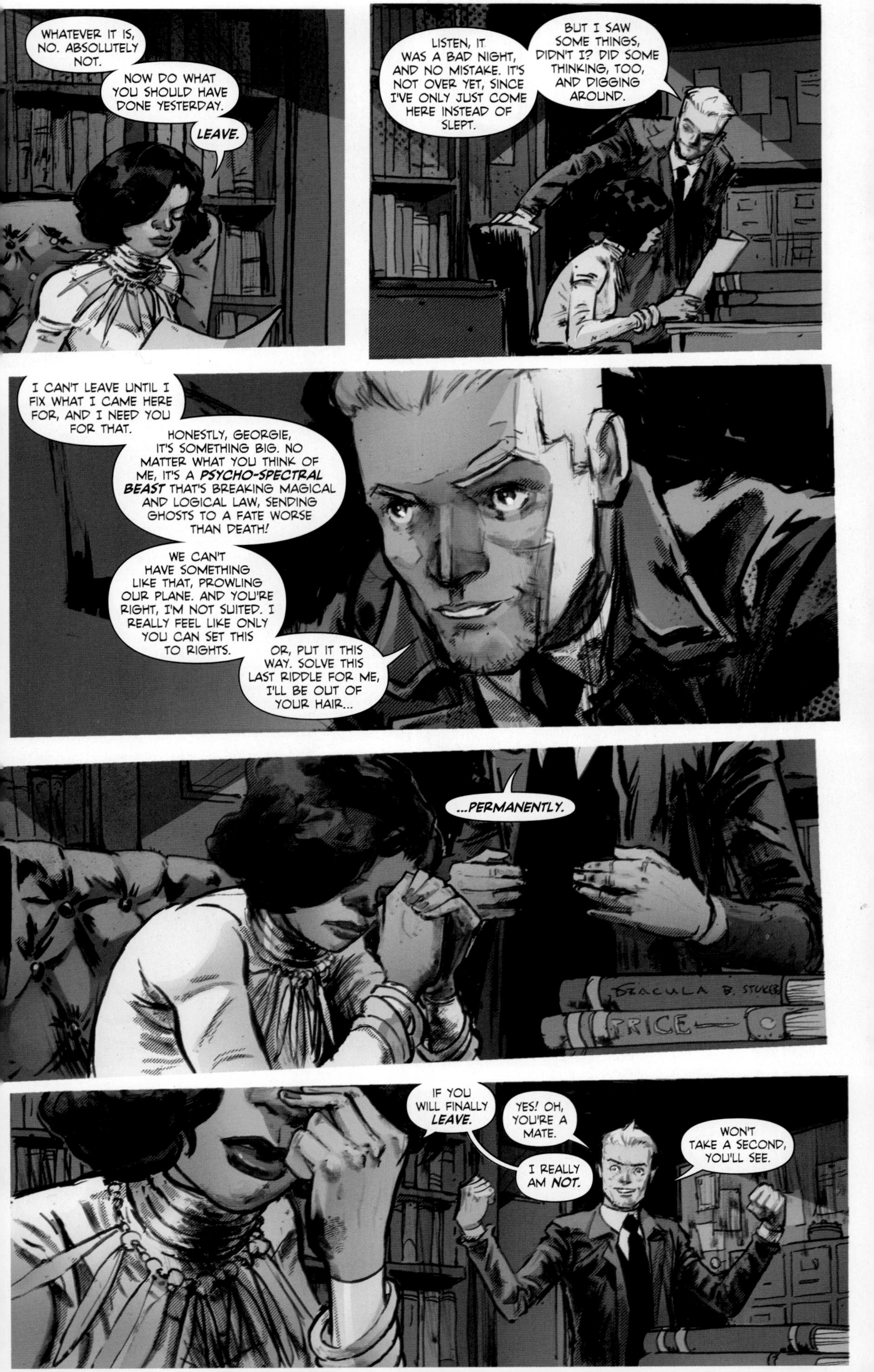
WHATEVER IT IS, NO. ABSOLUTELY NOT.
NOW DO WHAT YOU SHOULD HAVE DONE YESTERDAY.
LEAVE.
LISTEN, IT WAS A BAD NIGHT, AND NO MISTAKE. IT'S NOT OVER YET, SINCE I'VE ONLY JUST COME HERE INSTEAD OF SLEPT.
BUT I SAW SOME THINGS, DIDN'T I? DID SOME THINKING, TOO, AND DIGGING AROUND.
I CAN'T LEAVE UNTIL I FIX WHAT I CAME HERE FOR, AND I NEED YOU FOR THAT.
HONESTLY, GEORGIE, IT'S SOMETHING BIG. NO MATTER WHAT YOU THINK OF ME, IT'S A ***PSYCHO-SPECTRAL BEAST*** THAT'S BREAKING MAGICAL AND LOGICAL LAW, SENDING GHOSTS TO A FATE WORSE THAN DEATH!
WE CAN'T HAVE SOMETHING LIKE THAT, PROWLING OUR PLANE. AND YOU'RE RIGHT, I'M NOT SUITED. I REALLY FEEL LIKE ONLY YOU CAN SET THIS TO RIGHTS.
OR, PUT IT THIS WAY. SOLVE THIS LAST RIDDLE FOR ME, I'LL BE OUT OF YOUR HAIR...
...PERMANENTLY.
DRACULA B. STOKER
PRICE
IF YOU WILL FINALLY ***LEAVE.***
YES! OH, YOU'RE A MATE.
I REALLY AM ***NOT.***
WON'T TAKE A SECOND, YOU'LL SEE.

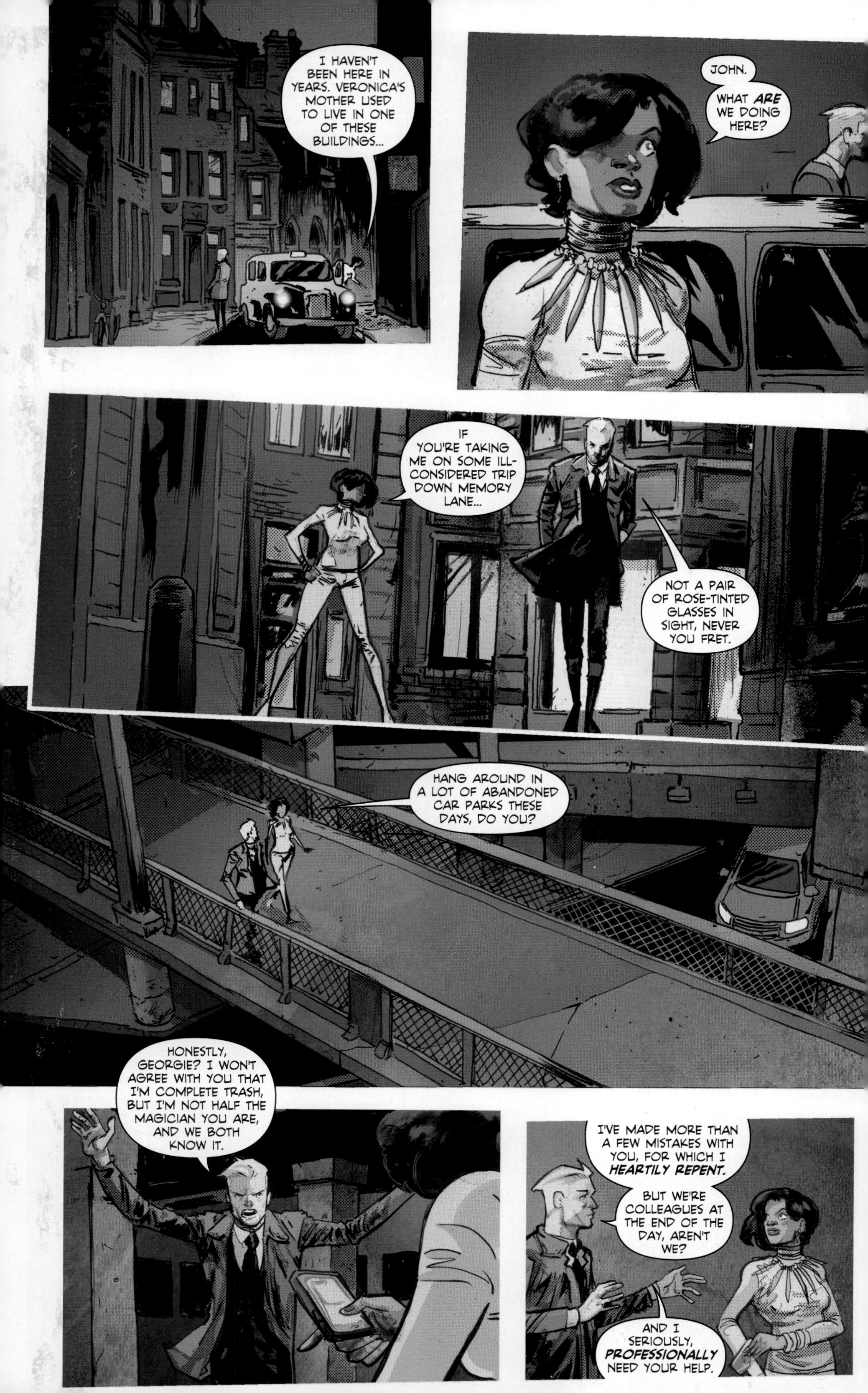
I HAVEN'T BEEN HERE IN YEARS. VERONICA'S MOTHER USED TO LIVE IN ONE OF THESE BUILDINGS...
JOHN.
WHAT ARE WE DOING HERE?
IF YOU'RE TAKING ME ON SOME ILL-CONSIDERED TRIP DOWN MEMORY LANE...
NOT A PAIR OF ROSE-TINTED GLASSES IN SIGHT, NEVER YOU FRET.
HANG AROUND IN A LOT OF ABANDONED CAR PARKS THESE DAYS, DO YOU?
HONESTLY, GEORGIE? I WON'T AGREE WITH YOU THAT I'M COMPLETE TRASH, BUT I'M NOT HALF THE MAGICIAN YOU ARE, AND WE BOTH KNOW IT.
I'VE MADE MORE THAN A FEW MISTAKES WITH YOU, FOR WHICH I HEARTILY REPENT.
BUT WE'RE COLLEAGUES AT THE END OF THE DAY, AREN'T WE?
AND I SERIOUSLY, PROFESSIONALLY NEED YOUR HELP.

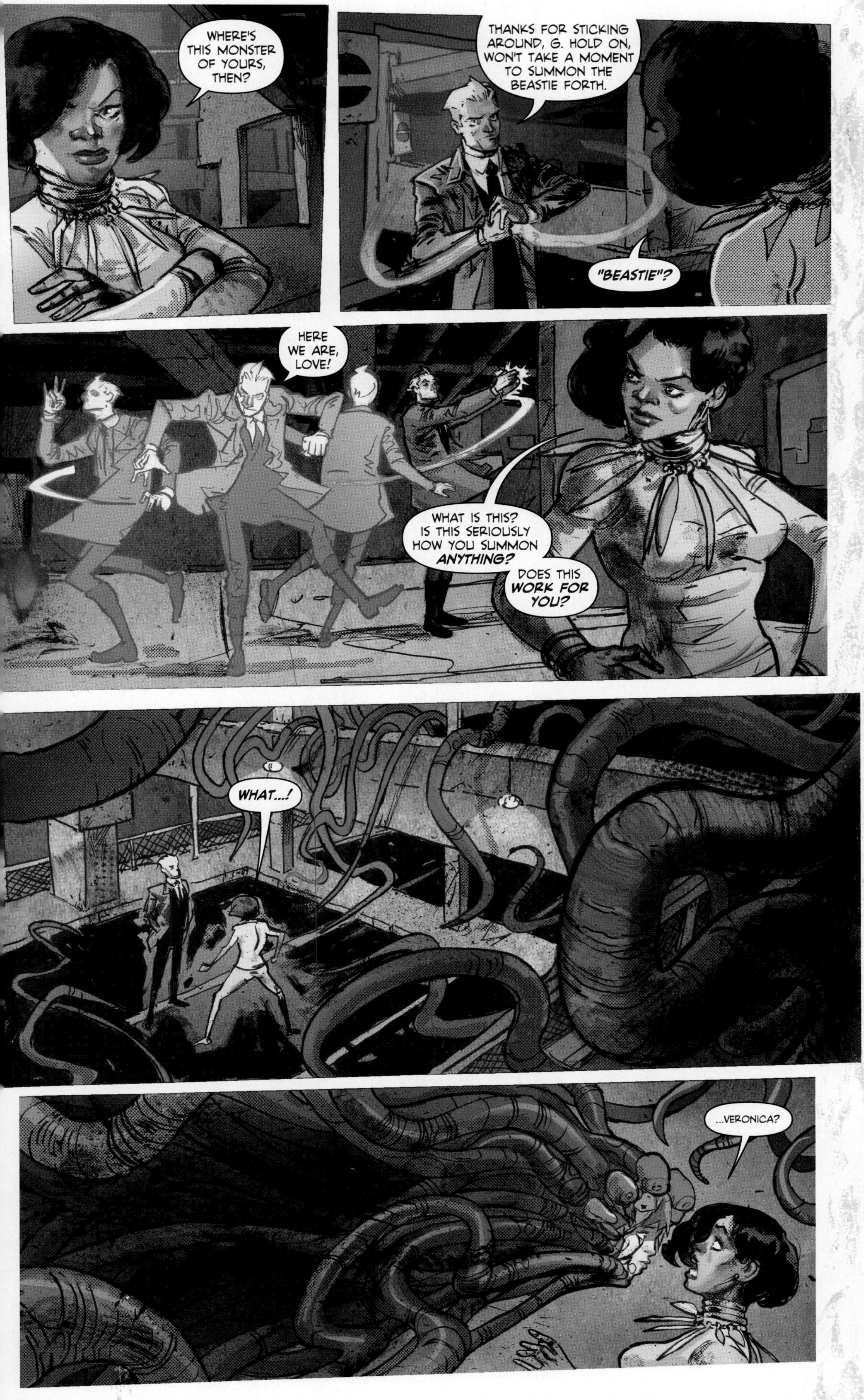
WHERE'S THIS MONSTER OF YOURS, THEN?
THANKS FOR STICKING AROUND, G. HOLD ON, WON'T TAKE A MOMENT TO SUMMON THE BEASTIE FORTH.
"BEASTIE"?
HERE WE ARE, LOVE!
WHAT IS THIS? IS THIS SERIOUSLY HOW YOU SUMMON ANYTHING?
DOES THIS WORK FOR YOU?
WHAT...!
...VERONICA?

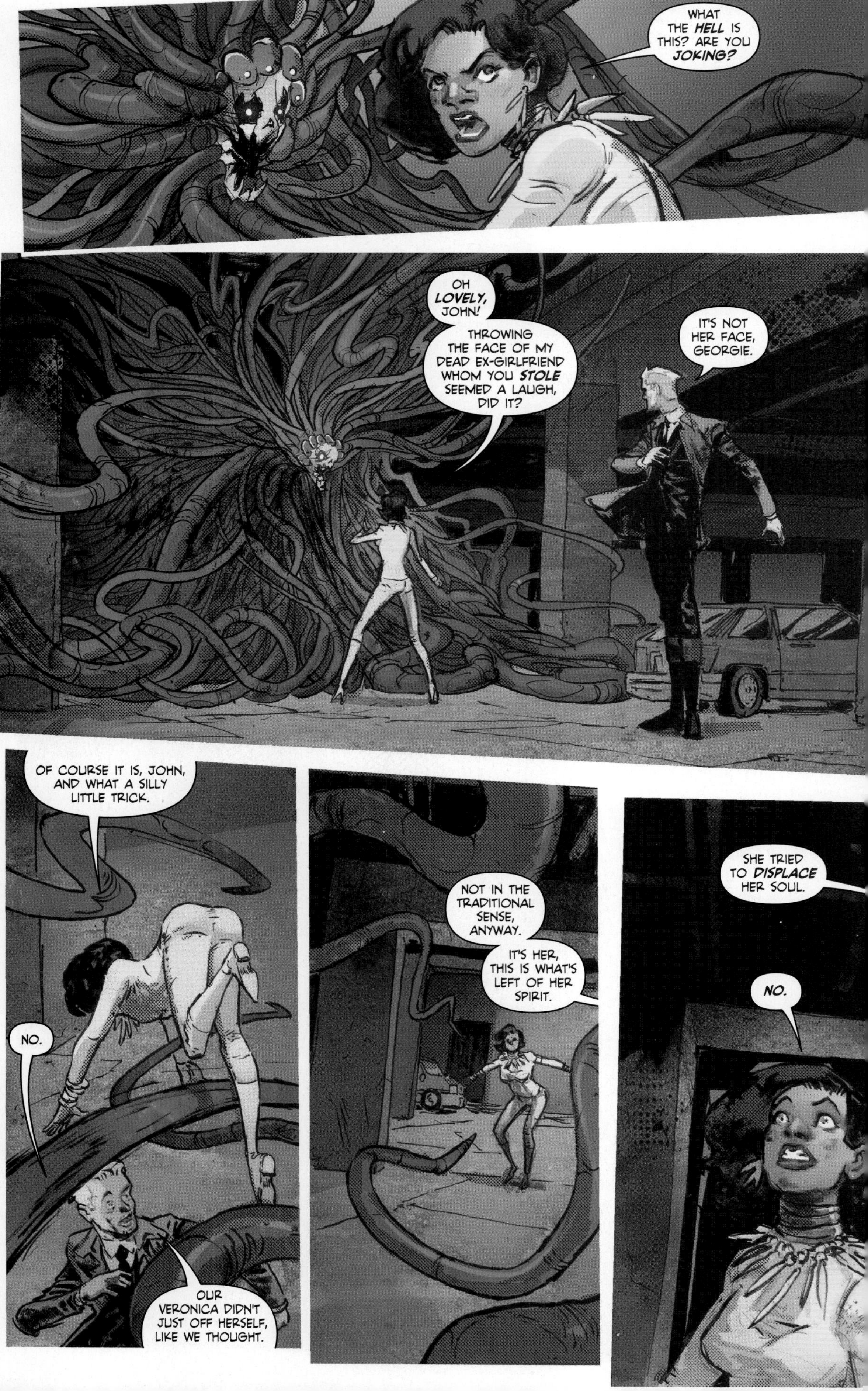
WHAT THE HELL IS THIS? ARE YOU JOKING?
OH LOVELY, JOHN!
THROWING THE FACE OF MY DEAD EX-GIRLFRIEND WHOM YOU STOLE SEEMED A LAUGH, DID IT?
IT'S NOT HER FACE, GEORGIE.
OF COURSE IT IS, JOHN, AND WHAT A SILLY LITTLE TRICK.
NO.
OUR VERONICA DIDN'T JUST OFF HERSELF, LIKE WE THOUGHT.
NOT IN THE TRADITIONAL SENSE, ANYWAY.
IT'S HER, THIS IS WHAT'S LEFT OF HER SPIRIT.
SHE TRIED TO DISPLACE HER SOUL.
NO.

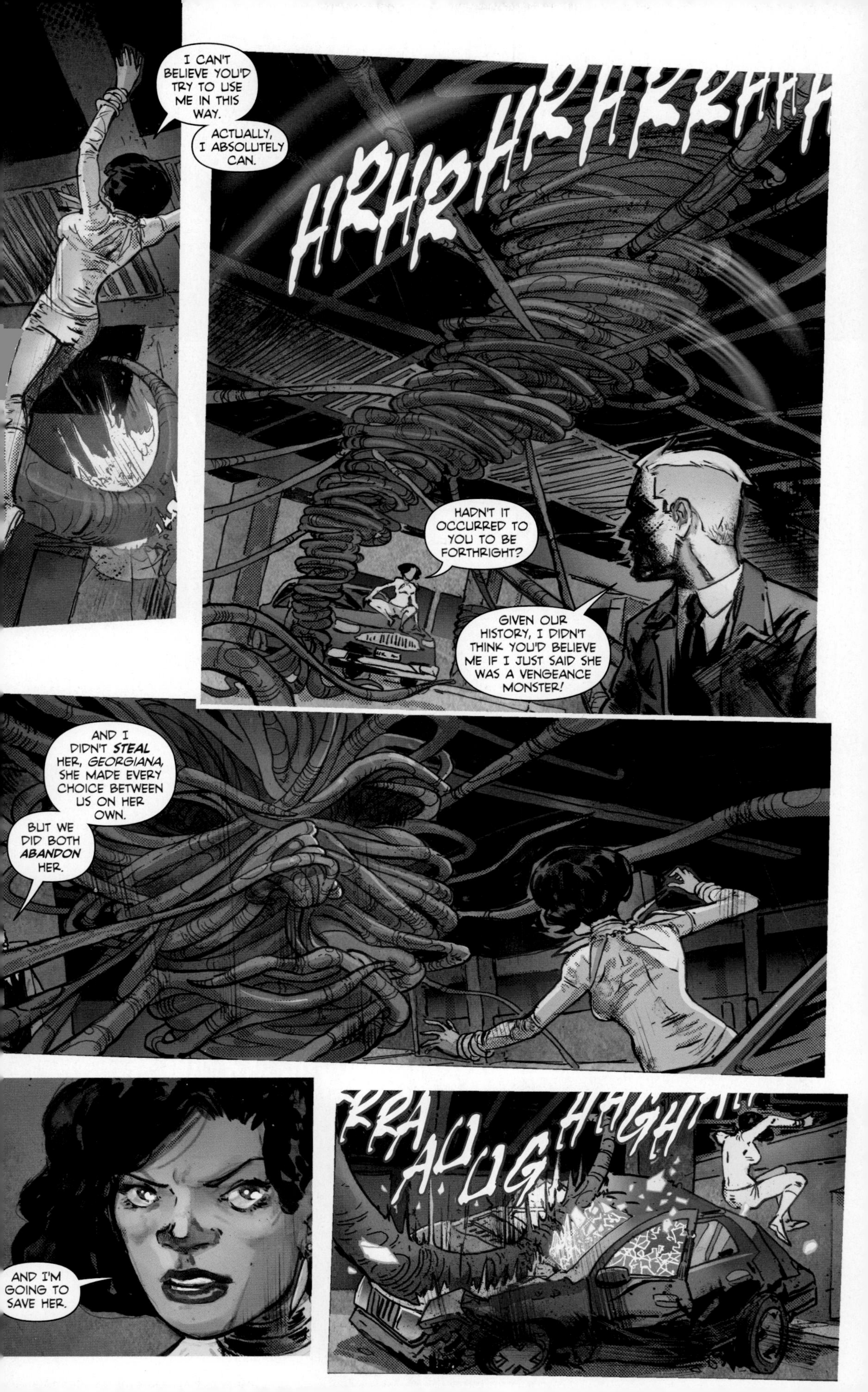
I CAN'T BELIEVE YOU'D TRY TO USE ME IN THIS WAY.
ACTUALLY, I ABSOLUTELY CAN.
HRHRHRHRRAHHH
HADN'T IT OCCURRED TO YOU TO BE FORTHRIGHT?
GIVEN OUR HISTORY, I DIDN'T THINK YOU'D BELIEVE ME IF I JUST SAID SHE WAS A VENGEANCE MONSTER!
AND I DIDN'T **STEAL** HER, *GEORGIANA*, SHE MADE EVERY CHOICE BETWEEN US ON HER OWN.
BUT WE DID BOTH **ABANDON** HER.
AND I'M GOING TO SAVE HER.
KRAAUUGHAGHH

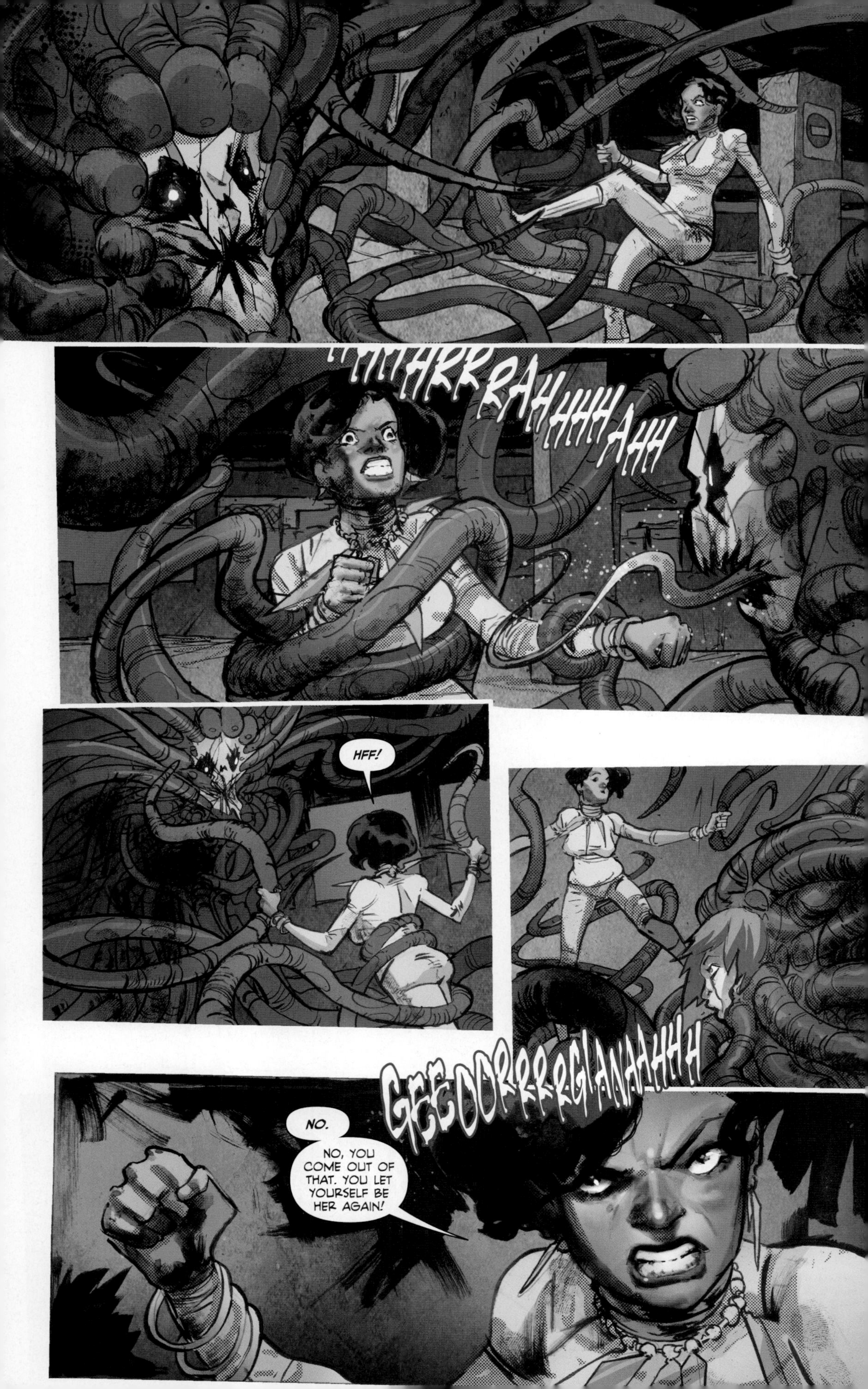
HRRRAHHHHAHH
HFF!
GEEDORRRRGLANAAHHH
NO.
NO, YOU COME OUT OF THAT. YOU LET YOURSELF BE HER AGAIN!

KRAK

YOU ARE HER! YOU'RE HERE, AND I SEE YOU! I SEE YOU, VERONICA!

GGGGEORRR-GIIEEEEE-IEEEEE

COME *HERE*, DO YOU HEAR ME, LOVE? COME RIGHT BACK HERE, *IRON TO BLOOD, CHALK TO BONE.*

CLAIM HEARTH, CLAIM HEART, CLAIM MORTAL HOME.

IIEEEE-IEEEE-IEEEEEEEE

GEORRR--!

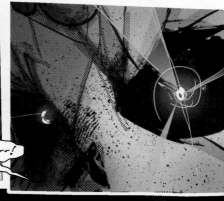

AH--!

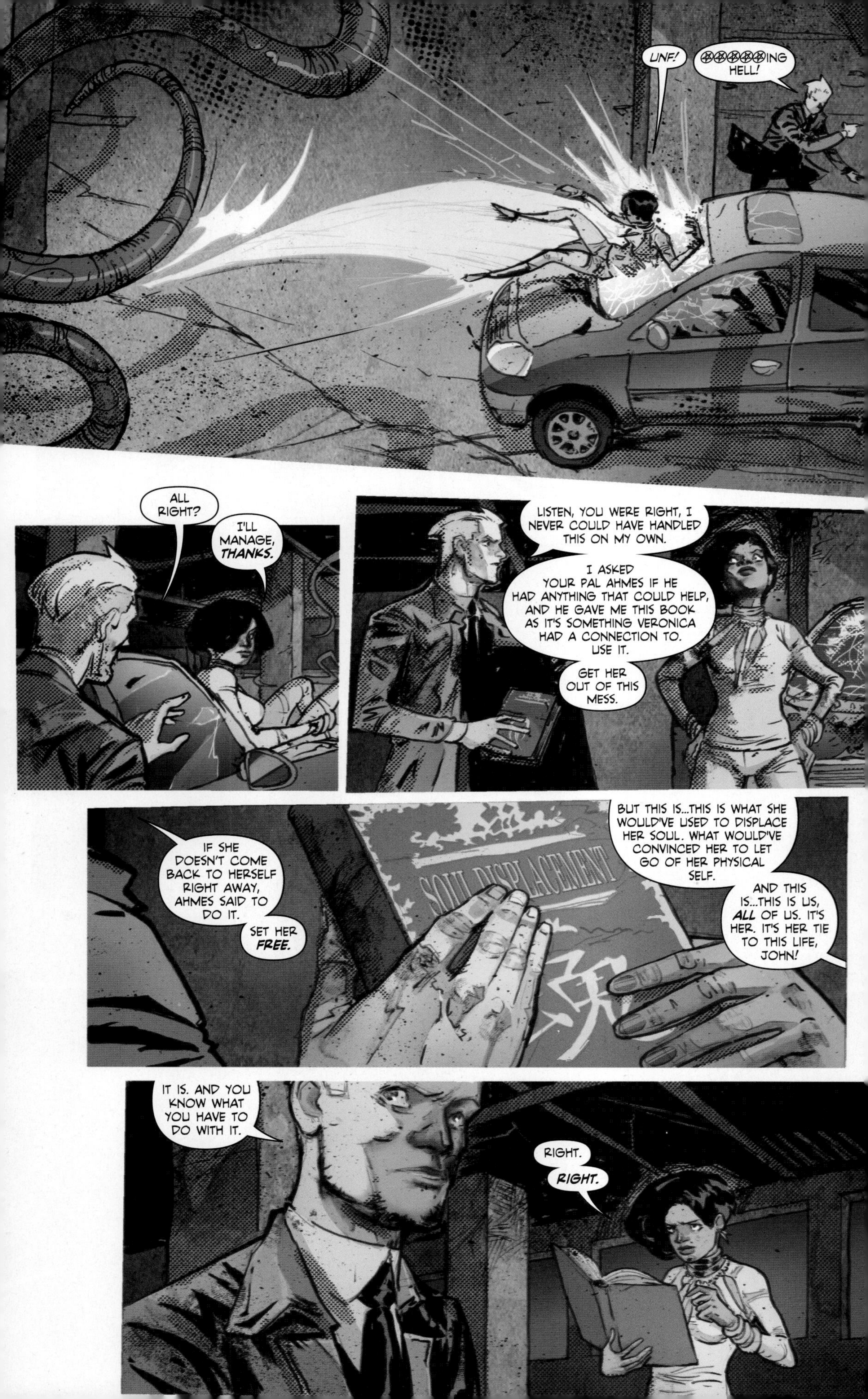
UNF!
⊗⊗⊗⊗⊗ING HELL!
ALL RIGHT?
I'LL MANAGE, THANKS.
LISTEN, YOU WERE RIGHT, I NEVER COULD HAVE HANDLED THIS ON MY OWN.
I ASKED YOUR PAL AHMES IF HE HAD ANYTHING THAT COULD HELP, AND HE GAVE ME THIS BOOK AS IT'S SOMETHING VERONICA HAD A CONNECTION TO. USE IT.
GET HER OUT OF THIS MESS.
IF SHE DOESN'T COME BACK TO HERSELF RIGHT AWAY, AHMES SAID TO DO IT.
SET HER FREE.
SOUL DISPLACEMENT
BUT THIS IS...THIS IS WHAT SHE WOULD'VE USED TO DISPLACE HER SOUL. WHAT WOULD'VE CONVINCED HER TO LET GO OF HER PHYSICAL SELF.
AND THIS IS...THIS IS US, ALL OF US. IT'S HER. IT'S HER TIE TO THIS LIFE, JOHN!
IT IS. AND YOU KNOW WHAT YOU HAVE TO DO WITH IT.
RIGHT. RIGHT.

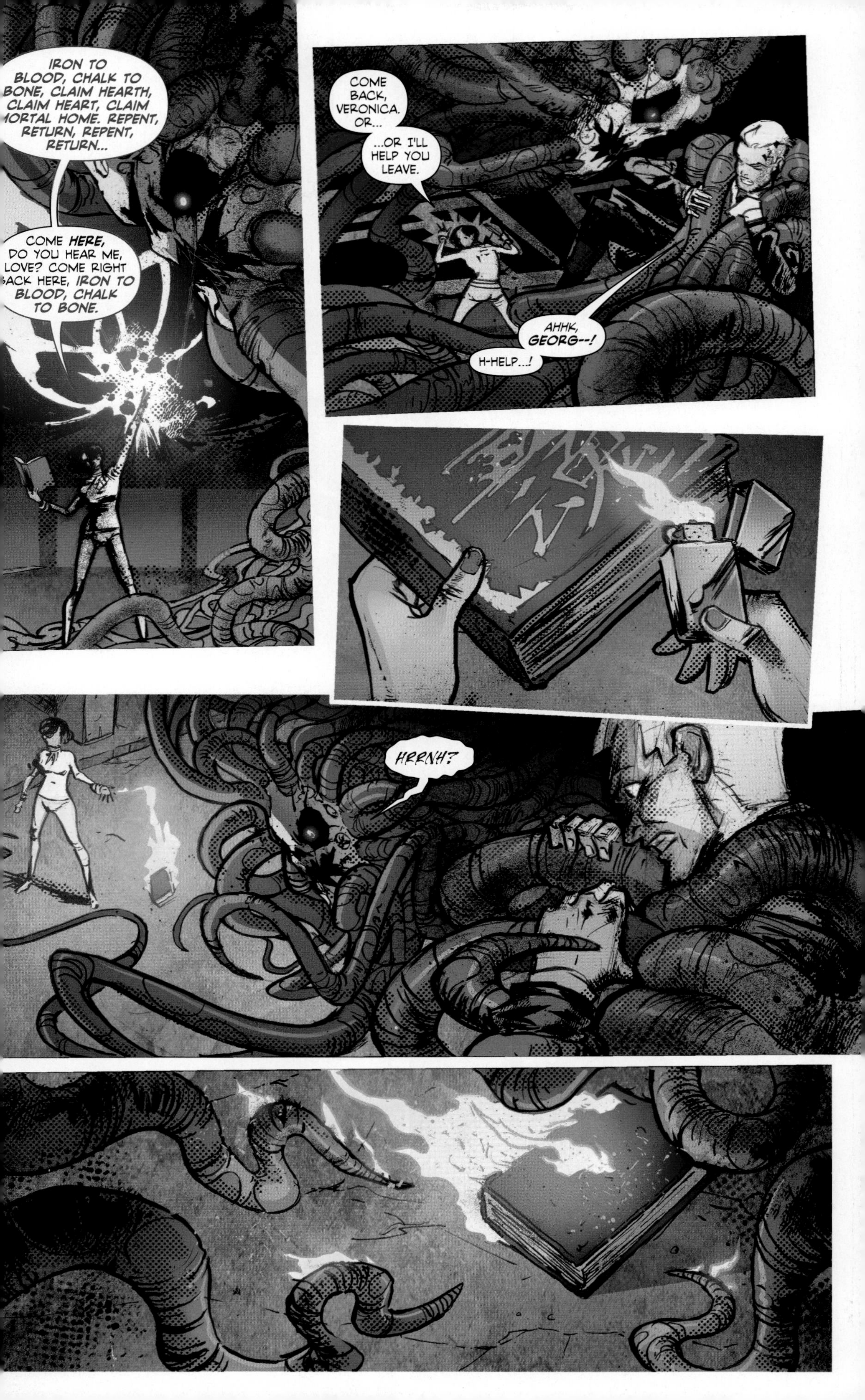

IRON TO BLOOD, CHALK TO BONE, CLAIM HEARTH, CLAIM HEART, CLAIM MORTAL HOME. REPENT, RETURN, REPENT, RETURN...
COME HERE, DO YOU HEAR ME, LOVE? COME RIGHT BACK HERE, IRON TO BLOOD, CHALK TO BONE.
COME BACK, VERONICA. OR...
...OR I'LL HELP YOU LEAVE.
AHHK, GEORG--!
H-HELP...!
HRRNH?

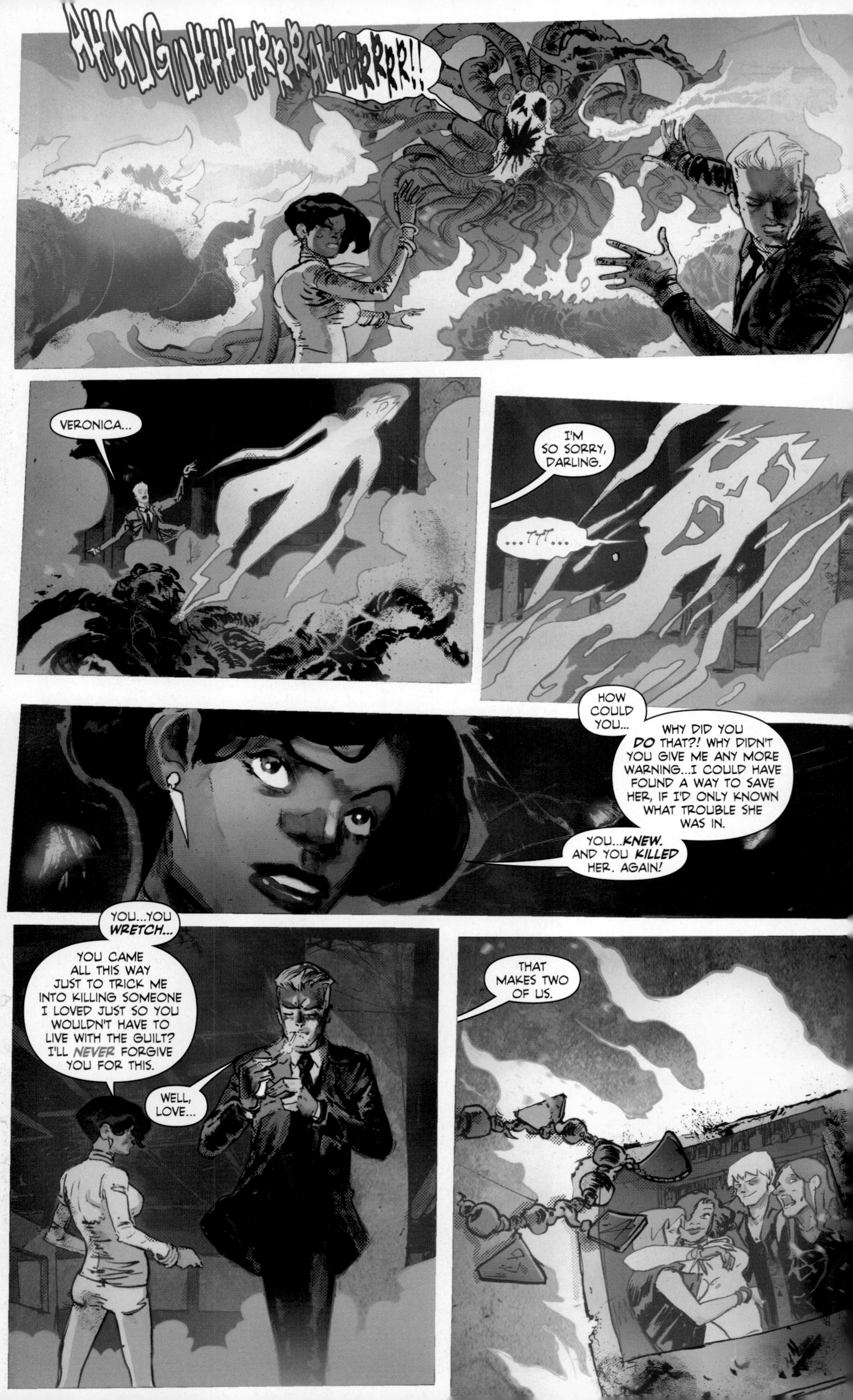
AHHADGIDHHHHRRRAHHHRRRR!!
VERONICA...
I'M SO SORRY, DARLING.
...TTT...
HOW COULD YOU...
WHY DID YOU **DO** THAT?! WHY DIDN'T YOU GIVE ME ANY MORE WARNING...I COULD HAVE FOUND A WAY TO SAVE HER, IF I'D ONLY KNOWN WHAT TROUBLE SHE WAS IN.
YOU...**KNEW.** AND YOU **KILLED** HER. AGAIN!
YOU...YOU **WRETCH...**
YOU CAME ALL THIS WAY JUST TO TRICK ME INTO KILLING SOMEONE I LOVED JUST SO YOU WOULDN'T HAVE TO LIVE WITH THE GUILT? I'LL **NEVER** FORGIVE YOU FOR THIS.
WELL, LOVE...
THAT MAKES TWO OF US.

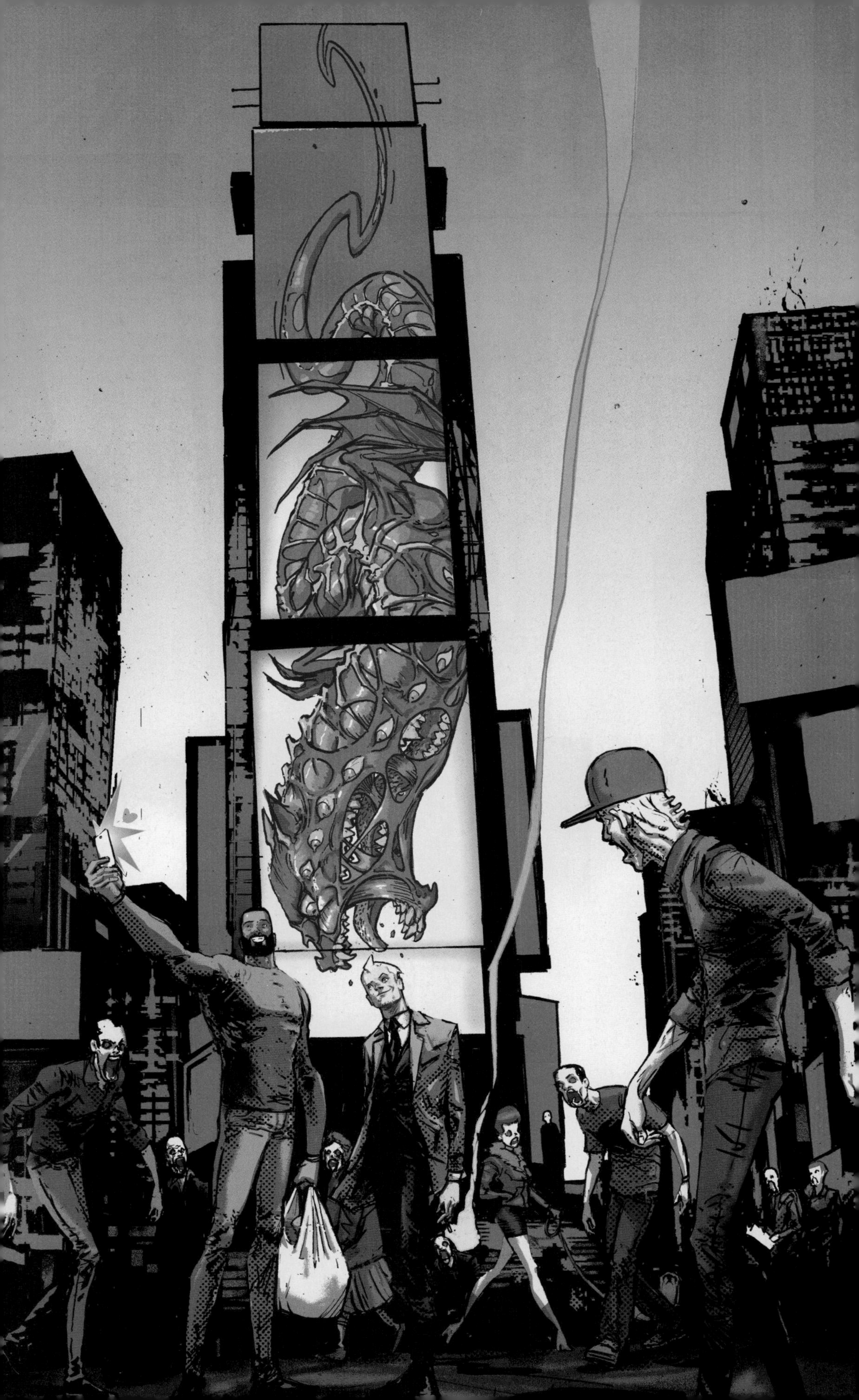

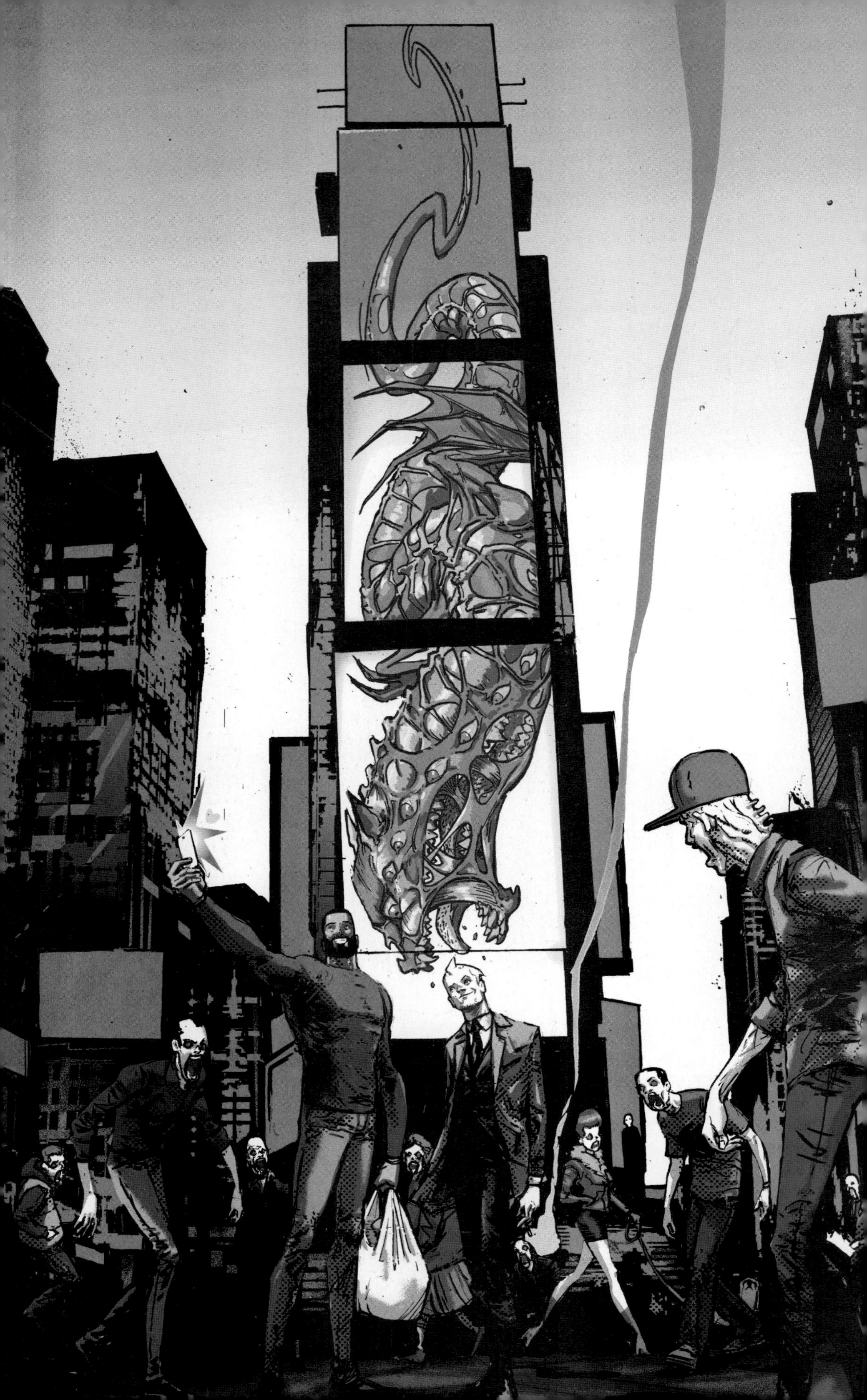

MISTER CONSTANTINE...
PLEASE BE HOME. I NEED YOUR HELP.
THE THING IN THE BASEMENT... IT'S BACK.
KNOCK KNOCK
GET A JOB
JAMES TYNION IV & MING DOYLE WRITERS
RILEY ROSSMO ART & COVER
IVAN PLASCENCIA COLORIST
TOM NAPOLITANO LETTERER

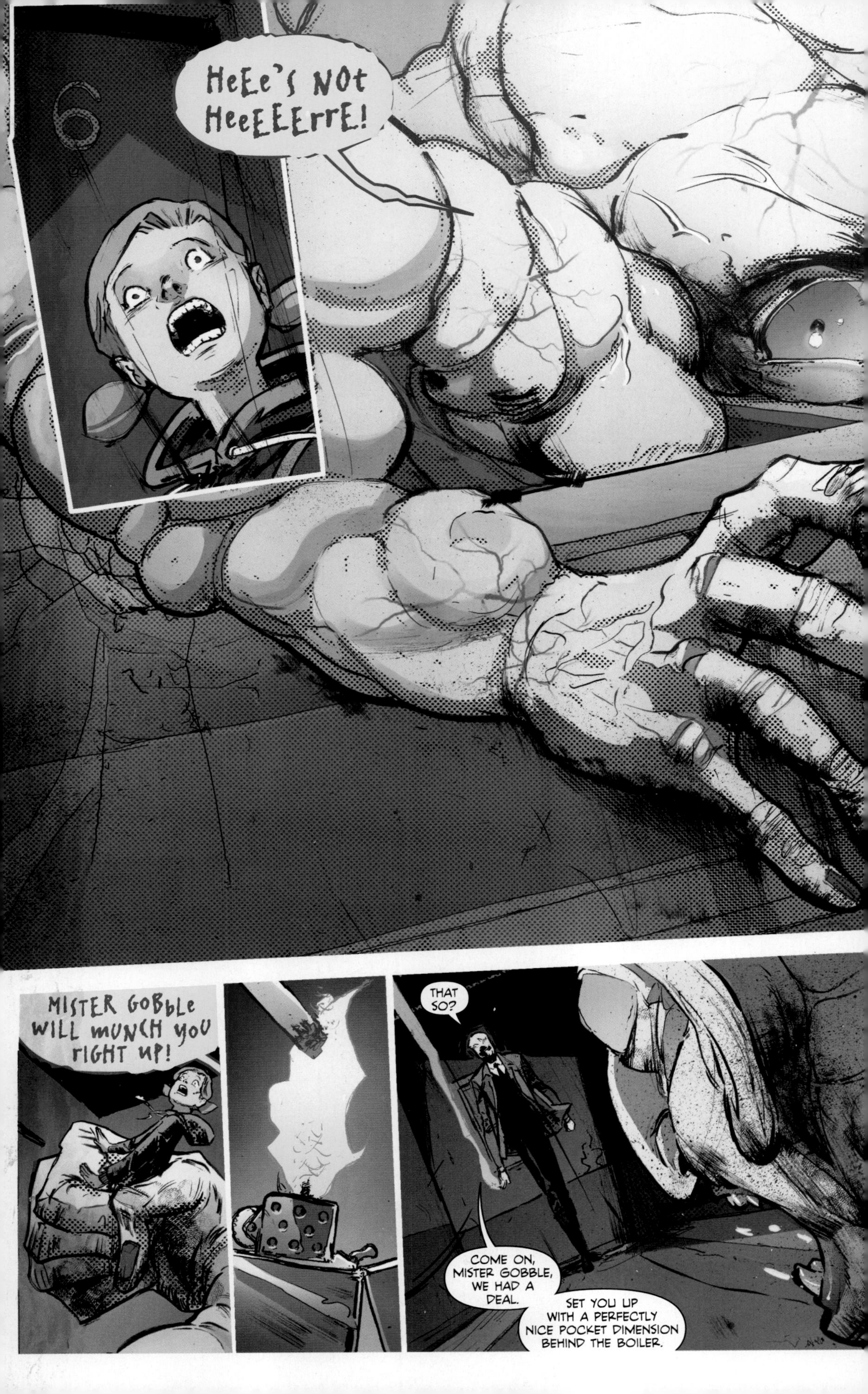
HeEe's NOt HeeEEErrE!
MISTER GOBbLe WILL mUNCH yOU rIGHT UP!
THAT SO?
COME ON, MISTER GOBBLE, WE HAD A DEAL.
SET YOU UP WITH A PERFECTLY NICE POCKET DIMENSION BEHIND THE BOILER.

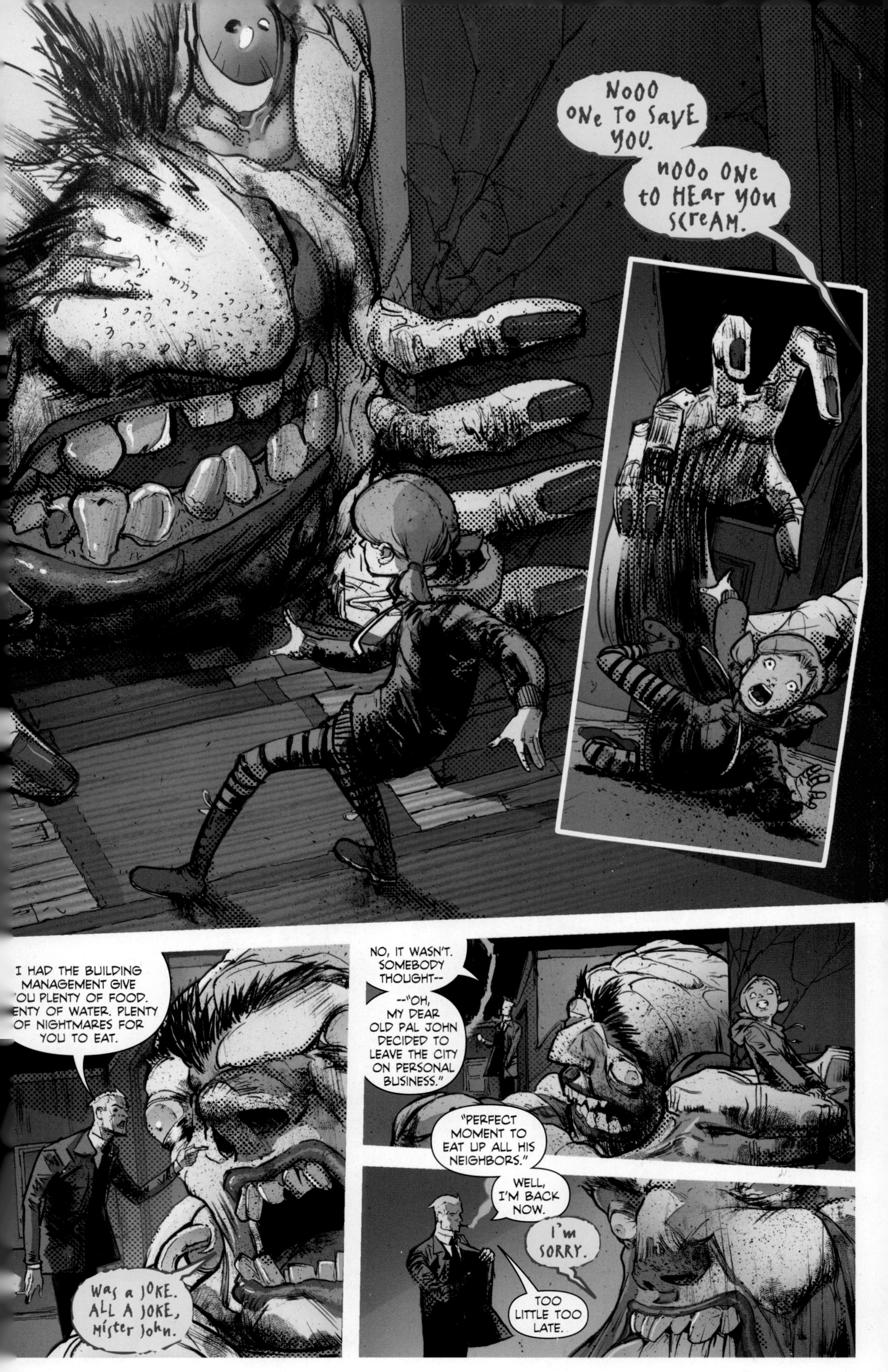

NOOO ONE TO SAVE YOU.
NOOO ONE TO HEAR YOU SCREAM.
I HAD THE BUILDING MANAGEMENT GIVE OU PLENTY OF FOOD. ENTY OF WATER. PLENTY OF NIGHTMARES FOR YOU TO EAT.
Was a JOKE. ALL A JOKE, Mister John.
NO, IT WASN'T. SOMEBODY THOUGHT--
--"OH, MY DEAR OLD PAL JOHN DECIDED TO LEAVE THE CITY ON PERSONAL BUSINESS."
"PERFECT MOMENT TO EAT UP ALL HIS NEIGHBORS."
WELL, I'M BACK NOW.
I'm SORRY.
TOO LITTLE TOO LATE.

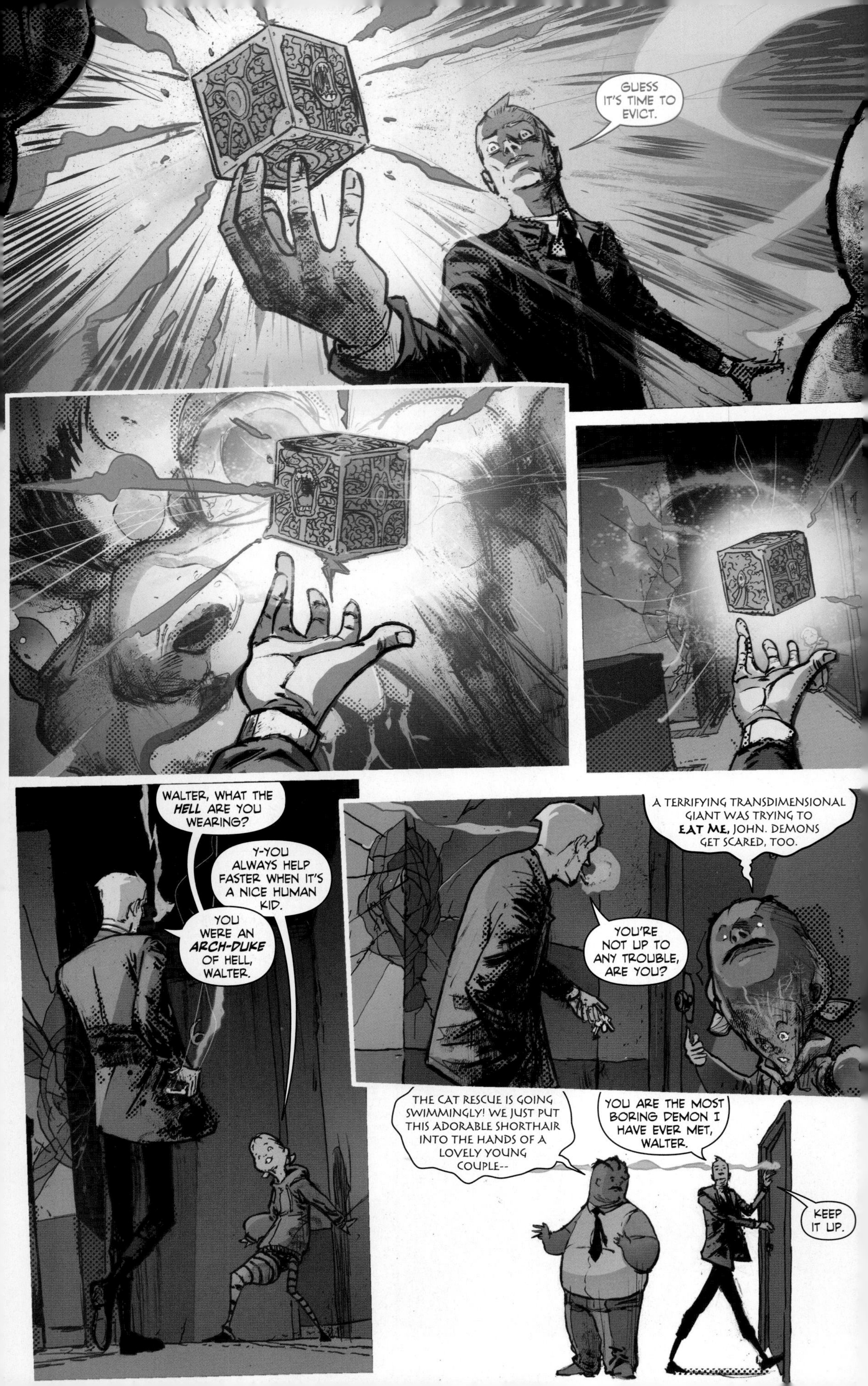
GUESS IT'S TIME TO EVICT.
WALTER, WHAT THE HELL ARE YOU WEARING?
Y-YOU ALWAYS HELP FASTER WHEN IT'S A NICE HUMAN KID.
YOU WERE AN ARCH-DUKE OF HELL, WALTER.
YOU'RE NOT UP TO ANY TROUBLE, ARE YOU?
A TERRIFYING TRANSDIMENSIONAL GIANT WAS TRYING TO EAT ME, JOHN. DEMONS GET SCARED, TOO.
THE CAT RESCUE IS GOING SWIMMINGLY! WE JUST PUT THIS ADORABLE SHORTHAIR INTO THE HANDS OF A LOVELY YOUNG COUPLE--
YOU ARE THE MOST BORING DEMON I HAVE EVER MET, WALTER.
KEEP IT UP.

IT HAPPENS EVERY TIME YOU SLIP AWAY FOR A SPELL. YOU GET BACK HOME AND YOUR LITTLE CORNER OF THE WORLD HAS KEPT MOVING ON WITHOUT YOU.

YOU WANT TO EASE IN, SLOWLY, BUT EVERYTHING AROUND YOU IS JUST BARRELING INTO THE DISTANCE. AND THE RESPONSIBILITIES JUST KEEP PILING UP.

MOMENTS LIKE THESE, FEELS LIKE THE UNIVERSE IS TRYING TO REMIND YOU THAT IT'S GOT A PLAN FOR YOU, AND IF YOU SLIPPED OUT OF THAT PLAN FOR JUST A SECOND, IT'S GOING TO ⊗⊗⊗⊗ YOU AS HARD AS IT CAN TO MAKE SURE YOU DON'T DO IT AGAIN.

SO THE BEST OPTION IS TO THROW OFF YOUR DIRTY CLOTHES AND LOUNGE LIKE A MONSTER AS LONG AS YOU CAN.

I COULD USE A BREATHER. JUST LAY IN FRONT OF THE TV, CATCH UP ON THE LATEST SEASON OF WHATEVER THE HELL THE PLEBES ARE WATCHING THESE DAYS.

...FRE IN MY FLAT.

ALONE WITH MY THOUGHTS.

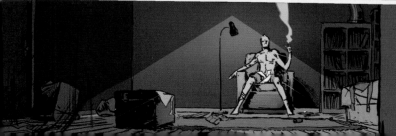

ALONE LIKE I HAVEN'T REALLY BEEN IN YEARS...

WITHOUT MY GHOSTS.

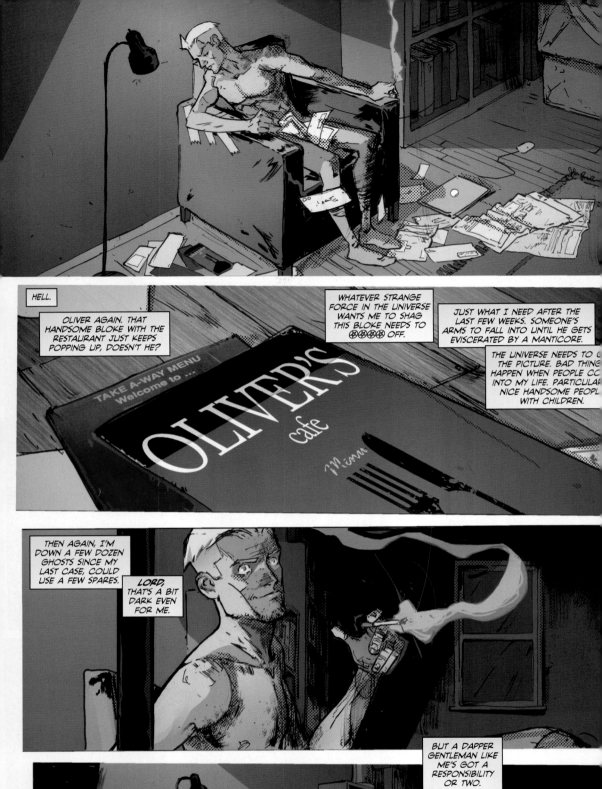

HELL.

OLIVER AGAIN. THAT HANDSOME BLOKE WITH THE RESTAURANT JUST KEEPS POPPING UP, DOESN'T HE?

WHATEVER STRANGE FORCE IN THE UNIVERSE WANTS ME TO SHAG THIS BLOKE NEEDS TO ⊗⊗⊗⊗ OFF.

JUST WHAT I NEED AFTER THE LAST FEW WEEKS. SOMEONE'S ARMS TO FALL INTO UNTIL HE GETS EVISCERATED BY A MANTICORE.

THE UNIVERSE NEEDS TO ~ THE PICTURE. BAD THING HAPPEN WHEN PEOPLE C~ INTO MY LIFE. PARTICULAR NICE HANDSOME PEOPL~ WITH CHILDREN.

TAKE A-WAY MENU
Welcome to ...
OLIVER'S cafe
Menu

THEN AGAIN, I'M DOWN A FEW DOZEN GHOSTS SINCE MY LAST CASE, COULD USE A FEW SPARES.

LORD, THAT'S A BIT DARK EVEN FOR ME.

BUT A DAPPER GENTLEMAN LIKE ME'S GOT A RESPONSIBILITY OR TWO.

IT'S ACTUALLY A BIT EASIER TO PAY RENT LEGITIMATELY THAN IT IS TO MAGICALLY REWRITE THE LANDLORD'S BRAIN TO THINK IT'S ALREADY PAID.

NOW, I DON'T CARE MUCH FOR THE TECH SIDE OF THINGS. WHEN MY SCHOOLMATES WERE LOOKING FOR PORN ON THEIR FIRST HOME P.C.S, I WAS OUT TRYING TO SUMMON MINOR DEMONS TO TEACH ME ALL THE RIGHT PICKUP LINES.

YOU FALL INTO ONE PART OF THE WORLD TOO HARD AND IT MAKES IT HARD TO CONNECT TOO MUCH WITH THE OTHERS. MAGIC AND TECHNOLOGY ARE A BIT LIKE OIL AND WATER. THEY DON'T QUITE BLEND.

(THAT SAID, I RAN THAT THOUGHT PAST A PAIR OF GOBLINS RUNNING A TECH START-UP IN TRIBECA, AND THEY JUST SAID I'M "SMALL-MINDED" AND AN "IDIOT".)

GUY I WAS SEEING MADE ME GET A SMARTPHONE FOR THE FIRST TIME LAST YEAR. HE ALSO LOOKED AT THE AD I HAD RUNNING IN THE BACK OF A FEW LOCAL PAPERS AND LAUGHED RIGHT IN MY FACE.

kregslist.com

Suggested Website

kregslist: New York area careers, condos, classifieds, sales, opportunities...

kregslist.com

Look for "kregslist.com"

SAID IF I WANTED WORK, EVEN WORK OF THE CREEPY-CRAWLY VARIETY, I NEEDED TO JOIN THE REST OF THEM IN THE 21ST CENTURY.

BIT OF AN ASSHOLE, REALLY. NOT THE BEST LAY, EITHER. BUT NICE SHOULDERS.

VERY HANDSOME EXORCIST, WILL SOLVE SPOOKIEST PROBLEMS

Monster hiding under your bed? Gremlins chewing through your walls? Daughter crawling on the ceiling cursing you out in a forgotten tongue? If you have the need for an expert in the paranormal, there is no better choice in the tri-state area than JOHN CONSTANTINE.

COST VARIES PER JOB. PLEASE INQUIRE.

AND 64 INQUIRIES. MORE THAN USUAL, BUT SOUNDS JUST LIKE WHAT GOOD OLD JOHN NEEDS.

NO TIME FOR SLEEP. NO TIME FOR THE UNIVERSE AND WHATEVER IT'S GOT UP ITS SLEEVES FOR ME.

IT'S TIME TO GET TO WORK...

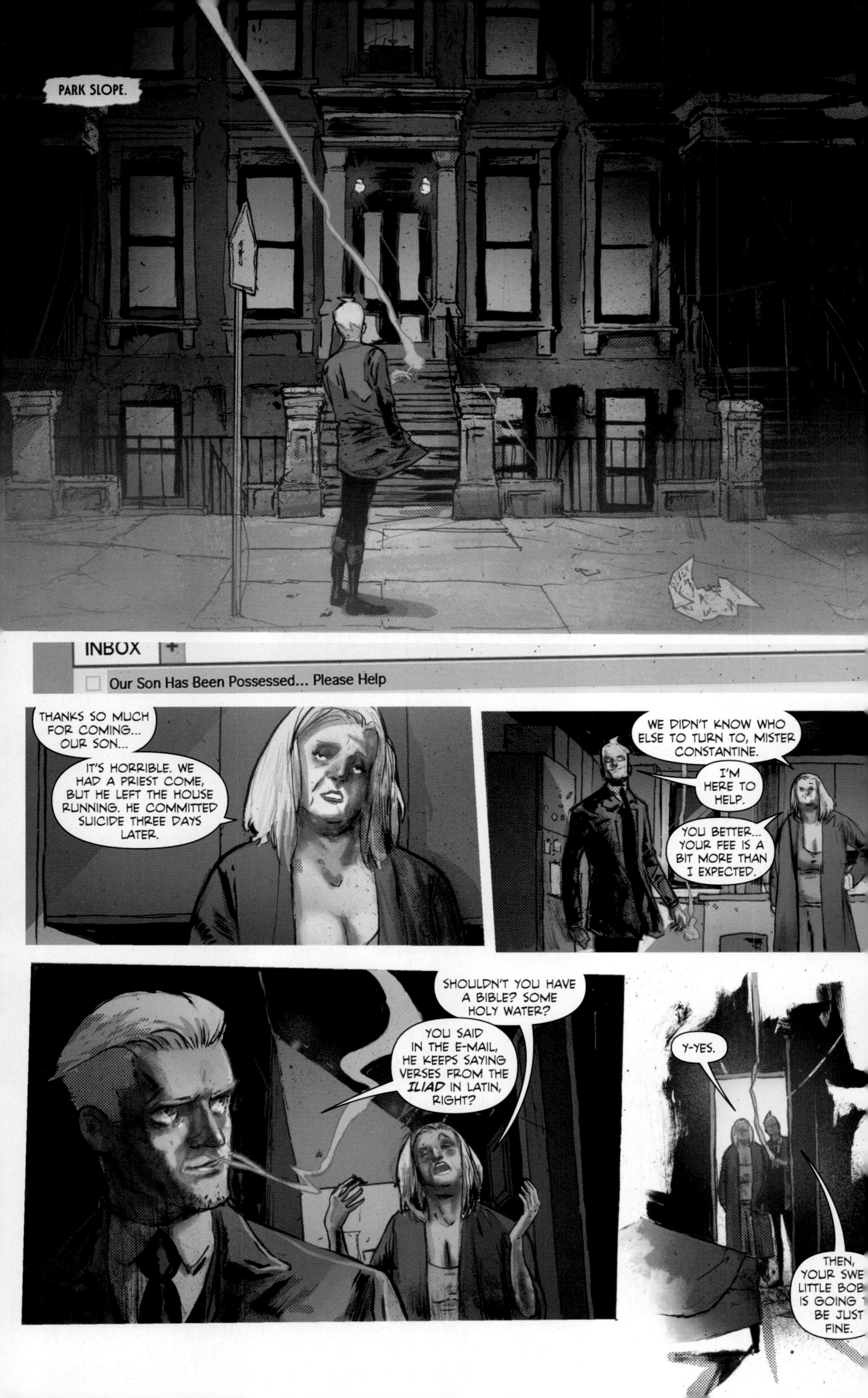
PARK SLOPE.
INBOX
Our Son Has Been Possessed... Please Help
THANKS SO MUCH FOR COMING... OUR SON...
IT'S HORRIBLE. WE HAD A PRIEST COME, BUT HE LEFT THE HOUSE RUNNING. HE COMMITTED SUICIDE THREE DAYS LATER.
WE DIDN'T KNOW WHO ELSE TO TURN TO, MISTER CONSTANTINE.
I'M HERE TO HELP.
YOU BETTER... YOUR FEE IS A BIT MORE THAN I EXPECTED.
SHOULDN'T YOU HAVE A BIBLE? SOME HOLY WATER?
YOU SAID IN THE E-MAIL, HE KEEPS SAYING VERSES FROM THE *ILIAD* IN LATIN, RIGHT?
Y-YES.
THEN, YOUR SWE LITTLE BOB IS GOING BE JUST FINE.

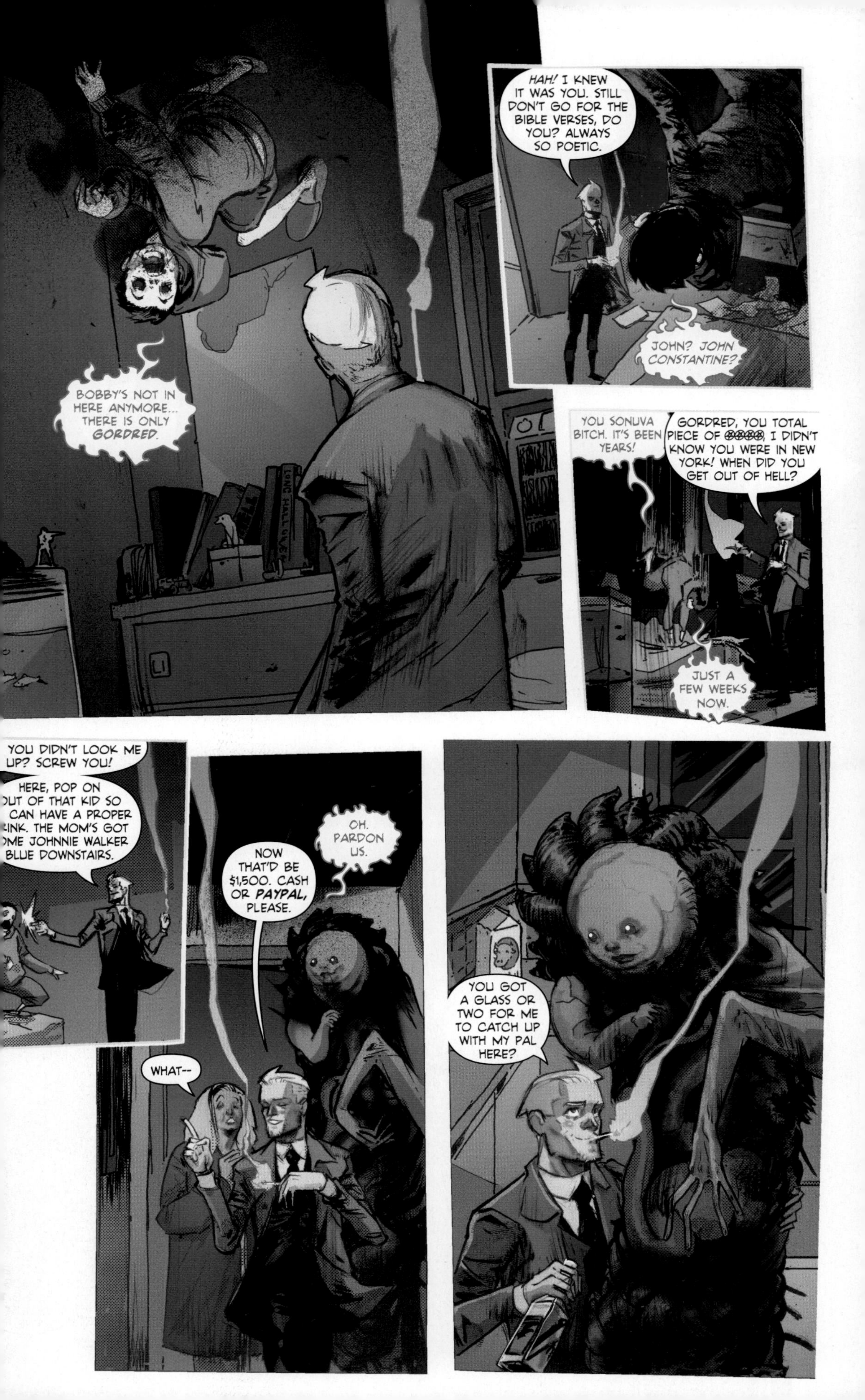
BOBBY'S NOT IN HERE ANYMORE... THERE IS ONLY GORDRED.
HAH! I KNEW IT WAS YOU. STILL DON'T GO FOR THE BIBLE VERSES, DO YOU? ALWAYS SO POETIC.
JOHN? JOHN CONSTANTINE?
YOU SONUVA BITCH. IT'S BEEN YEARS!
GORDRED, YOU TOTAL PIECE OF ⊗⊗⊗⊗, I DIDN'T KNOW YOU WERE IN NEW YORK! WHEN DID YOU GET OUT OF HELL?
JUST A FEW WEEKS NOW.
YOU DIDN'T LOOK ME UP? SCREW YOU!
HERE, POP ON OUT OF THAT KID SO CAN HAVE A PROPER RINK. THE MOM'S GOT OME JOHNNIE WALKER BLUE DOWNSTAIRS.
NOW THAT'D BE $1,500. CASH OR PAYPAL, PLEASE.
OH. PARDON US.
WHAT--
YOU GOT A GLASS OR TWO FOR ME TO CATCH UP WITH MY PAL HERE?

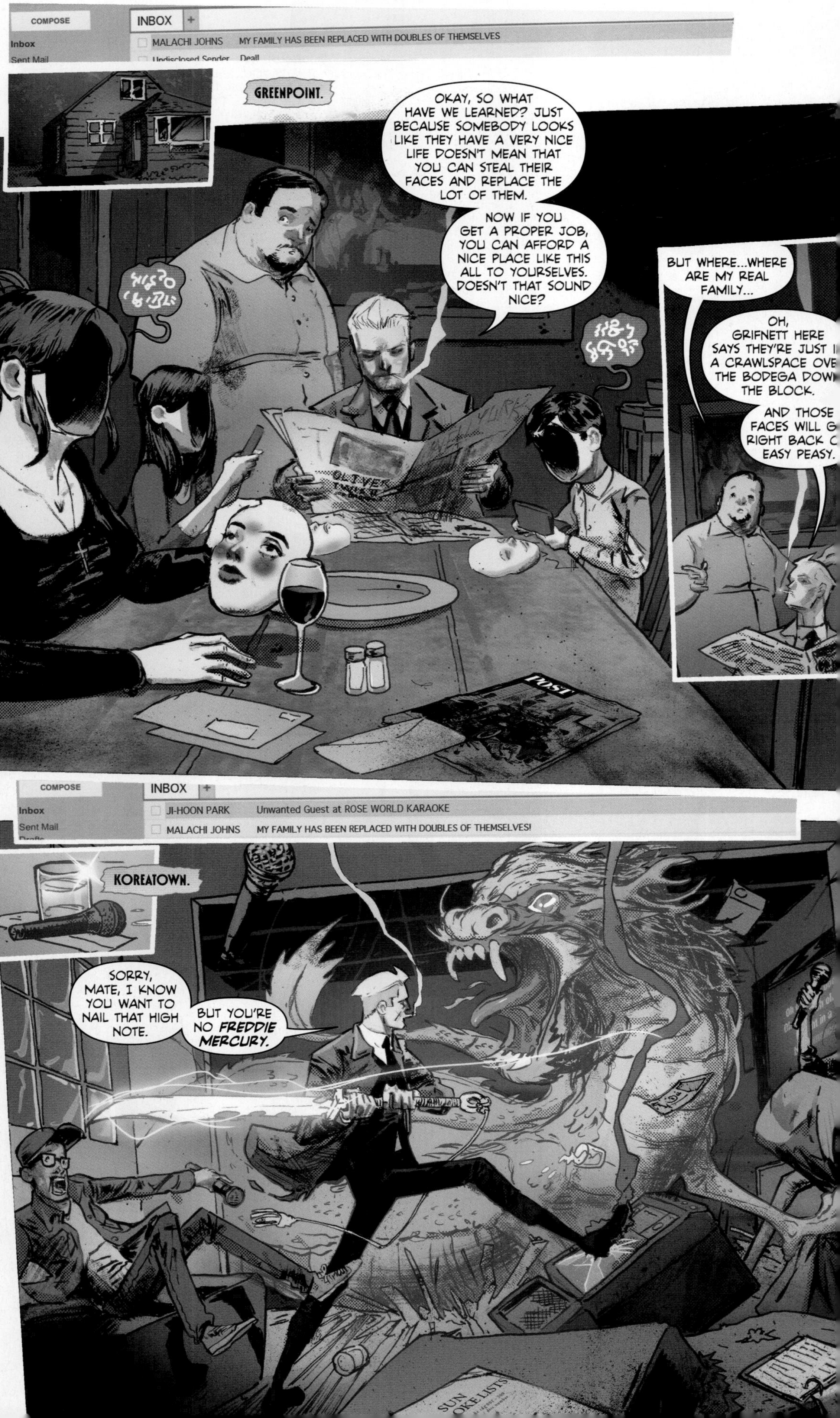
COMPOSE
INBOX
Inbox
Sent Mail
MALACHI JOHNS MY FAMILY HAS BEEN REPLACED WITH DOUBLES OF THEMSELVES
Undisclosed Sender Deal!
GREENPOINT.
OKAY, SO WHAT HAVE WE LEARNED? JUST BECAUSE SOMEBODY LOOKS LIKE THEY HAVE A VERY NICE LIFE DOESN'T MEAN THAT YOU CAN STEAL THEIR FACES AND REPLACE THE LOT OF THEM.
NOW IF YOU GET A PROPER JOB, YOU CAN AFFORD A NICE PLACE LIKE THIS ALL TO YOURSELVES. DOESN'T THAT SOUND NICE?
BUT WHERE...WHERE ARE MY REAL FAMILY...
OH, GRIFNETT HERE SAYS THEY'RE JUST I A CRAWLSPACE OVE THE BODEGA DOW THE BLOCK.
AND THOSE FACES WILL G RIGHT BACK C EASY PEASY.
POST
COMPOSE
INBOX
Inbox
Sent Mail
JI-HOON PARK Unwanted Guest at ROSE WORLD KARAOKE
MALACHI JOHNS MY FAMILY HAS BEEN REPLACED WITH DOUBLES OF THEMSELVES!
KOREATOWN.
SORRY, MATE, I KNOW YOU WANT TO NAIL THAT HIGH NOTE.
BUT YOU'RE NO *FREDDIE MERCURY.*

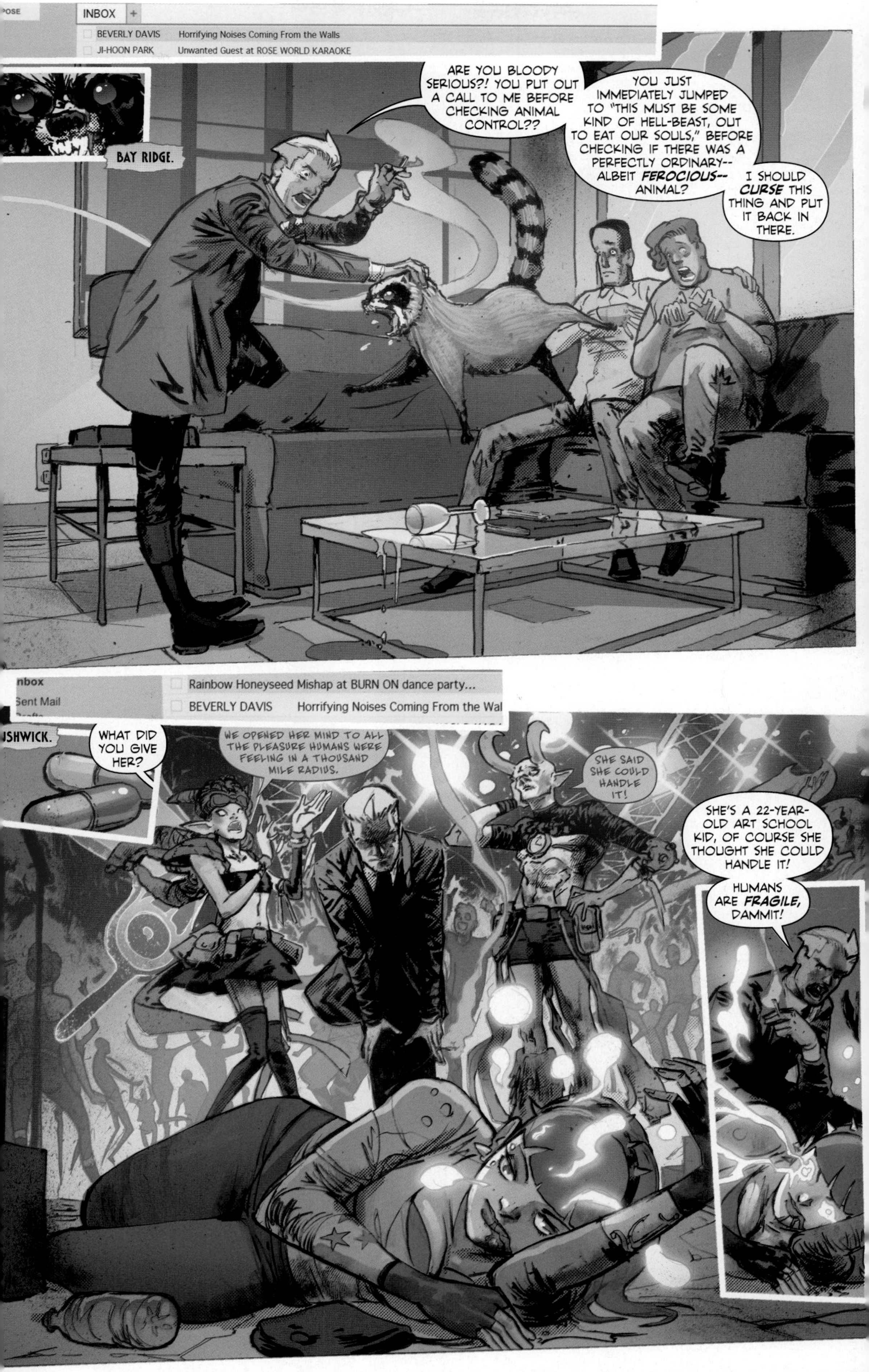
INBOX
BEVERLY DAVIS Horrifying Noises Coming From the Walls
JI-HOON PARK Unwanted Guest at ROSE WORLD KARAOKE
BAY RIDGE.
ARE YOU BLOODY SERIOUS?! YOU PUT OUT A CALL TO ME BEFORE CHECKING ANIMAL CONTROL??
YOU JUST IMMEDIATELY JUMPED TO "THIS MUST BE SOME KIND OF HELL-BEAST, OUT TO EAT OUR SOULS," BEFORE CHECKING IF THERE WAS A PERFECTLY ORDINARY-- ALBEIT FEROCIOUS-- ANIMAL?
I SHOULD CURSE THIS THING AND PUT IT BACK IN THERE.
Rainbow Honeyseed Mishap at BURN ON dance party...
Sent Mail
BEVERLY DAVIS Horrifying Noises Coming From the Wal
WHAT DID YOU GIVE HER?
WE OPENED HER MIND TO ALL THE PLEASURE HUMANS WERE FEELING IN A THOUSAND MILE RADIUS.
SHE SAID SHE COULD HANDLE IT!
SHE'S A 22-YEAR-OLD ART SCHOOL KID, OF COURSE SHE THOUGHT SHE COULD HANDLE IT!
HUMANS ARE FRAGILE, DAMMIT!

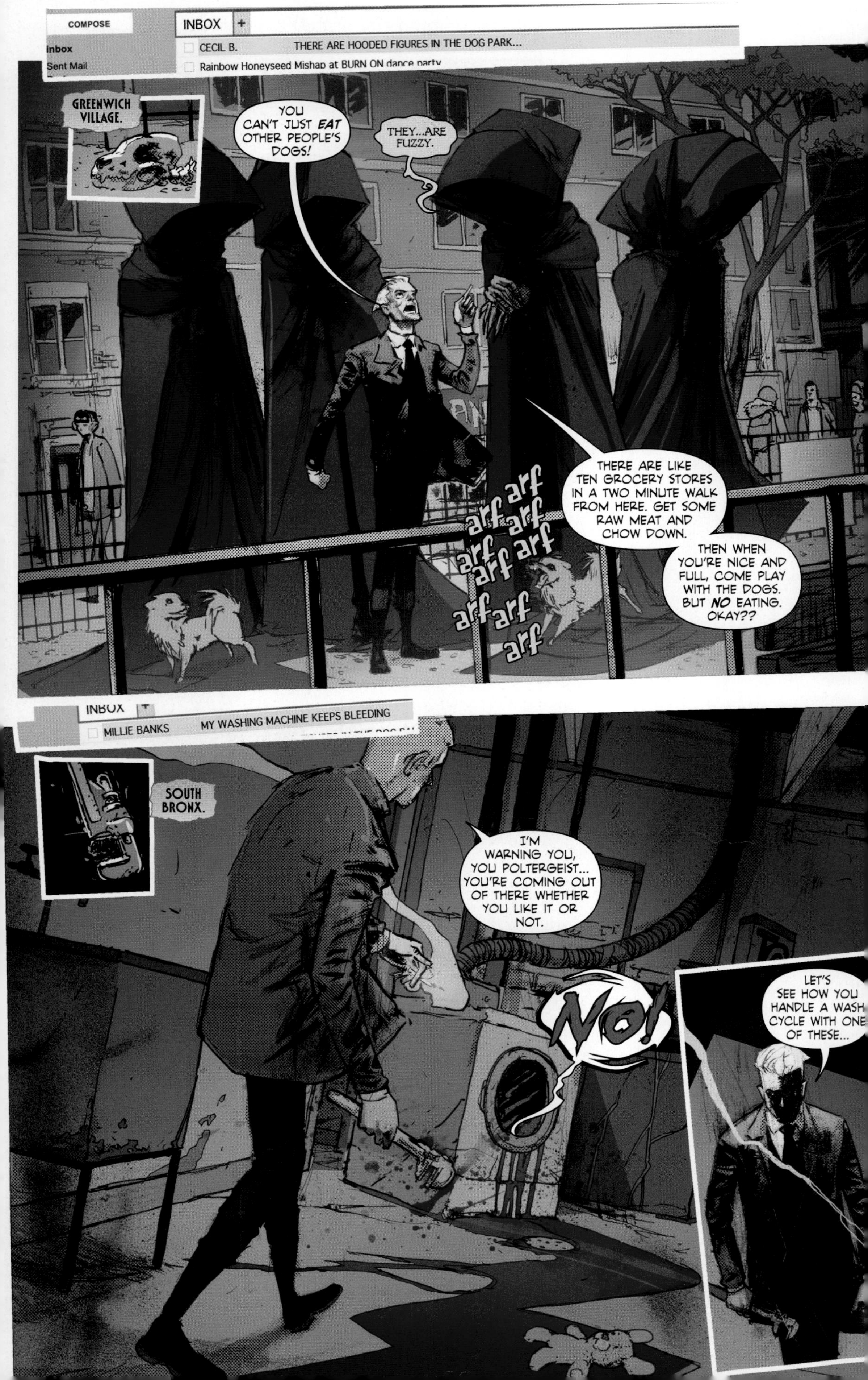
COMPOSE
INBOX
+
Inbox
Sent Mail
CECIL B.
THERE ARE HOODED FIGURES IN THE DOG PARK...
Rainbow Honeyseed Mishap at BURN ON dance party
GREENWICH VILLAGE.
YOU CAN'T JUST EAT OTHER PEOPLE'S DOGS!
THEY...ARE FUZZY.
THERE ARE LIKE TEN GROCERY STORES IN A TWO MINUTE WALK FROM HERE. GET SOME RAW MEAT AND CHOW DOWN.
arf arf arf arf arf arf arf arf arf arf arf
THEN WHEN YOU'RE NICE AND FULL, COME PLAY WITH THE DOGS. BUT NO EATING. OKAY??
INBOX
+
MILLIE BANKS
MY WASHING MACHINE KEEPS BLEEDING
SOUTH BRONX.
I'M WARNING YOU, YOU POLTERGEIST... YOU'RE COMING OUT OF THERE WHETHER YOU LIKE IT OR NOT.
NO!
LET'S SEE HOW YOU HANDLE A WASH CYCLE WITH ONE OF THESE...

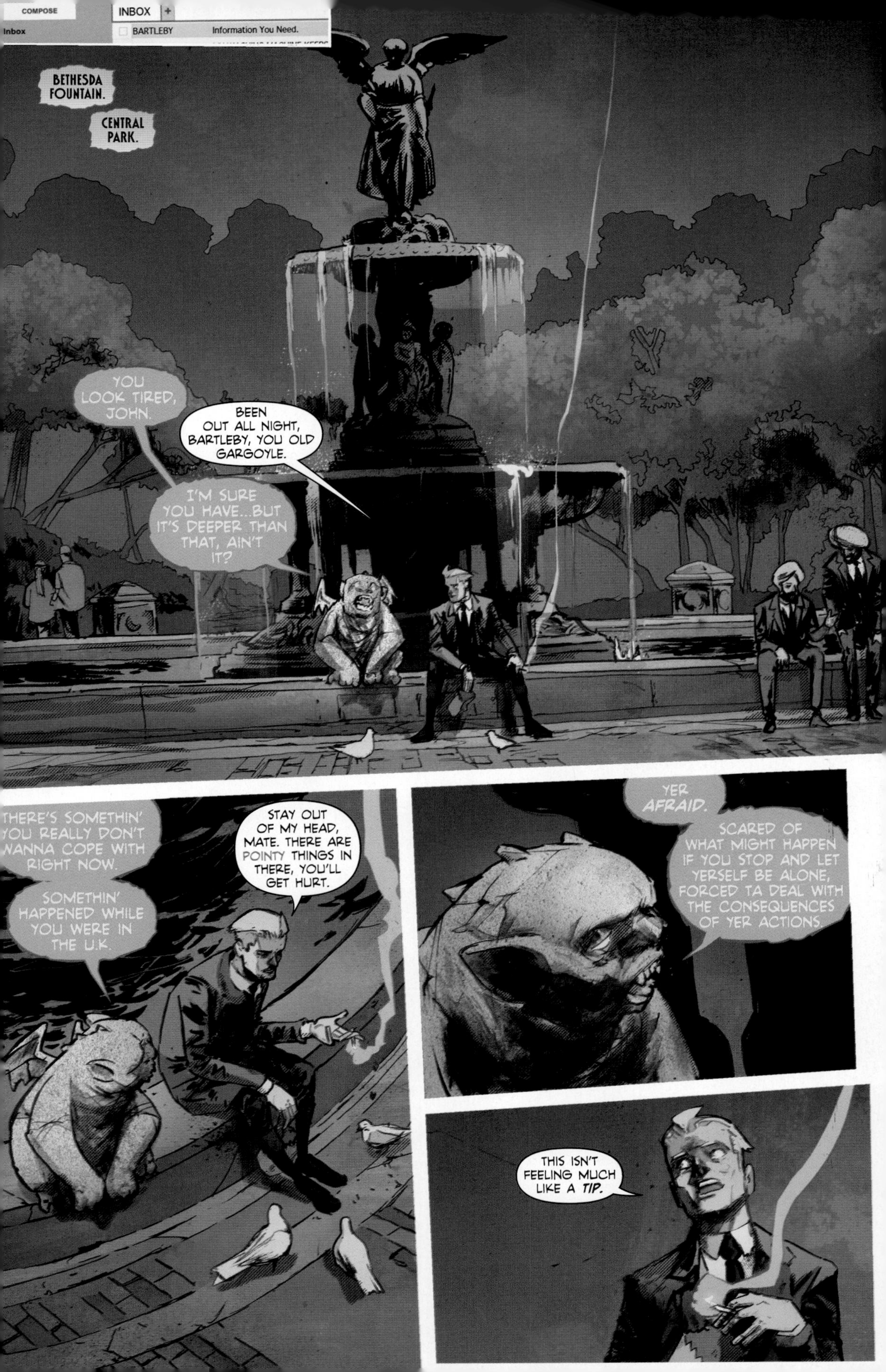
COMPOSE
INBOX
Inbox
BARTLEBY
Information You Need.
BETHESDA FOUNTAIN.
CENTRAL PARK.
YOU LOOK TIRED, JOHN.
BEEN OUT ALL NIGHT, BARTLEBY, YOU OLD GARGOYLE.
I'M SURE YOU HAVE...BUT IT'S DEEPER THAN THAT, AIN'T IT?
THERE'S SOMETHIN' YOU REALLY DON'T WANNA COPE WITH RIGHT NOW.
SOMETHIN' HAPPENED WHILE YOU WERE IN THE U.K.
STAY OUT OF MY HEAD, MATE. THERE ARE POINTY THINGS IN THERE, YOU'LL GET HURT.
YER AFRAID.
SCARED OF WHAT MIGHT HAPPEN IF YOU STOP AND LET YERSELF BE ALONE, FORCED TA DEAL WITH THE CONSEQUENCES OF YER ACTIONS.
THIS ISN'T FEELING MUCH LIKE A TIP.

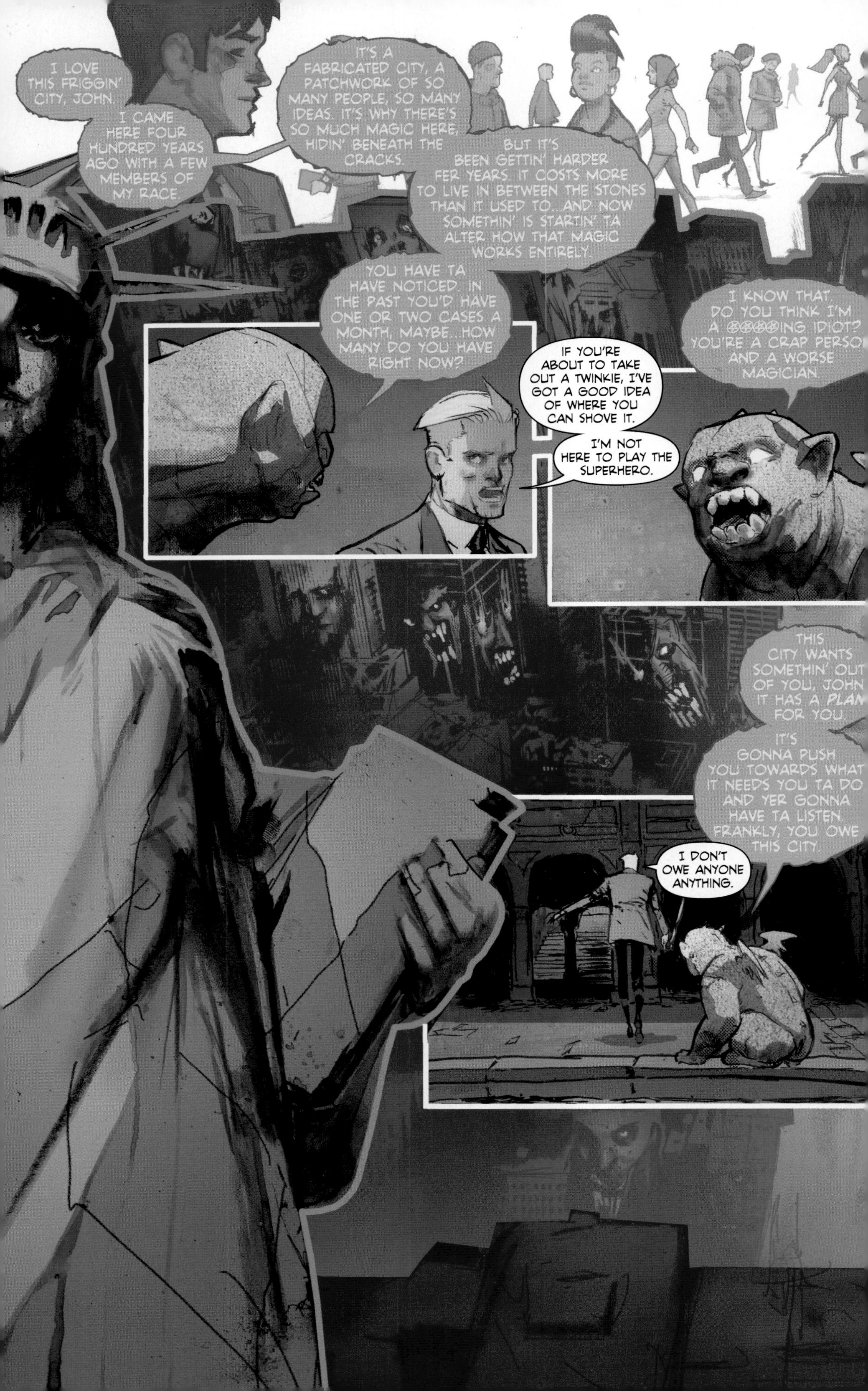

I LOVE THIS FRIGGIN' CITY, JOHN.
I CAME HERE FOUR HUNDRED YEARS AGO WITH A FEW MEMBERS OF MY RACE.
IT'S A FABRICATED CITY, A PATCHWORK OF SO MANY PEOPLE, SO MANY IDEAS. IT'S WHY THERE'S SO MUCH MAGIC HERE, HIDIN' BENEATH THE CRACKS.
BUT IT'S BEEN GETTIN' HARDER FER YEARS. IT COSTS MORE TO LIVE IN BETWEEN THE STONES THAN IT USED TO...AND NOW SOMETHIN' IS STARTIN' TA ALTER HOW THAT MAGIC WORKS ENTIRELY.
YOU HAVE TA HAVE NOTICED. IN THE PAST YOU'D HAVE ONE OR TWO CASES A MONTH, MAYBE...HOW MANY DO YOU HAVE RIGHT NOW?
IF YOU'RE ABOUT TO TAKE OUT A TWINKIE, I'VE GOT A GOOD IDEA OF WHERE YOU CAN SHOVE IT.
I'M NOT HERE TO PLAY THE SUPERHERO.
I KNOW THAT. DO YOU THINK I'M A ⊛⊛⊛⊛ING IDIOT? YOU'RE A CRAP PERSO AND A WORSE MAGICIAN.
THIS CITY WANTS SOMETHIN' OUT OF YOU, JOHN IT HAS A *PLAN* FOR YOU.
IT'S GONNA PUSH YOU TOWARDS WHAT IT NEEDS YOU TA DO AND YER GONNA HAVE TA LISTEN. FRANKLY, YOU OWE THIS CITY.
I DON'T OWE ANYONE ANYTHING.

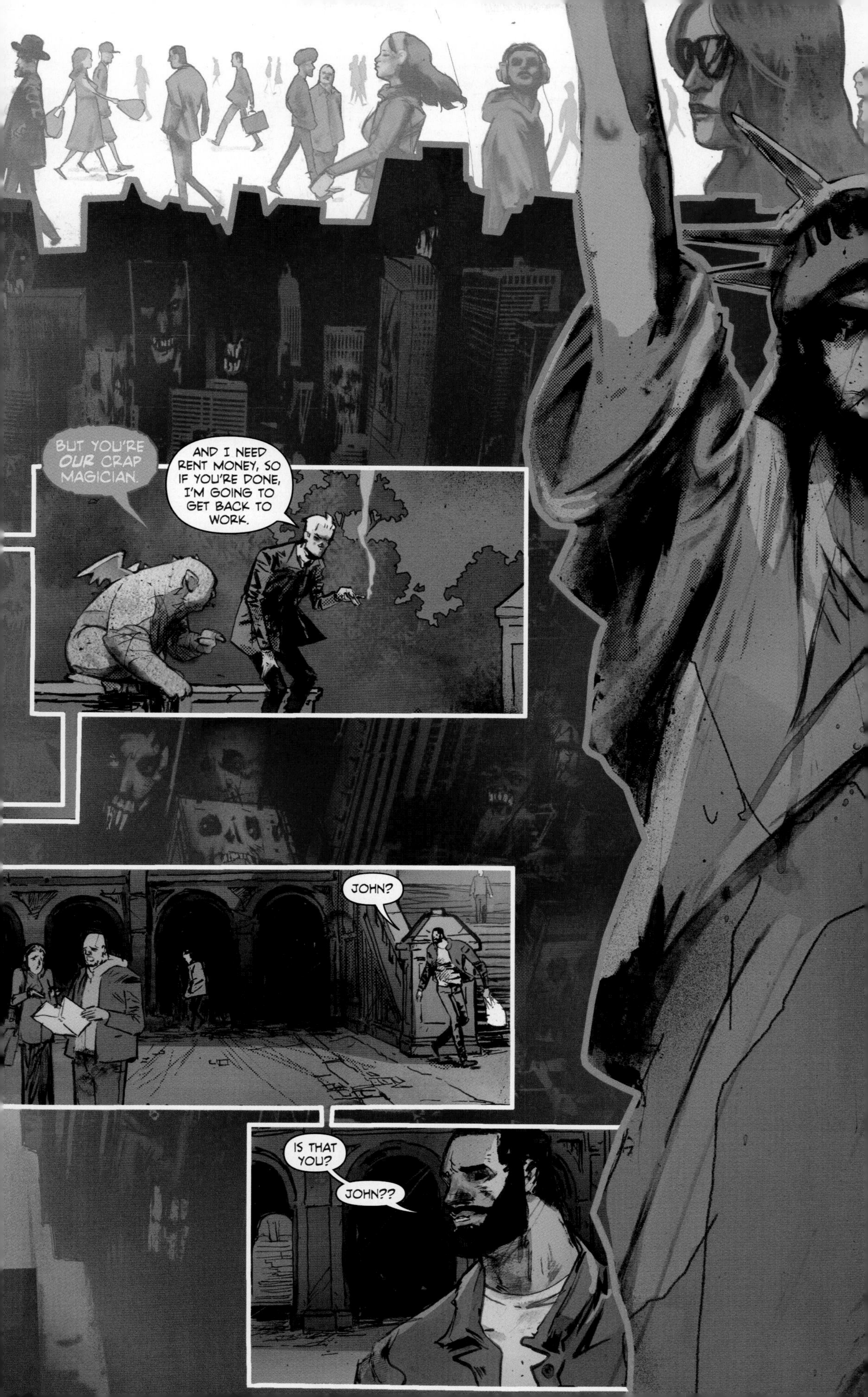
BUT YOU'RE *OUR* CRAP MAGICIAN.
AND I NEED RENT MONEY, SO IF YOU'RE DONE, I'M GOING TO GET BACK TO WORK.
JOHN?
IS THAT YOU?
JOHN??

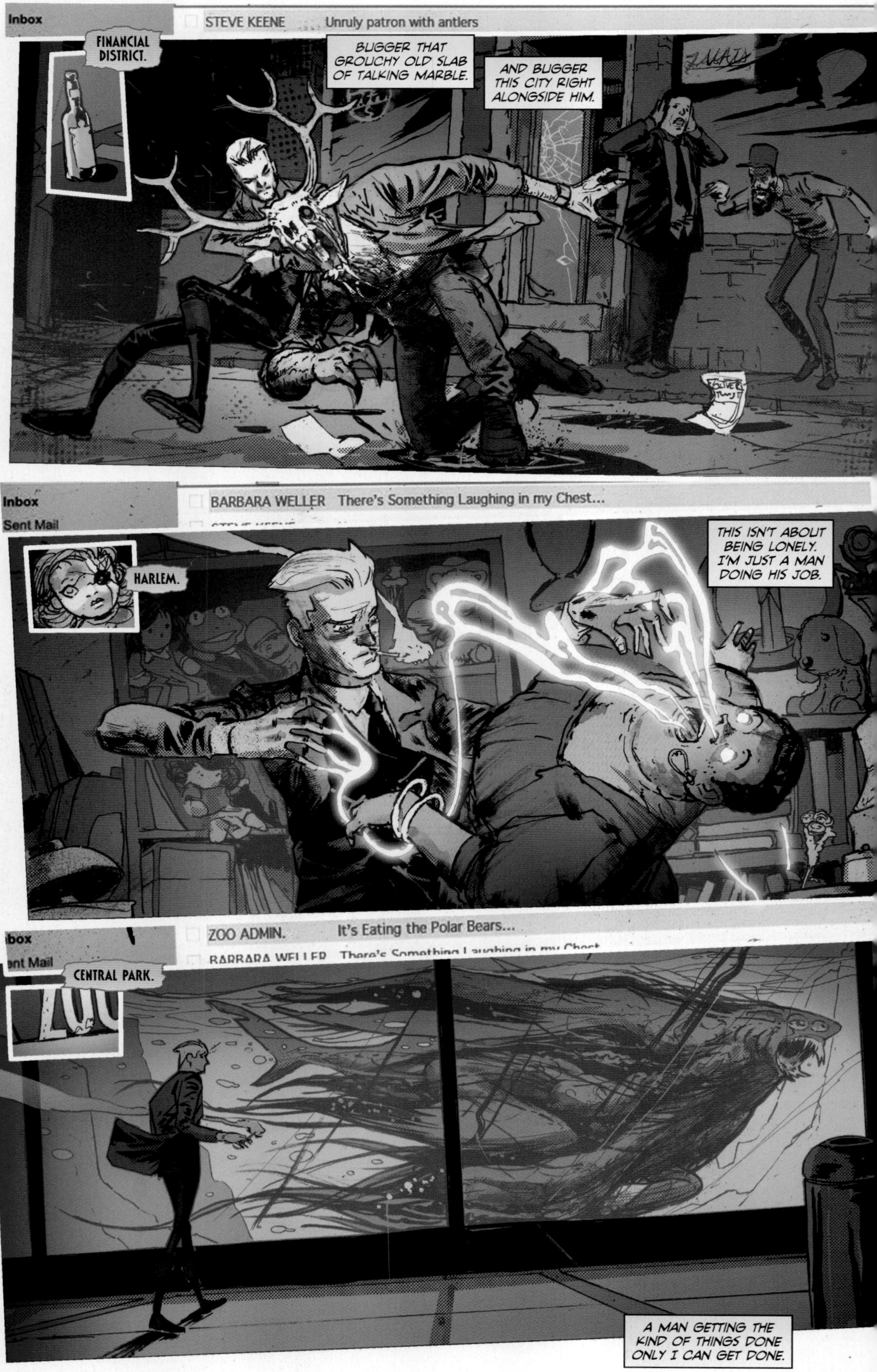
Inbox
STEVE KEENE Unruly patron with antlers
FINANCIAL DISTRICT.
BUGGER THAT GROUCHY OLD SLAB OF TALKING MARBLE.
AND BUGGER THIS CITY RIGHT ALONGSIDE HIM.
Inbox
Sent Mail
BARBARA WELLER There's Something Laughing in my Chest...
HARLEM.
THIS ISN'T ABOUT BEING LONELY. I'M JUST A MAN DOING HIS JOB.
ZOO ADMIN. It's Eating the Polar Bears...
CENTRAL PARK.
A MAN GETTING THE KIND OF THINGS DONE ONLY I CAN GET DONE.

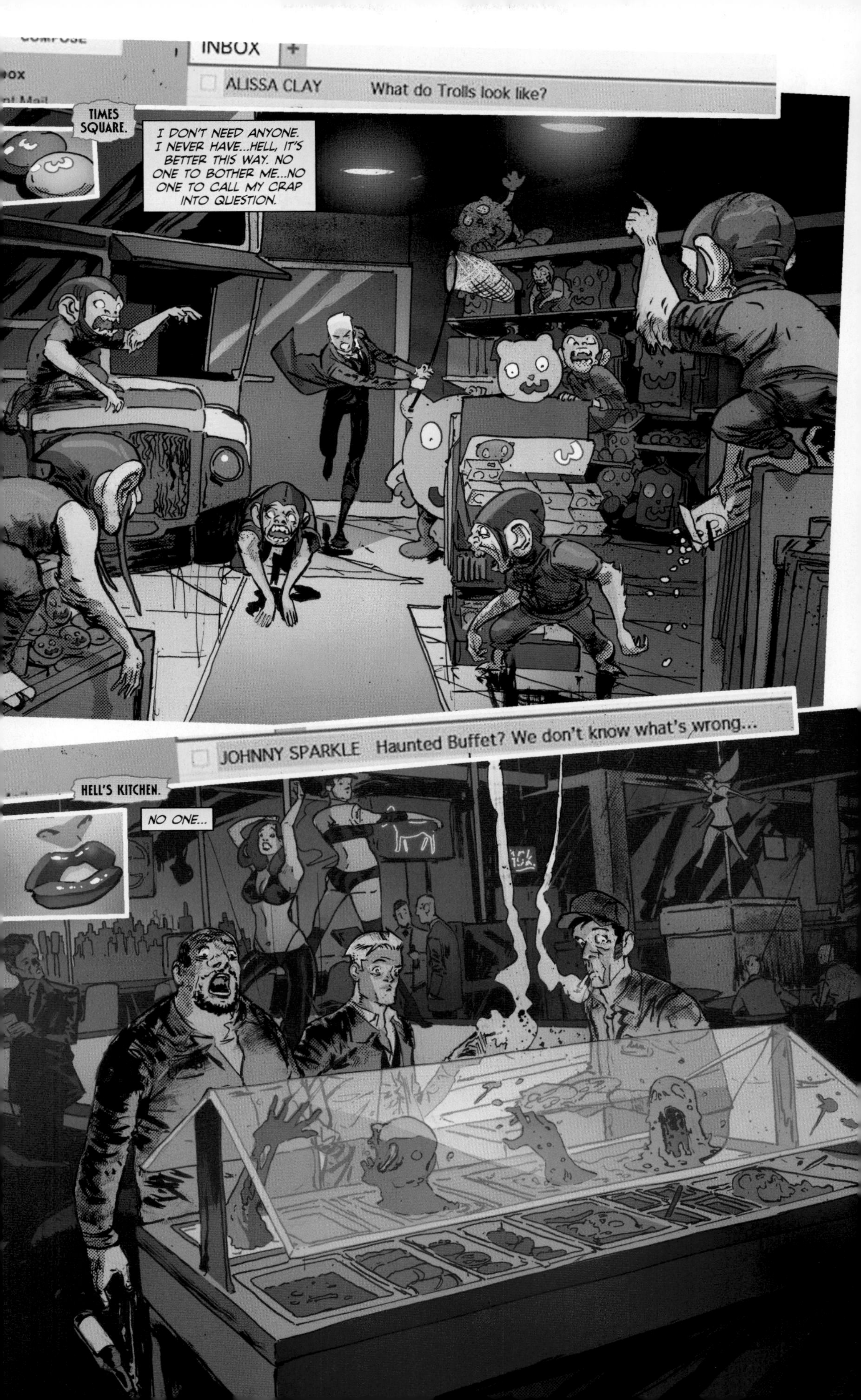

INBOX
+
ALISSA CLAY What do Trolls look like?
TIMES SQUARE.
I DON'T NEED ANYONE. I NEVER HAVE...HELL, IT'S BETTER THIS WAY. NO ONE TO BOTHER ME...NO ONE TO CALL MY CRAP INTO QUESTION.
JOHNNY SPARKLE Haunted Buffet? We don't know what's wrong...
HELL'S KITCHEN.
NO ONE...

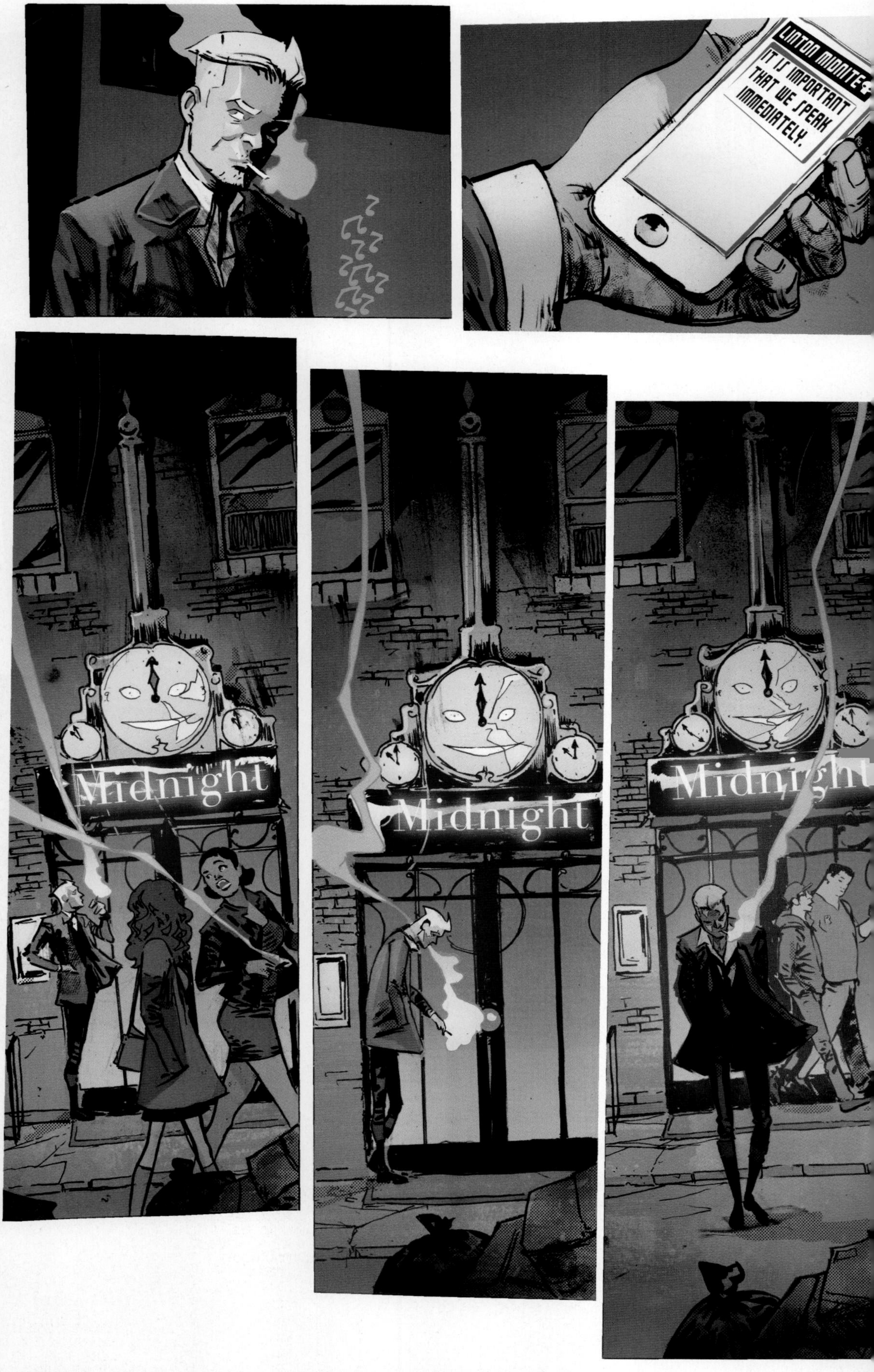
LINTON MIDNITE:
IT IS IMPORTANT THAT WE SPEAK IMMEDIATELY.
Midnight
Midnight
Midnight

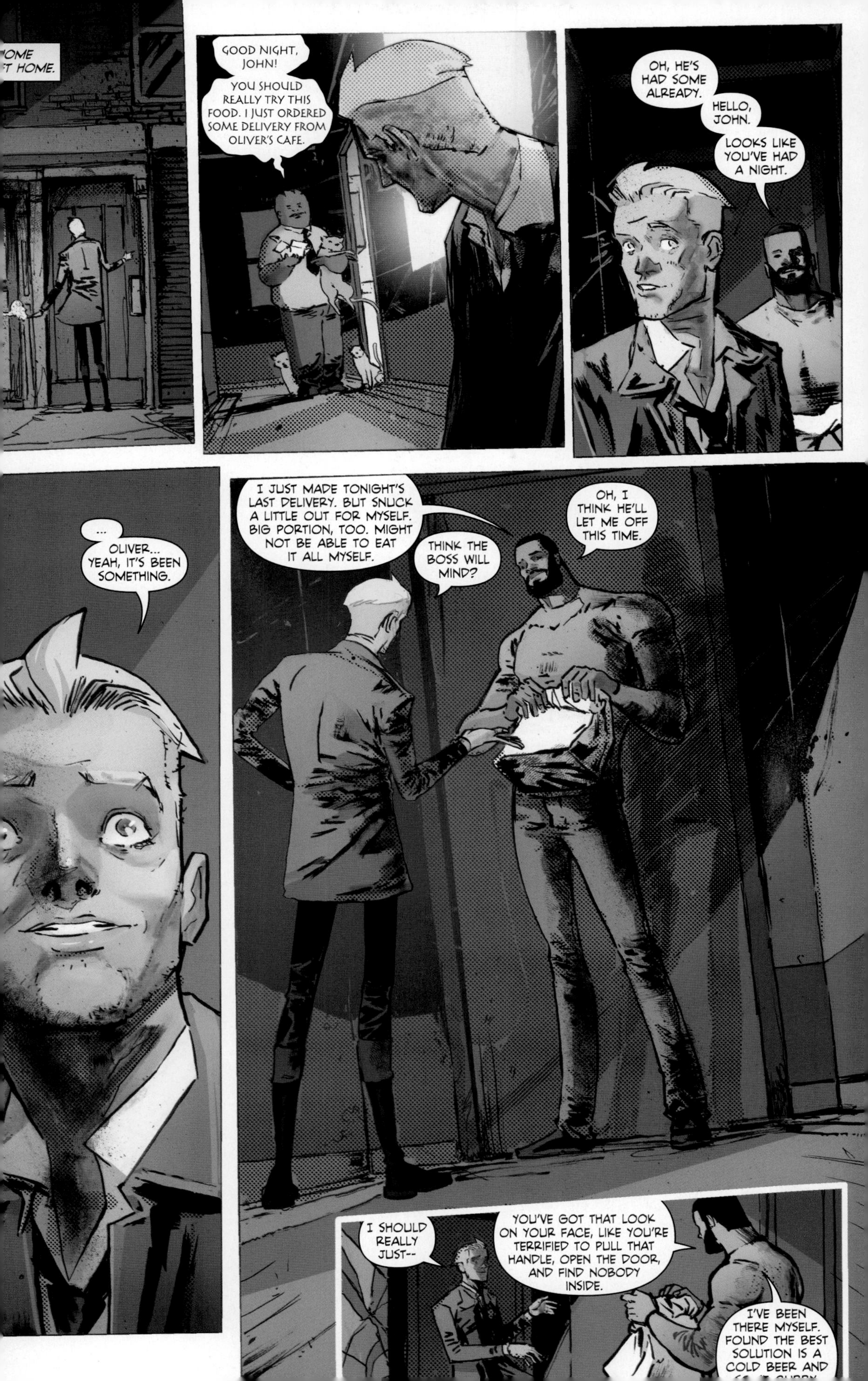
OME
T HOME.
GOOD NIGHT, JOHN!
YOU SHOULD REALLY TRY THIS FOOD. I JUST ORDERED SOME DELIVERY FROM OLIVER'S CAFE.
OH, HE'S HAD SOME ALREADY.
HELLO, JOHN.
LOOKS LIKE YOU'VE HAD A NIGHT.
...
OLIVER... YEAH, IT'S BEEN SOMETHING.
I JUST MADE TONIGHT'S LAST DELIVERY. BUT SNUCK A LITTLE OUT FOR MYSELF. BIG PORTION, TOO. MIGHT NOT BE ABLE TO EAT IT ALL MYSELF.
THINK THE BOSS WILL MIND?
OH, I THINK HE'LL LET ME OFF THIS TIME.
I SHOULD REALLY JUST--
YOU'VE GOT THAT LOOK ON YOUR FACE, LIKE YOU'RE TERRIFIED TO PULL THAT HANDLE, OPEN THE DOOR, AND FIND NOBODY INSIDE.
I'VE BEEN THERE MYSELF. FOUND THE BEST SOLUTION IS A COLD BEER AND

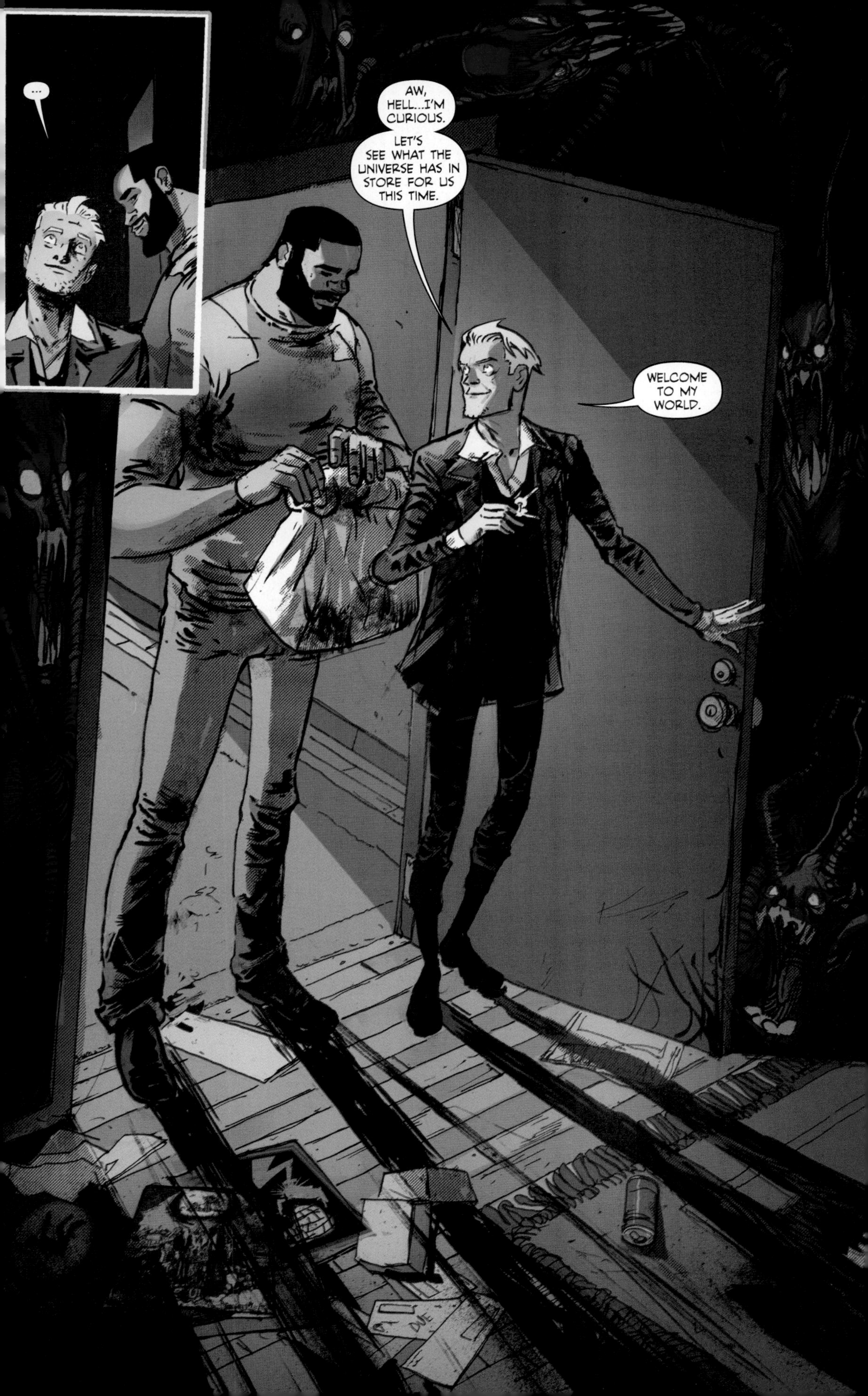
...
AW, HELL...I'M CURIOUS.
LET'S SEE WHAT THE UNIVERSE HAS IN STORE FOR US THIS TIME.
WELCOME TO MY WORLD.

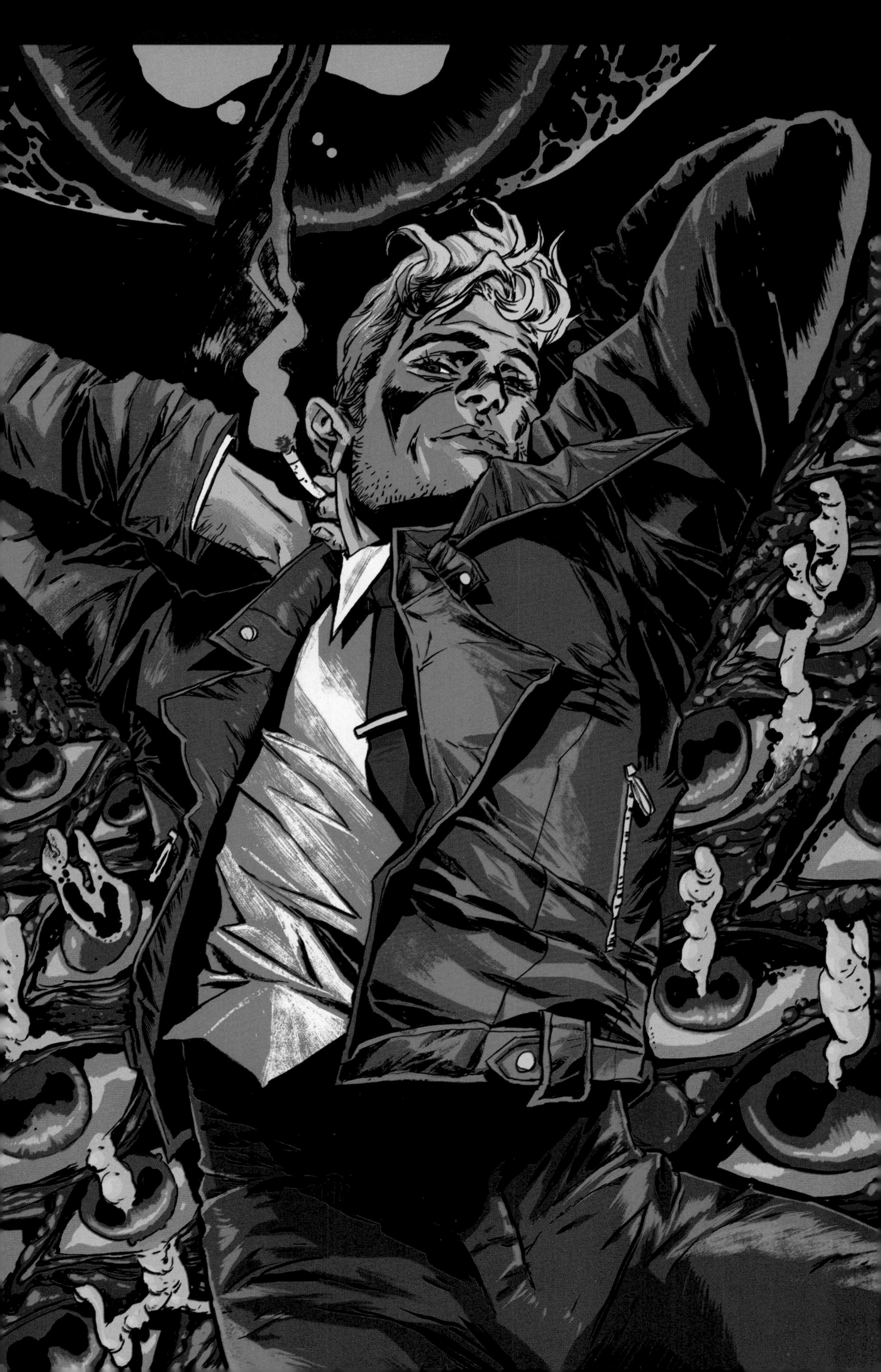

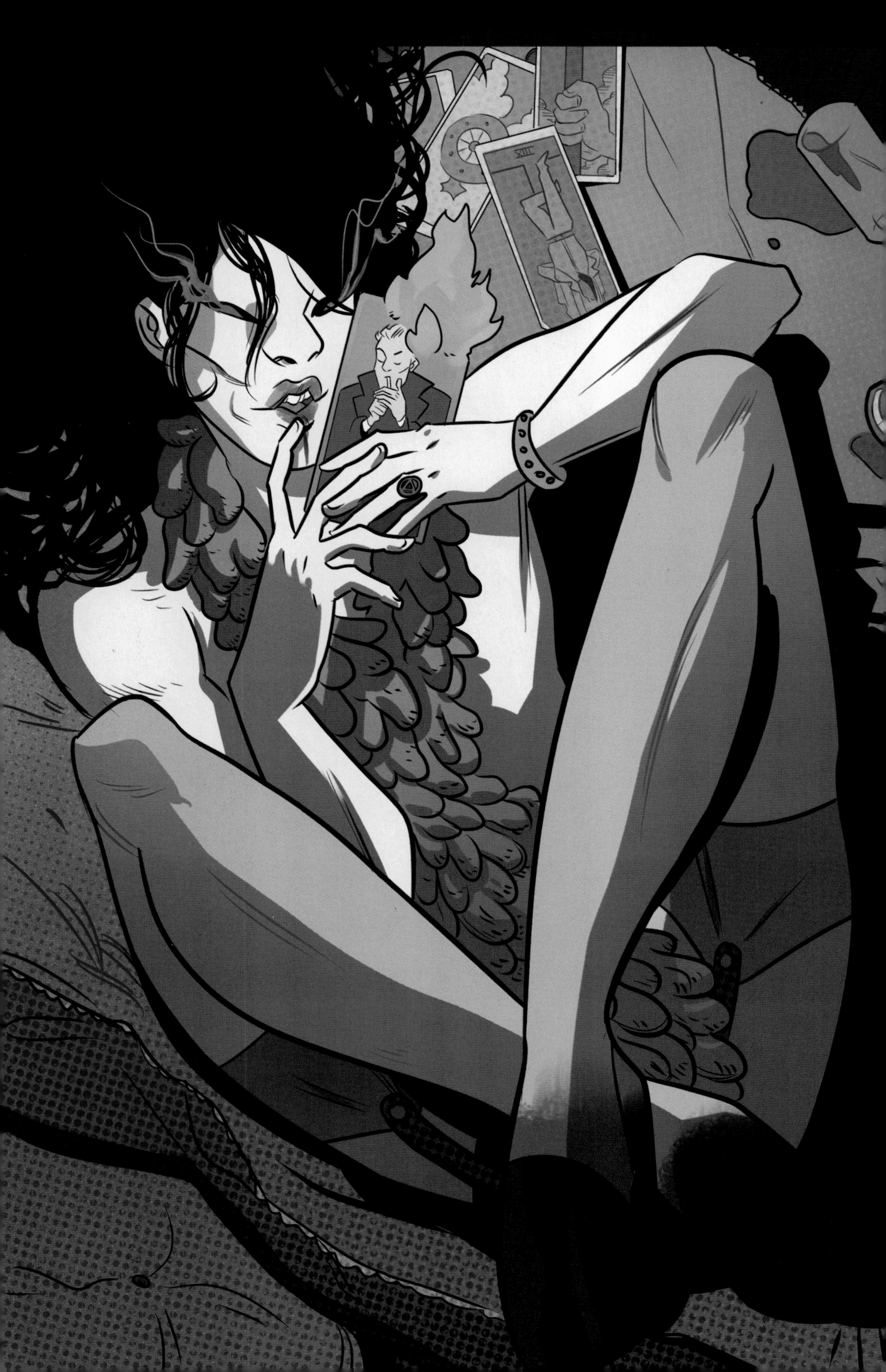

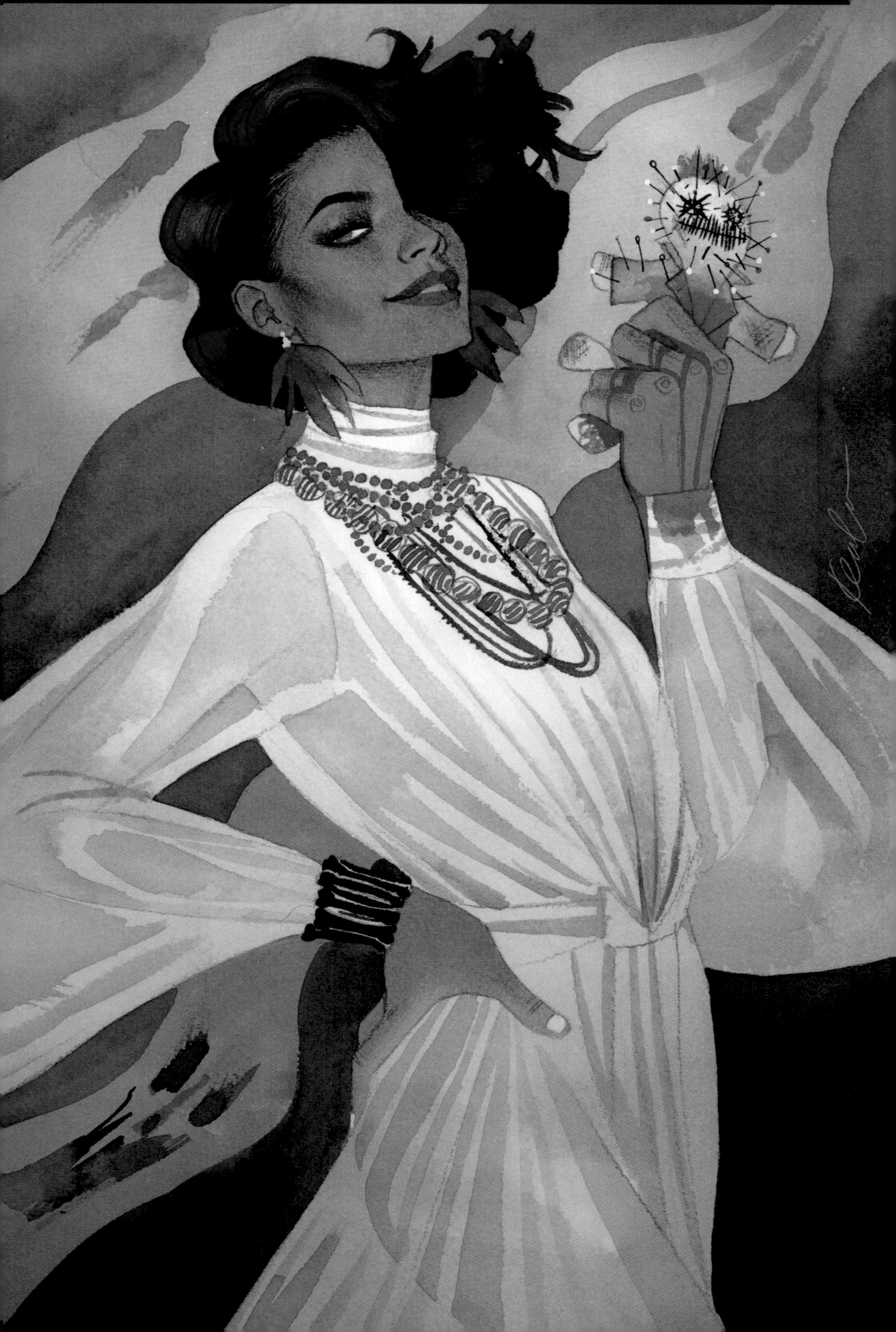

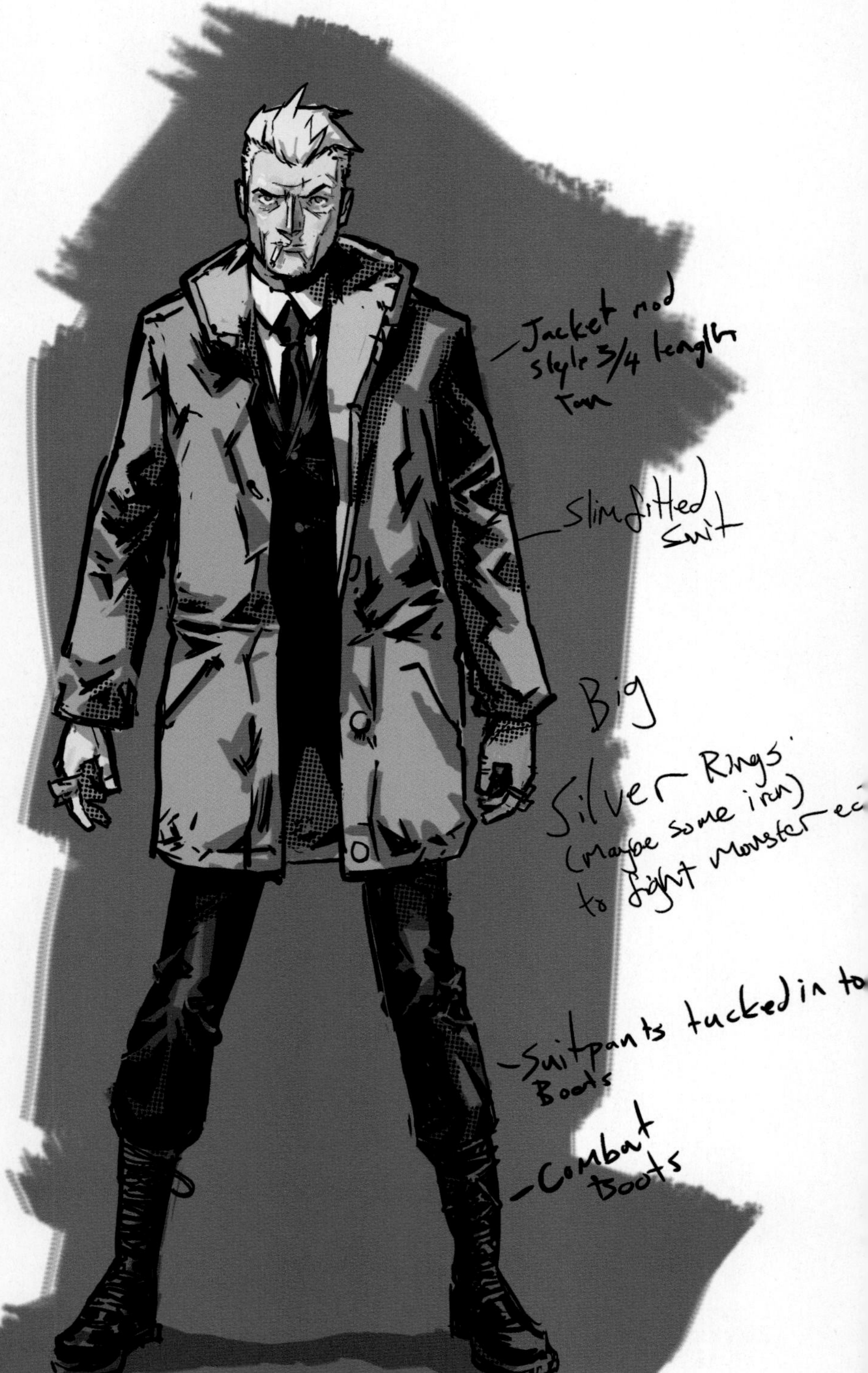
Jacket mod style 3/4 length Tan
Slim fitted suit
Big Silver Rings (maybe some iron) to fight monster etc
Suitpants tucked in to Boots
Combat Boots

John's defining design element has always been his jacket, so I spent a lot of time trying different iterations of it that felt fresh but also familiar. In order to make John's silhouette more distinct, I gave his hair a specific, angular shape, and tucked his pants into his boots to create a little flair mid-calf (later I changed this to cuffs).

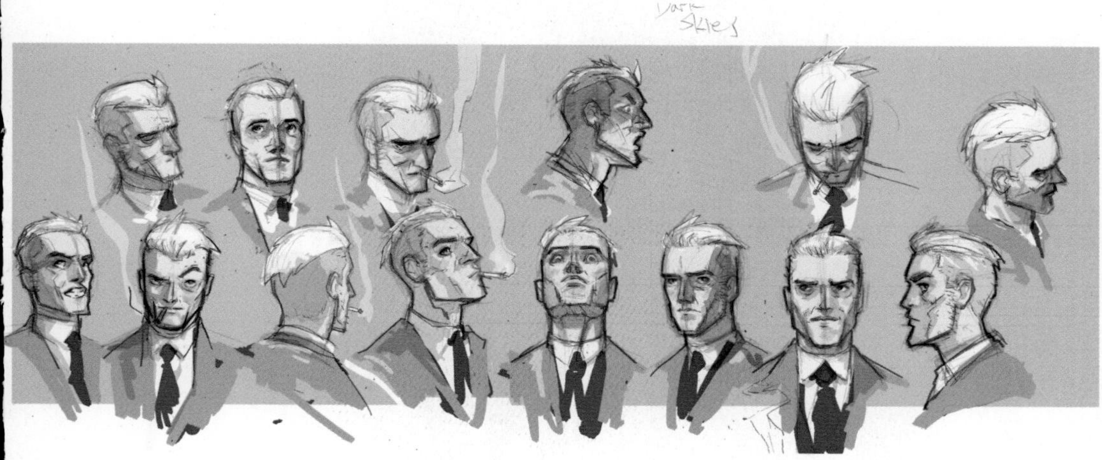

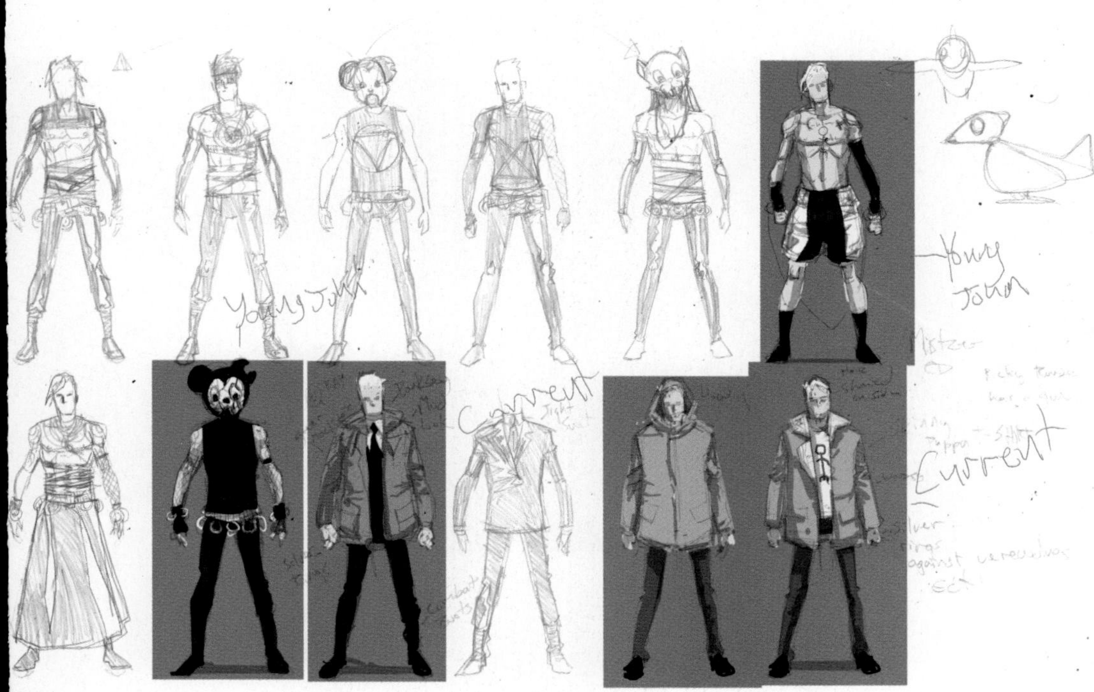
Young John
Young John
Current
Current

John's face was noticeably more weathered in my early designs, but we decided to make John more youthful so I dropped all those harsh lines. I liked the idea of John wearing silver rings for punching werewolves and vampires, but thought John would look too clunky if he always wore giant rings.

A redesign of the old DC villain Baron Winters, who we haven't yet seen in our series.

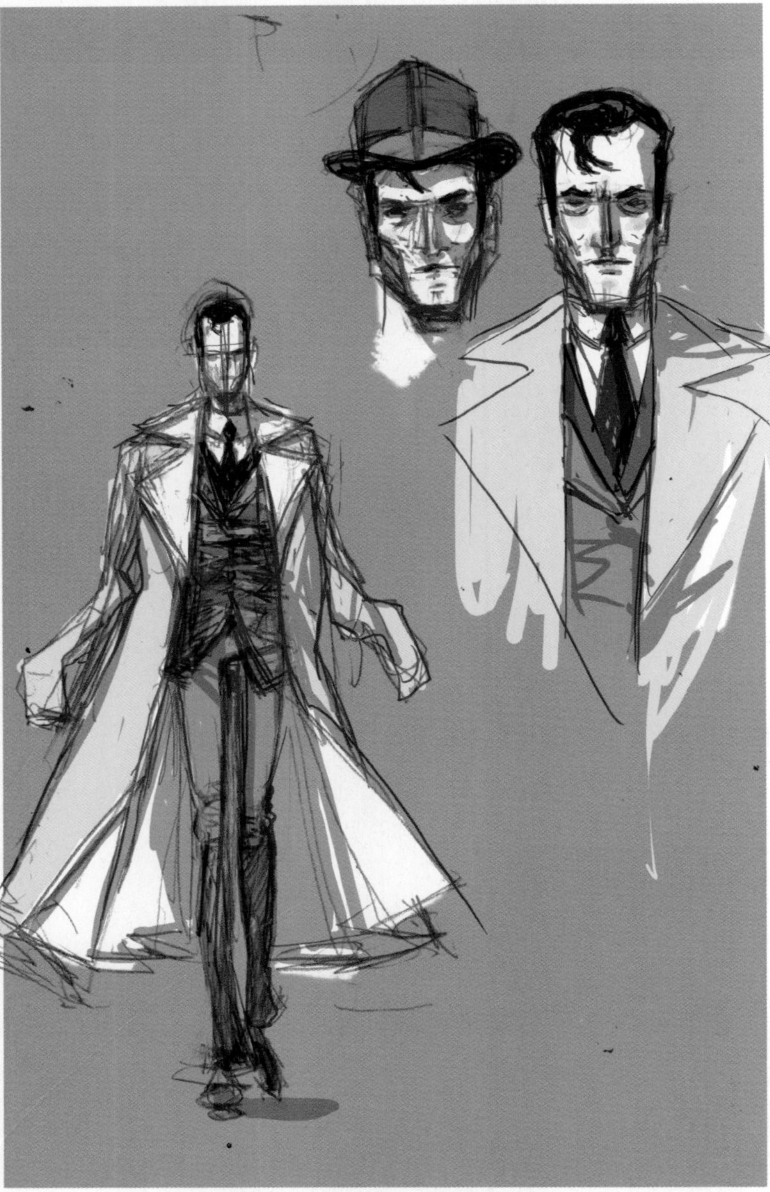

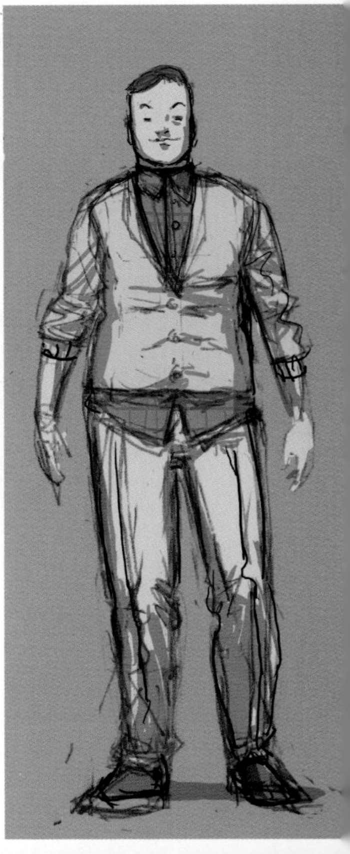

An early version of John's new love interest, Oliver. His look completely changed but we always knew he'd be more put together than John.

A new character created for our book, Georgiana Snow was envisioned as the anti-Constantine (or "Heckblazer" as editor Andy Khouri likes to say), wearing white, possessing good manners, is friendly with superheroes, and is generally far more respectable a magician. So of course they hate each other.

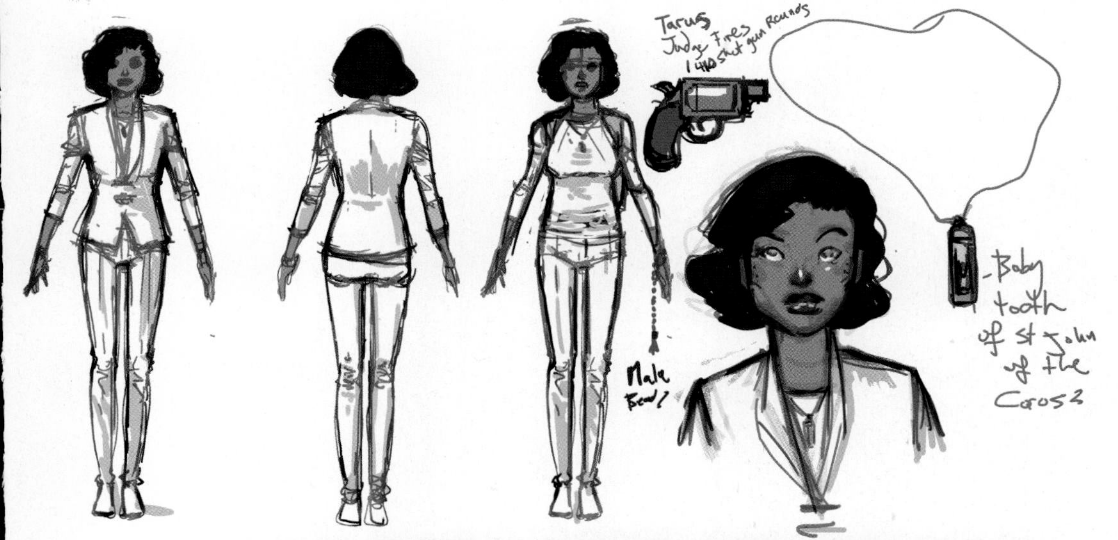
Tarus
Male
Baby
tooth

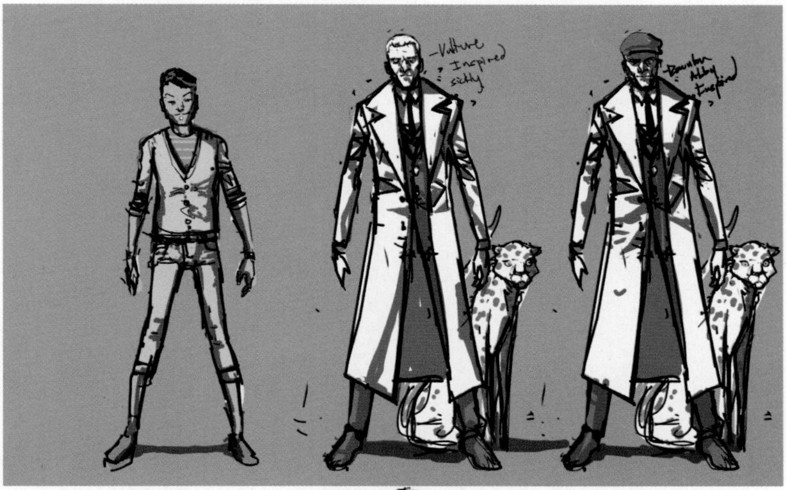

...mbers of John's punk band, Mucus Membrane.

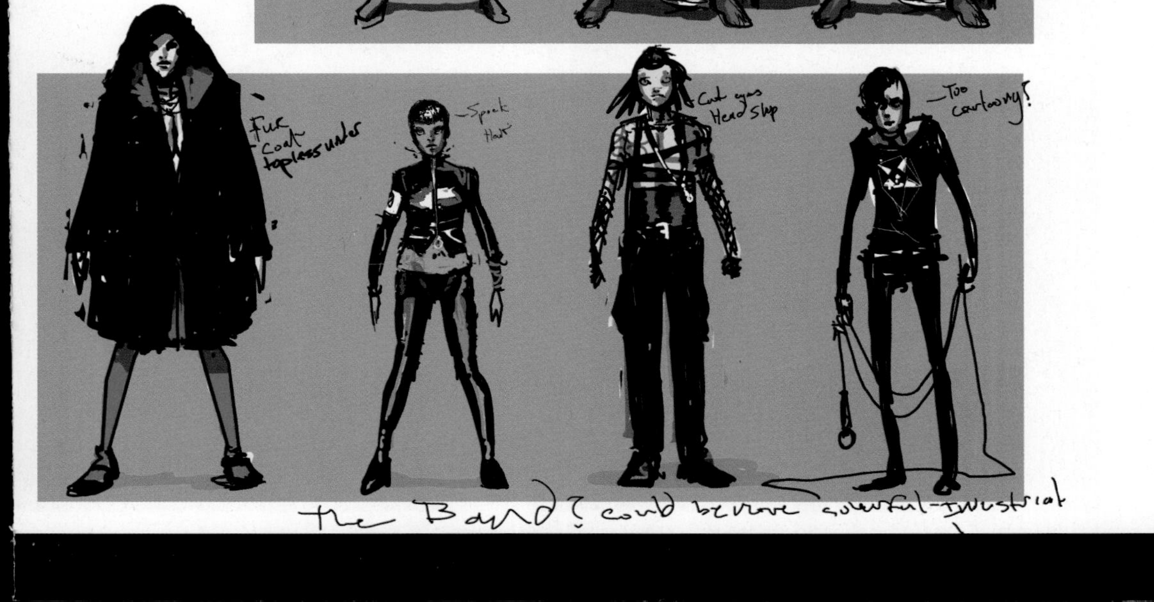
Fur
coat
topless under
-Spock
Hair
-Too
cartoony!
The Band?

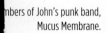

CONSTANTINE: THE HELLBLAZER #5
COVER CONCEPT SKETCH

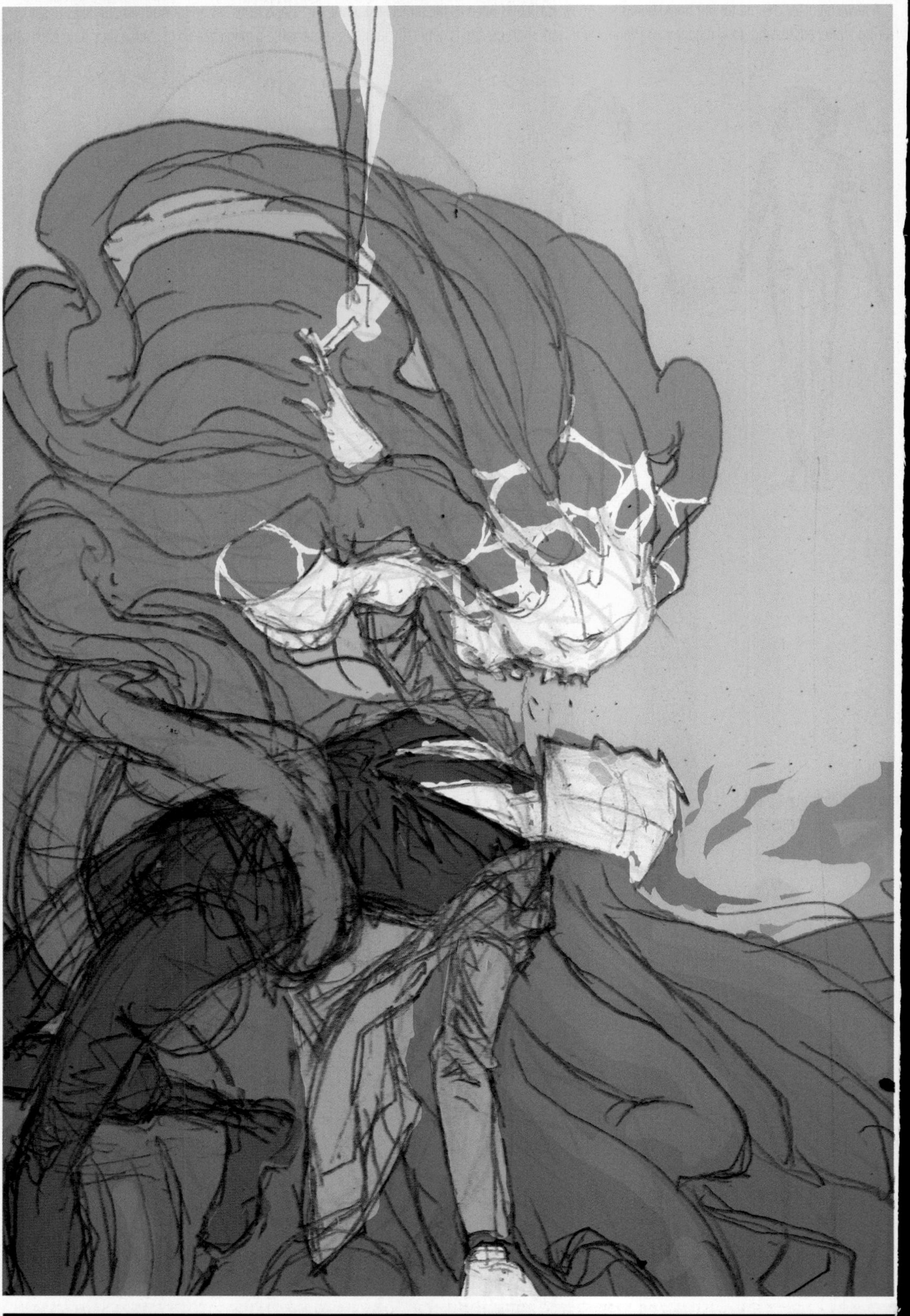

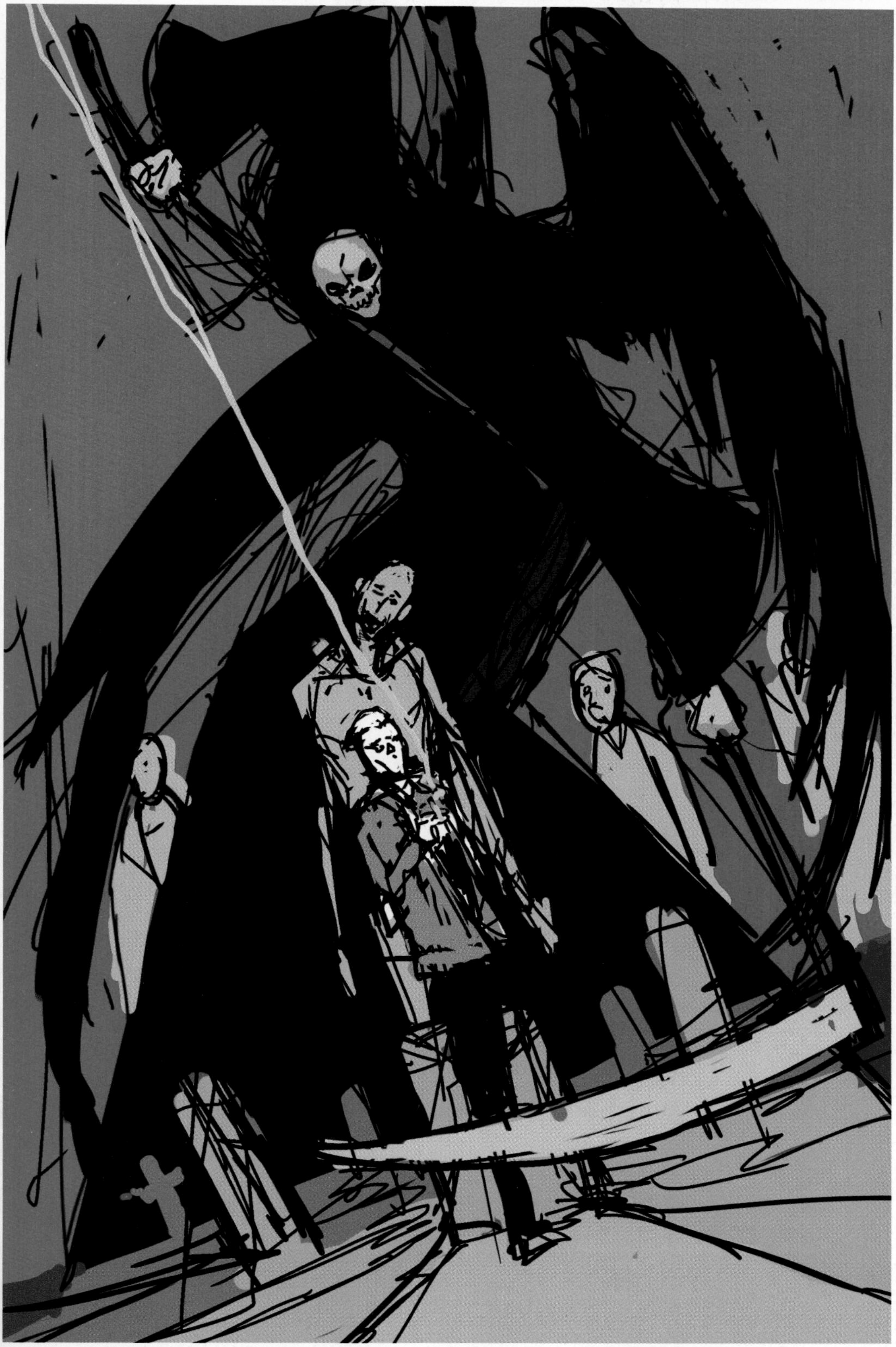

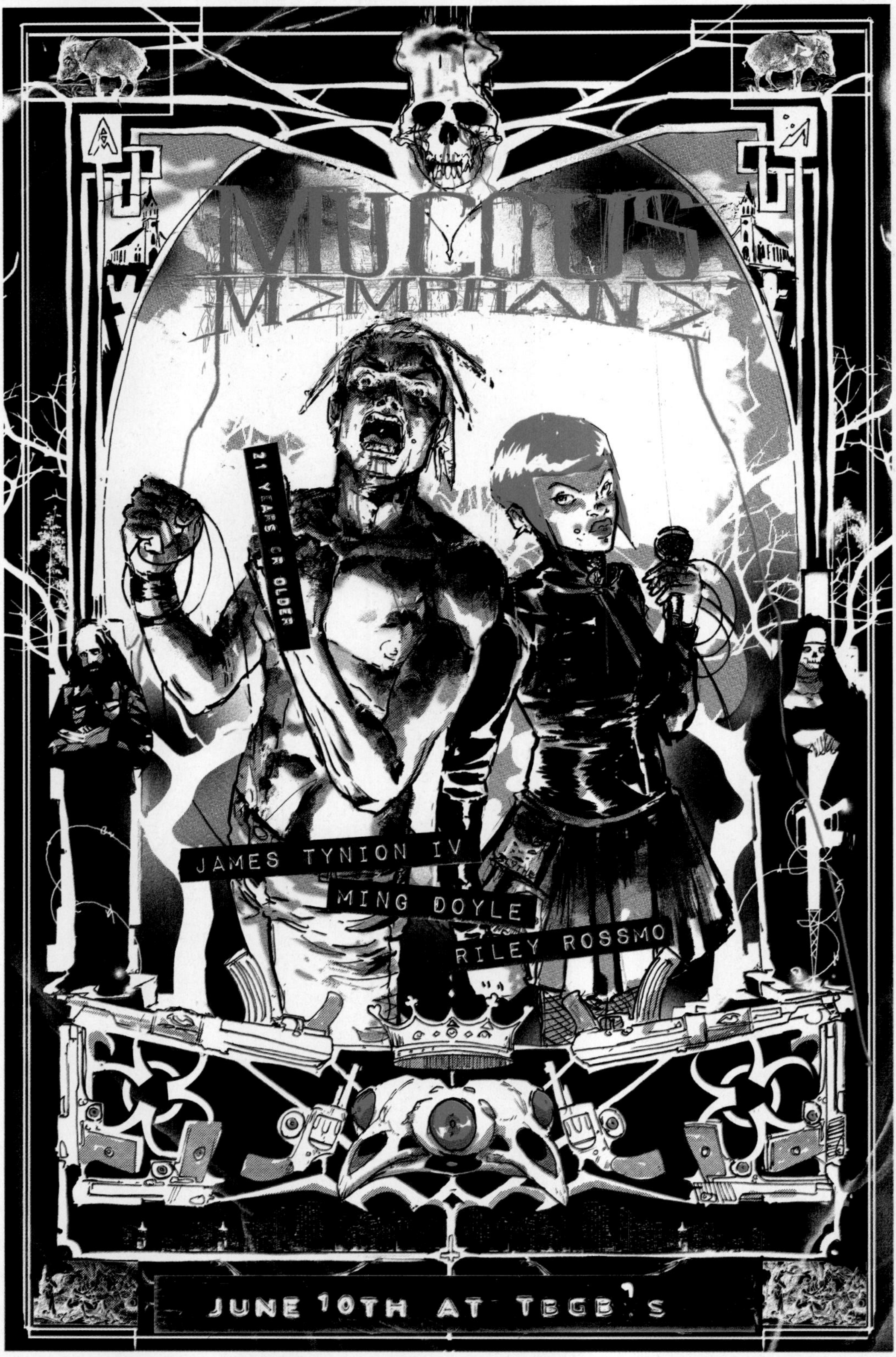
MUCOUS
MEMBRANE
21 YEARS OR OLDER
JAMES TYNION IV
MING DOYLE
RILEY ROSSMO
JUNE 10TH AT TBGB'S

I start my pages in non-photo blue pencil in a sketchbook. Once the figures are established and I feel like the page is flowing well, I scan it into Manga Studio and print it onto Bristol board for inking. Then I scan the inked page so I can add gray-tones.

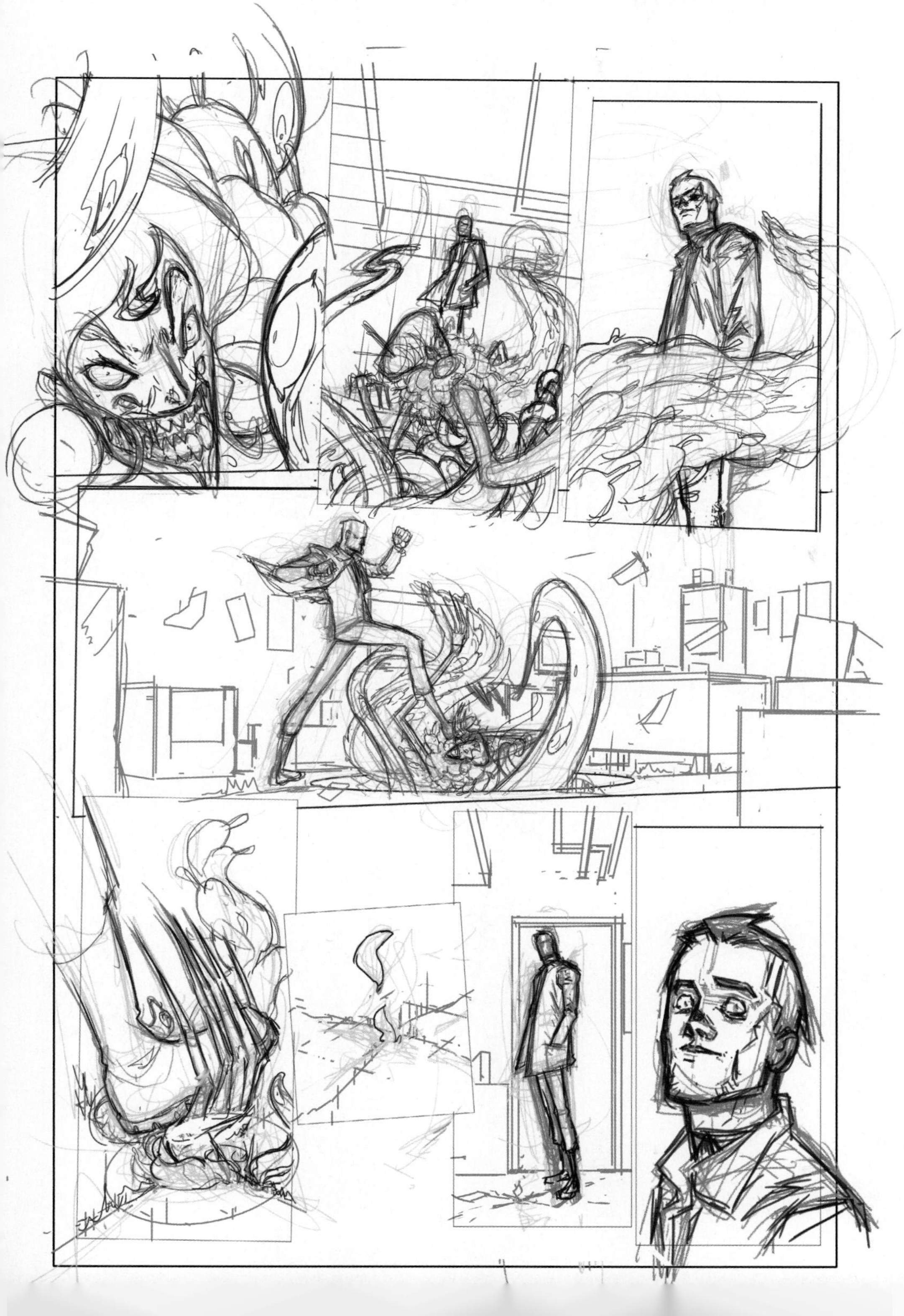

TWO VERSIONS OF PENCIL ART FOR CONSTANTINE: THE HELLBLAZER #2
PAGE 1

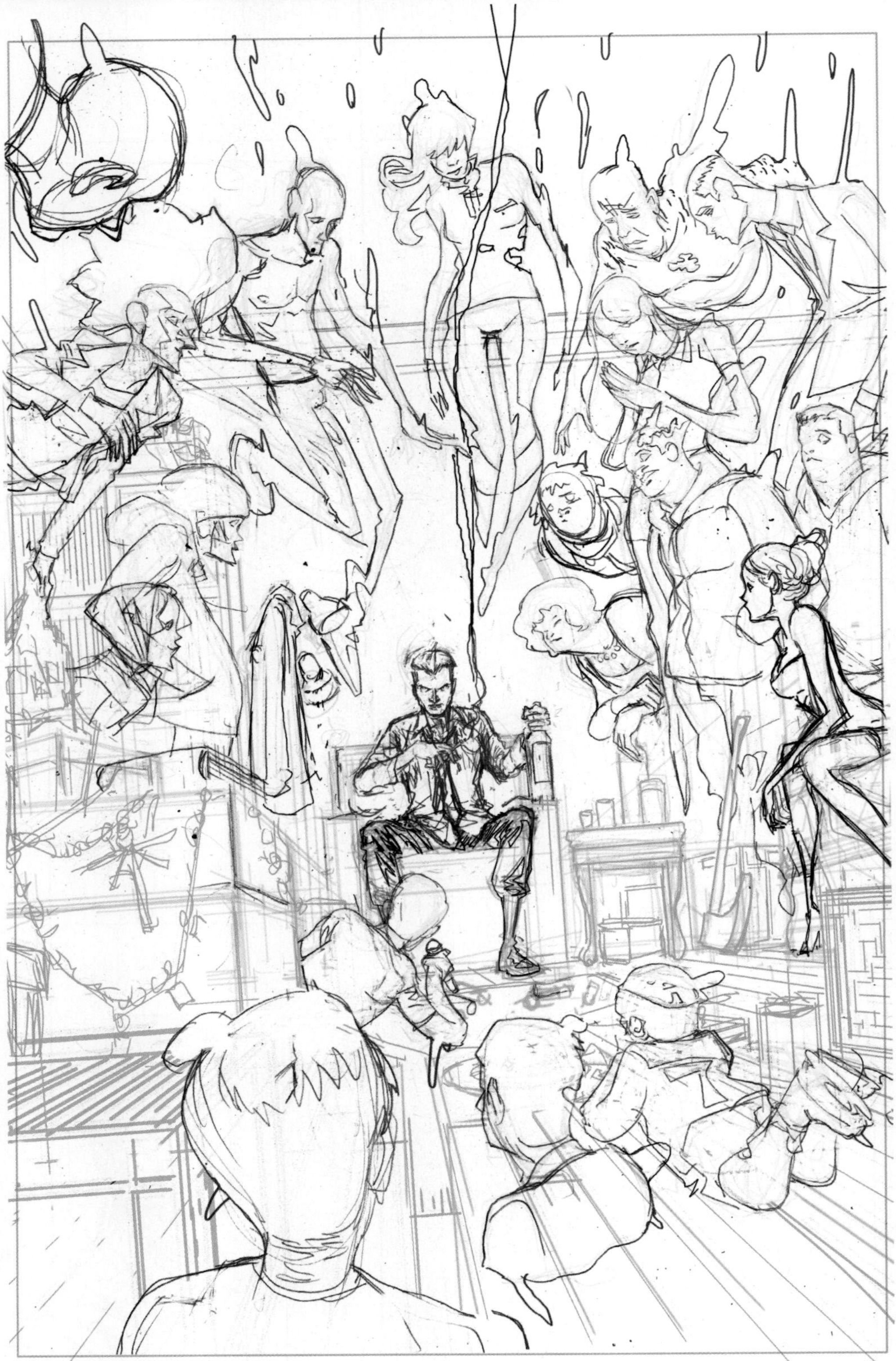

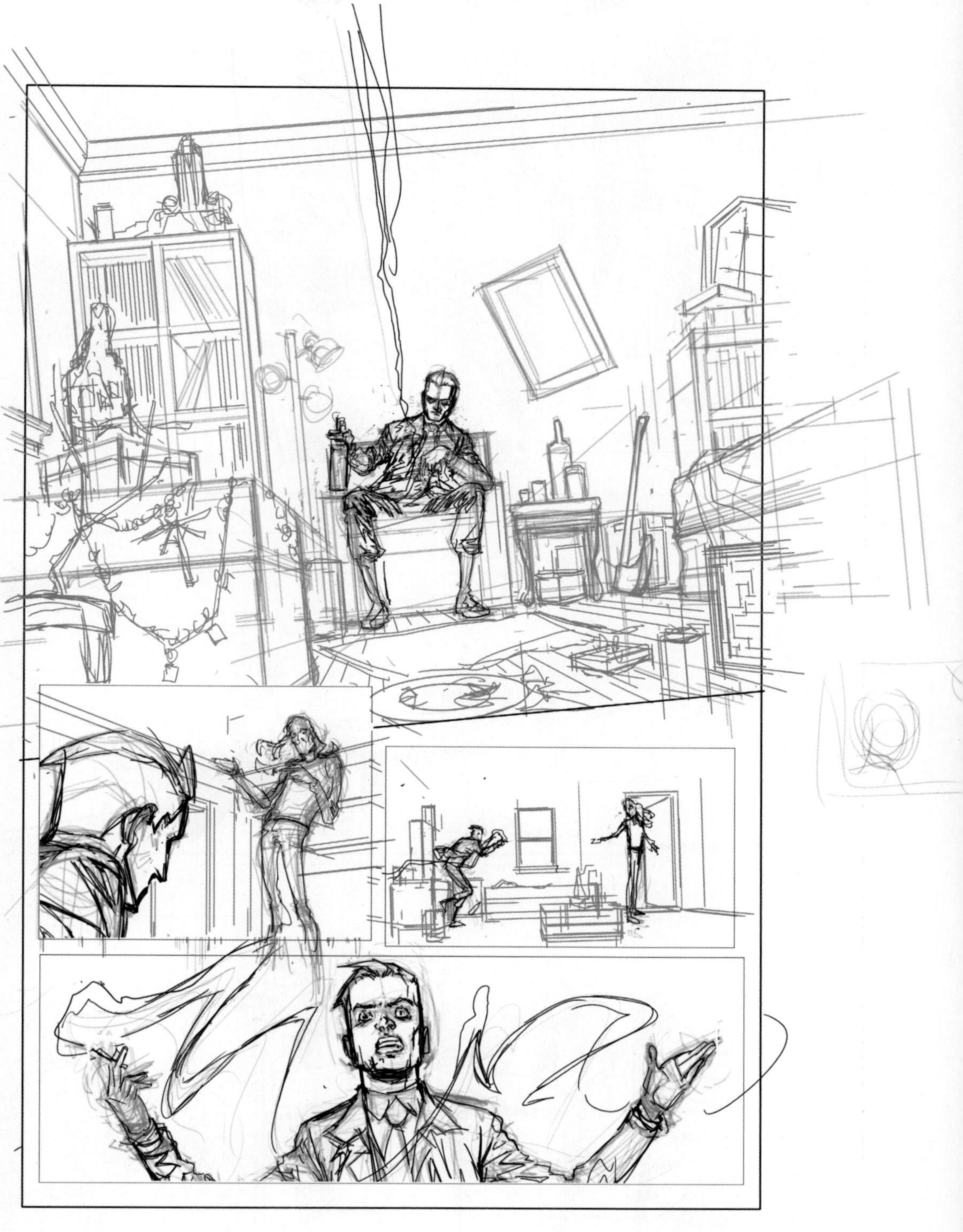

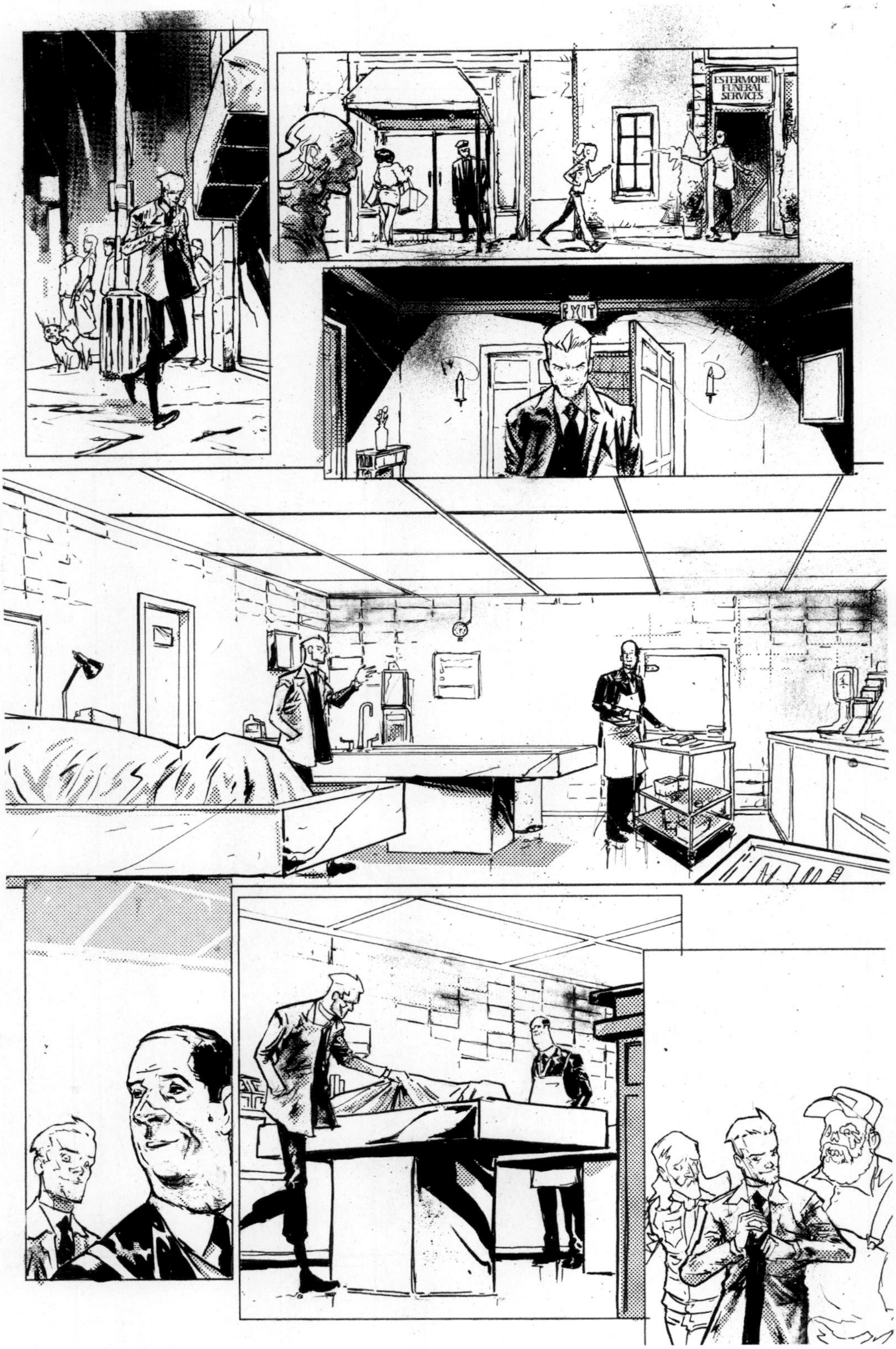
ESTERMORE FUNERAL SERVICES
EXIT

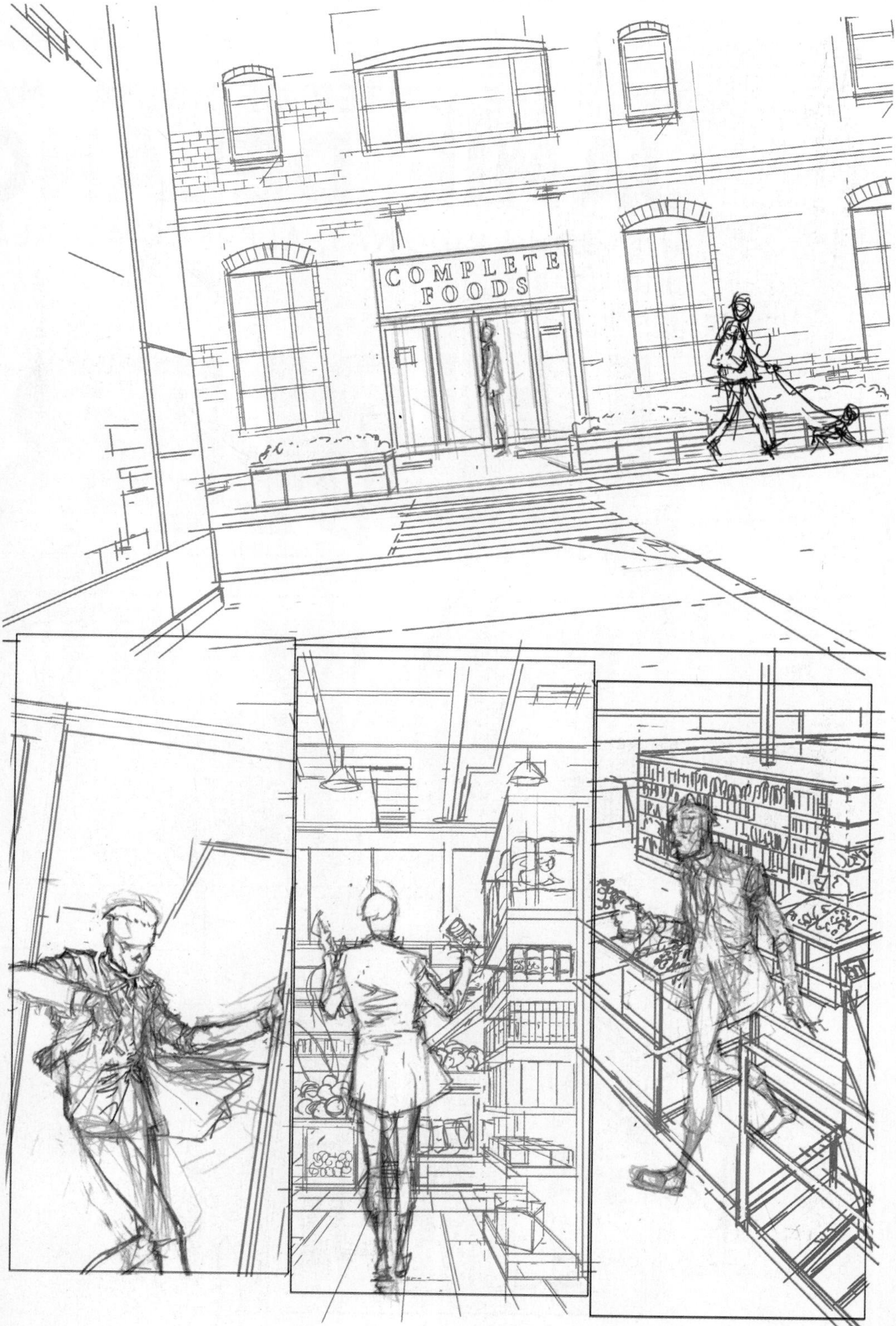
COMPLETE
FOODS

"Marvelous storytelling."—PUBLISHERS WEEK[

*"Jamie Delano introduced John Constantine's solo title with breath[
pace and little mercy."*—PASTE MAGAZ[

FROM THE WRITER OF *ANIMAL MAN*
JAMIE DELANO
with JOHN RIDGWAY, ALFREDO ALCALA
and others

JOHN CONSTANTINE,
HELLBLAZER VOL. 2:
THE DEVIL YOU KNOW

with DAVID LLOYD, MARK
BUCKINGHAM and others

JOHN CONSTANTINE,
HELLBLAZER VOL. 3:
THE FEAR MACHINE

with MARK BUCKINGHAM,
RICHARD PIERS RAYNER
and others

JOHN CONSTANTINE,
HELLBLAZER VOL. 4:
THE FAMILY MAN

with GRANT MORRISON,
NEIL GAIMAN and others

JOHN CONSTANTINE
HELLBLAZER
ORIGINAL SINS

VERTIGO

Jamie Delano   John Ridgway
Alfredo Alcala   Rick Veitch   Tom Mandrake